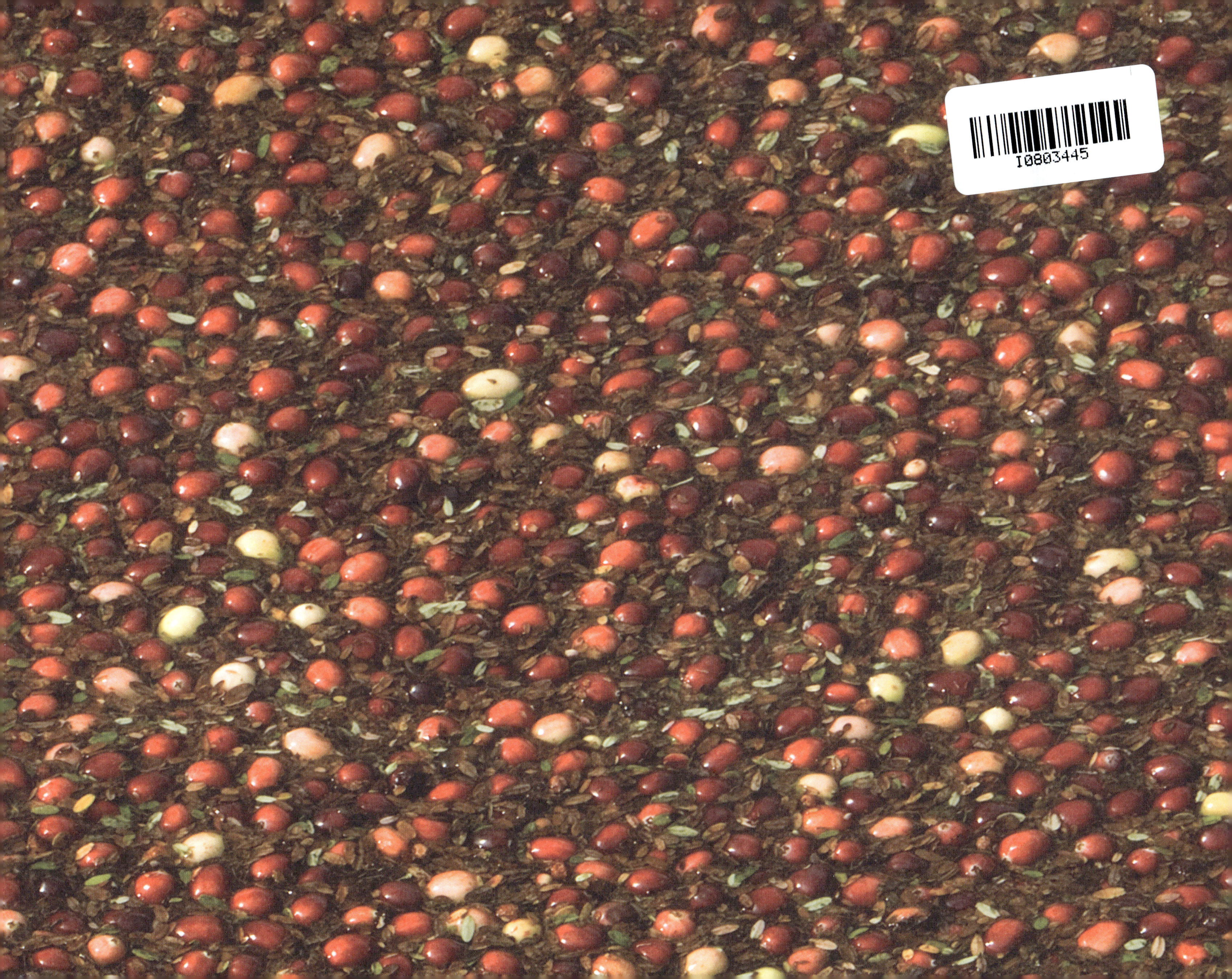

SOUTH SHORE WIDE

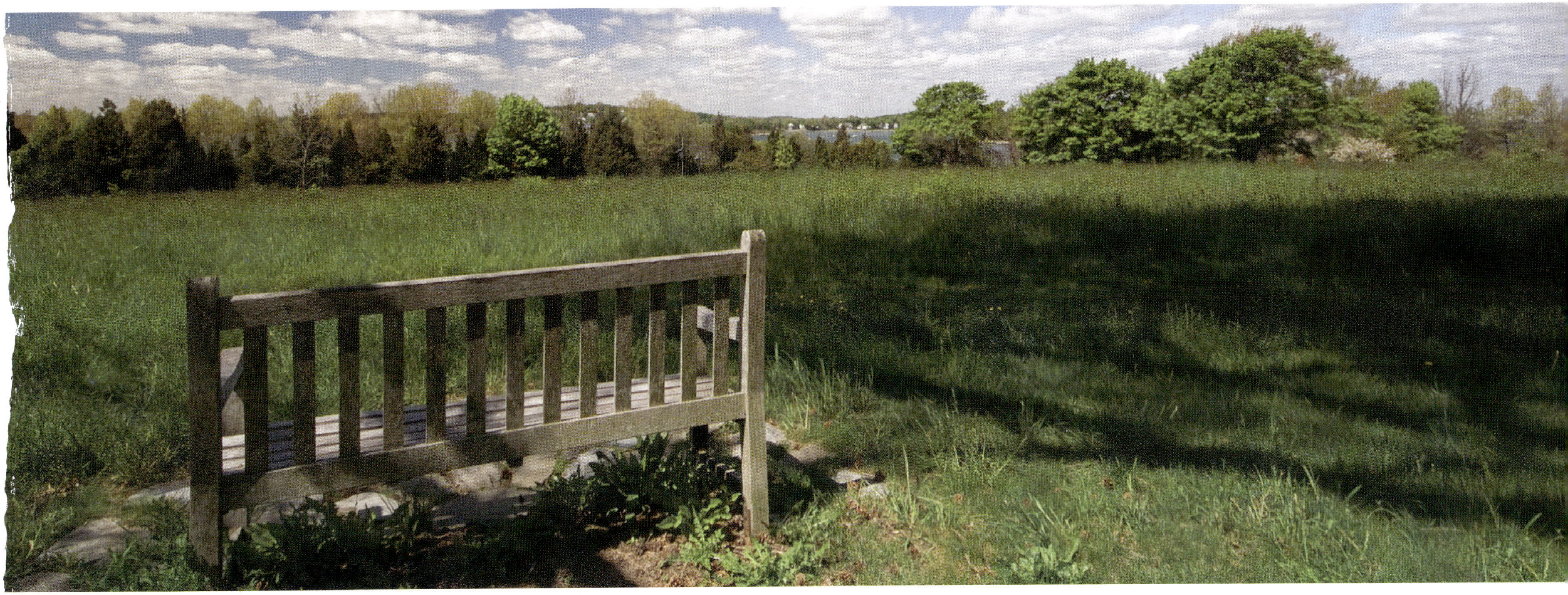

Schiffer Publishing Ltd
4880 Lower Valley Road, Atglen, Pennsylvania 19310

The Panoramas of
A. P. Richmond

This book is dedicated to Ava Elizabeth.

Schiffer Books are available at special discounts for bulk purchases for sales promotions or premiums. Special editions, including personalized covers, corporate imprints, and excerpts can be created in large quantities for special needs. For more information contact the publisher:

Published by Schiffer Publishing Ltd.
4880 Lower Valley Road
Atglen, PA 19310
Phone: (610) 593-1777; Fax: (610) 593-2002
E-mail: Info@schifferbooks.com

For the largest selection of fine reference books on this and related subjects, please visit our web site at **www.schifferbooks.com**
We are always looking for people to write books on new and related subjects. If you have an idea for a book please contact us at the above address.

This book may be purchased from the publisher.
Include $5.00 for shipping.
Please try your bookstore first.
You may write for a free catalog.

In Europe, Schiffer books are distributed by
Bushwood Books
6 Marksbury Ave.
Kew Gardens
Surrey TW9 4JF England
Phone: 44 (0) 20 8392-8585; Fax: 44 (0) 20 8392-9876
E-mail: info@bushwoodbooks.co.uk
Website: www.bushwoodbooks.co.uk
Free postage in the U.K., Europe; air mail at cost.

Front Endsheet: Cranberries floating in a bog ready for harvest.
Title Page: A bench in World's End Reservation, Hingham, overlooking the harbor.

Library of Congress Control Number: 2008939389

Designed by Mark David Bowyer
Type set in Americana BT / Zurich BT

ISBN: 978-0-7643-3184-8
Printed in China

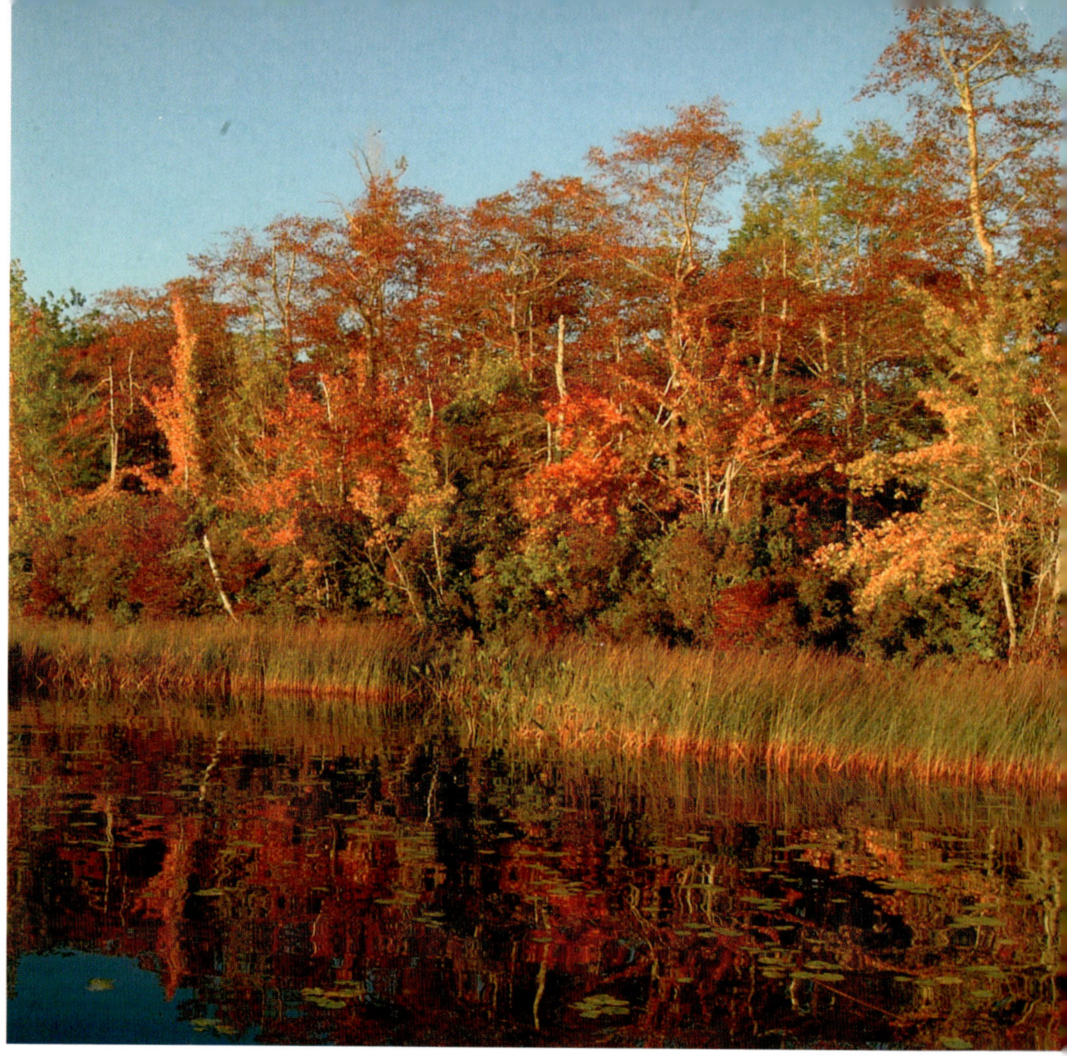

Acknowledgments

Although it's only my name on the cover, a book of this size and undertaking requires the expertise and assistance of many individuals. This is the third volume in the Wide series, and the inspiration and motivation to complete these projects would not have been possible without the support, guidance, and encouragement of Schiffer Publishing.

To Carol, for her encouragement and inspiration.

To Tony Pane for his continued assistance.

To Doug, Jared, Nicole and Brandi.

To the anonymous guides and locals who have offered their expertise.

To Salty Dog, my best friend.

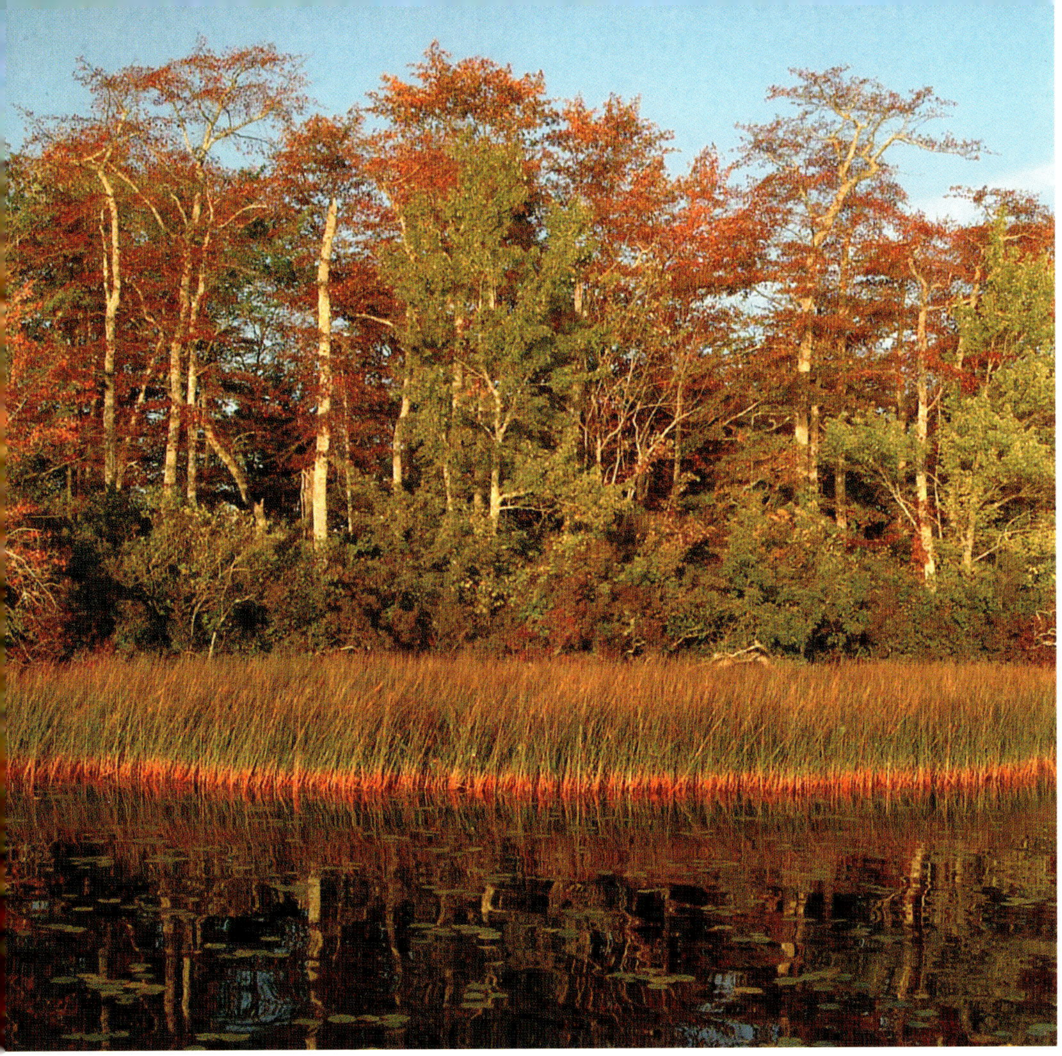

Contents

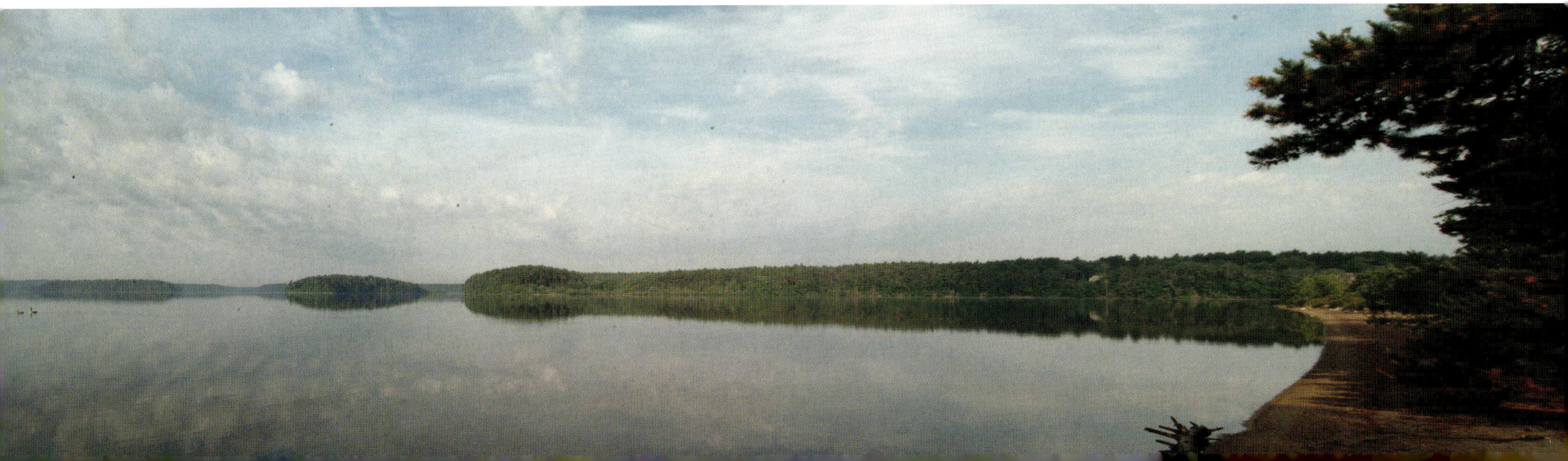

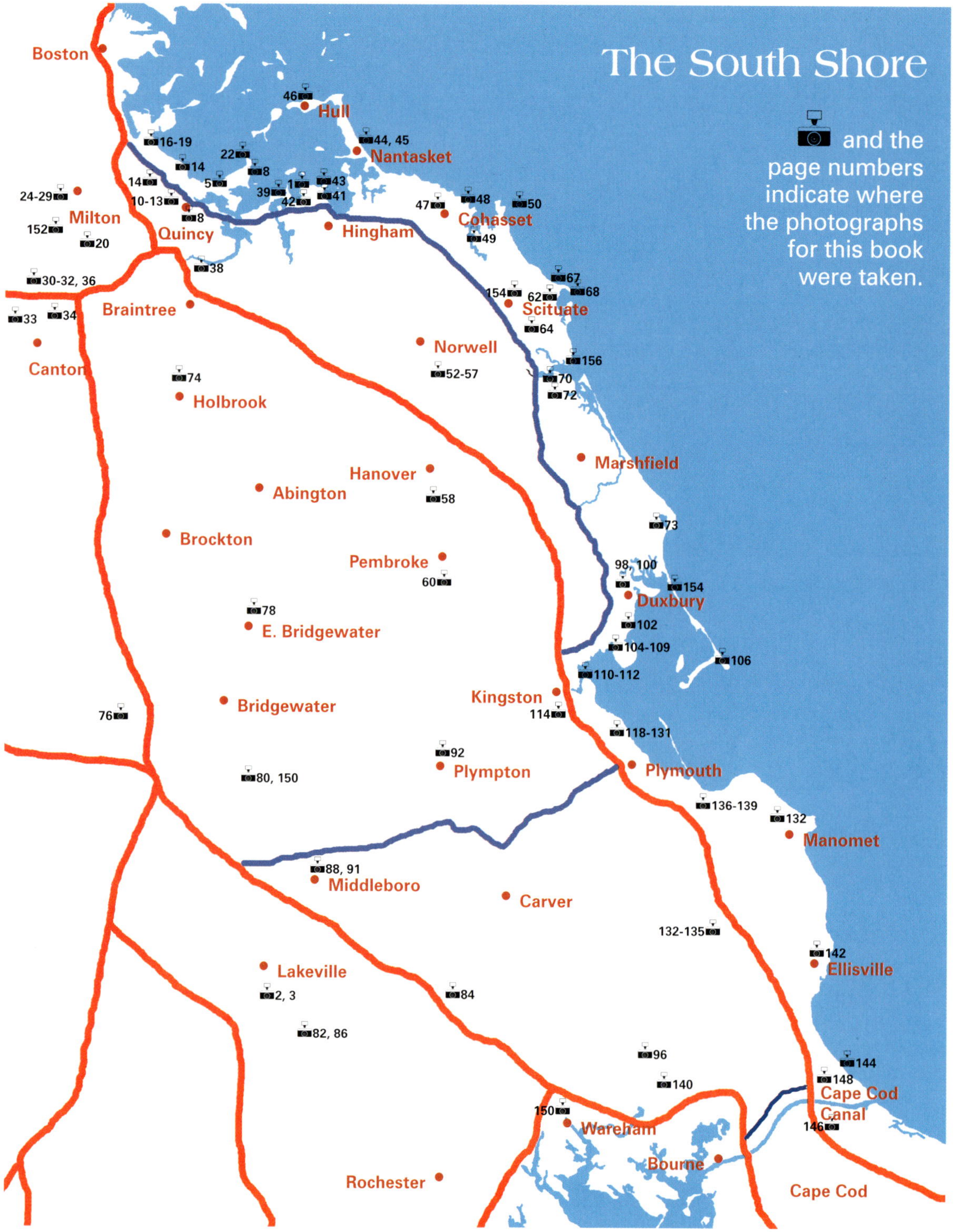
The South Shore
and the page numbers indicate where the photographs for this book were taken.
Boston
Hull
Nantasket
Milton
Quincy
Hingham
Cohasset
Braintree
Scituate
Norwell
Canton
Holbrook
Marshfield
Hanover
Abington
Brockton
Pembroke
Duxbury
E. Bridgewater
Bridgewater
Kingston
Plympton
Plymouth
Manomet
Middleboro
Carver
Ellisville
Lakeville
Cape Cod Canal
Wareham
Bourne
Rochester
Cape Cod
46
44, 45
16-19
22
14
8
14
5
1
43
24-29
39
42
41
10-13
47
48
50
8
152
49
20
38
30-32, 36
67
154
62
68
33
34
64
156
74
52-57
70
72
58
73
98, 100
154
60
78
102
104-109
106
110-112
76
114
118-131
92
80, 150
136-139
132
88, 91
132-135
142
2, 3
84
82, 86
96
144
148
140
150
146

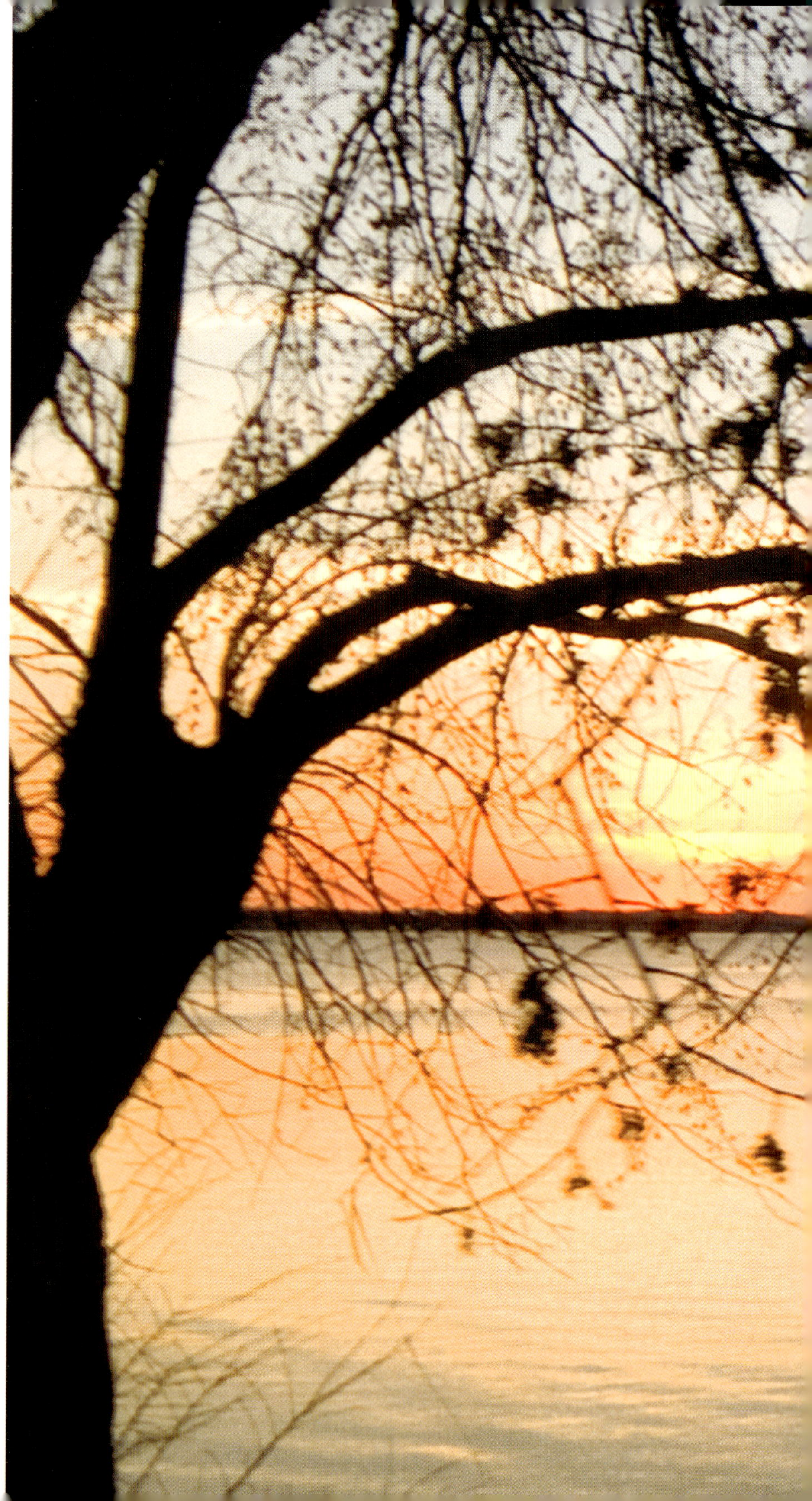

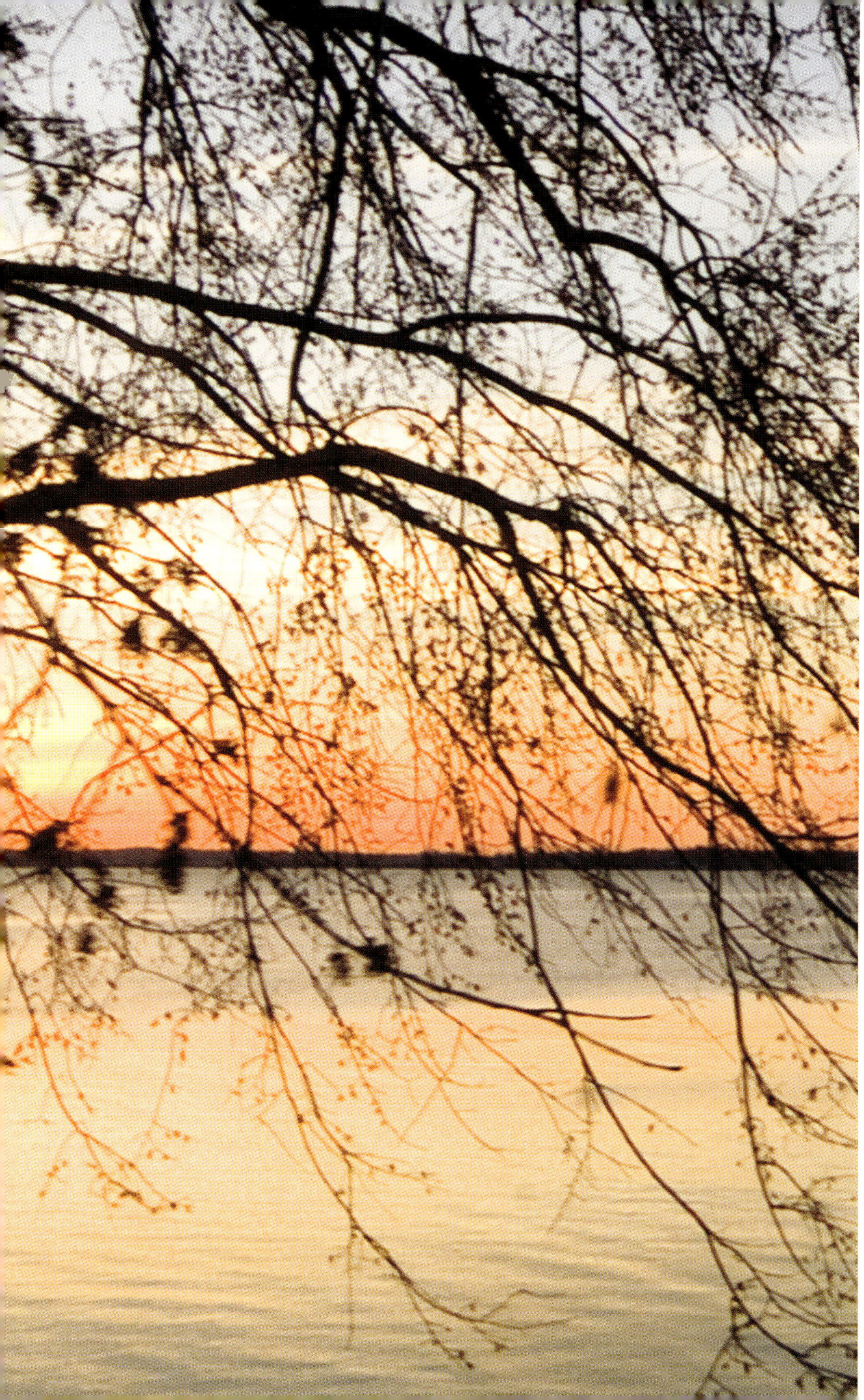

Introduction

Welcome to the South Shore of Massachusetts, which offers numerous opportunities for visitors and photographers. Often bypassed as people head to the Cape, this area of Massachusetts has some truly magnificent and remarkable locations. It is a diverse area that includes colonial seafaring villages that retain their coastal charm, cities rich in history, and forests, lakes and farmland that provide scenic vistas. Enormous parks, forests, and recreation regions are found throughout this area, providing residents and visitors with a wide variety of activities. The Massachusetts Audubon and the Trustees of the Reservation own and maintain significant properties throughout the region that are both historically important and environmentally sensitive. Both the Massachusetts Department of Conservation and Recreation and the United States National Park Service also own important, noteworthy, and substantial properties that attract visitors from around the world. Many of the images in this book were captured in these pristine locales.

This region is the birthplace of America. Quincy, with views of Boston from its shore, is the only city in America to be the home of two United States presidents: John Adams and John Quincy Adams. Along the coast, Hingham, Hull, Cohasset, and Scituate preserve and maintain their past with distinctive homes, safe harbors, and colonial architecture. Brockton and surrounding towns were once the centers of shoe manufacturing. Plymouth, an important tourist destination, was the first permanent settlement in America. In neighboring Duxbury there are numerous sites to visit that are nearly 400 years old. Lakeville, Middleborough, and Wareham, with numerous bogs, produce most of the state's cranberries.

Historically rich, the area abounds with original buildings constructed in the 1600s as well as replicas built to show the way life used to be. The Mayflower II and Plimoth Plantation recreate the Pilgrims' voyage to a new land, and how they lived in the early 1620s.

More recently, household names known throughout America have had their origins on the South Shore. Internationally, Dunkin Donuts has been an early morning stop for many; Howard Johnson's is famous for its 58 flavors of ice cream, and Ocean Spray cranberries are a must for the Thanksgiving meal, which had its beginnings in Plymouth with the Native Americans and the Pilgrims.

The beauty in this book is not only in the marvelous and splendid panoramas, but in the realization that what you see on these pages is what you would see if you were there. Enjoy and experience again scenes familiar to you or explore and find the same vistas that I have captured.

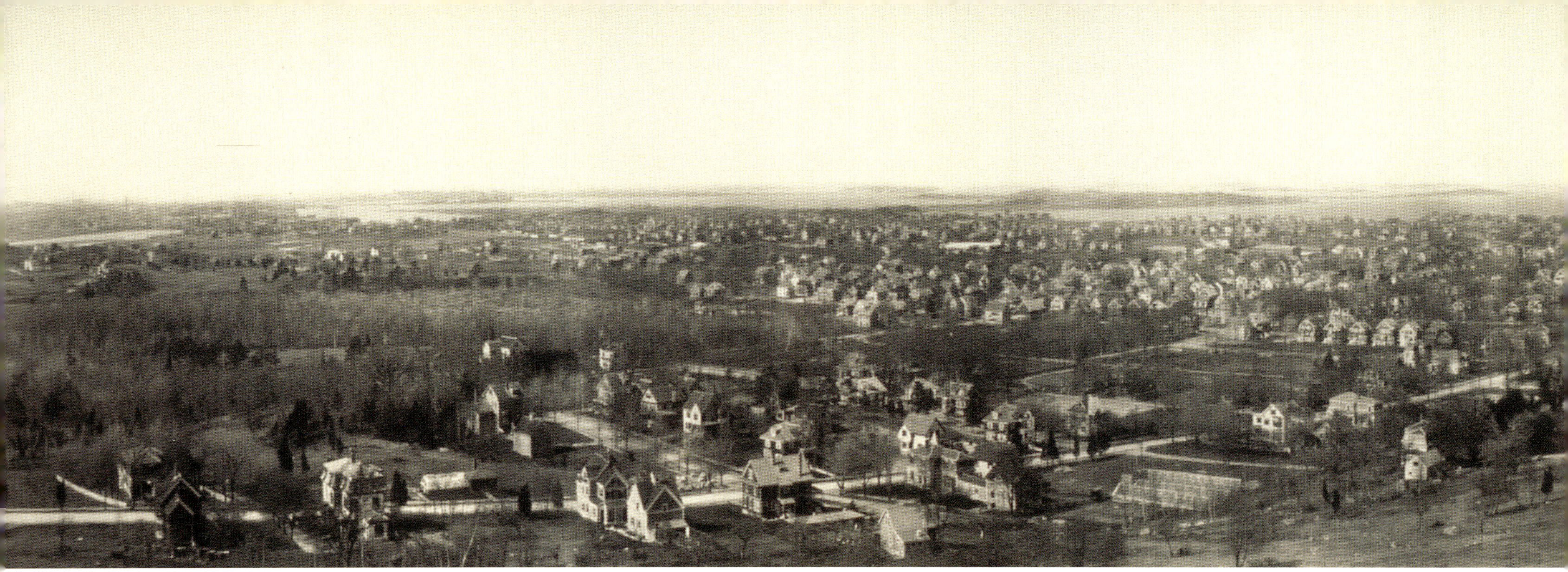

Panoramic photography has been of interest to photographers ever since Louis Daguerre was able to capture an image on a metal plate in the late 1830s. Early attempts that were made to capture local scenes naturally progressed to record wide-angle views. These three early panoramas were shot on the South Shore and record vistas and events that occurred almost 100 years ago. It is also interesting to note that photographic paper long enough to print these early images was not produced at the time. The vertical white line in the middle represents the size of the paper that was available then. (All images courtesy of Library of Congress).

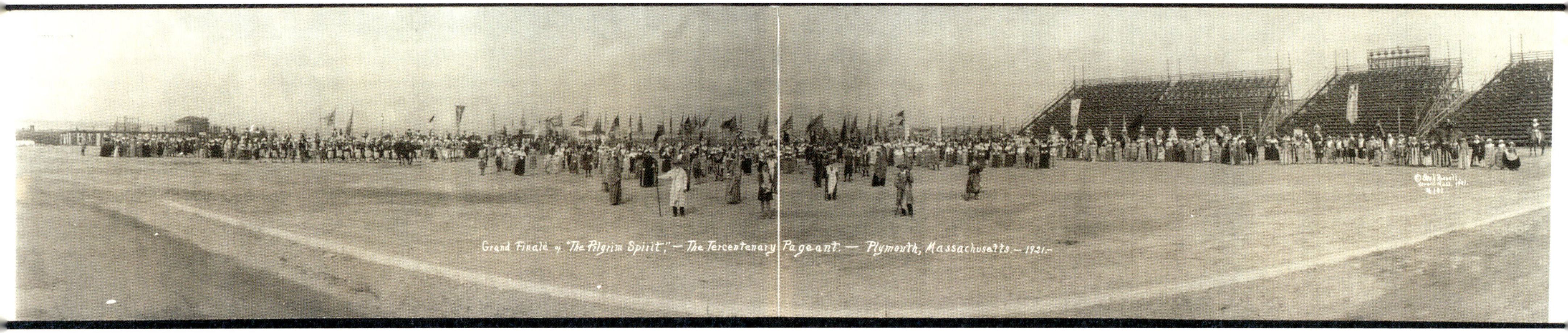

The title of this panorama is the Grand Finale of "The Pilgrim Spirit"— The Tercentenary Pageant—and was shot by George H. Russell in July 1921. The print size was 7" by 40".

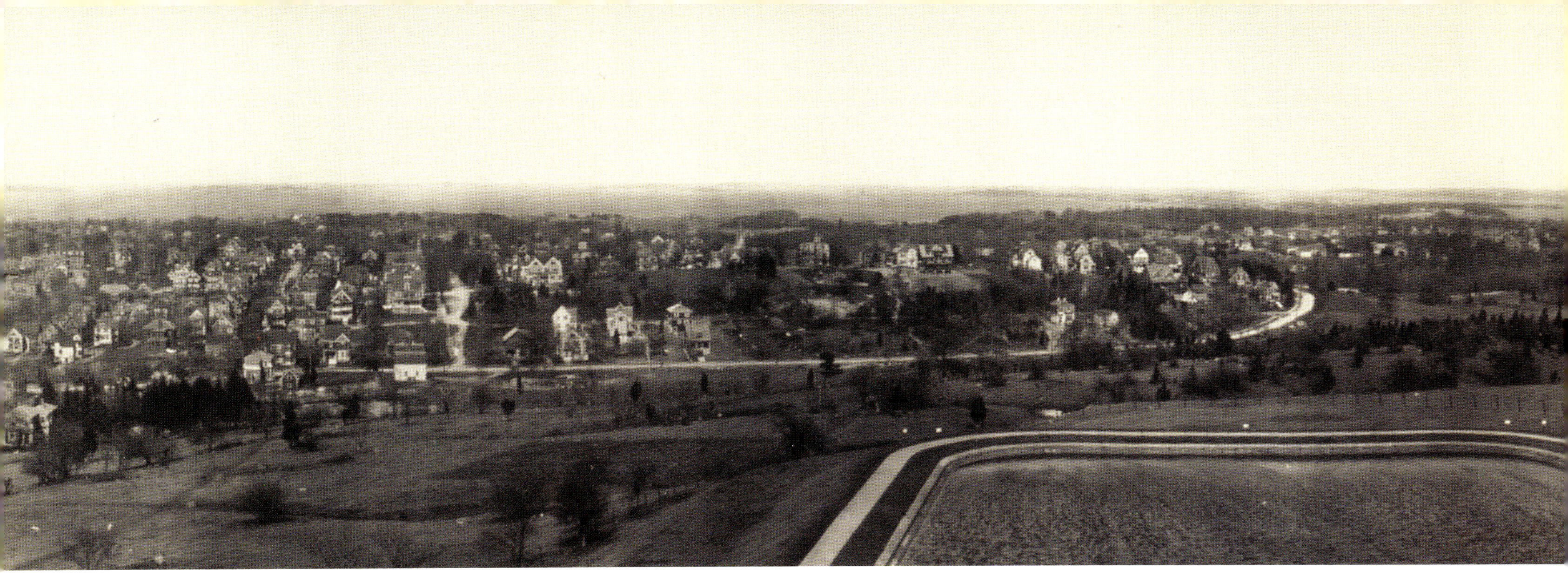

The original size of this gelatin silver print of Wollaston was 7.5" by 41.5", and was shot by K.F. Harriman in April 1910. Boston Harbor and the islands can be seen in the distance.

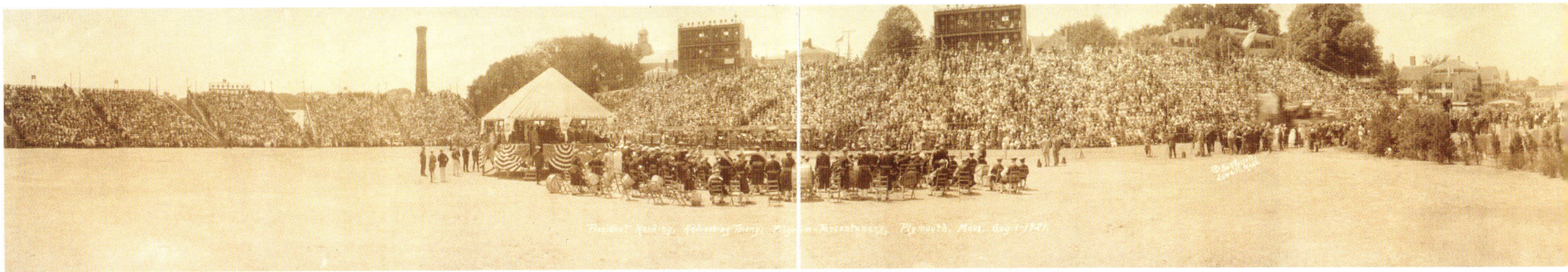

Another view of the Pilgrim Tercentenary captured by George H. Russell, this panorama measured 8" by 46", and recorded President Harding in the covered gazebo addressing the audience on August 1, 1921.

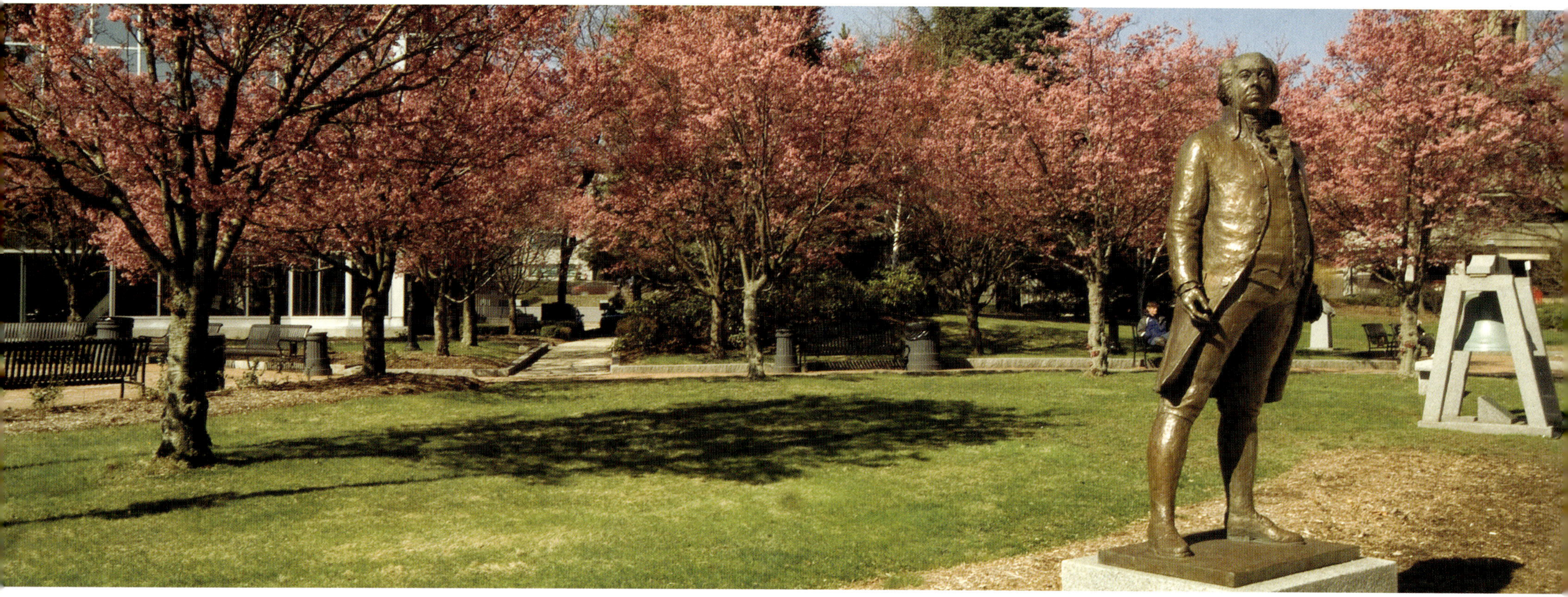

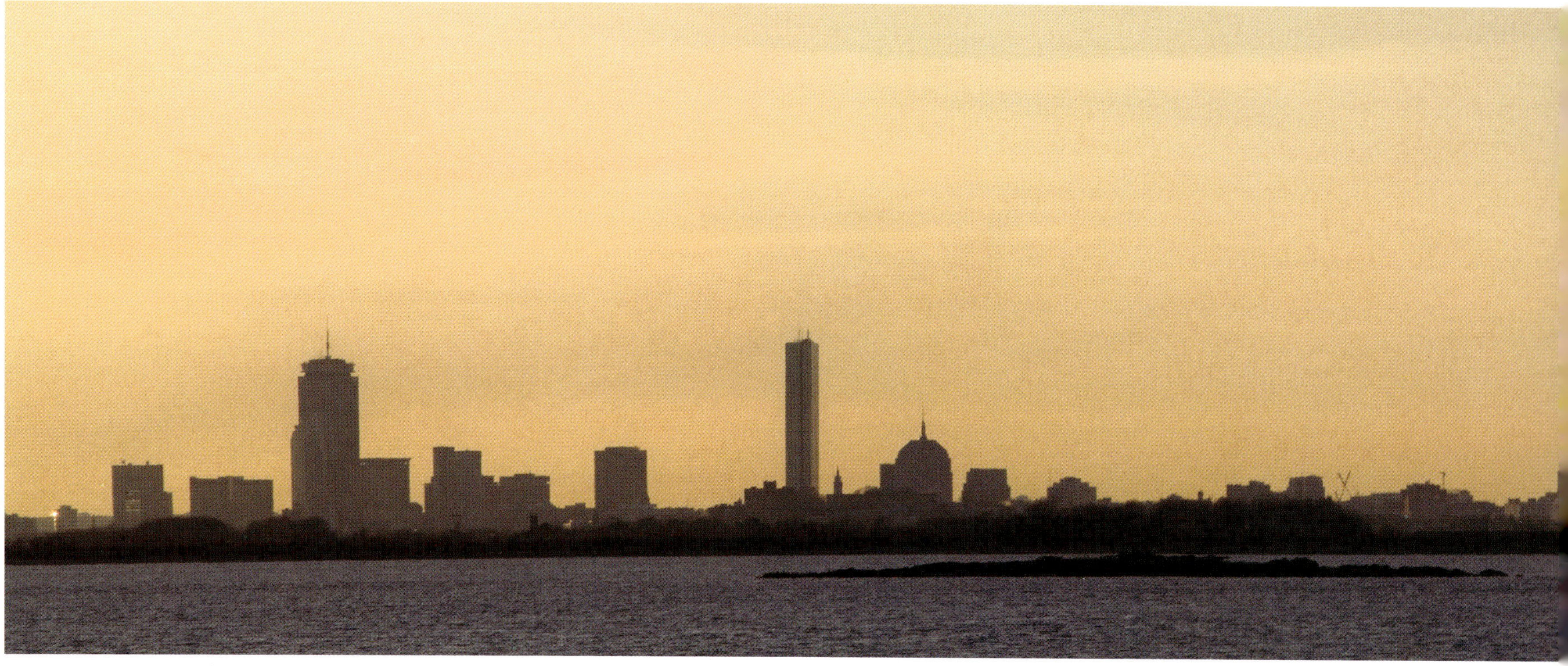

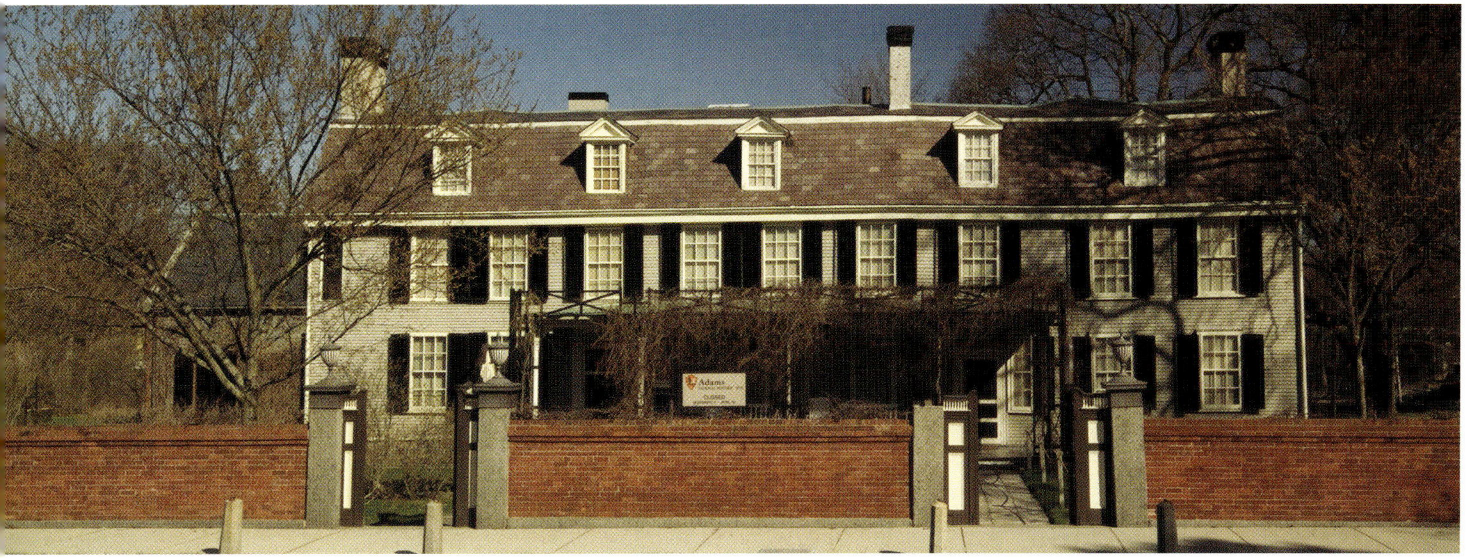

This is the Adams National Historic Site, built in 1731, purchased by John in 1787; it would be the "summer Whitehouse" for two Presidents. Ironically, John died here on the fourth of July, 1826, just a few hours after Thomas Jefferson passed away at his home, Monticello, in Virginia. The house was lived in by the Adams family descendents until 1927. It was later turned over to the federal government and is now maintained by the National Park Service.

Opposite:
A statue of John Adams, our second President, stands in front of the City Hall in downtown Quincy.

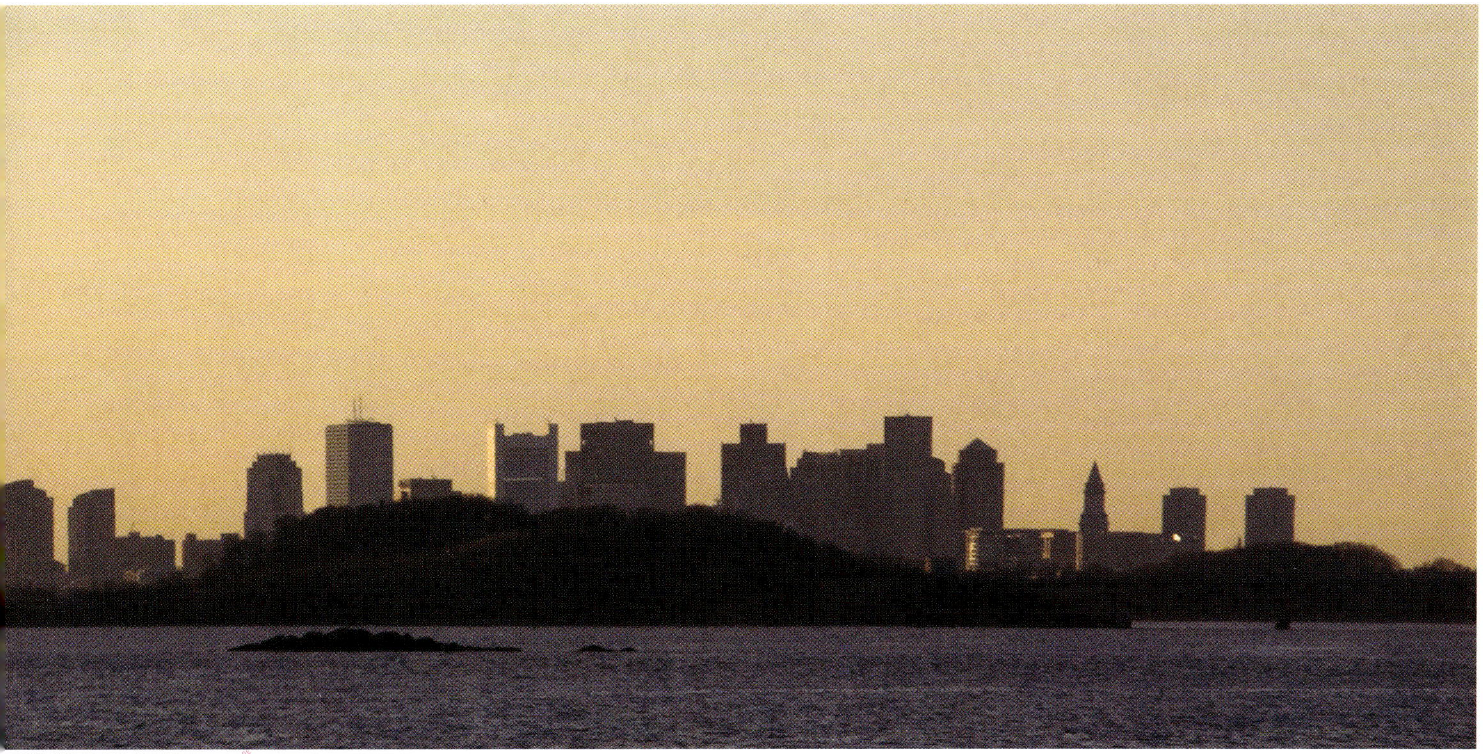

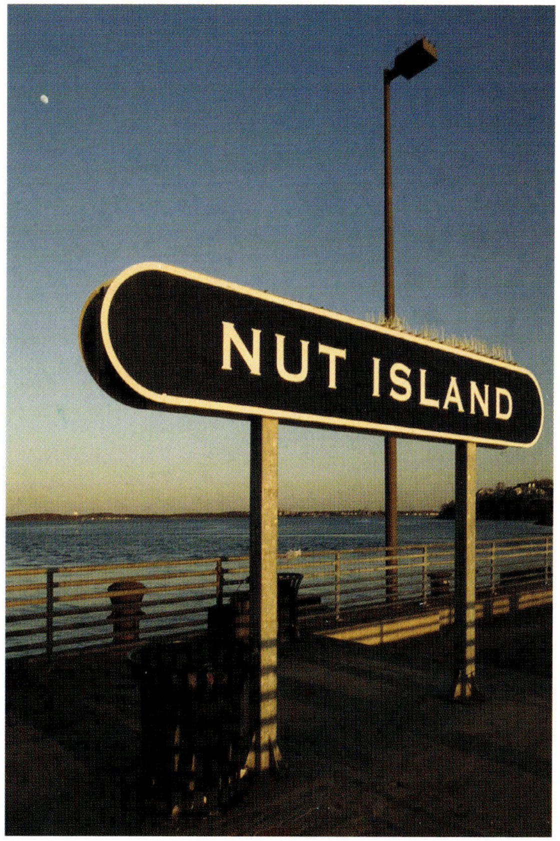

This view of the Boston skyline across Quincy Bay was taken from Nut Island, a park located at the end of Hough's Neck, in Quincy. With walking trails and a fishing pier, this tip of land offers panoramic views of Boston and the harbor islands.

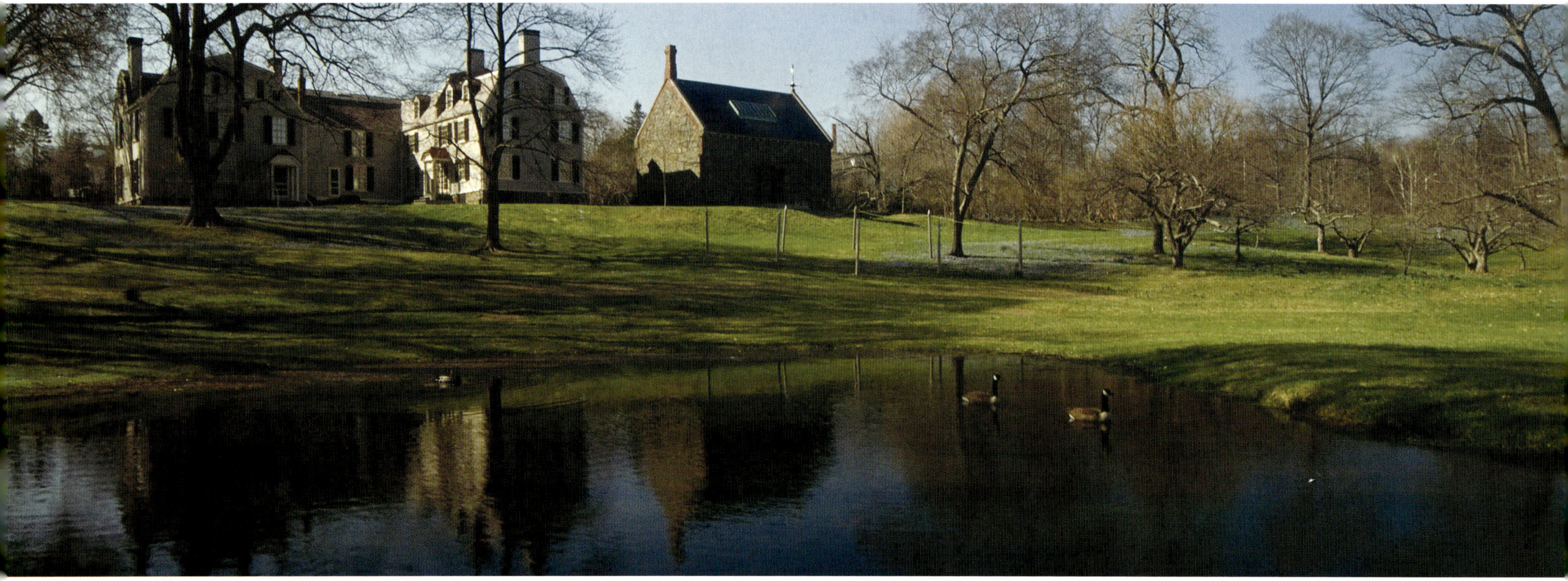

These two views show the house and gardens of the Adams estate. The slate-roofed granite (from local quarries) building is fire and waterproof and contains the 14,000 volume Adams Library. It also has the desks used by both father and son.

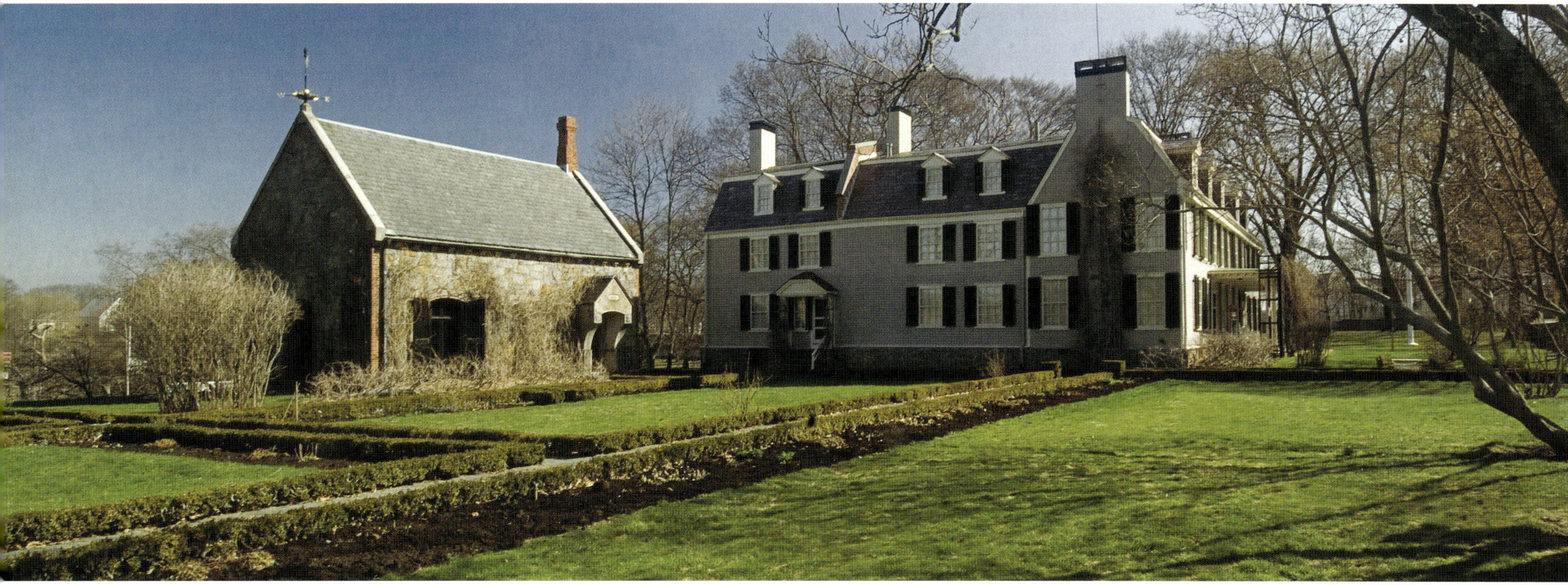

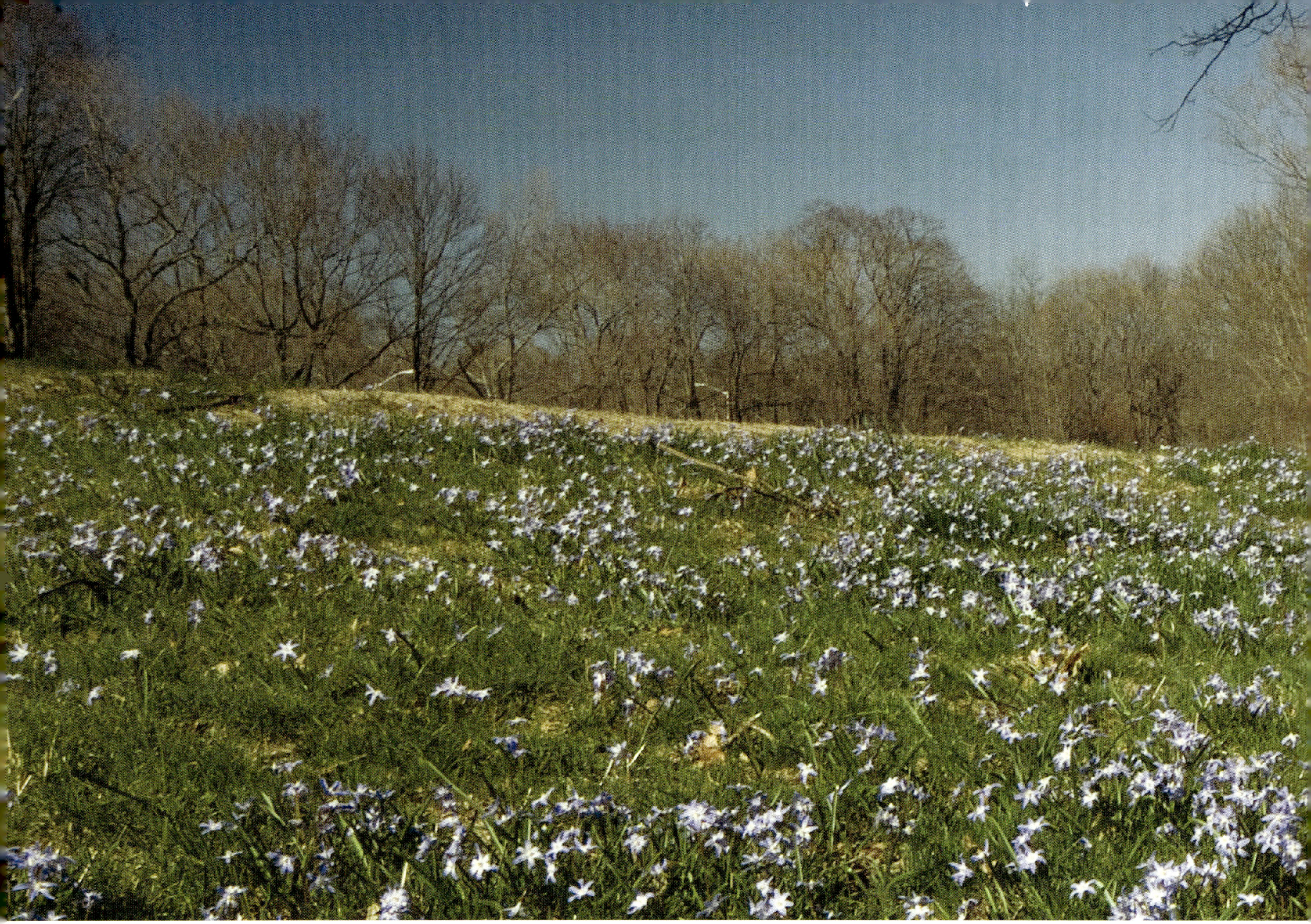
Blue flowers bloom in the spring with the Beale house in the background.
It is now the administrative headquarters for the Adams Historical Site.

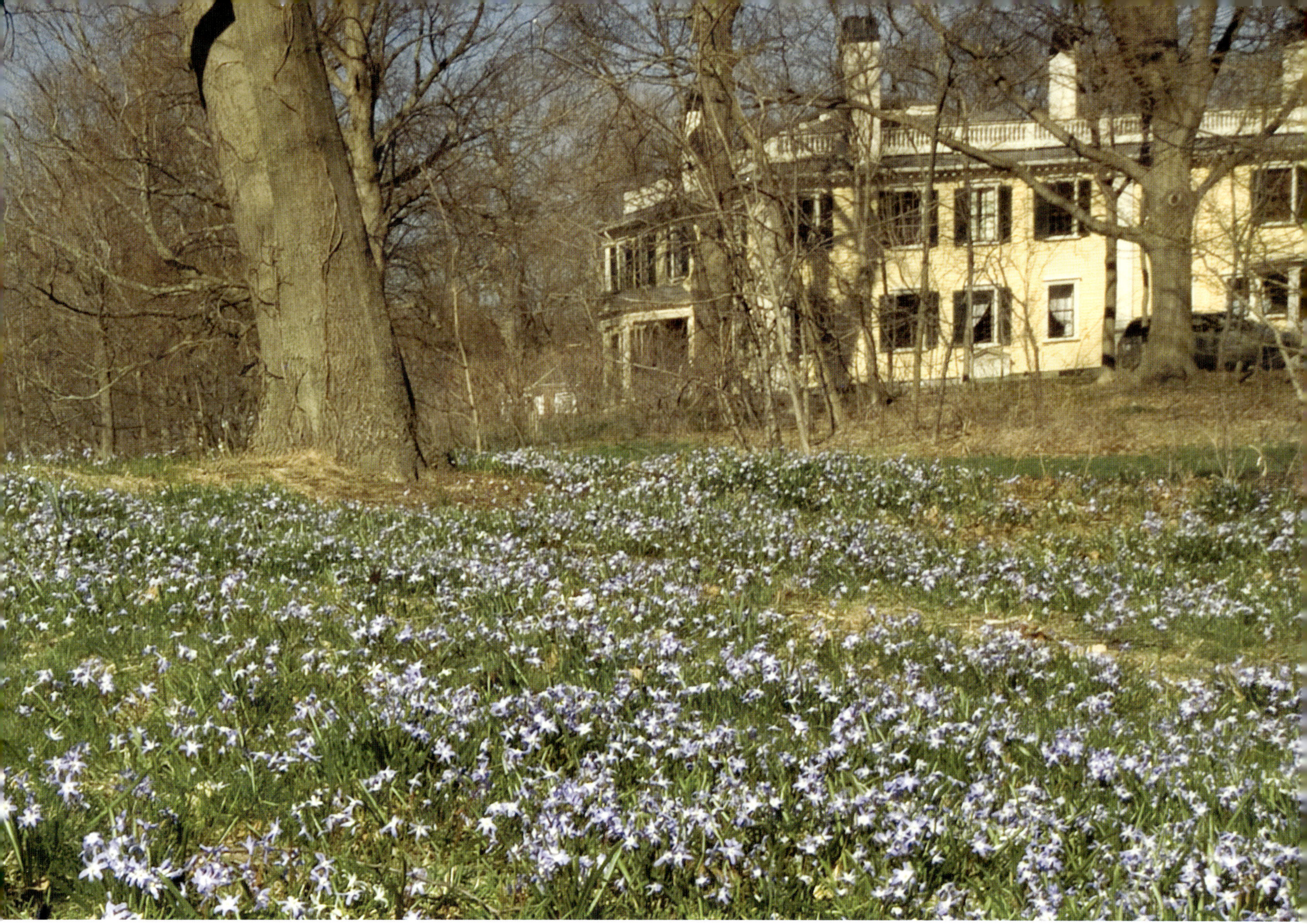

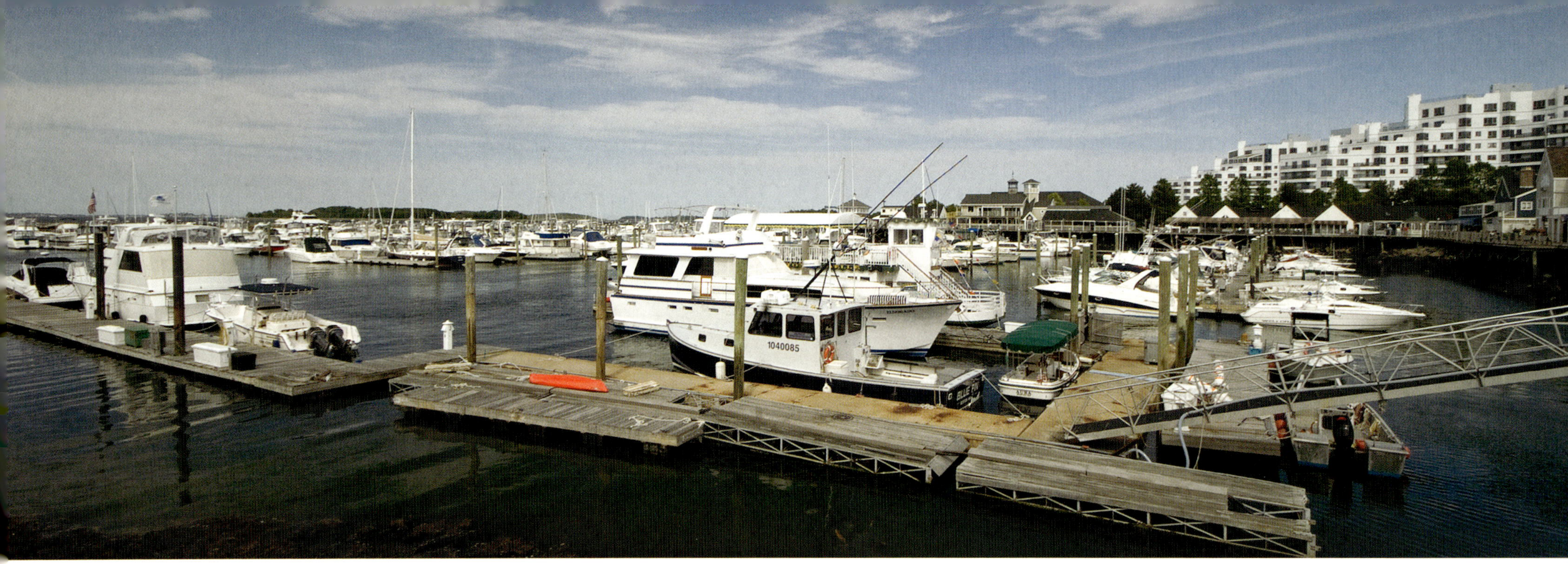

Marina Bay, in the Squantum section of Quincy, is a Nantucket-like community with boardwalks, boutiques, shops, restaurants, condominiums, and a marina. During the boating season, the nearly 700 slips are filled with a variety of craft.

Granite Links Golf Course offers spectacular panoramic views across the South Shore. This view is looking north with the Boston skyline in the distance.

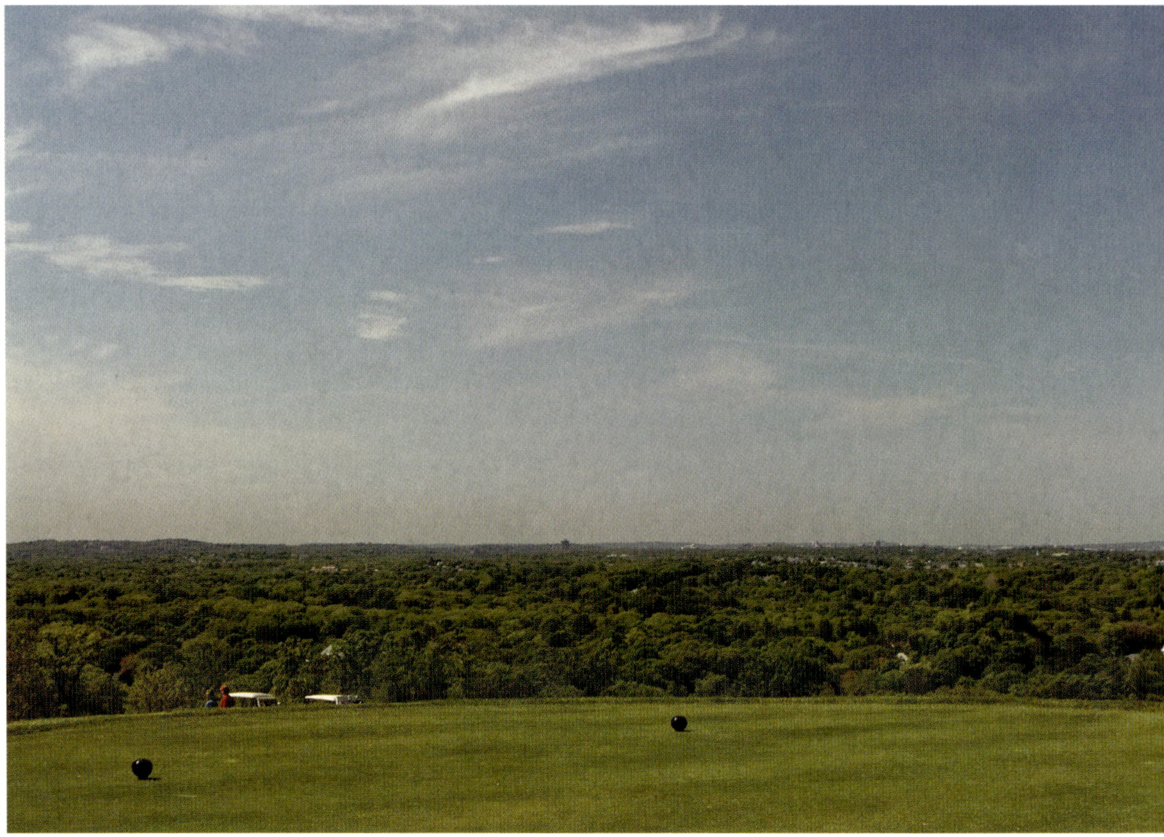

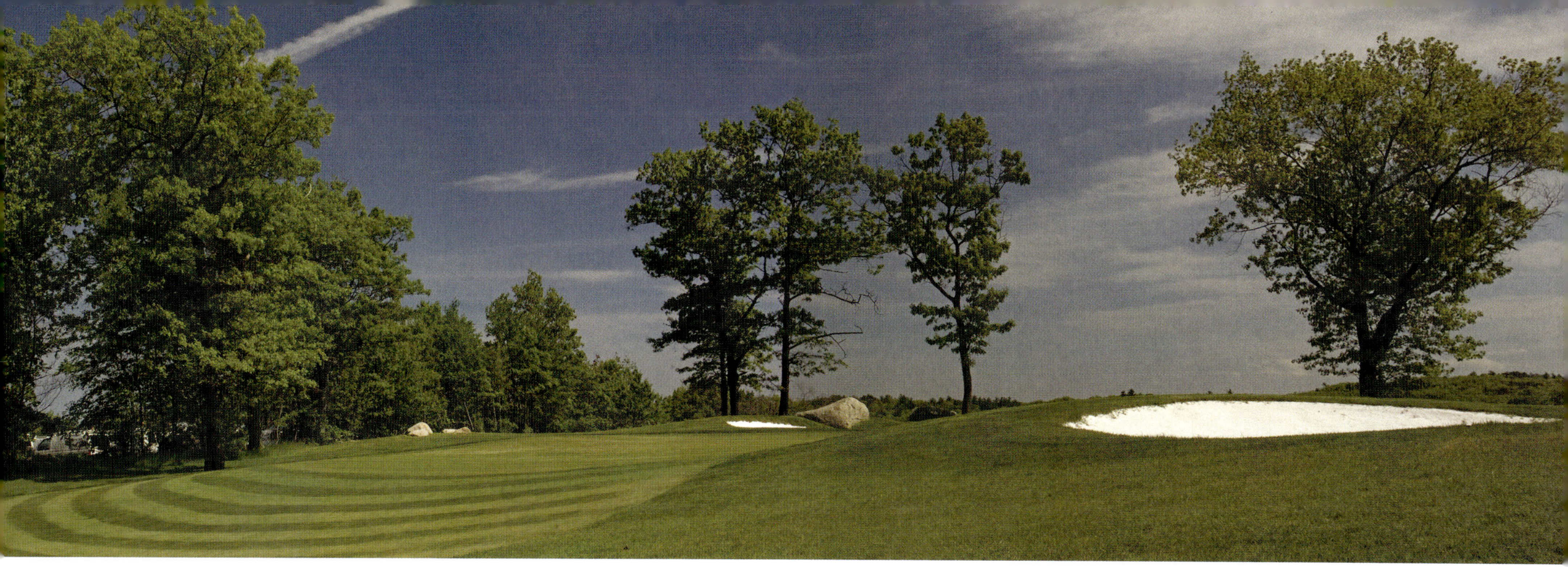

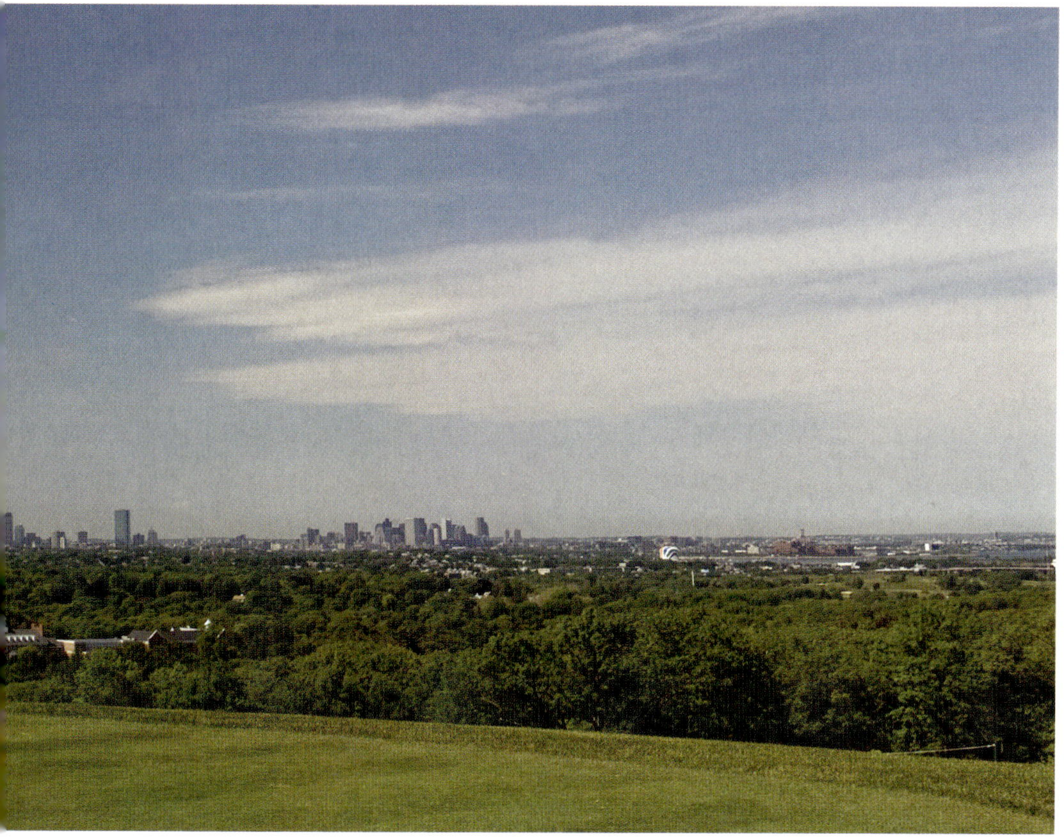

Another view of the Granite Links Golf Course.

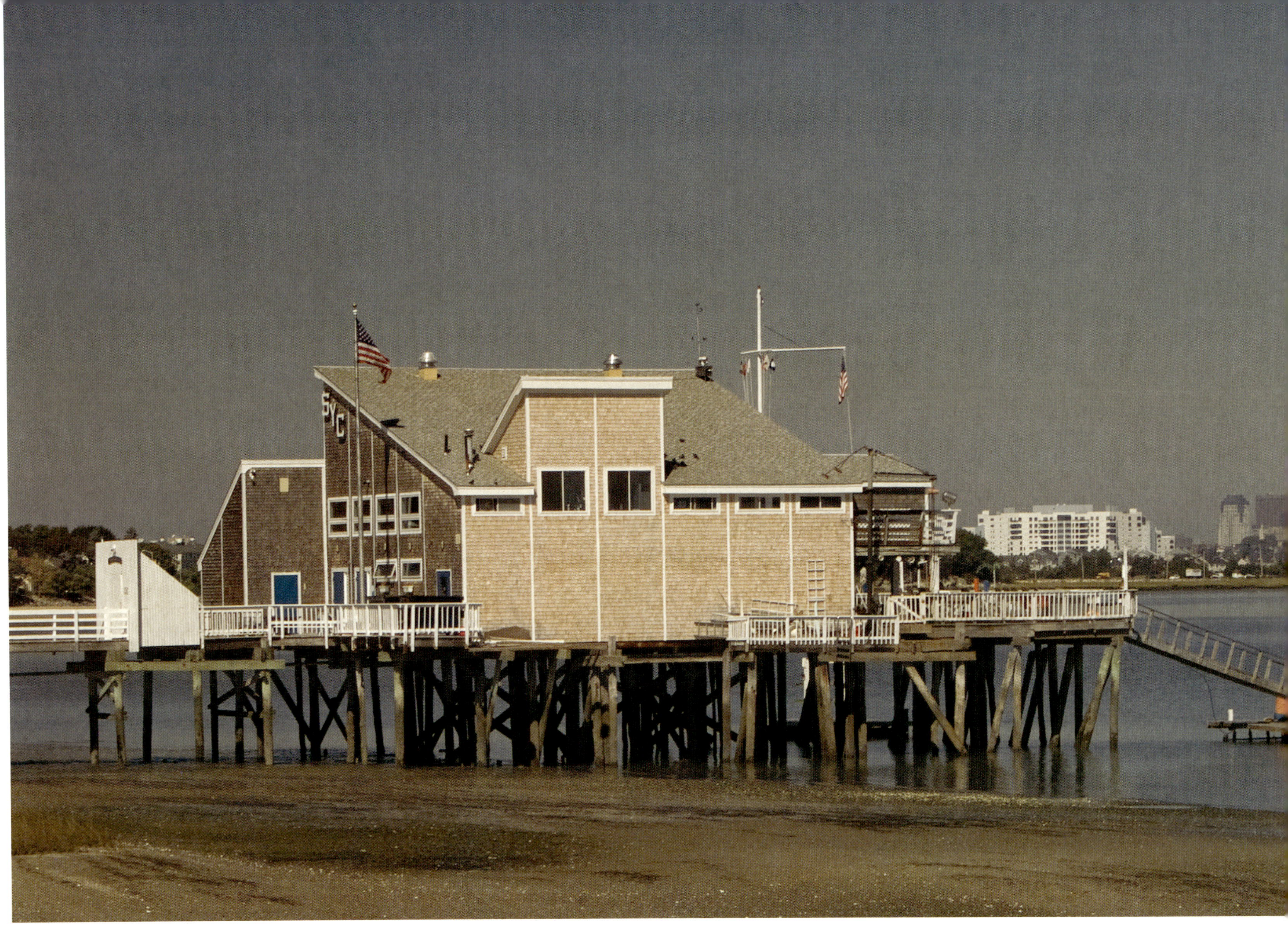

Along Wollaston Beach, Squantum Yacht Club is one of the marinas on the bay. The Boston skyline can be seen in the distance.

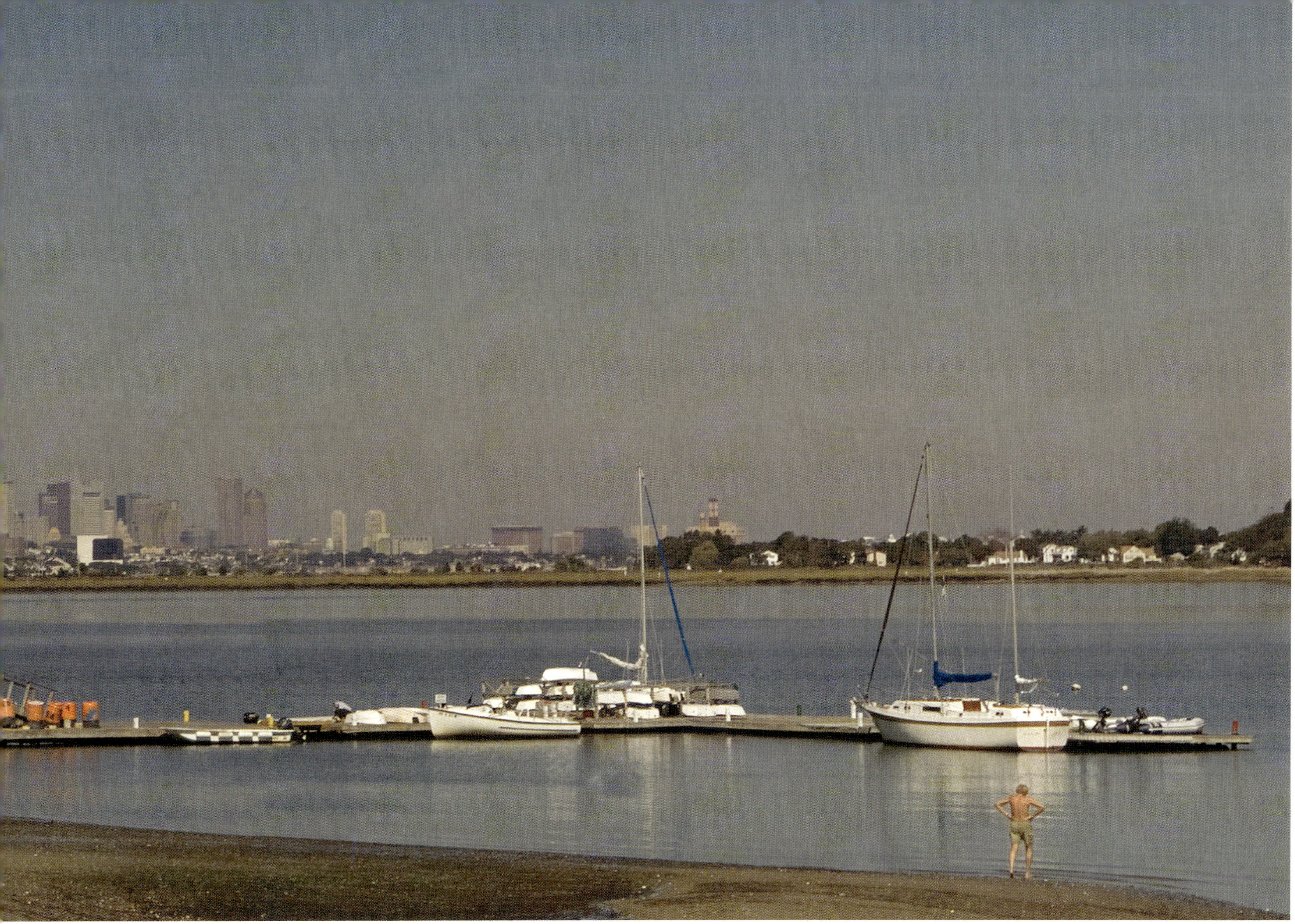

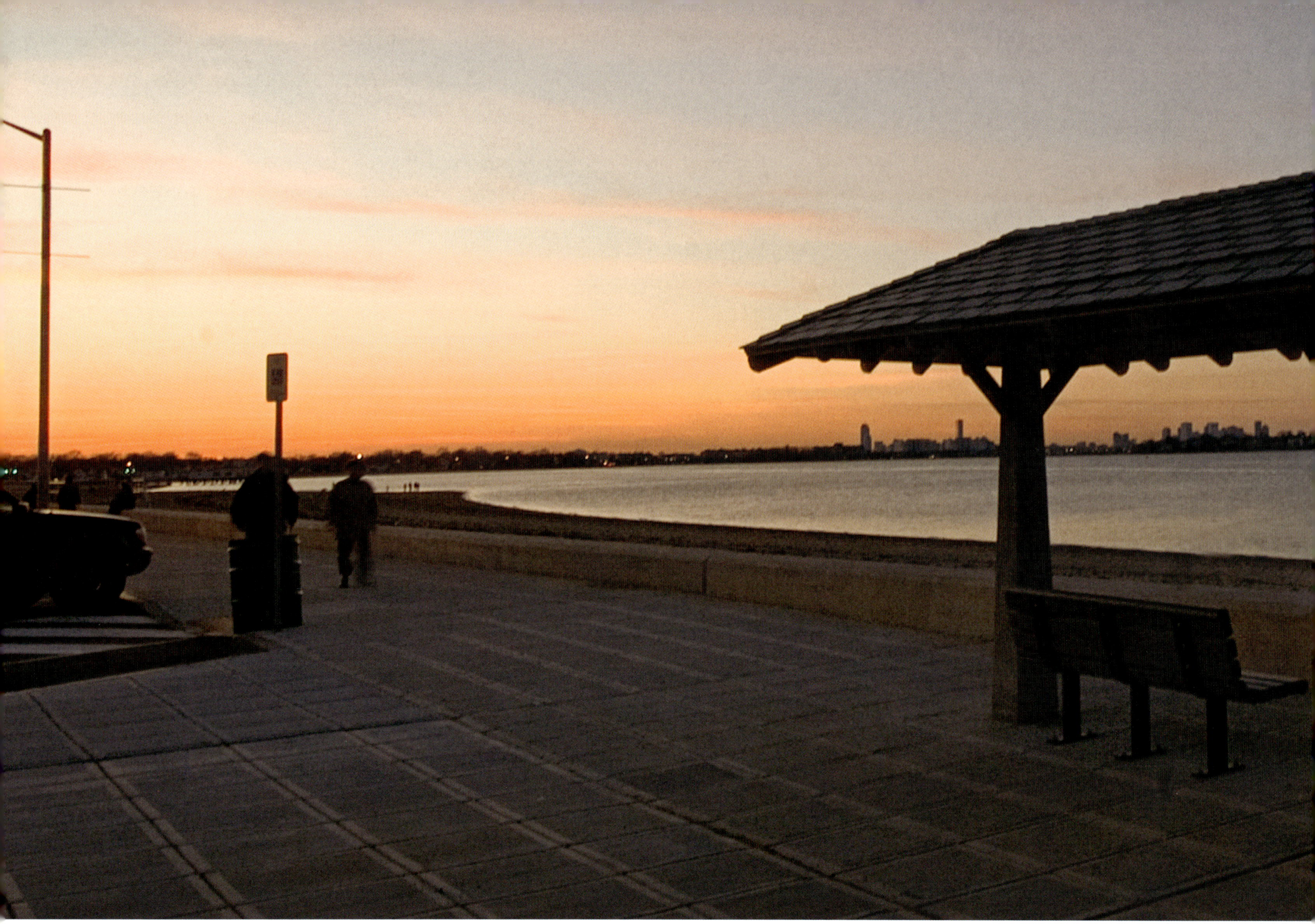

With a large walkway, rest areas, nearby restaurants, and plenty of parking, Wollaston Beach is a favorite for residents and a great place to watch the sunset.

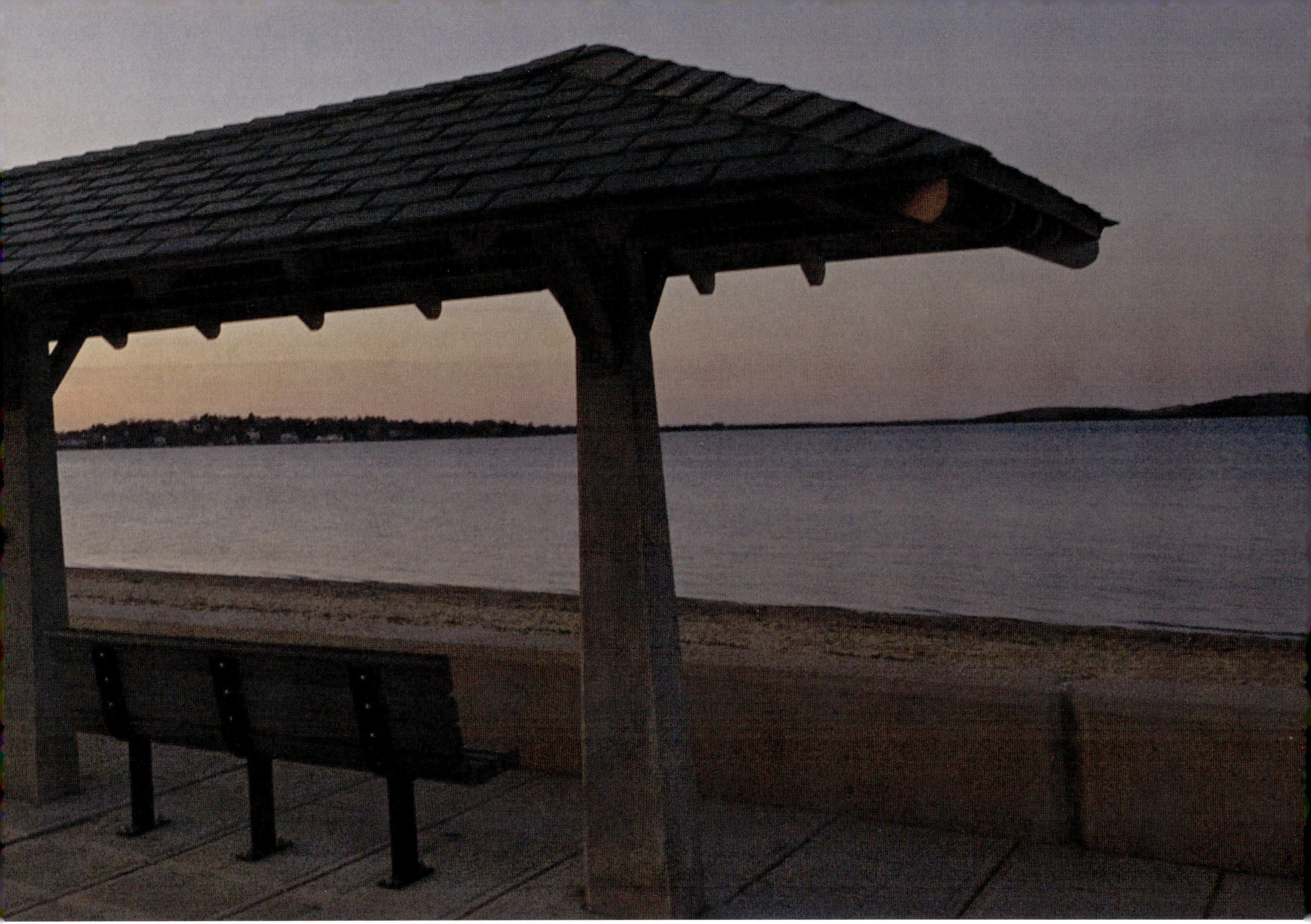

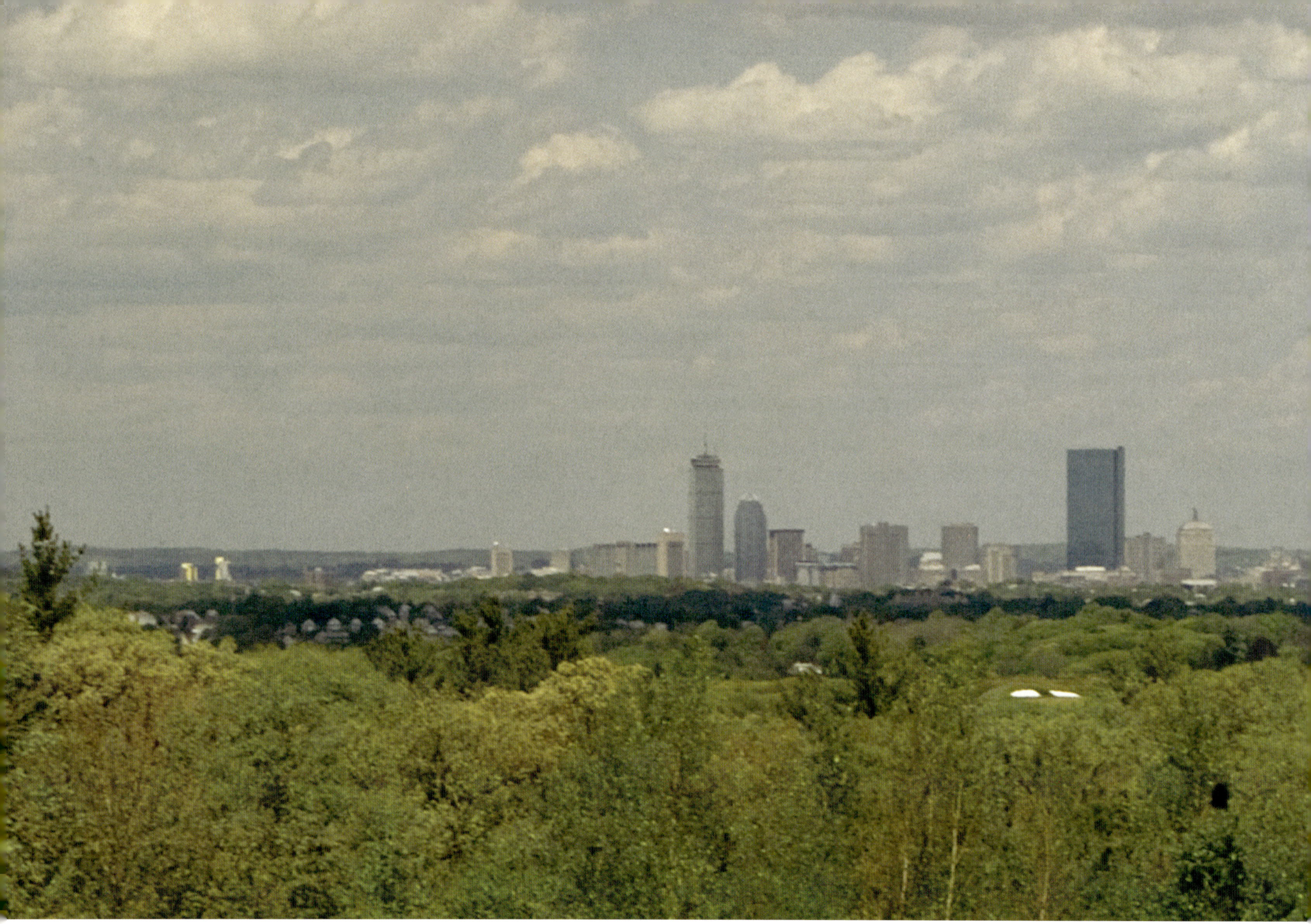

Chickatawbut Hill in the Blue Hills Reservation offers views of Boston.

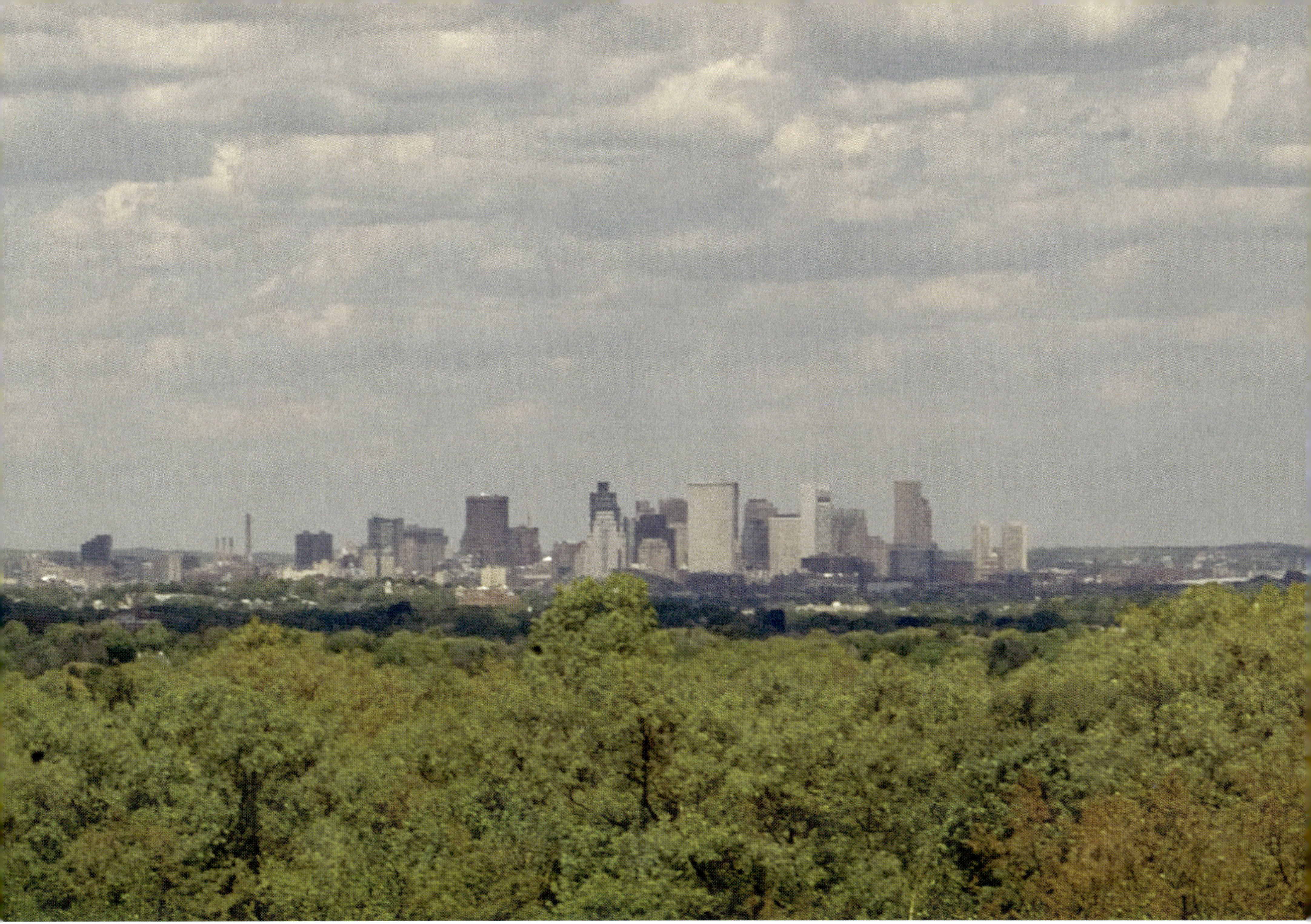

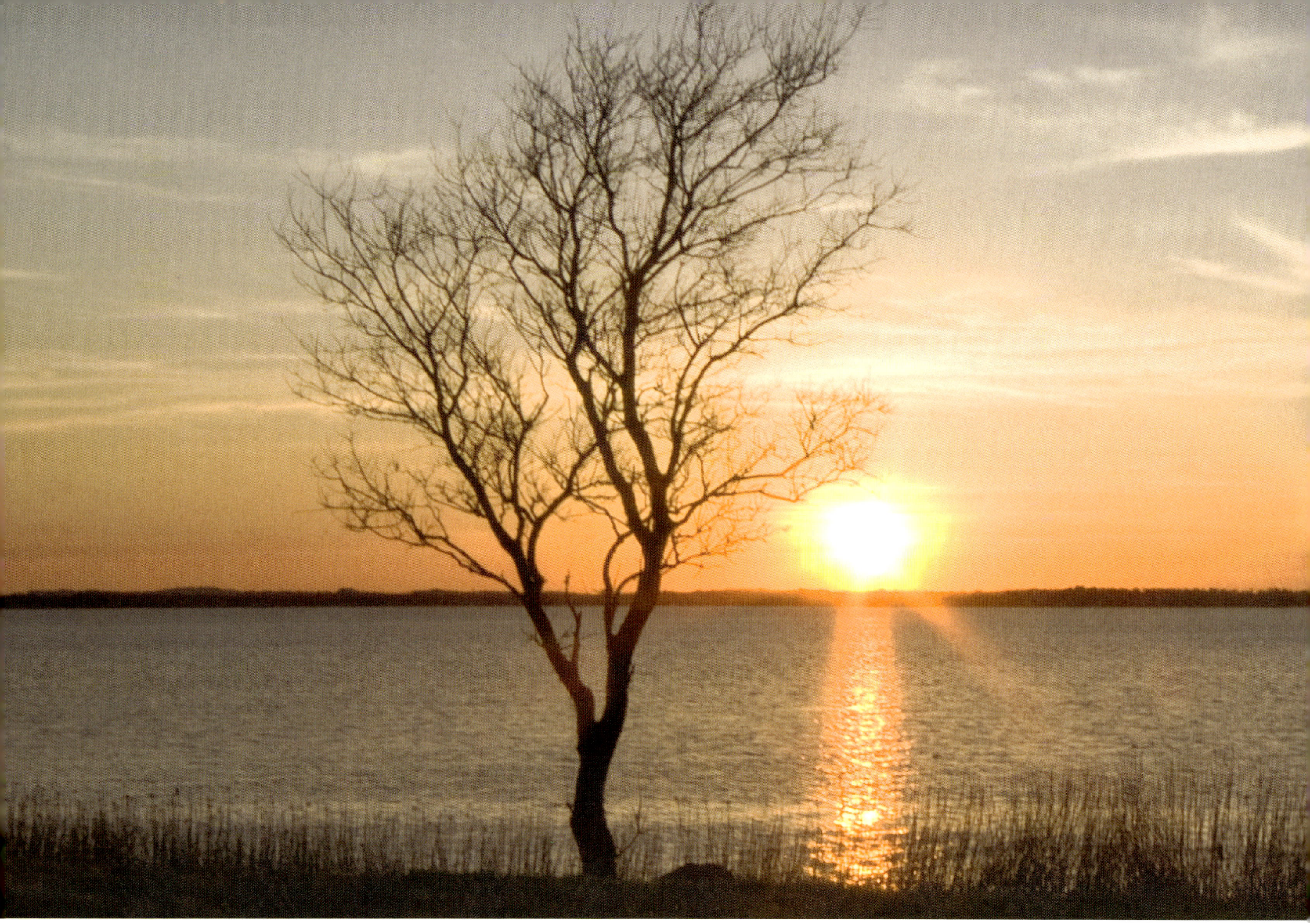

A sunset over Quincy Bay.

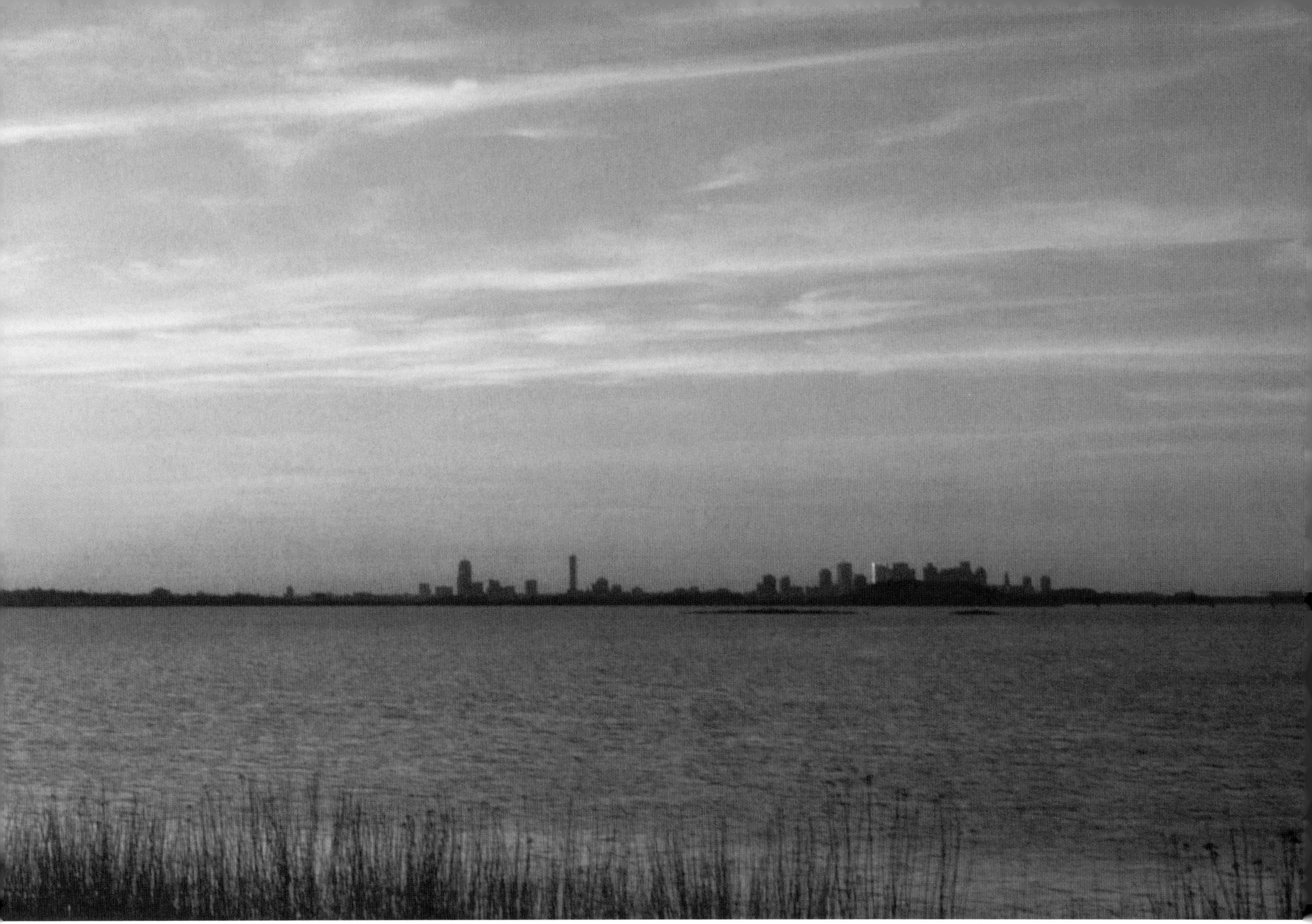

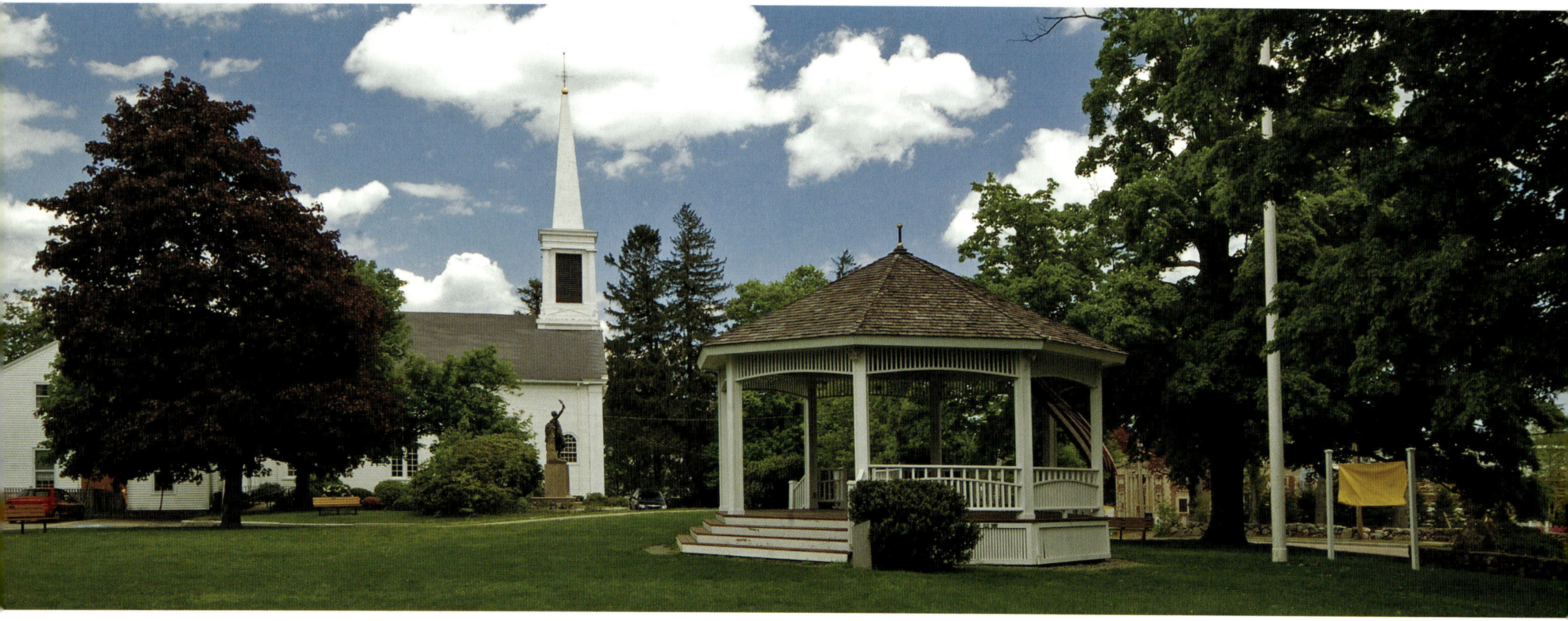

Two views of the Milton green in front of the Town Hall with the distinctive white churches.

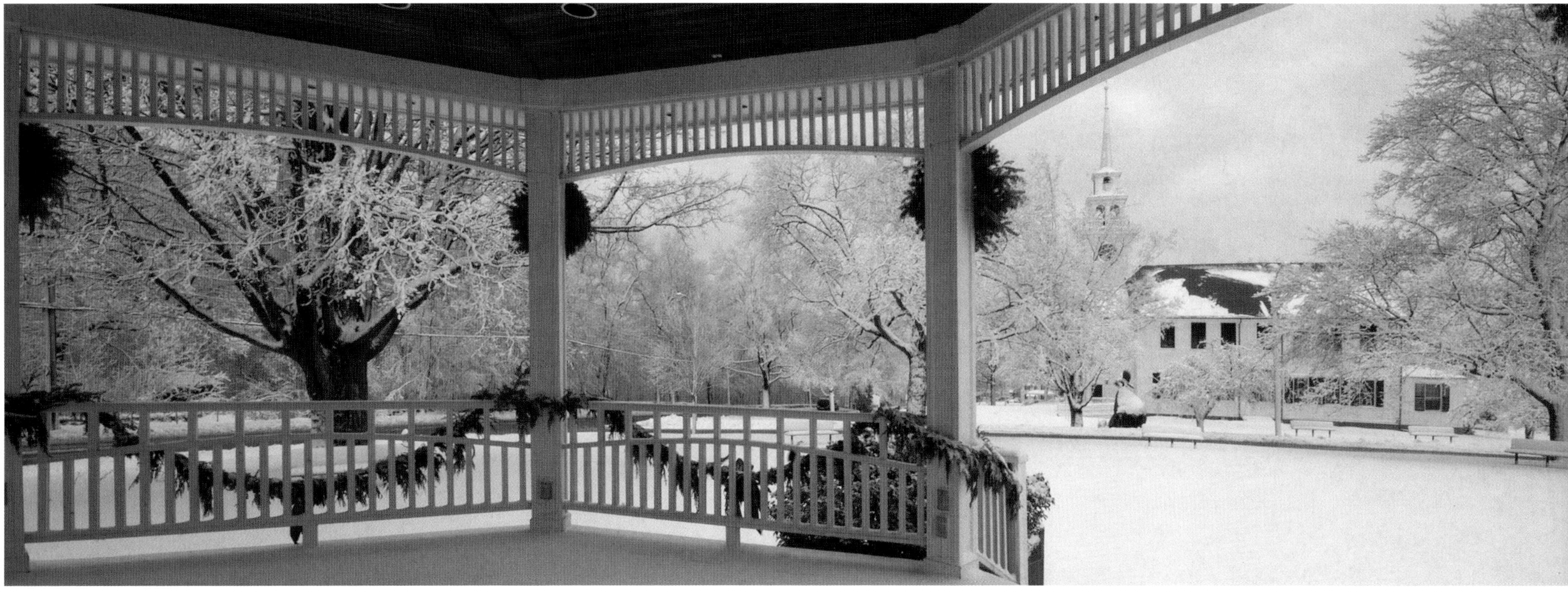

The gazebo in Milton, decorated for the holiday season.

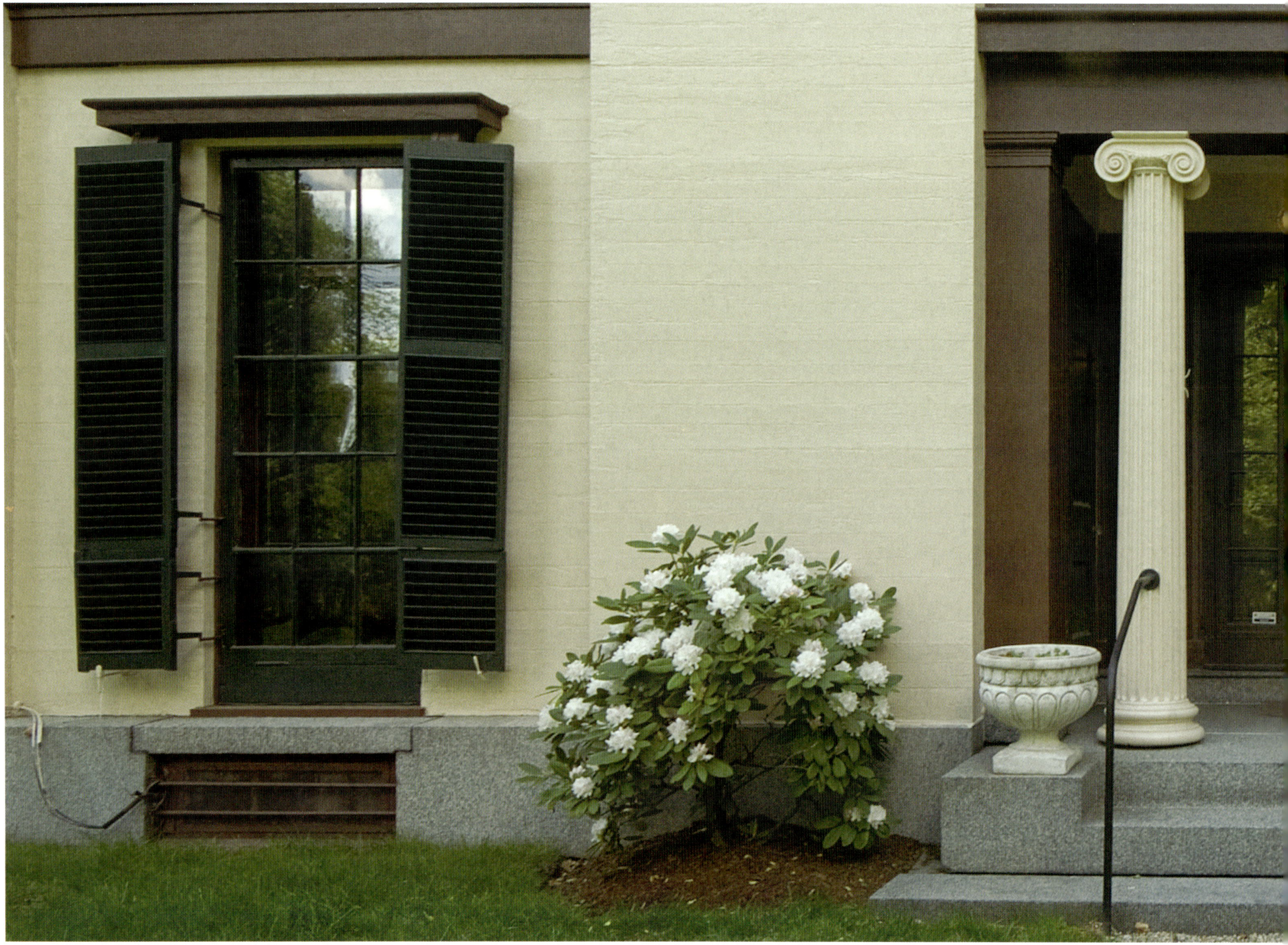

The front door of the Forbes House Museum.

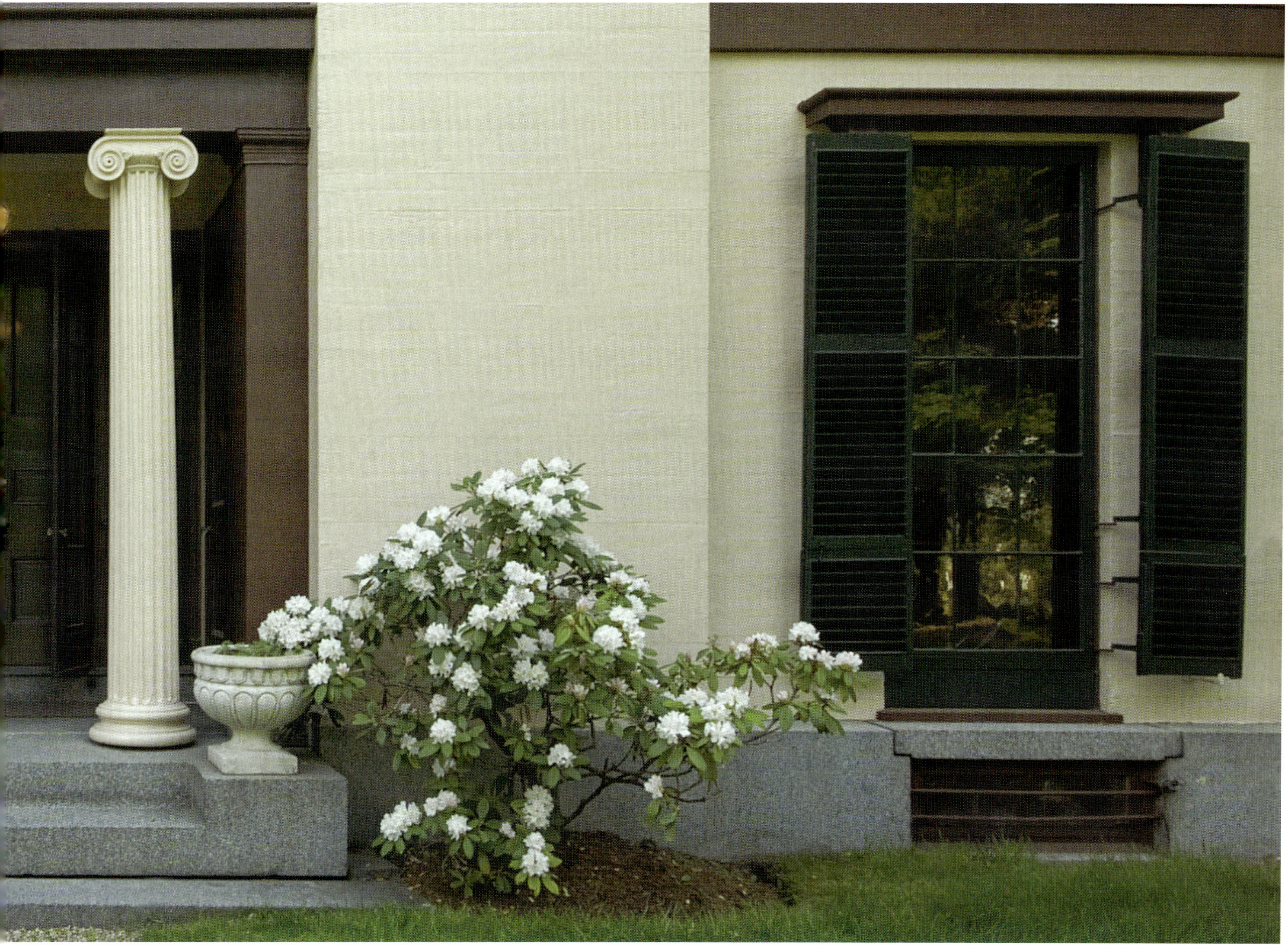

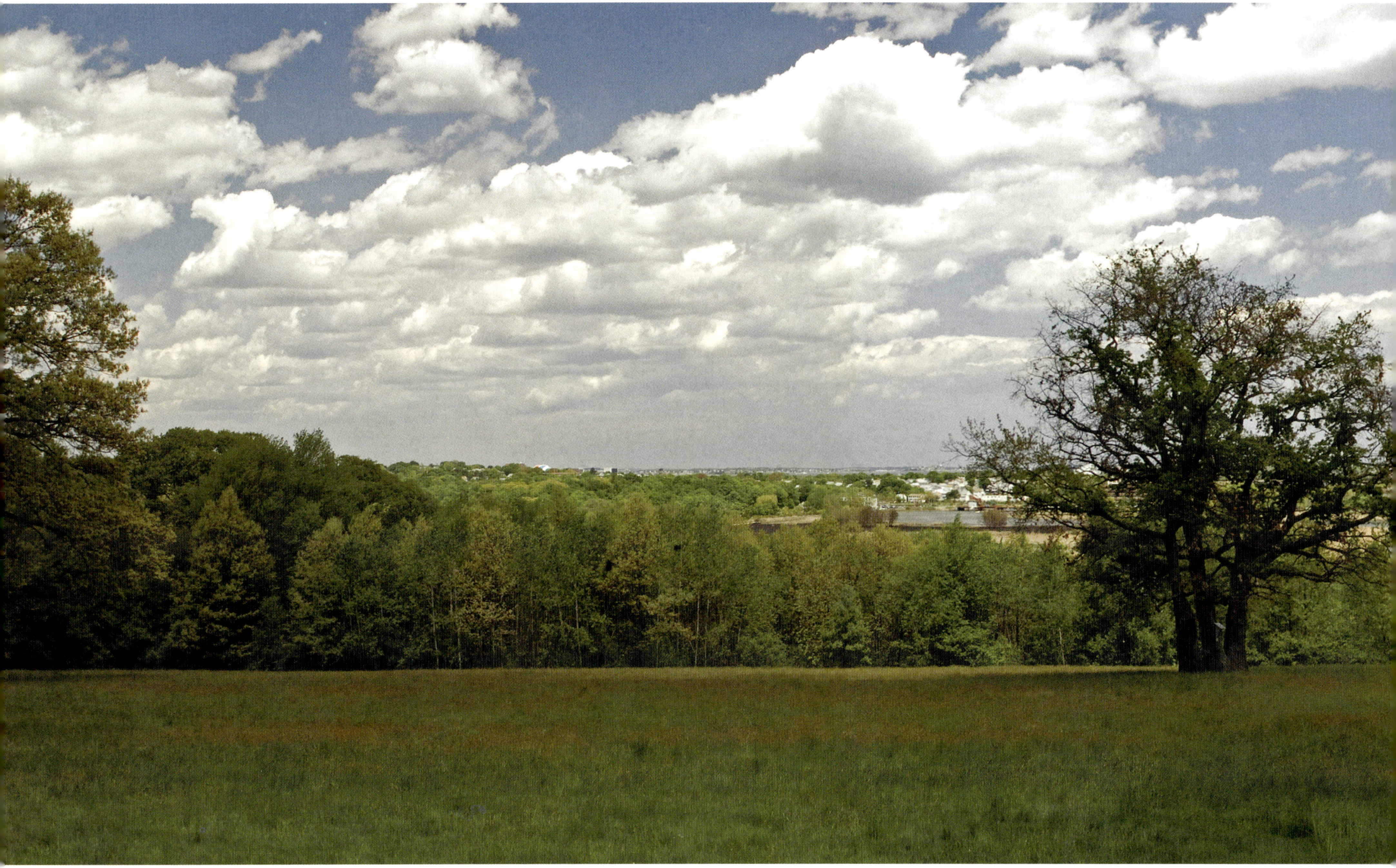

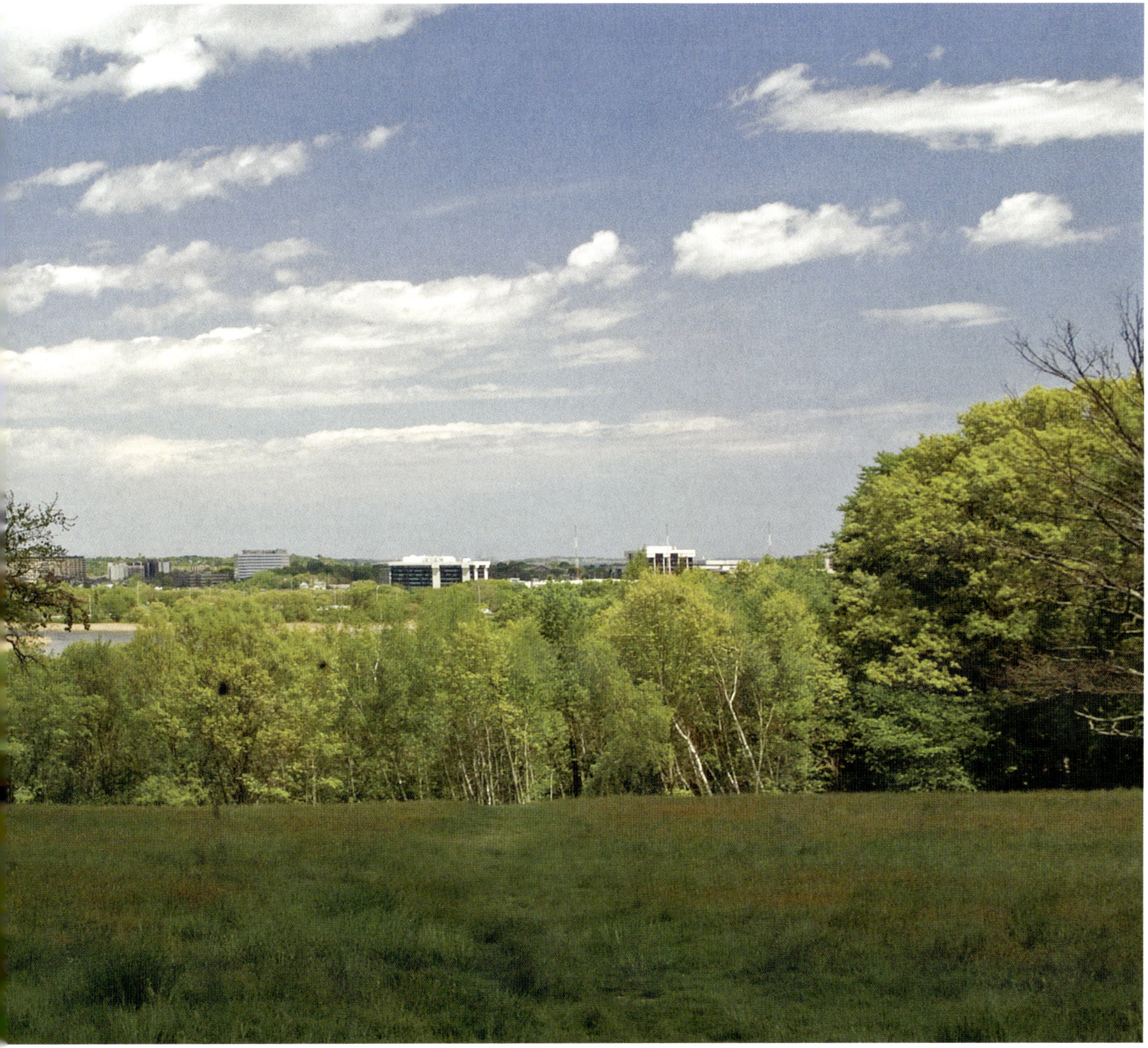

Governor Hutchinson's Field is on Adams Street in Milton and overlooks the Neponset River with the Boston skyline in the distance. Named for the owner, who was the last Royal Governor of the Massachusetts Bay Colony and loyal to the British Crown, Thomas Hutchinson built a modest estate in 1743 in this field. After the Boston Tea Party in 1774, he fled to England, where he died.

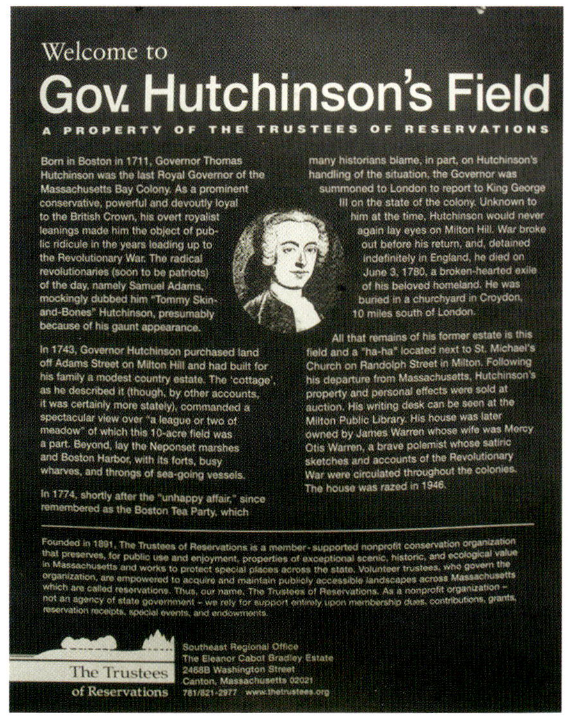

Looking southeast from the top of Big Blue, Ponkapoag Pond can be seen in the middle distance. At 635 feet, Big Blue offers views as far as 150 miles.

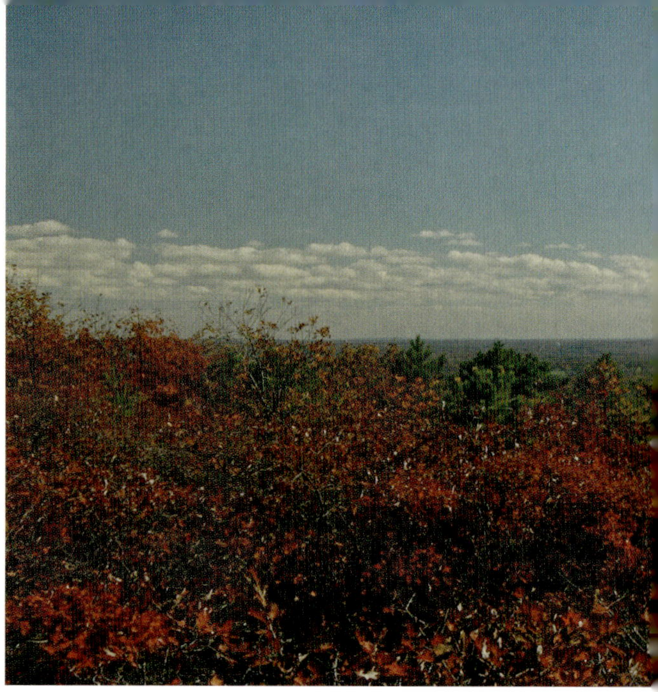

A great horned owl stares at the camera at the Trailside Museum in the Blue Hills Reservation.

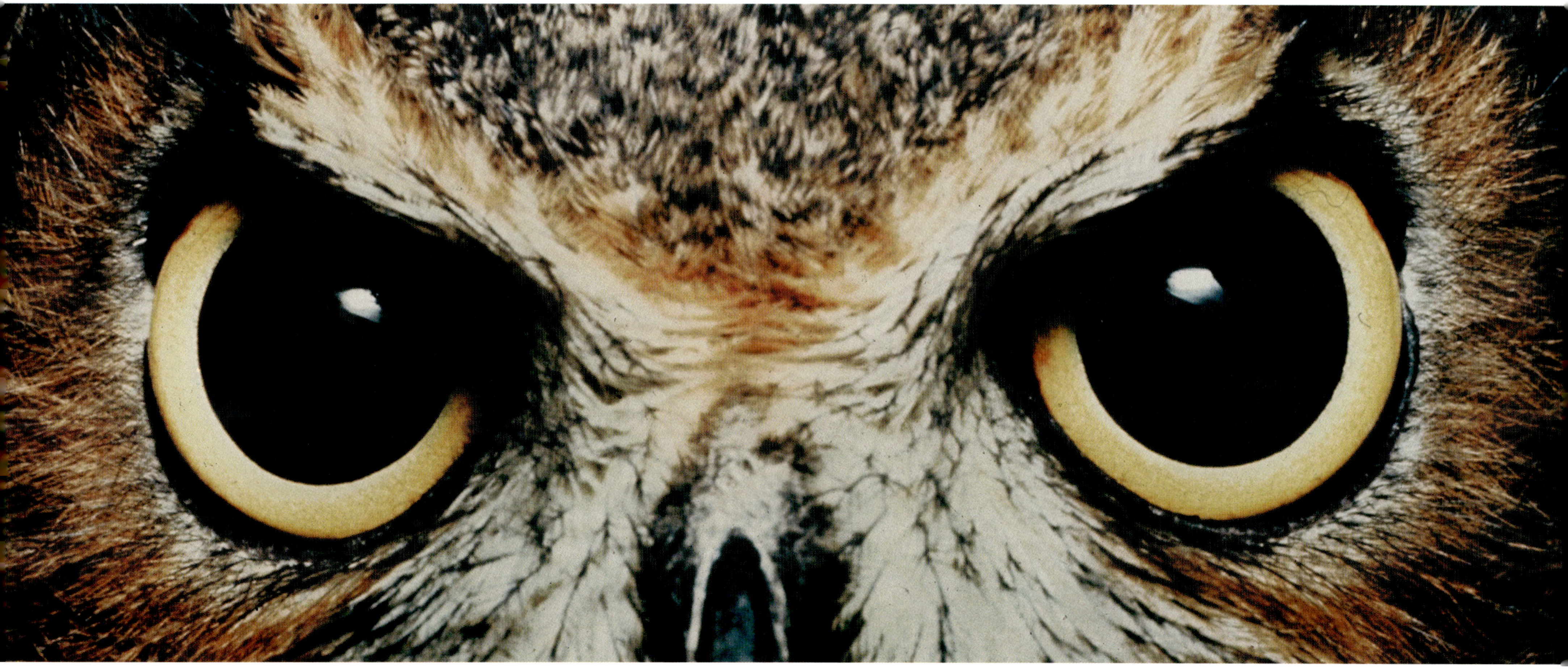

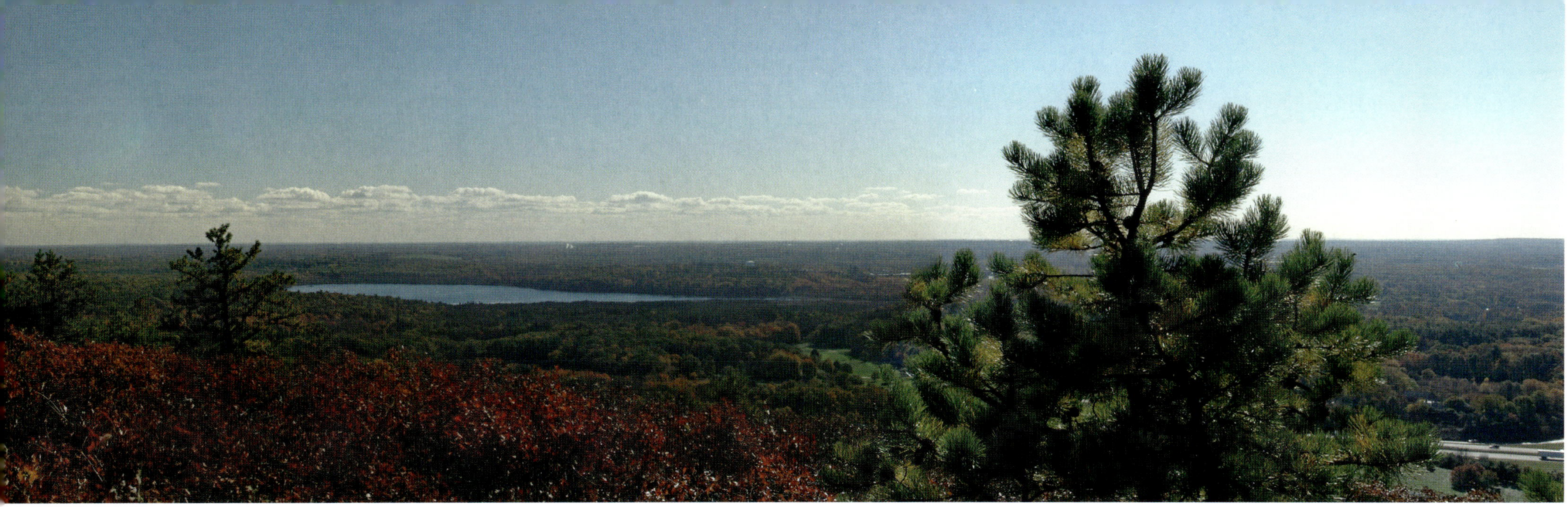

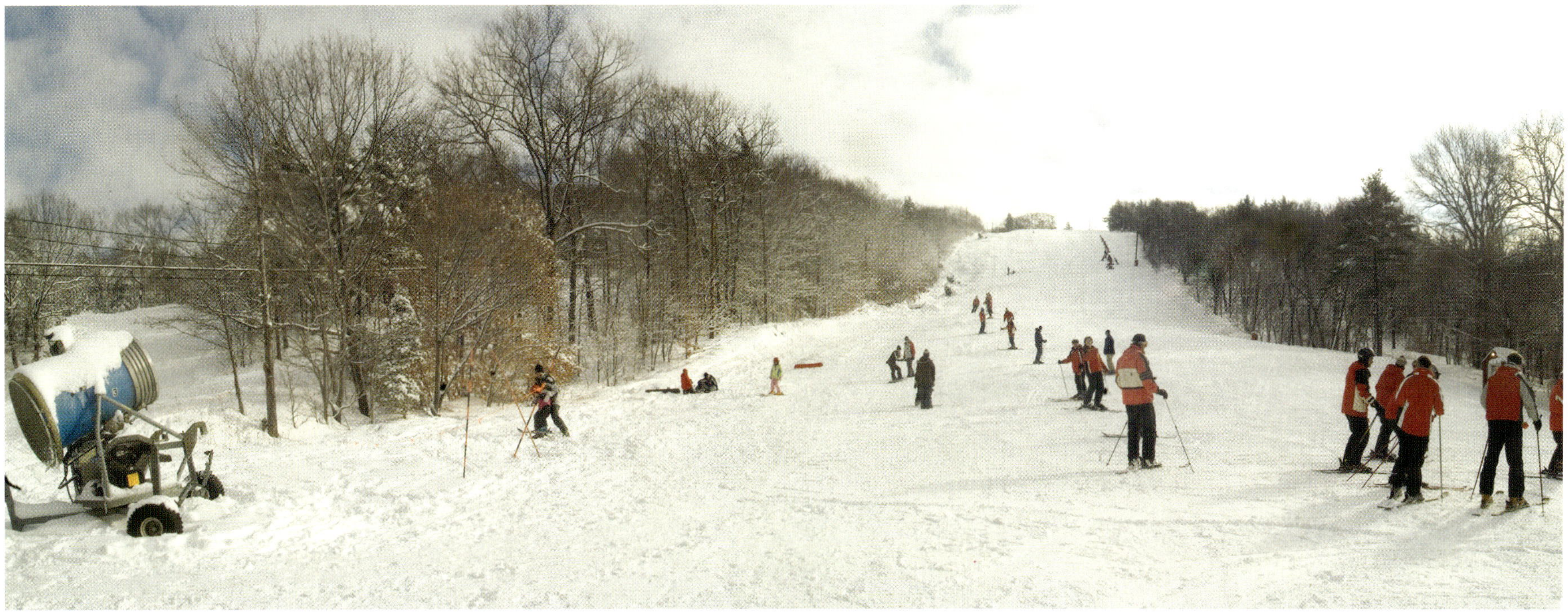

In the winter, the slopes of Big Blue provide an opportunity to ski and snowboard.

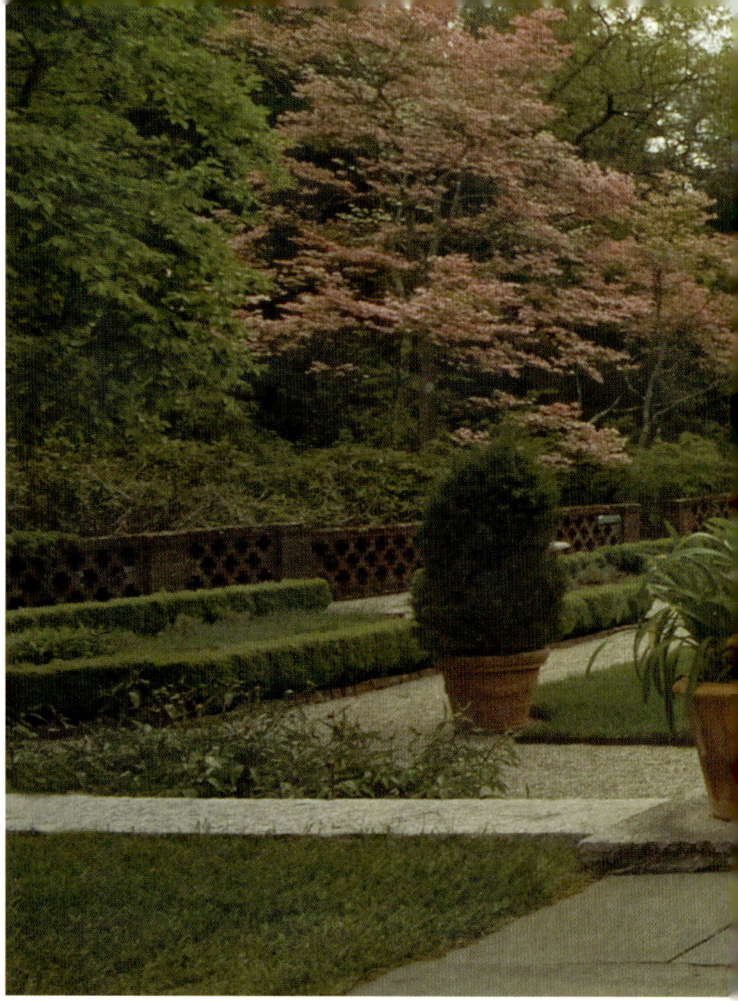

Houghton's Pond, also in the Blue Hills Reservation, provides a year-round location for a variety of activities.

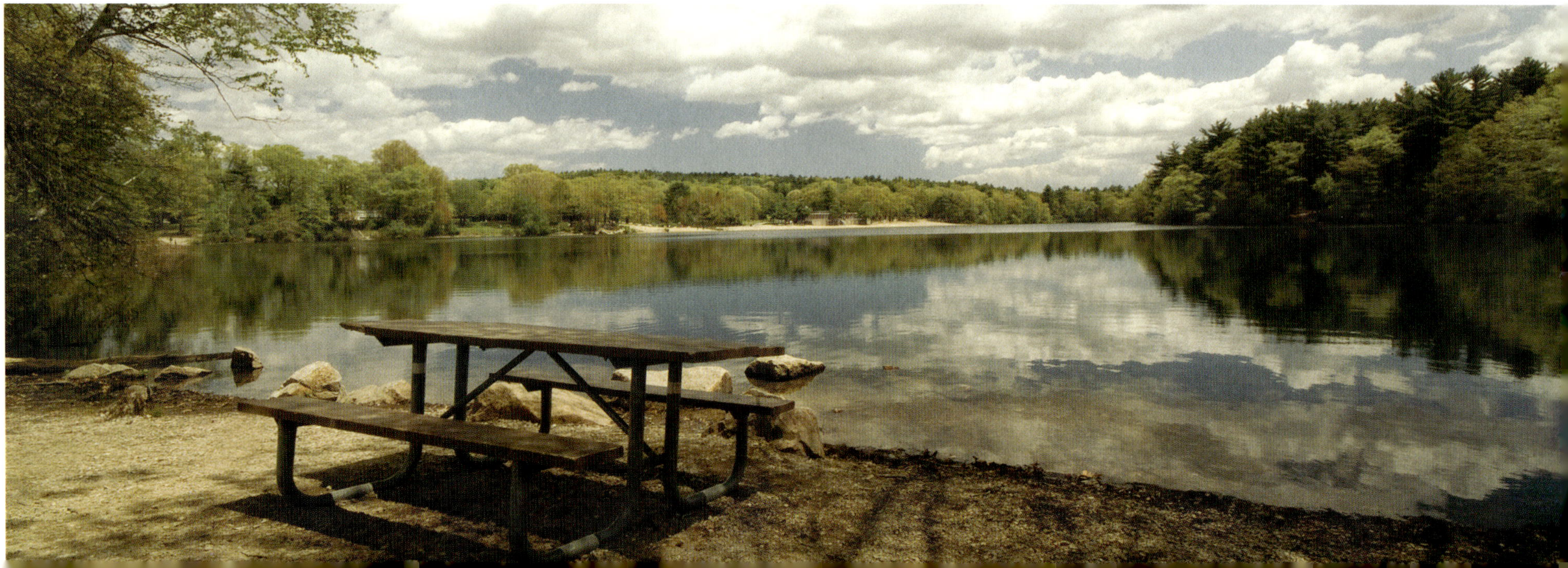

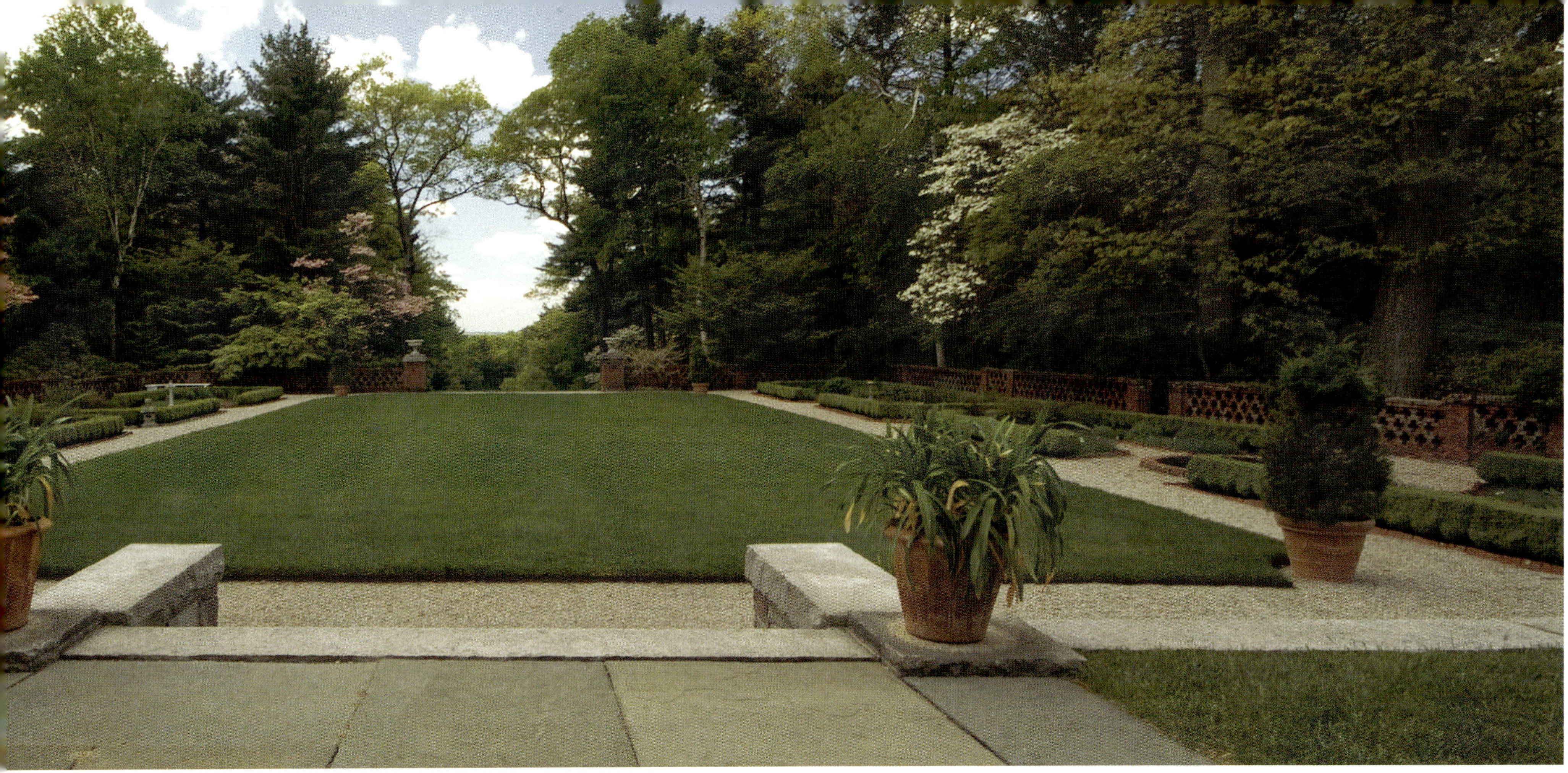

These two views of the Eleanor Cabot Bradley Estate in Canton, show the front and the formal garden with a manicured lawn in the rear. Built in the early 20th century, it was once the site of a colonial farm and now has over 3 miles of trails, ponds and gardens. It is owned and maintained by the Trustees of the Reservation.

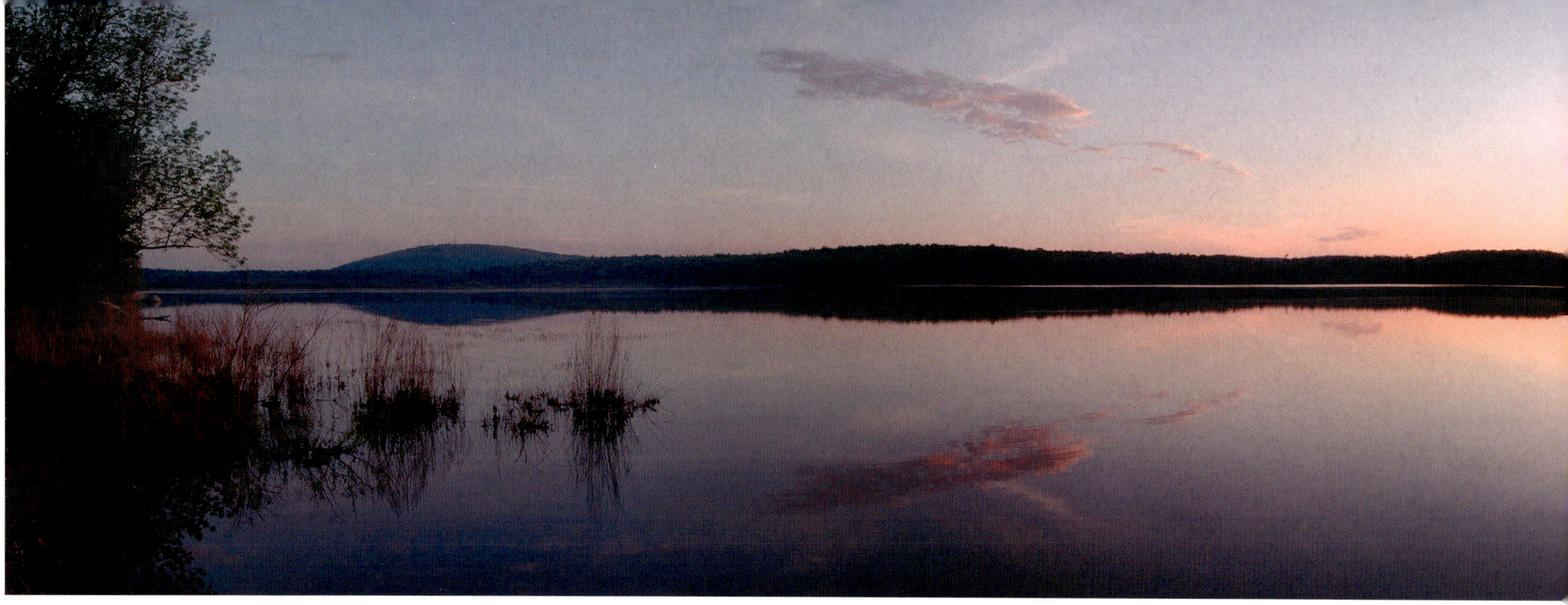

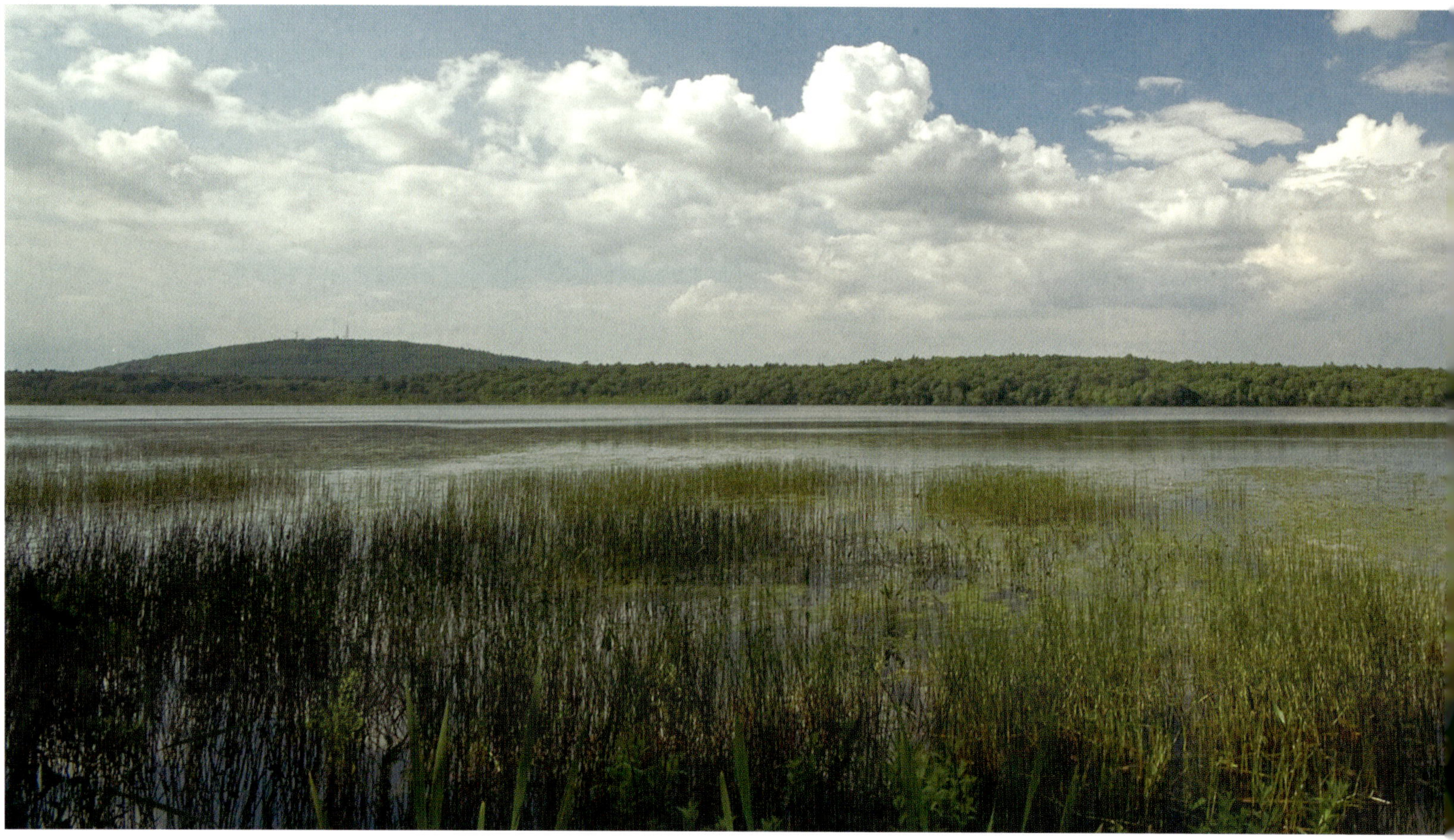

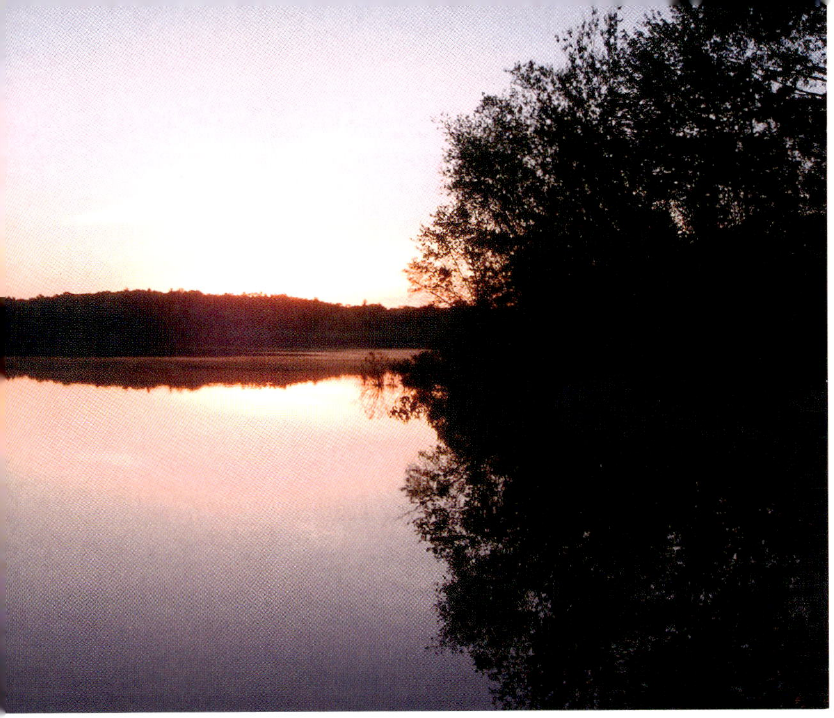

Ponkapoag Pond just before sunrise. Big Blue is the hill on the left in the distance.

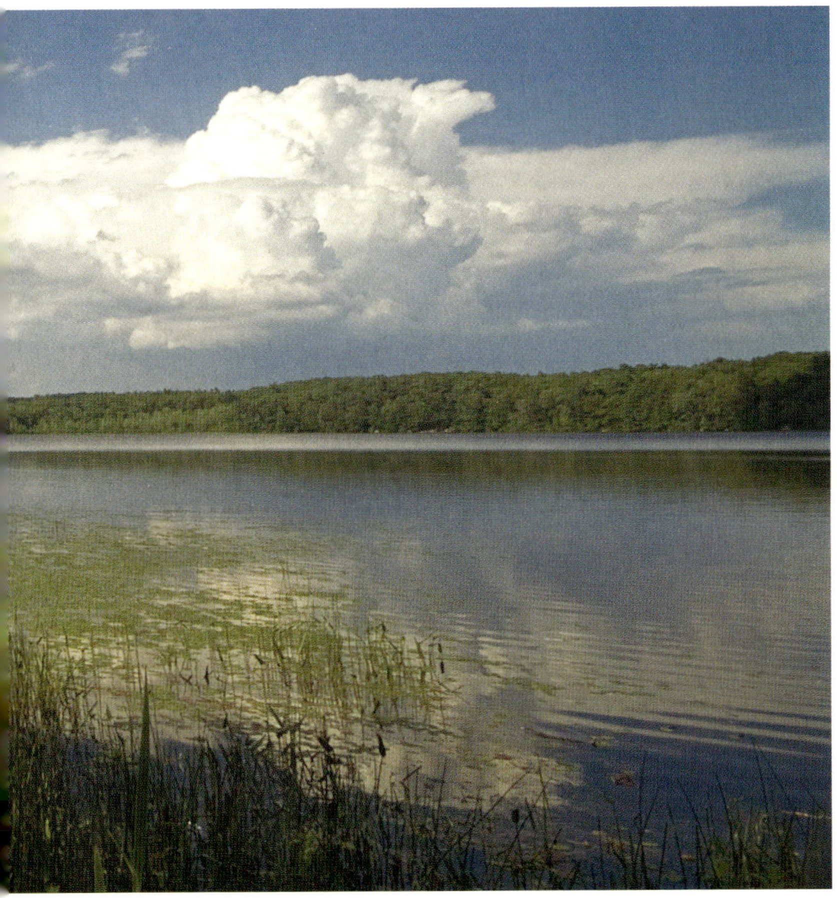

Two views along the shore of Ponkapoag Pond.

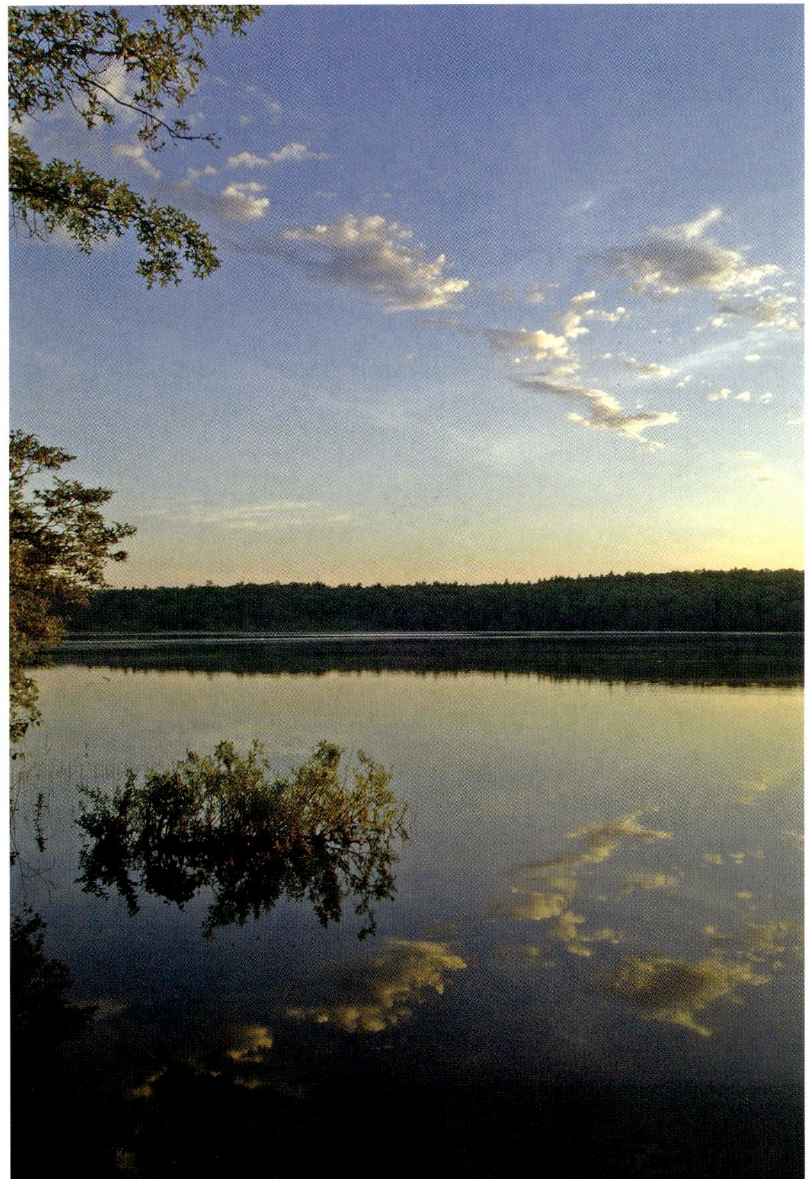

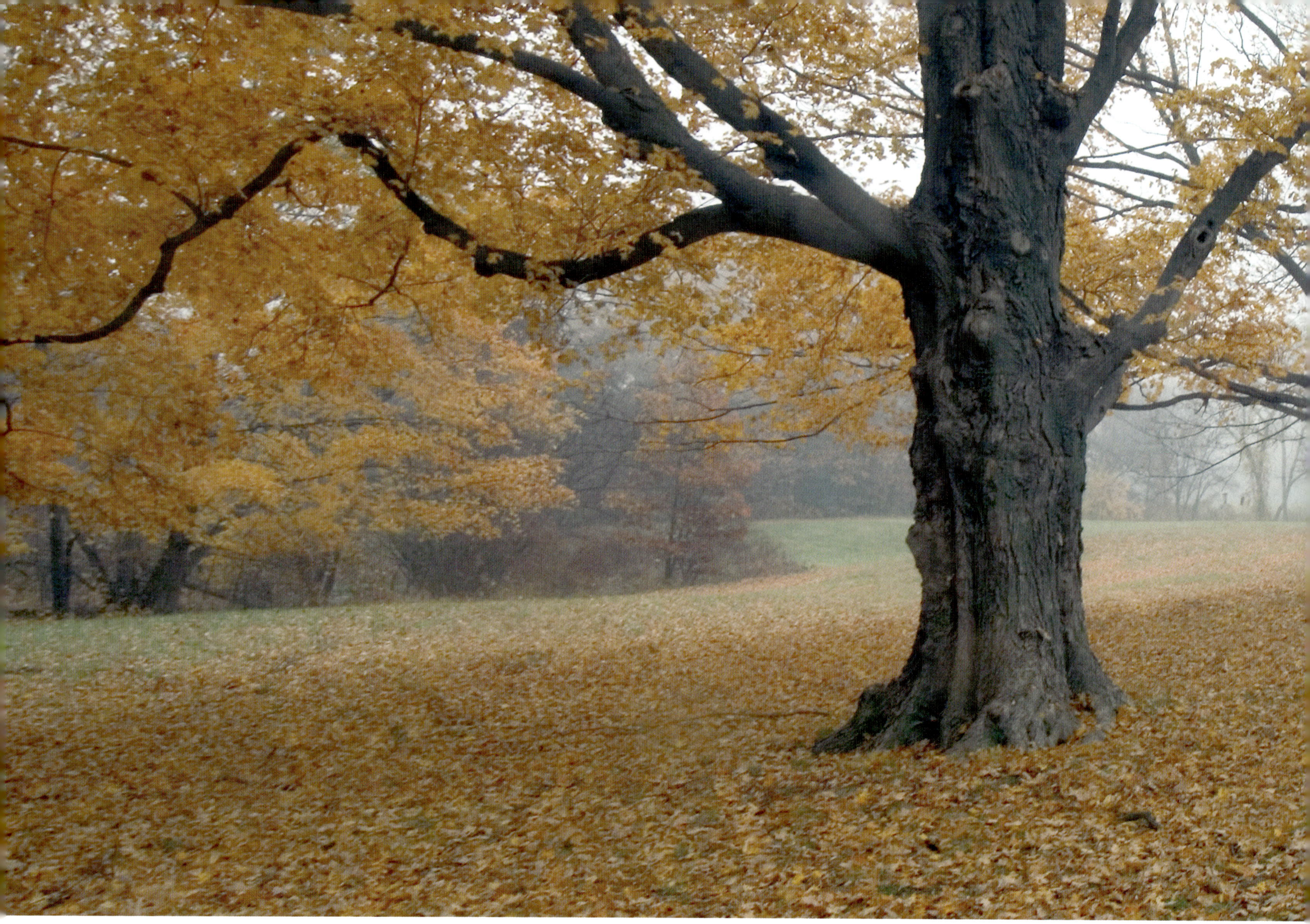

A path in Buttonwood Farm in Canton on a foggy, autumn day.

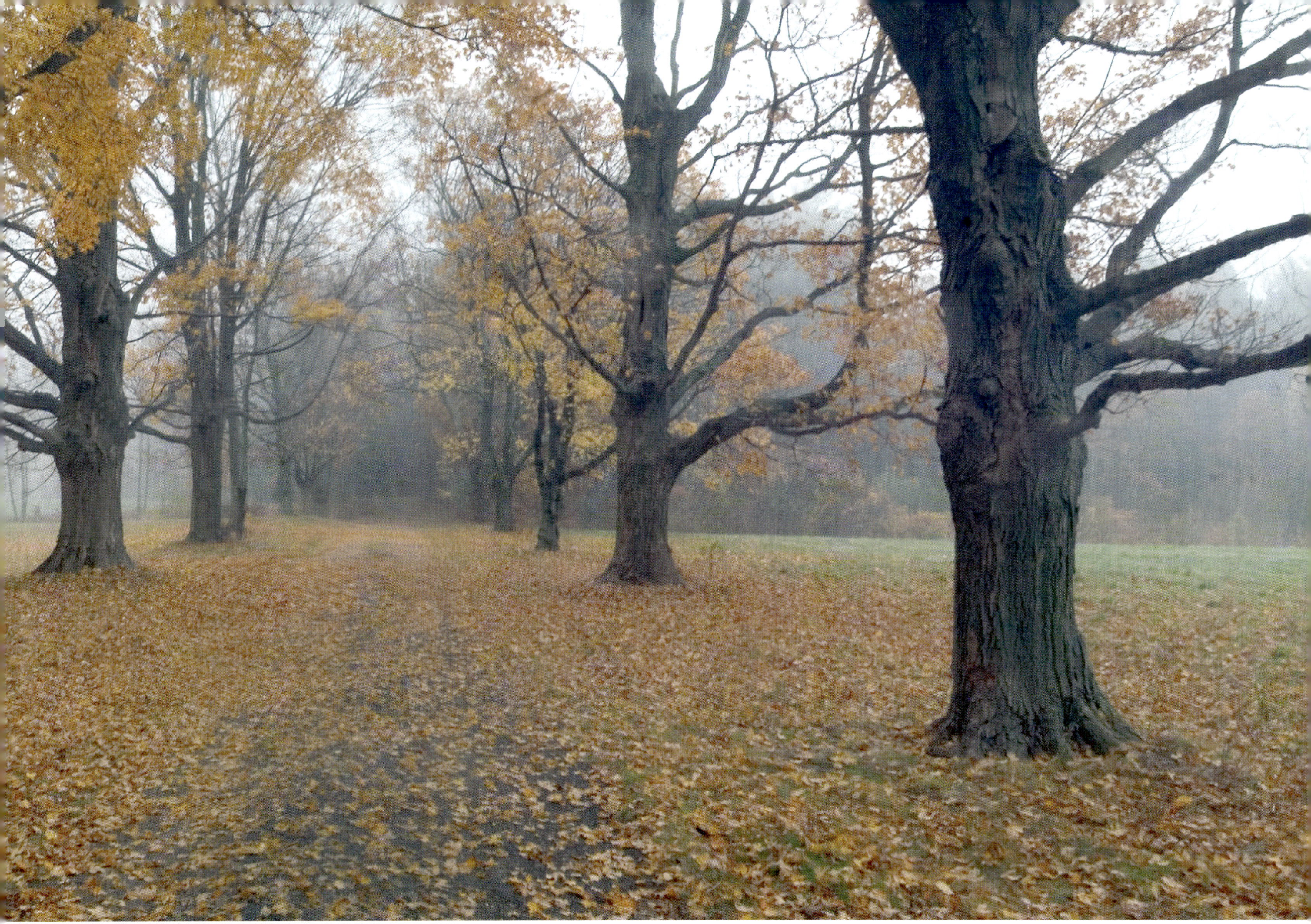

A passenger plane flying over the South Shore headed for Logan Airport.

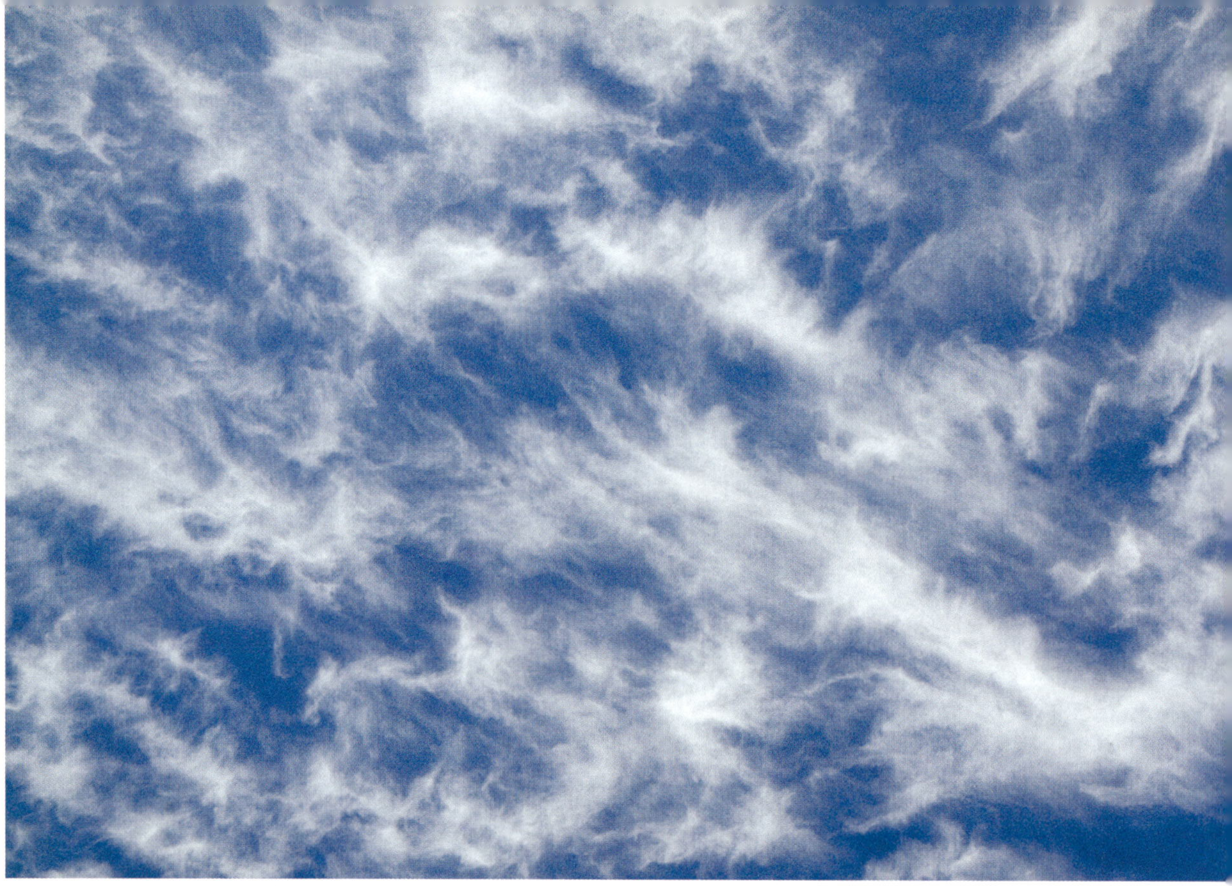

Boats line the slips at the Braintree Yacht Club on the Weymouth Fore River, which leads to Hingham Bay.

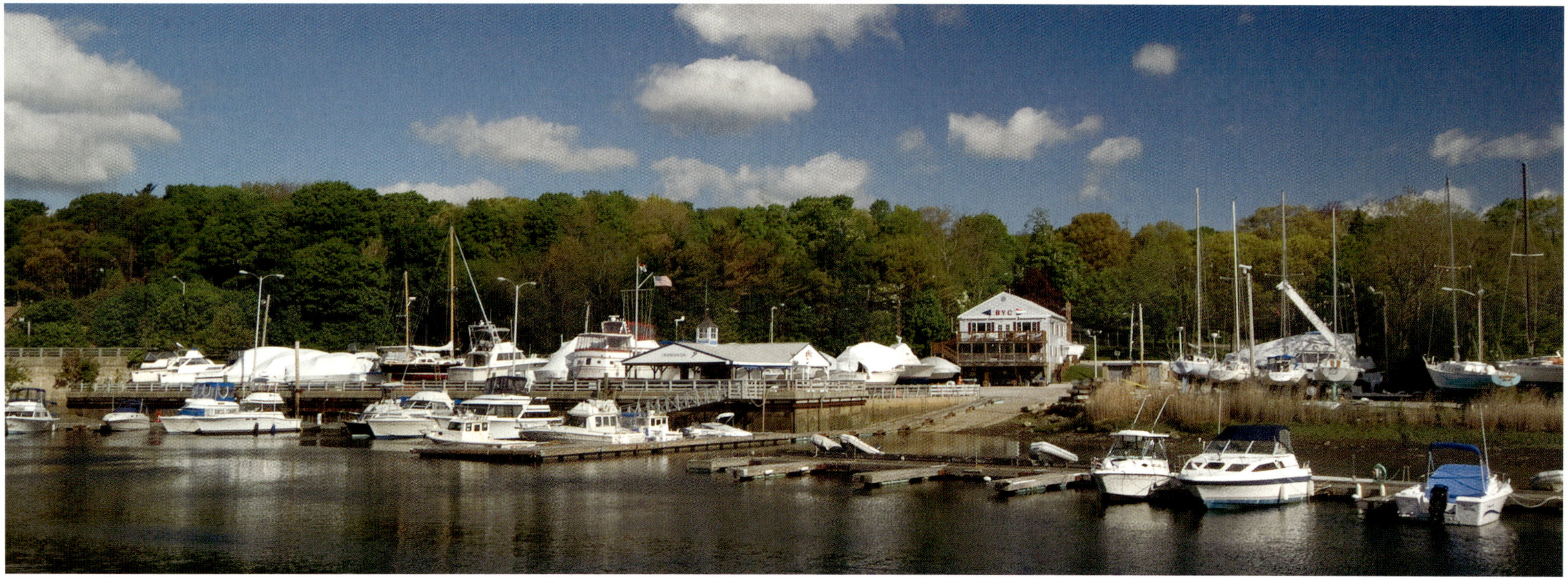

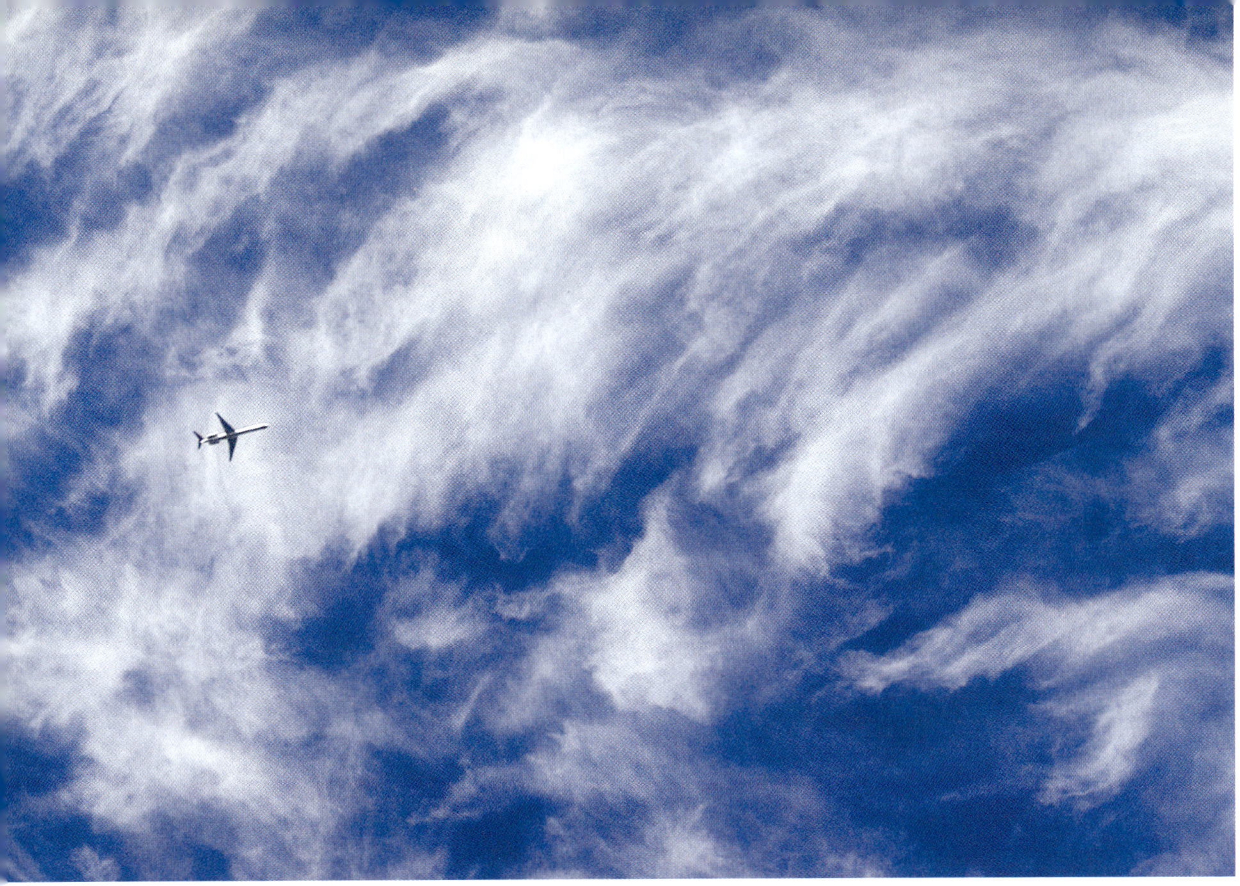

Webb Memorial Park, in North Weymouth, overlooks Boston Harbor between Quincy and Hingham Bays. Once an Indian summer camping area, it was a Nike missile site before it was restored to its present 36-acre park. Spectacular views. walking trails, picnicking, and fishing are some of the recreational activities available to visitors.

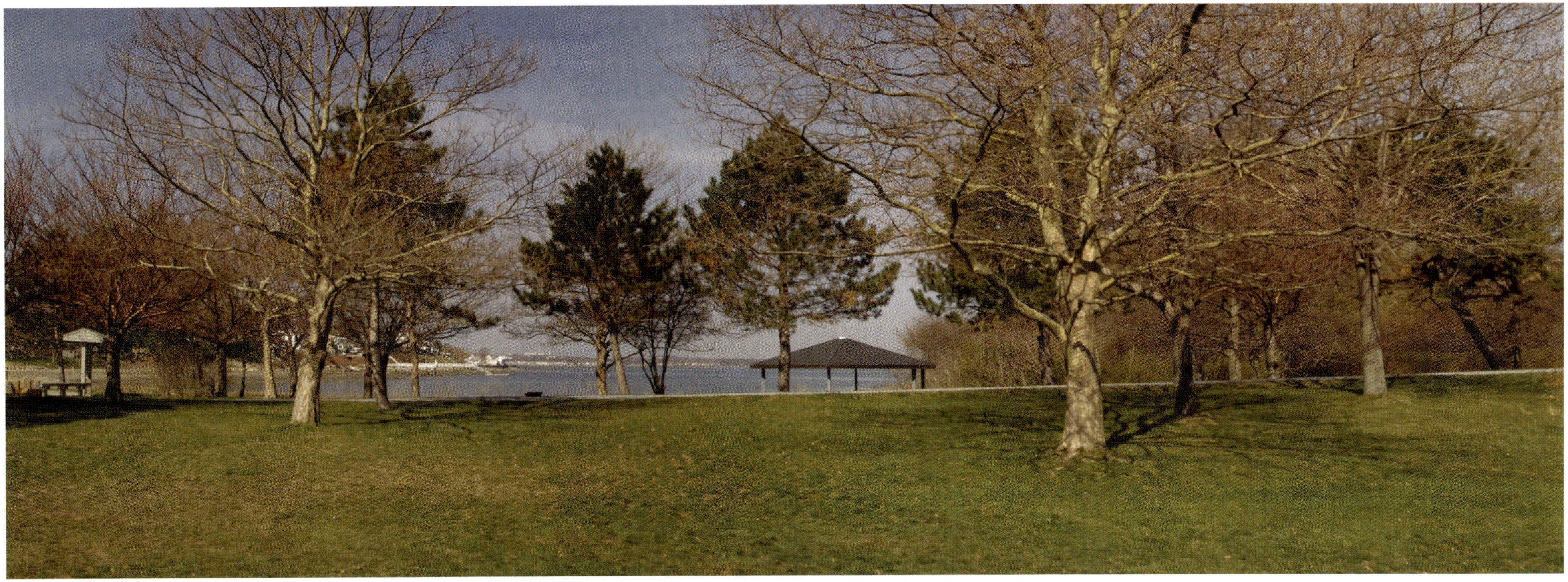

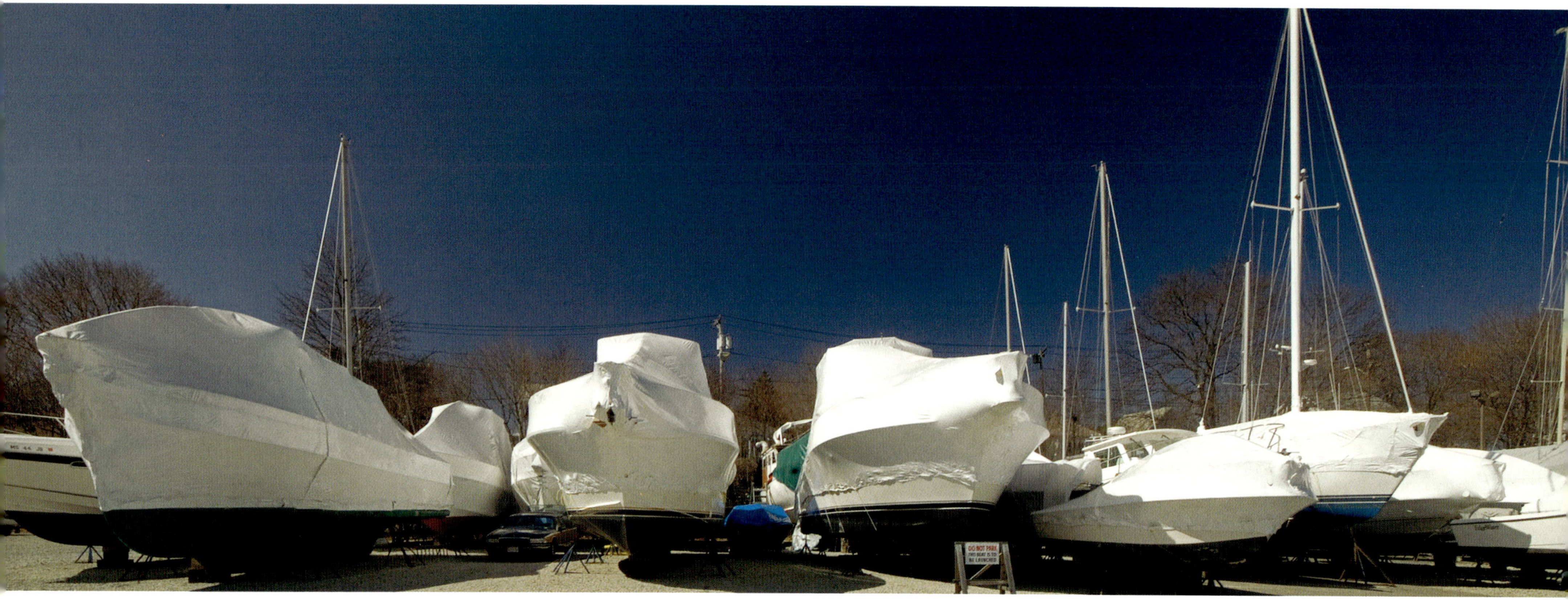

Shrink-wrapped boats at a local marina.

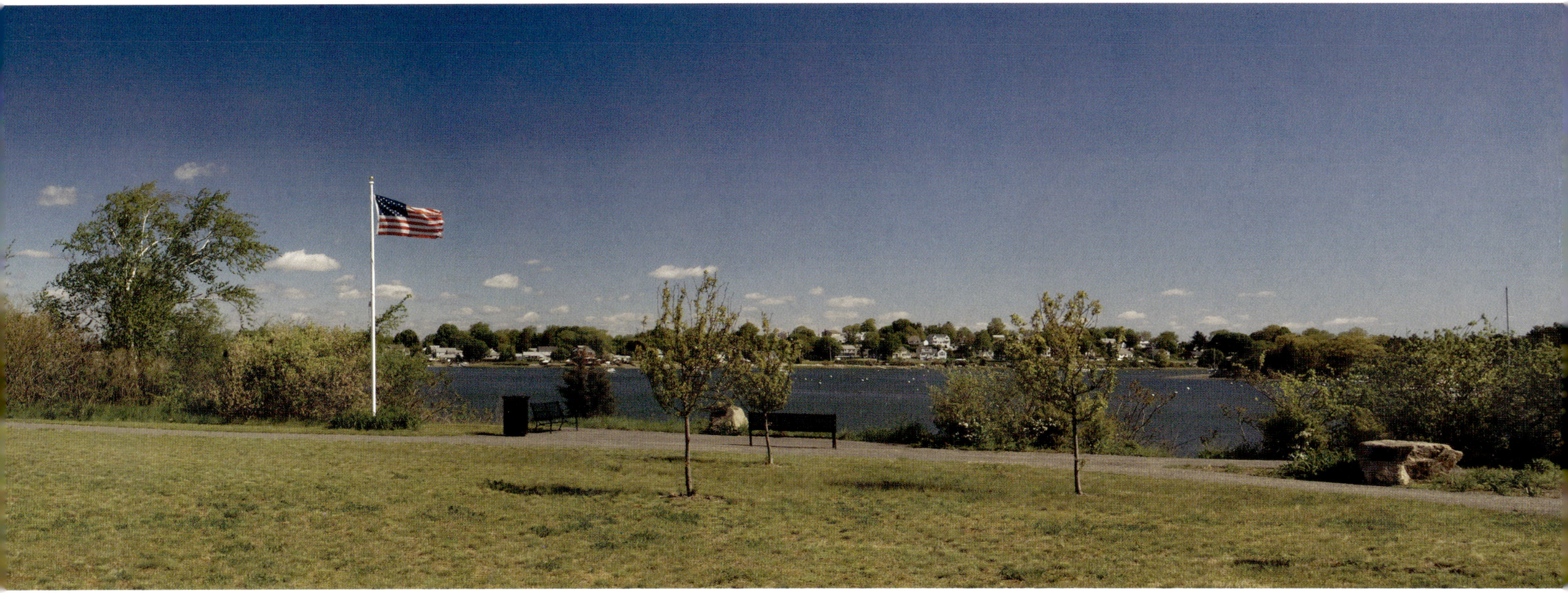

Abigail Adams Park, in Hingham on the Back River, overlooks Weymouth on the far shore.

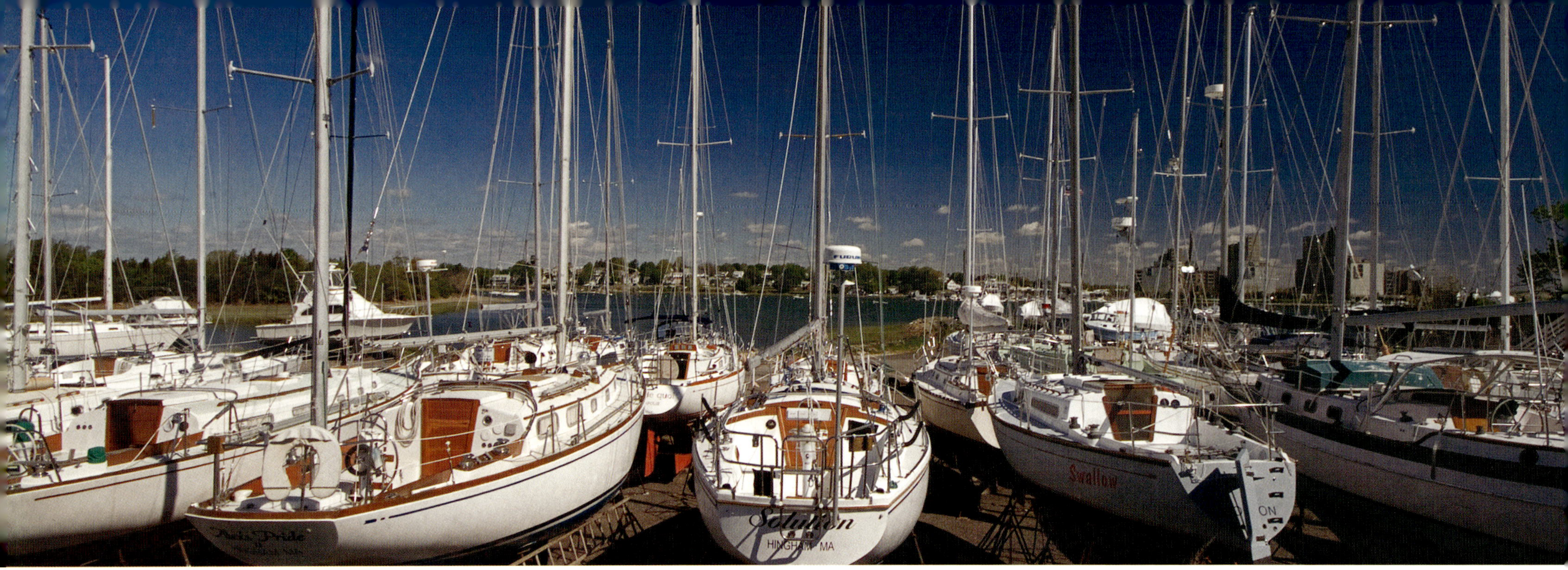

Sailboats wait to be launched in Hewitt's Cove Marina in Hingham.

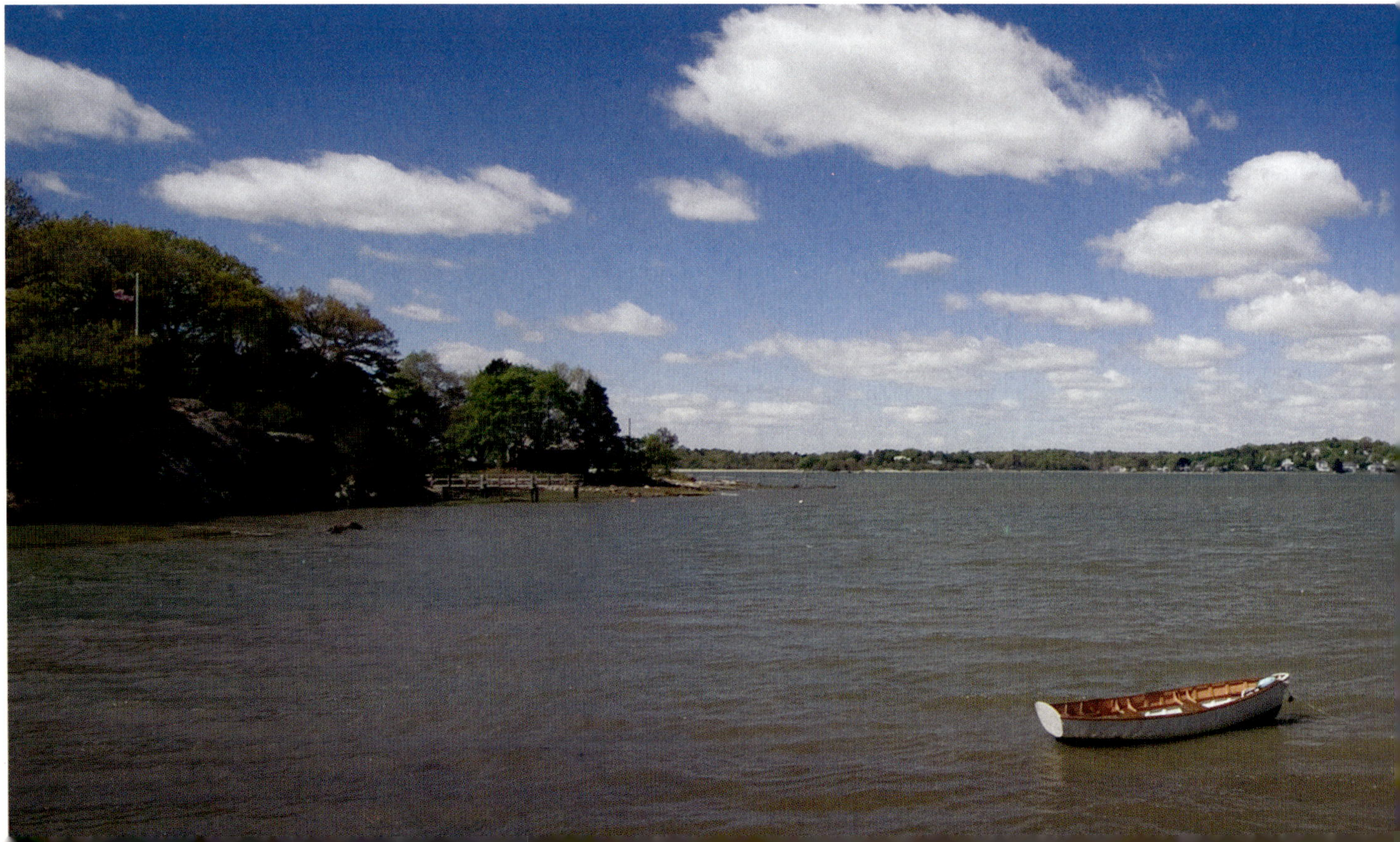

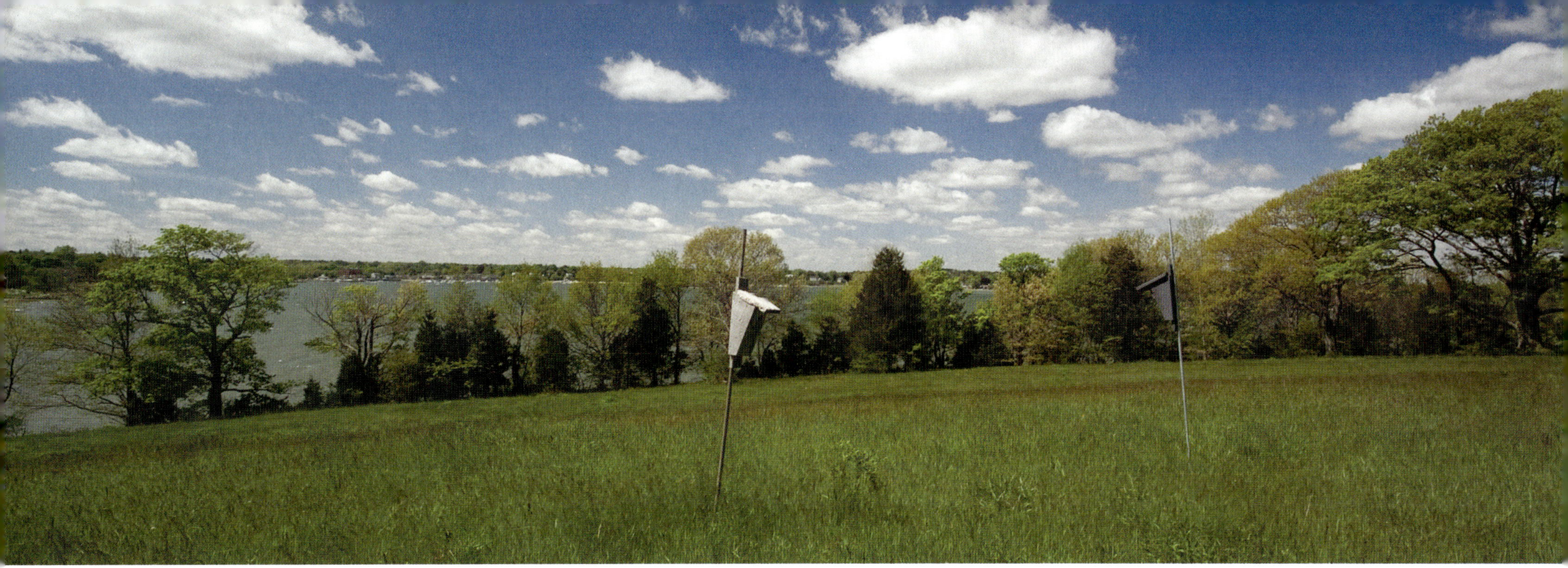

World's End Reservation in Hingham, which overlooks Dorchester Bay and Boston Harbor, is 249 acres of magnificent land that is owned and maintained by The Trustees of The Reservation. It offers visitors an extensive network of trails and walkways on this picturesque peninsula. Views of Hingham Harbor, Hull, Weymouth, Quincy, and far to the north, the hills of Cape Ann on the North Shore can be seen from the footpaths.

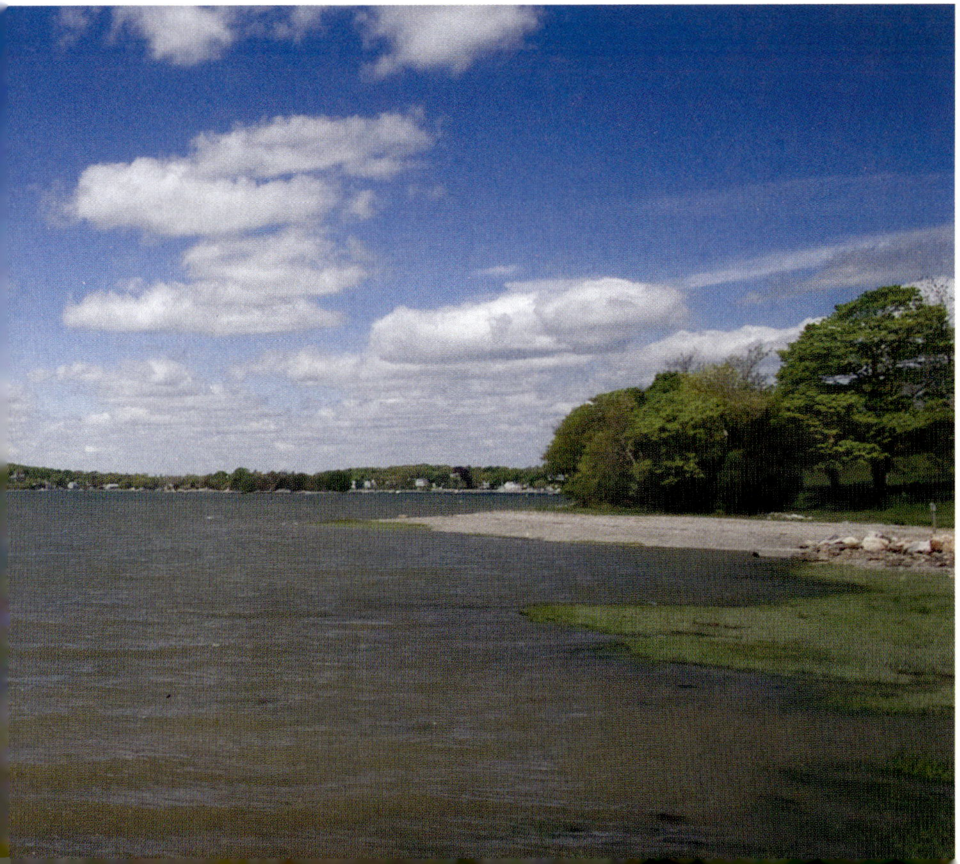

A classic dinghy floats in Martins Well just off Hingham Bay.

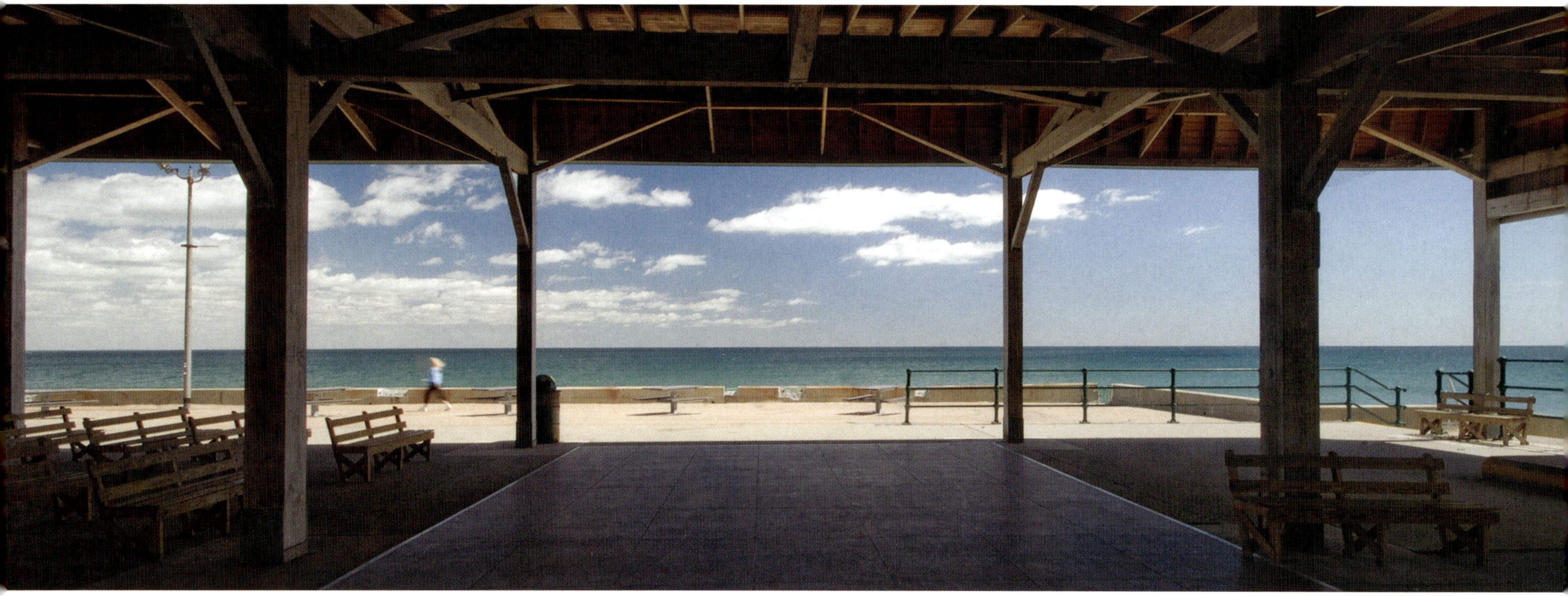

A pavilion overlooks Nantasket Beach in Hull.

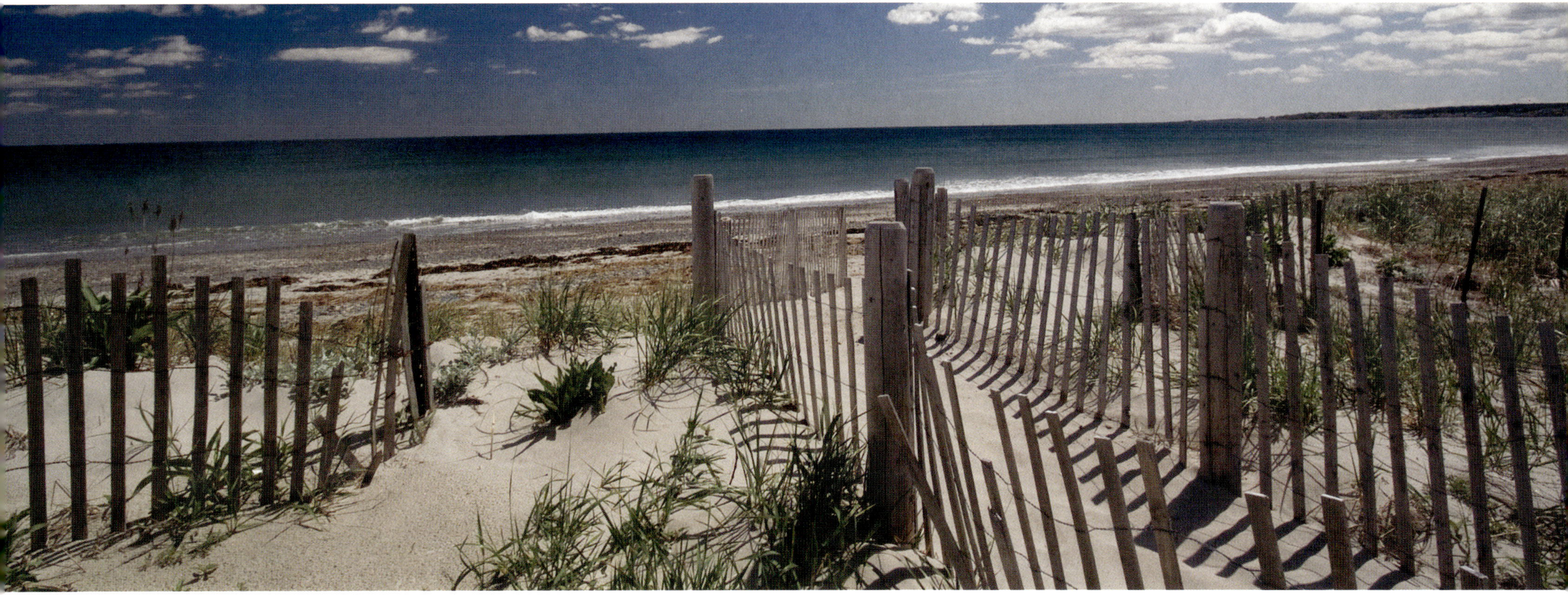

A sandy walkway leads to Nantasket Beach in Hull.

This covered rest area overlooks Pemberton Beach in Hull.

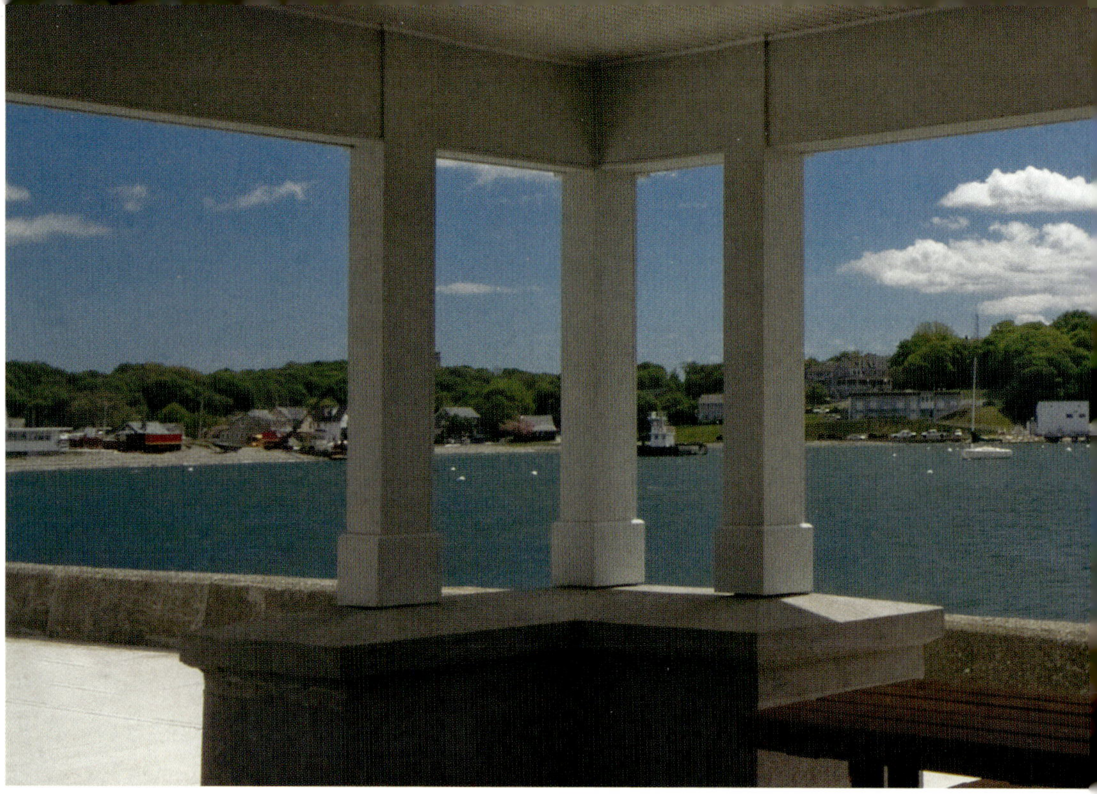

In 1848, the red building was both the first town hall and school in Hull.

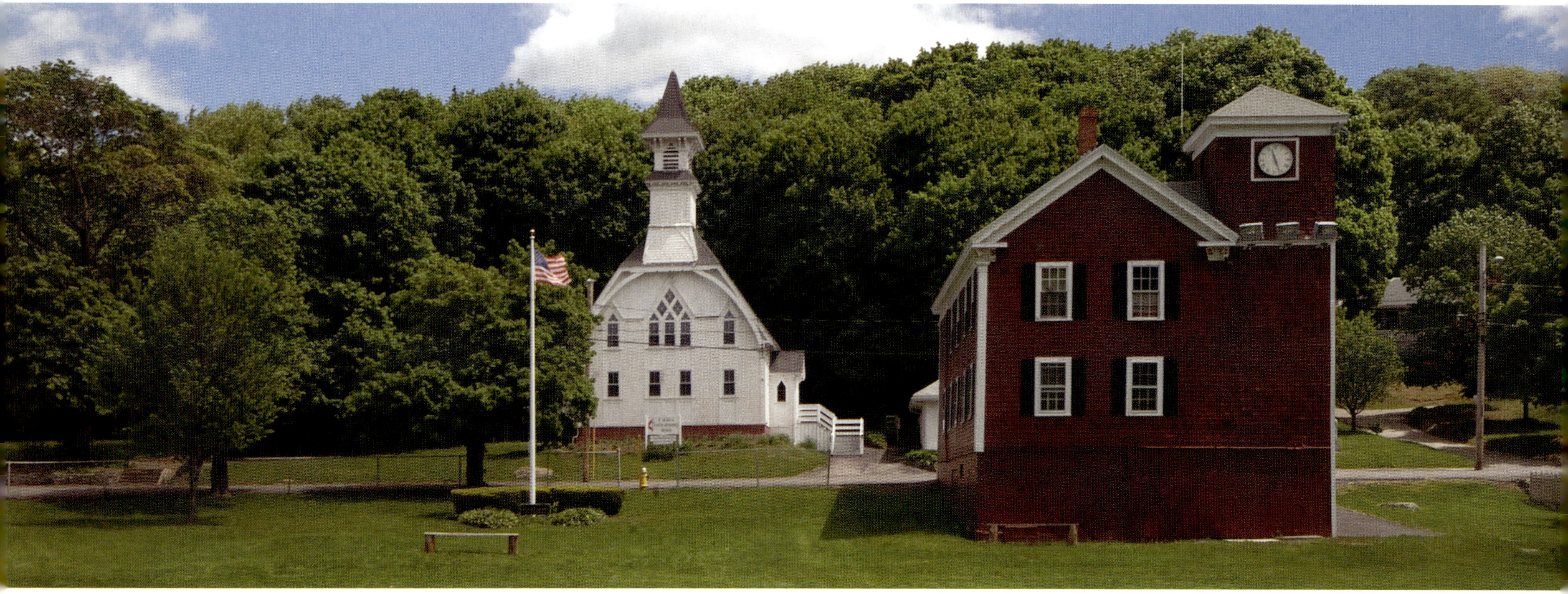

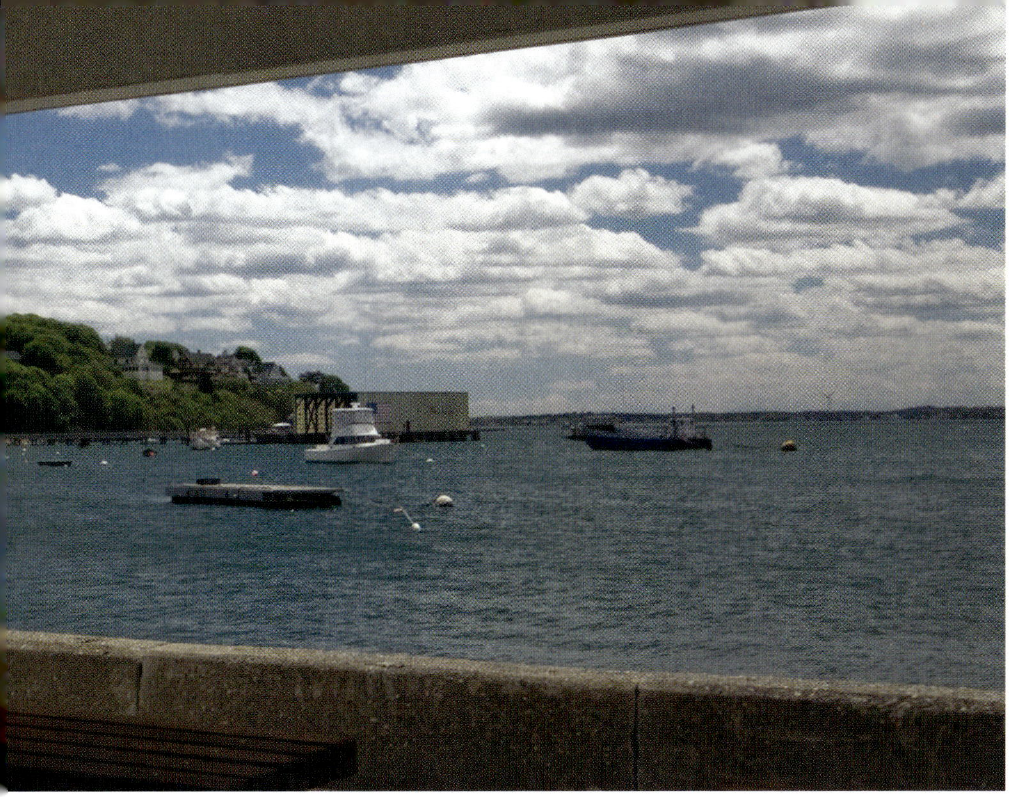

Dating to as early as 1683, three churches, the Town Hall, and historical homes overlook this pond on Cohasset Common. The harbor may have been the commercial center of the town, but it was the Common that provided a peaceful, unifying influence on the community. The architecture of the nearby homes, for residences of sea-captains, merchants, and early ministers, includes Colonial, Georgian, Federal, Greek Revival, and Italianate.

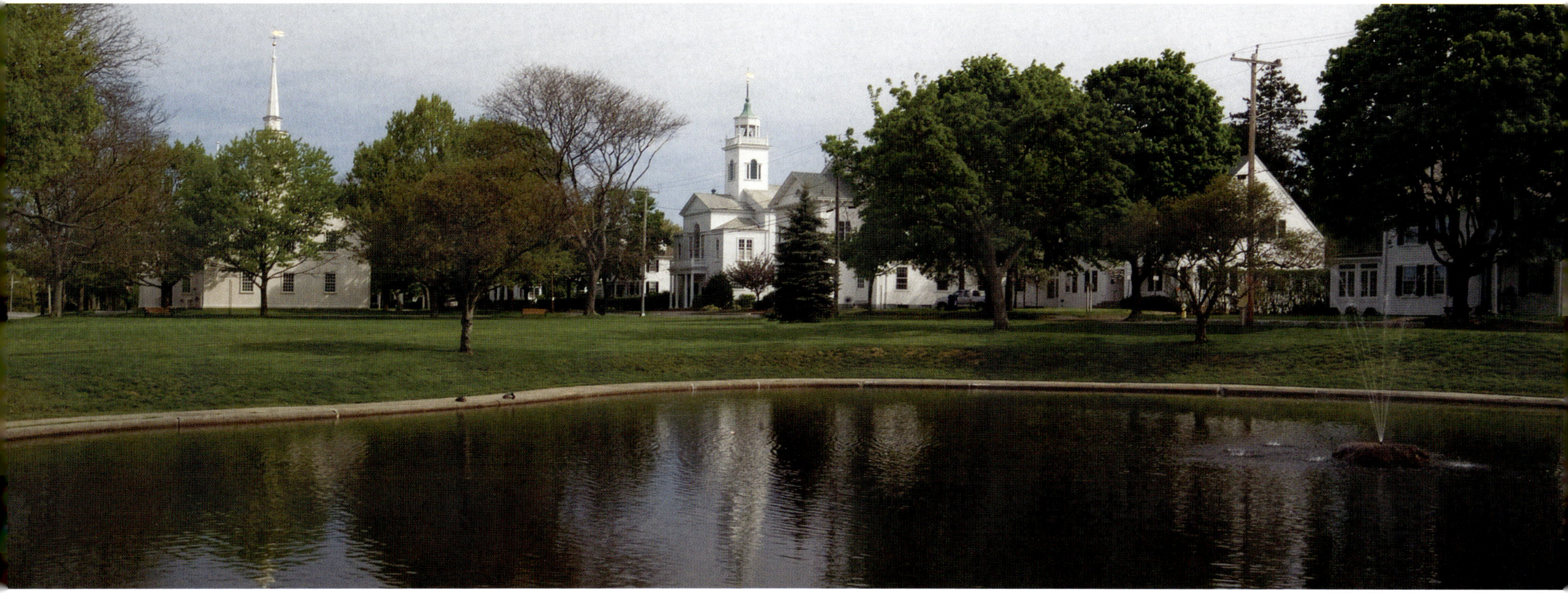

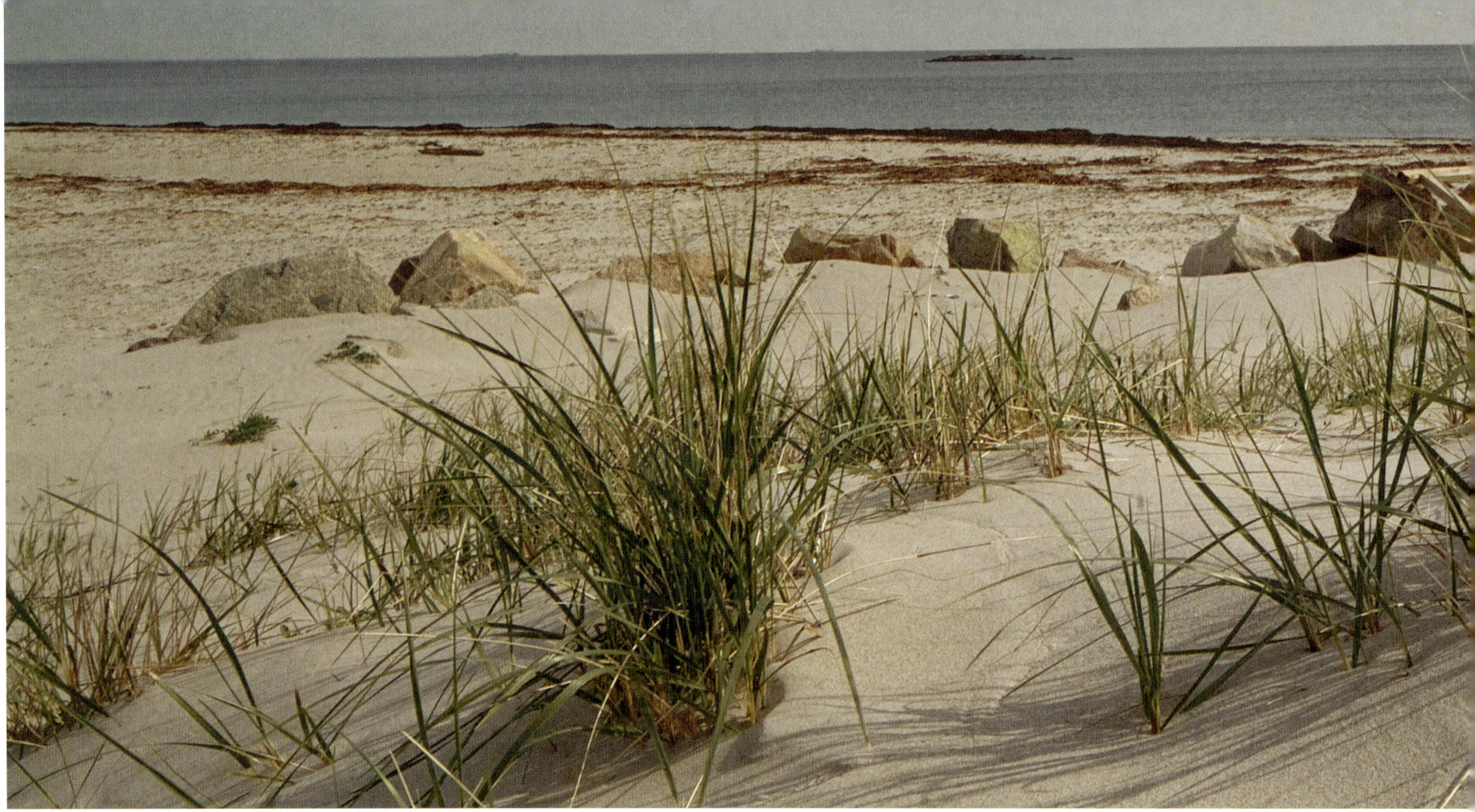

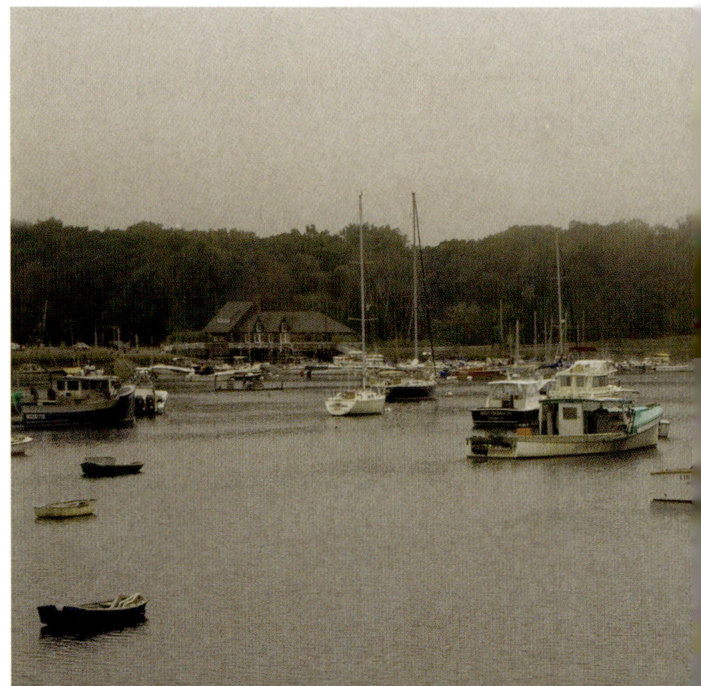

Cohasset Harbor looking out the inlet on a foggy morning.

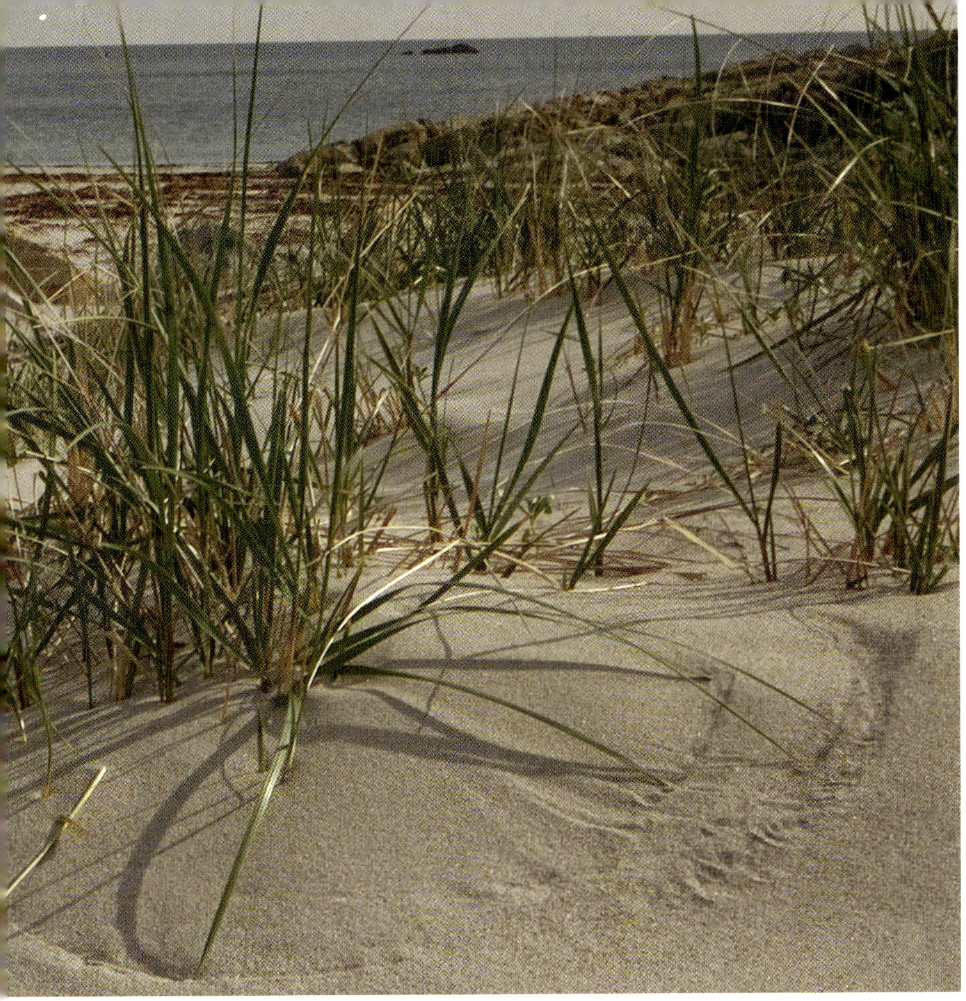

Sandy Beach in Cohasset, on Massachusetts Bay.

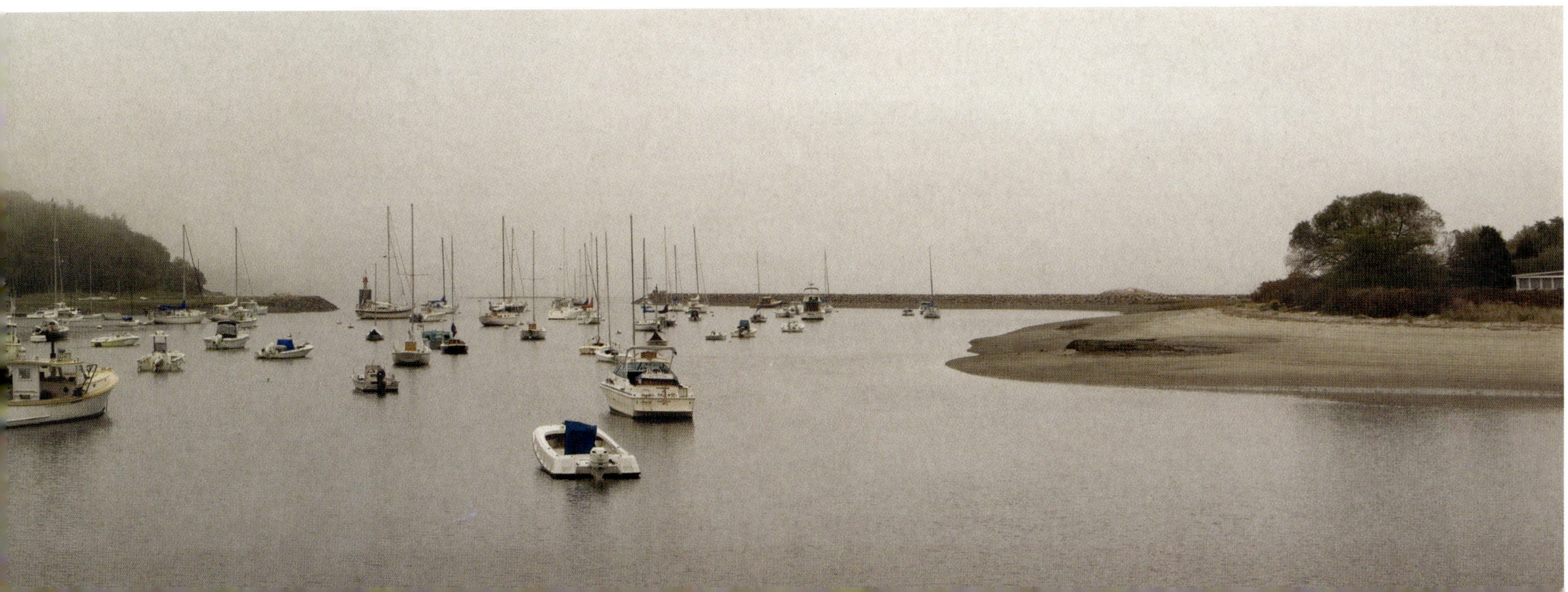

Minot Lighthouse stands just off the Cohasset shore and warns mariners of dangerous and treacherous ledges. The lighthouse was first built in 1850; a storm in 1851 claimed the tower and its' two keepers. The tower in this image was built in 1860.

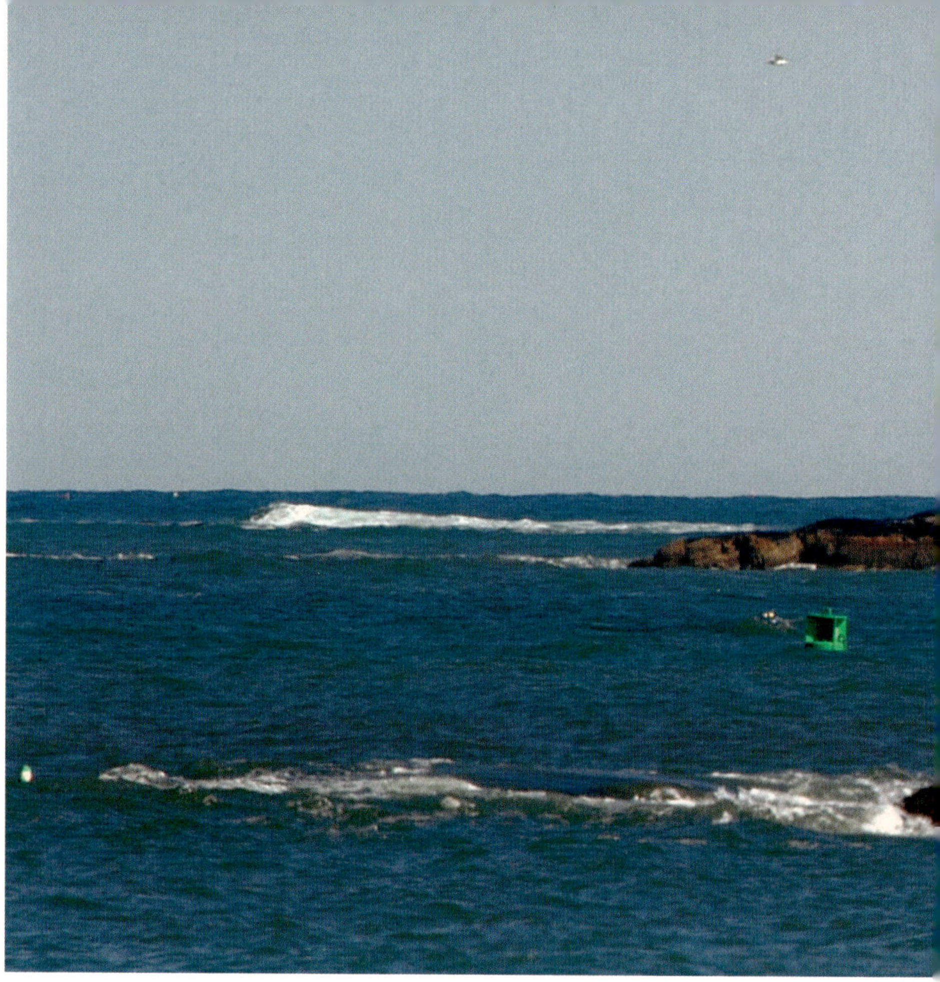

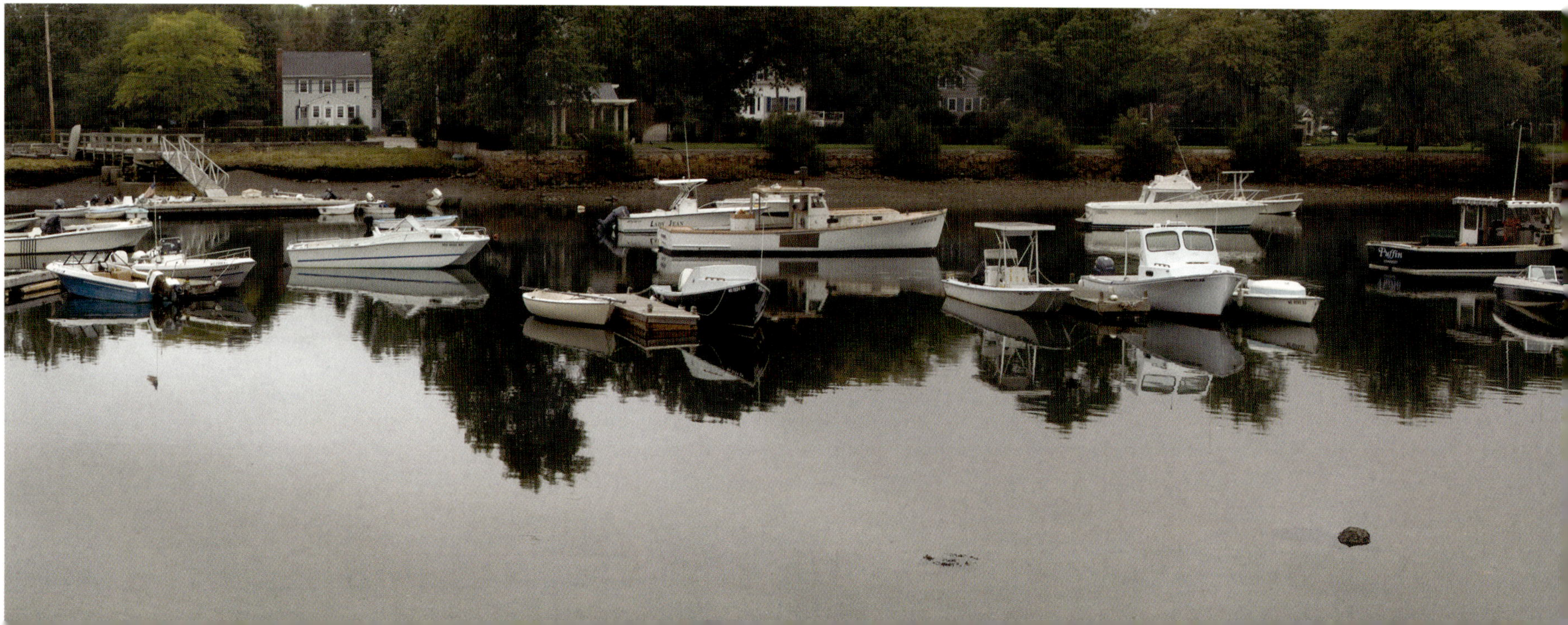

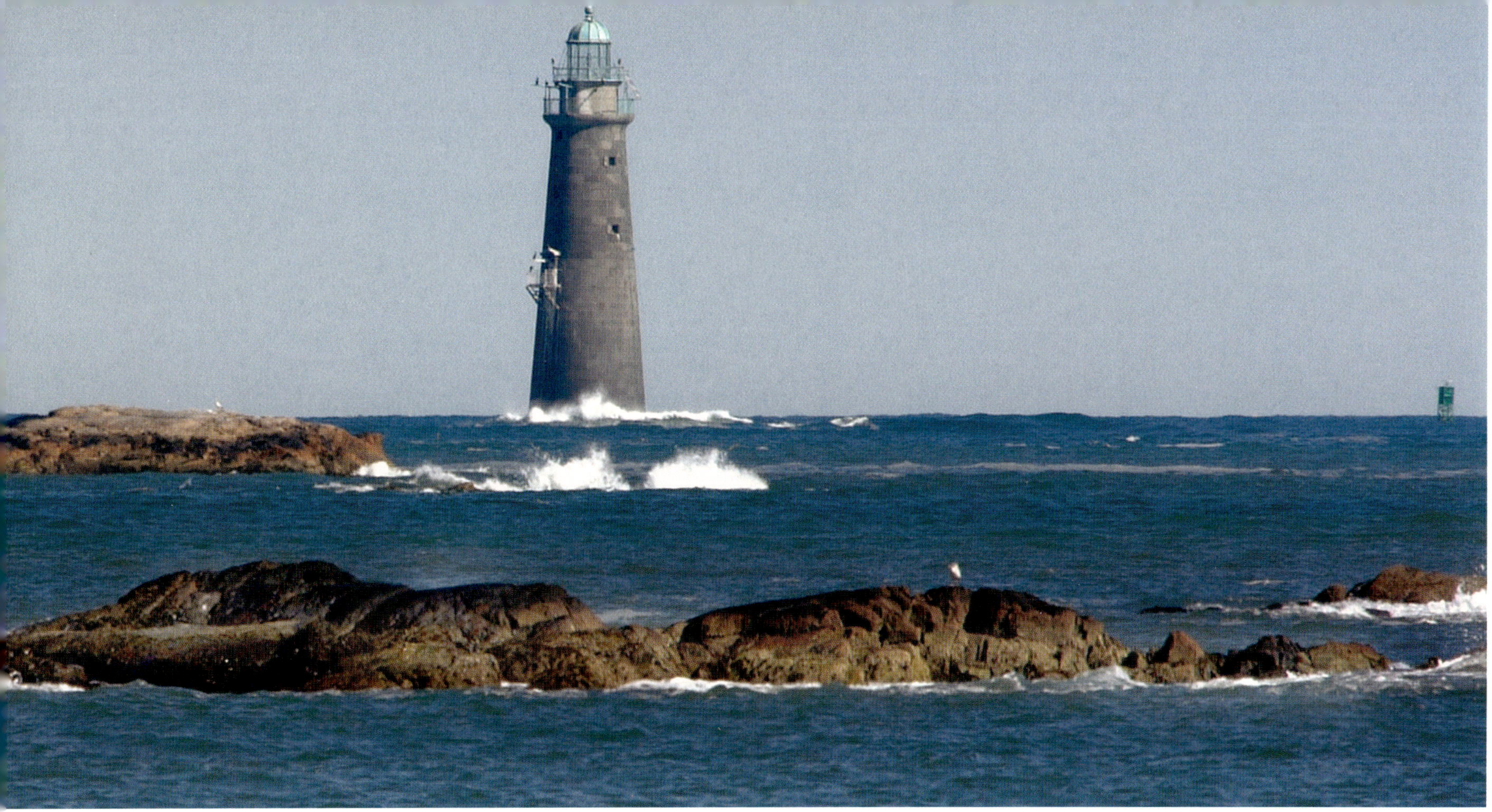

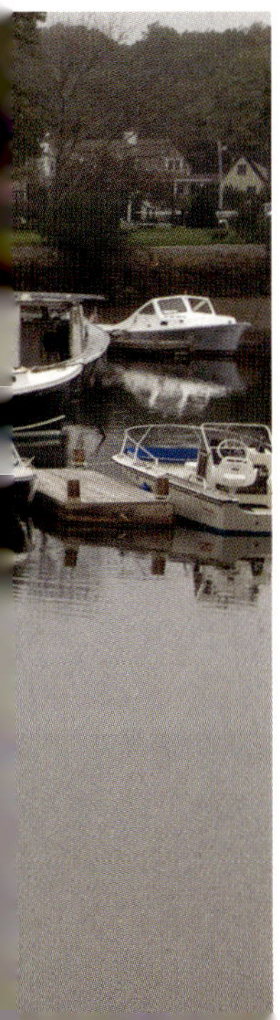

Boats quietly swing at anchor in Cohasset Harbor.

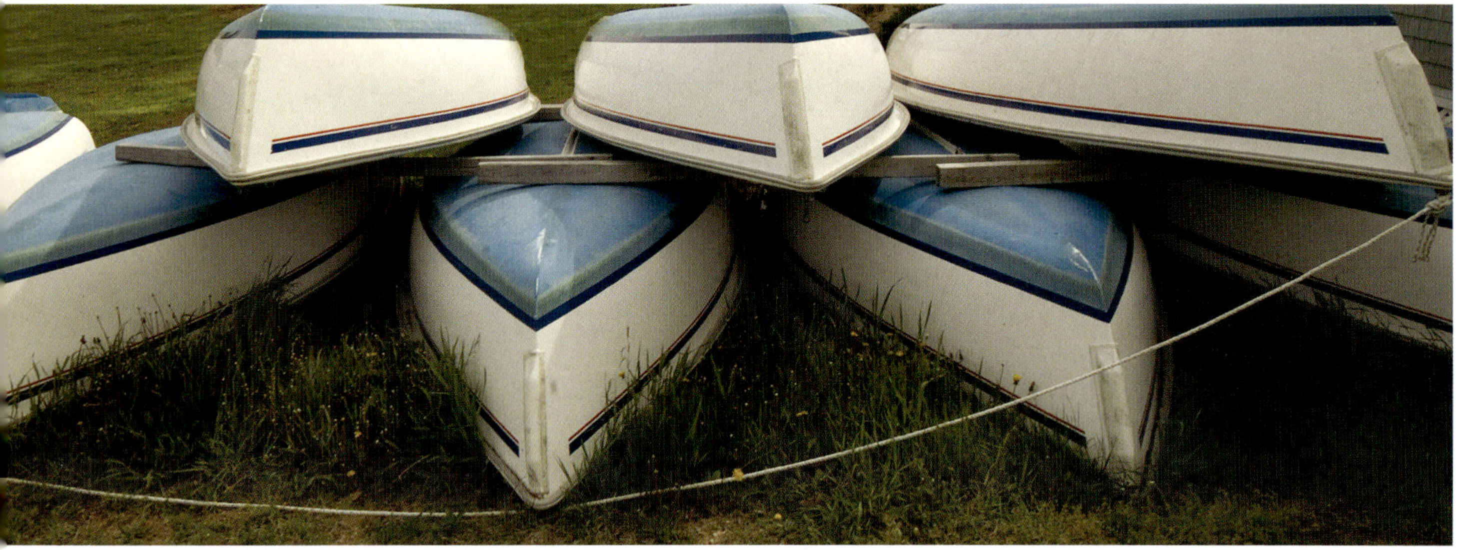

Sailboats are stacked at a local yacht club.

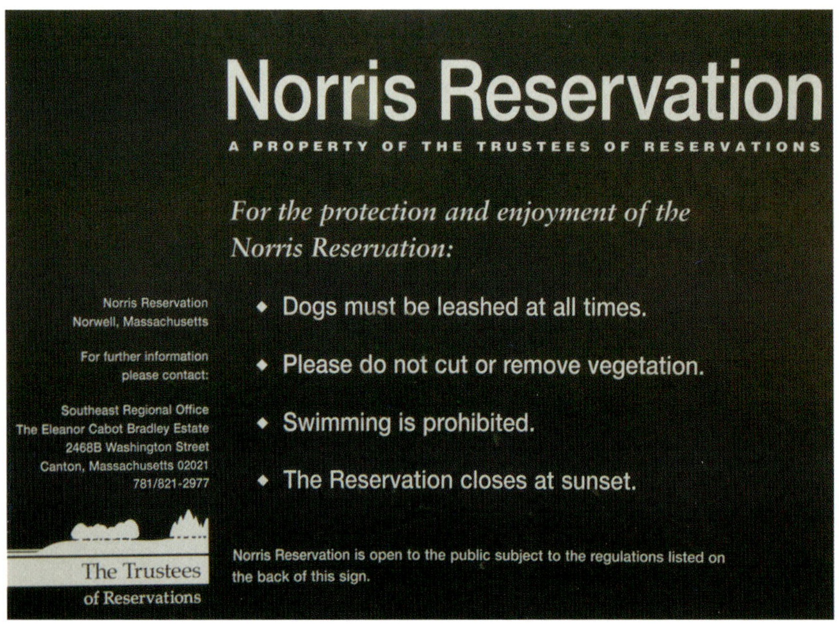

The Norris Reservation in Norwell includes more than 120 acres and extends from near the town center to the North River. Numerous trails lead through the woods and along the shore of the river.

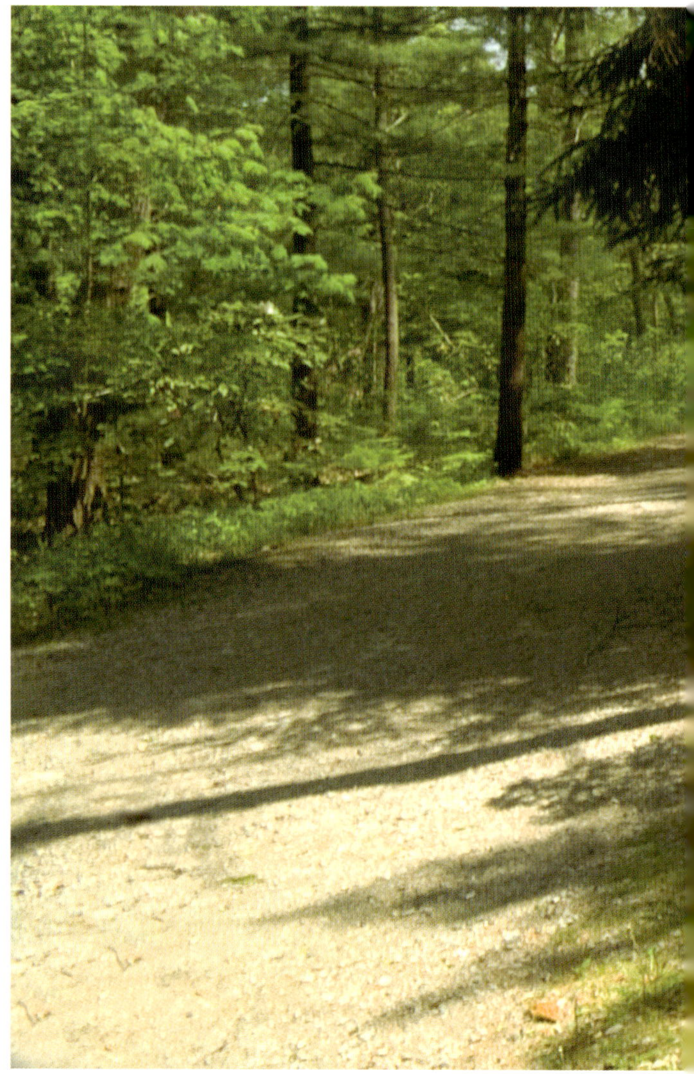

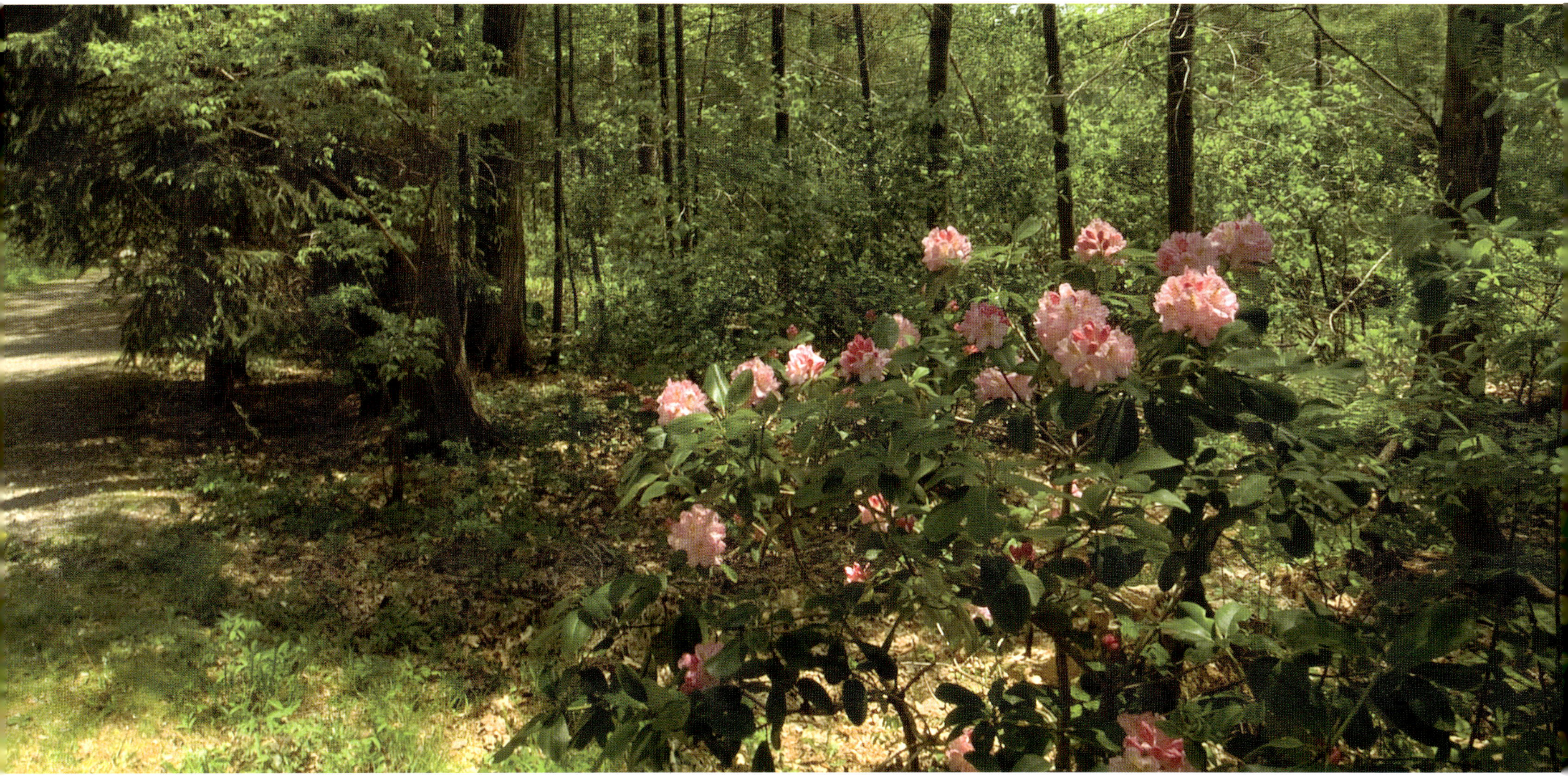

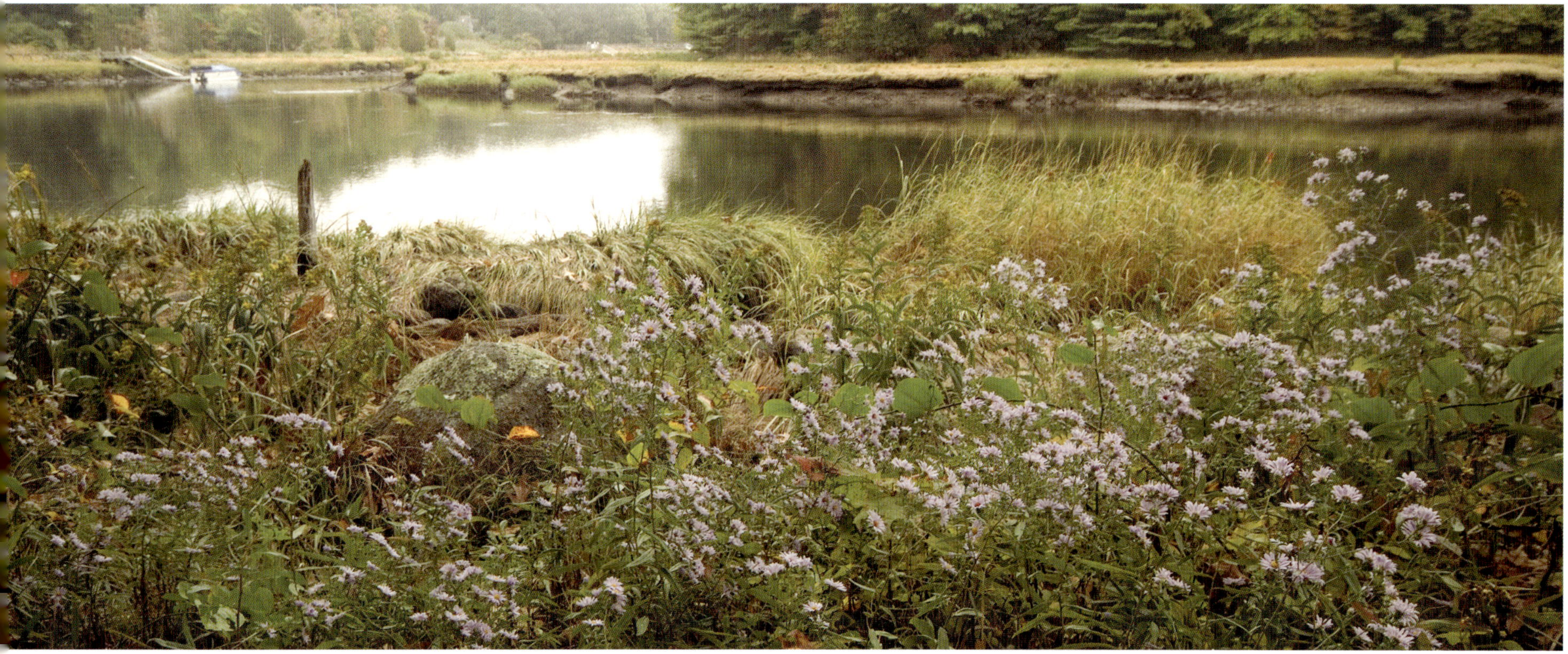

A view of the North River in the fall, with asters blooming on the bank.

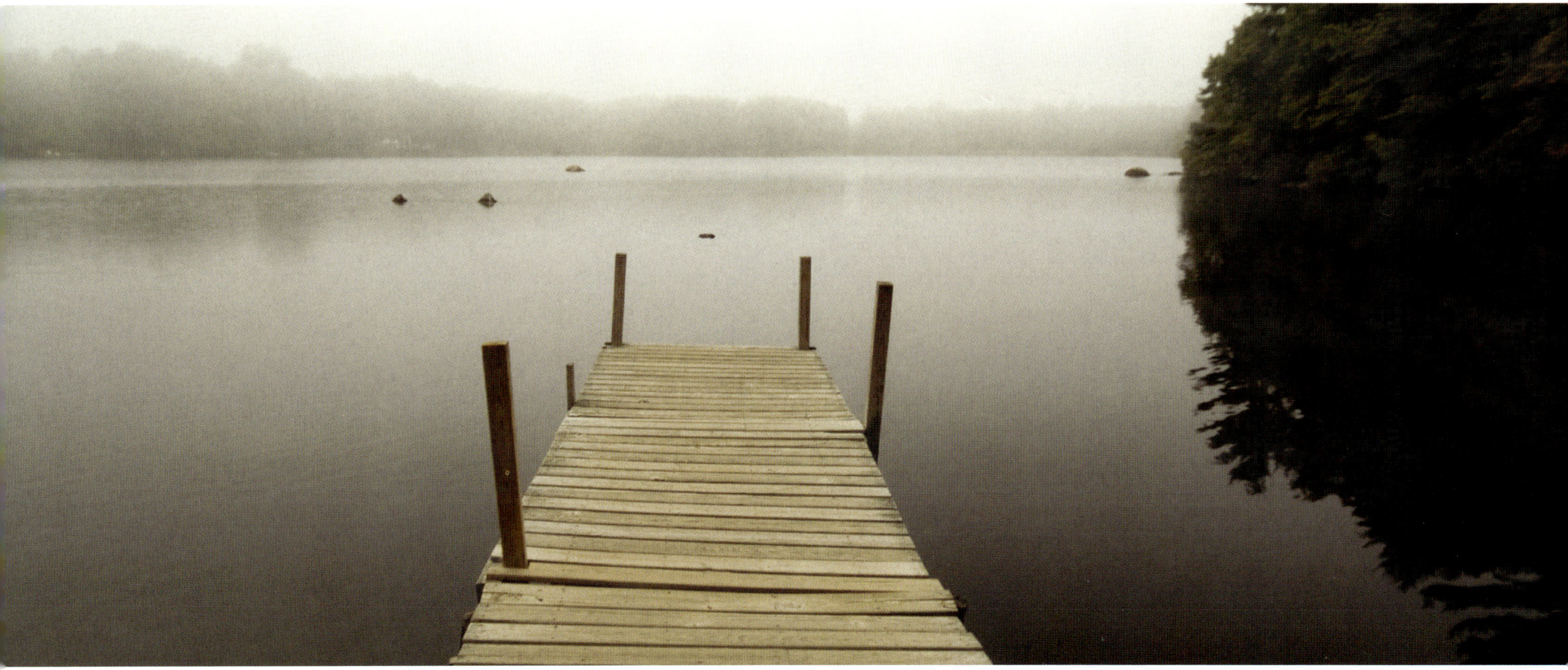

Jacob's Pond is a conservation area in Norwell.

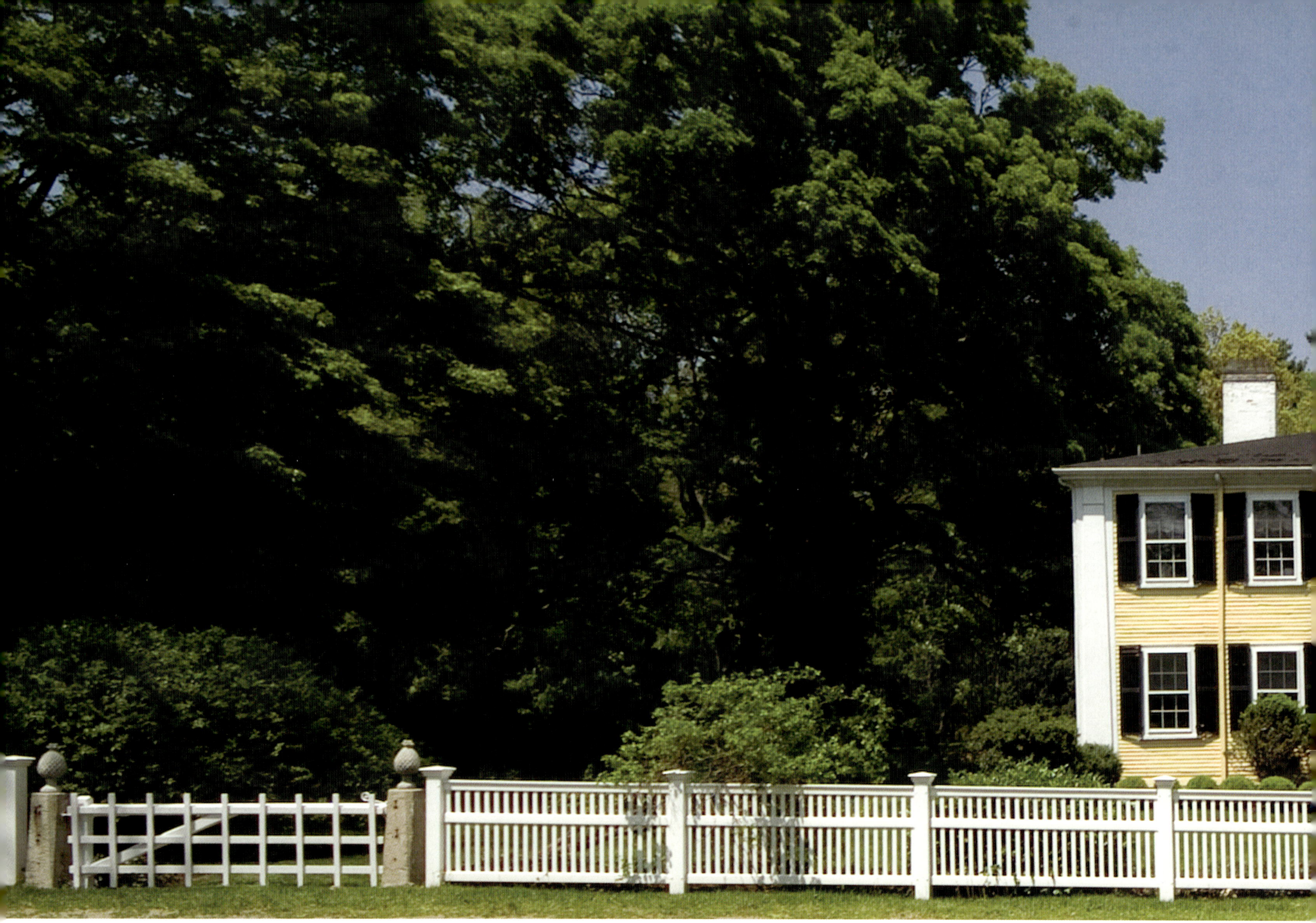

Many historic homes can be seen on the roads throughout Norwell.

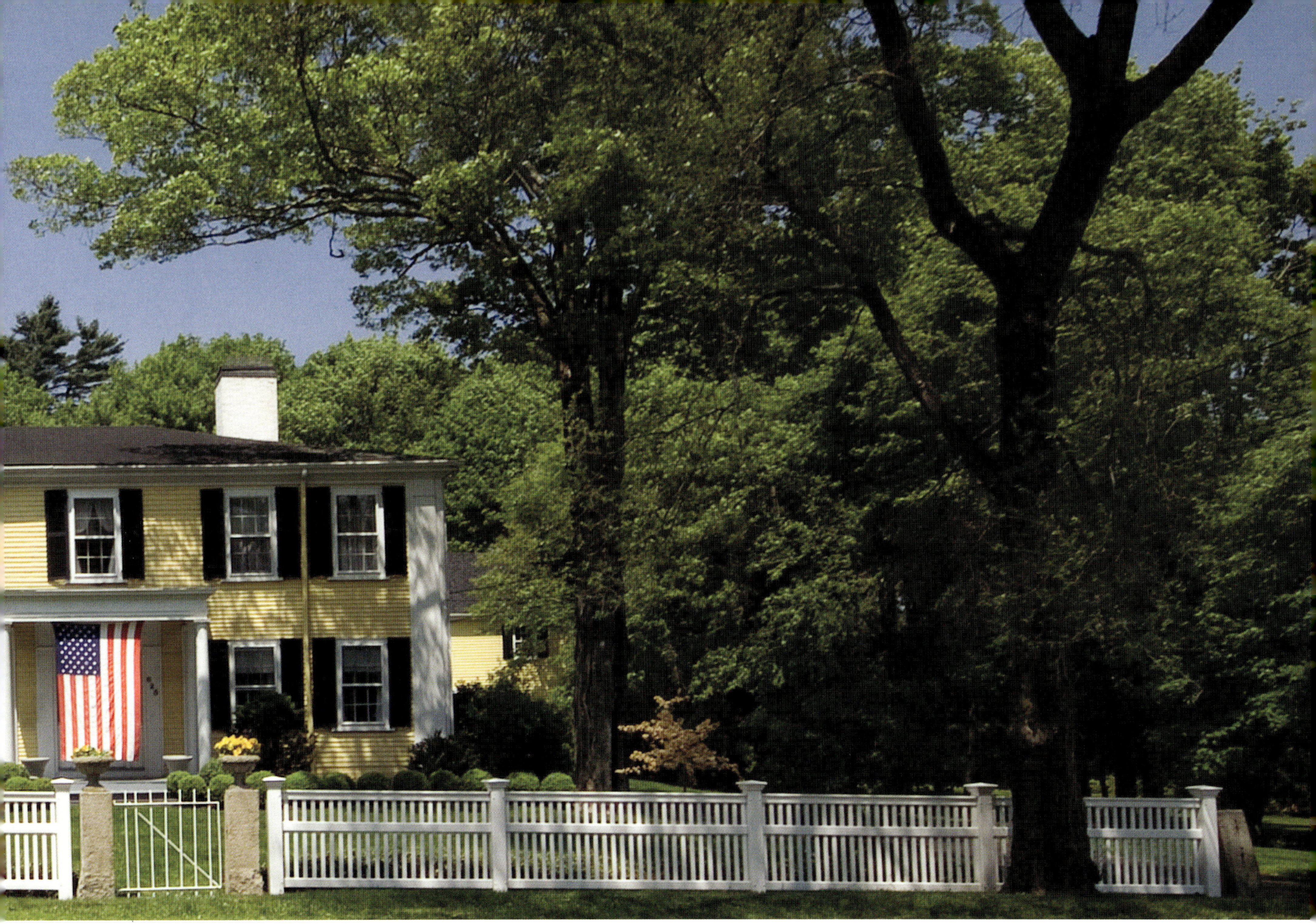

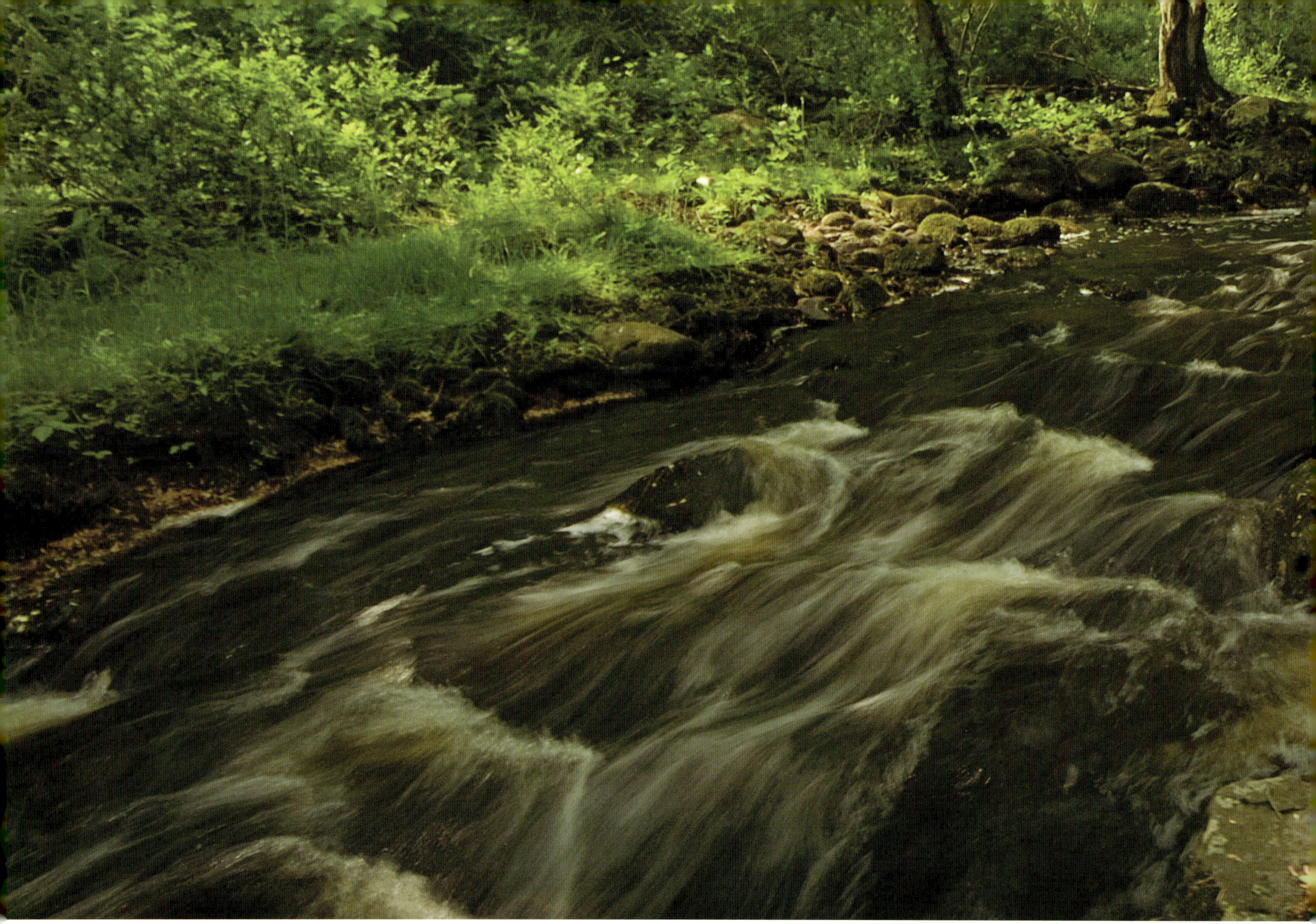

The Indian Head River, which eventually becomes the North River, at this point is the boundary between the towns of Hanover and Pembroke.

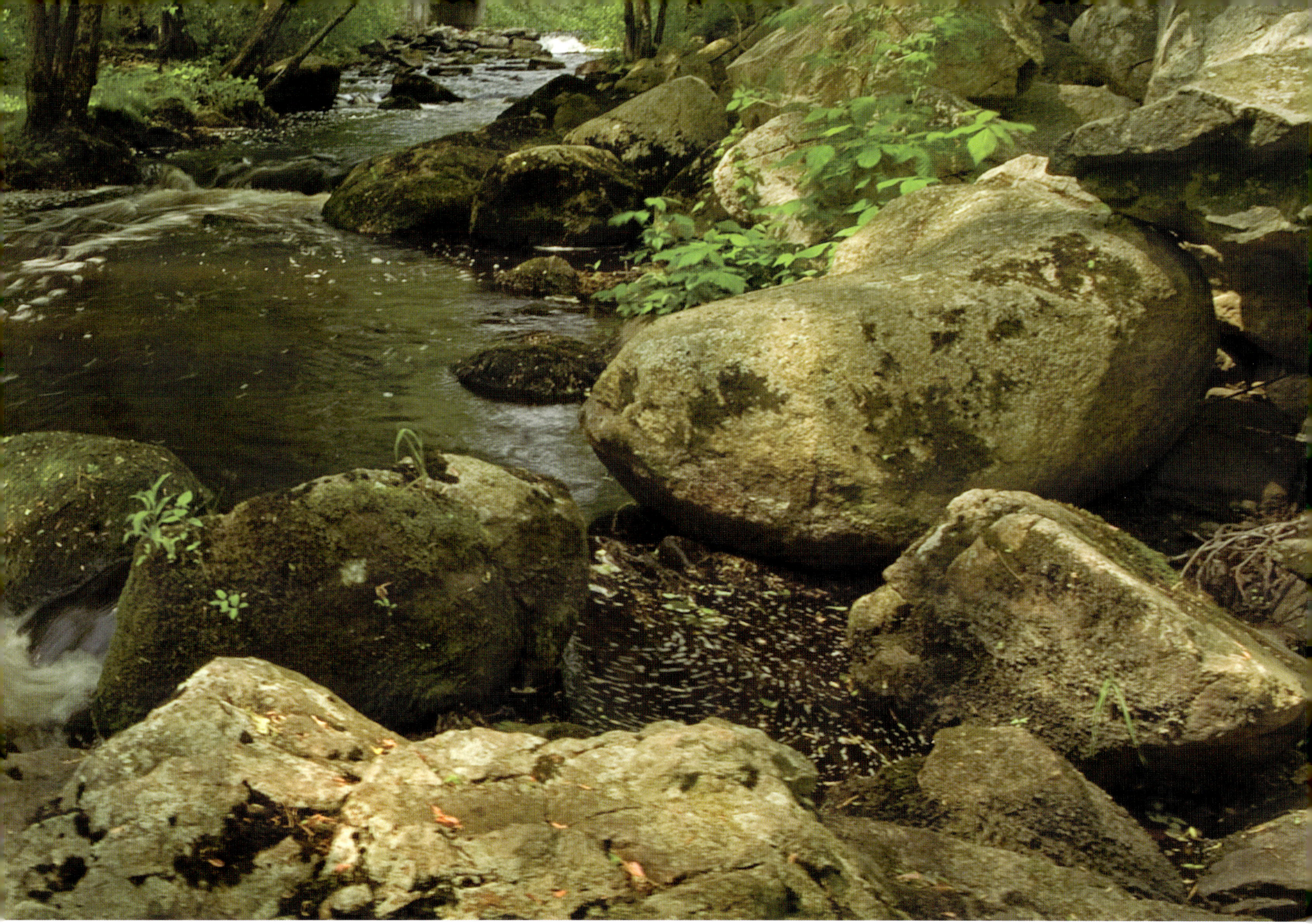

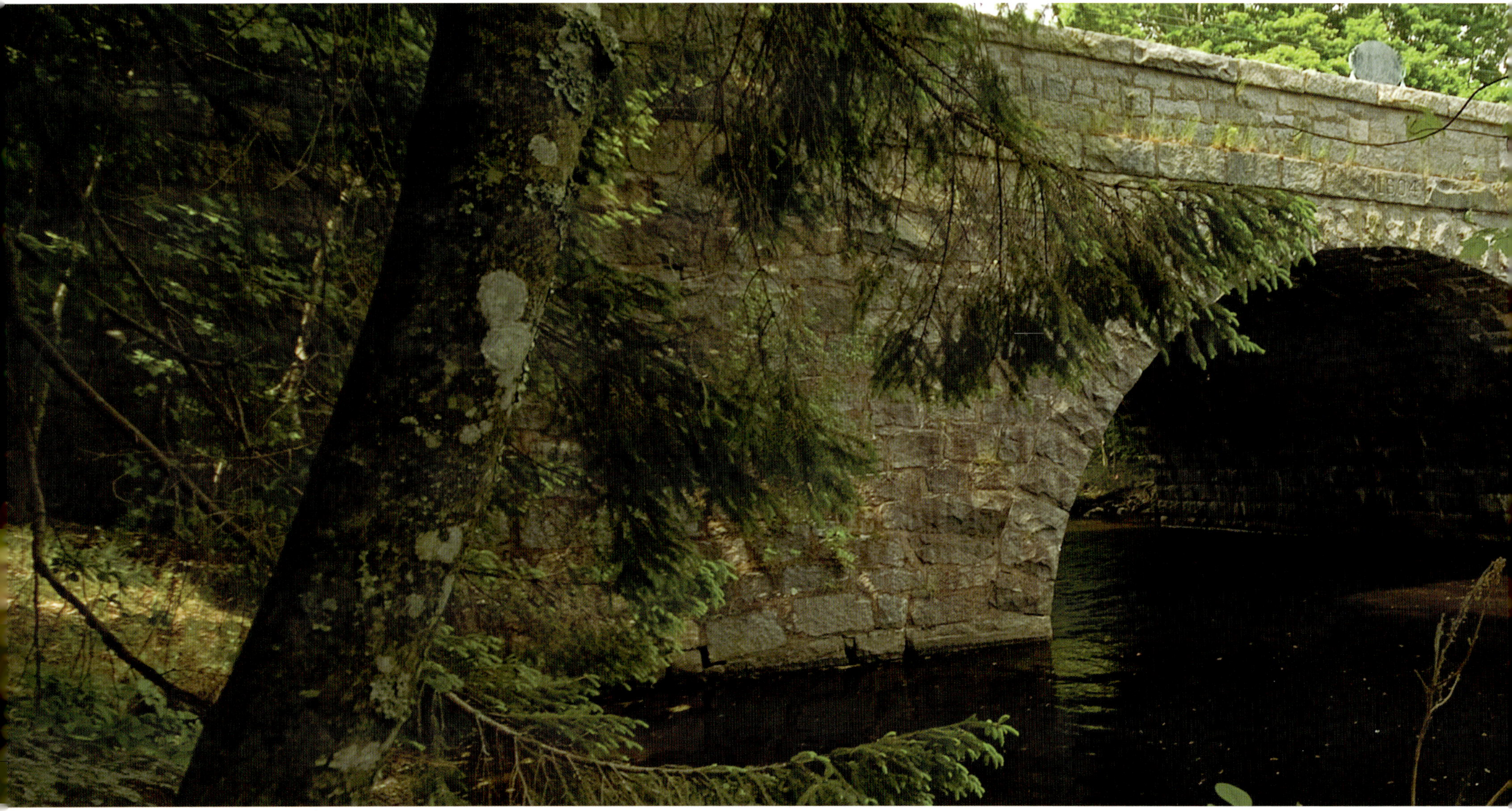

The Washington Street Bridge in Pembroke, which spans the North River, has had an historic maritime past.

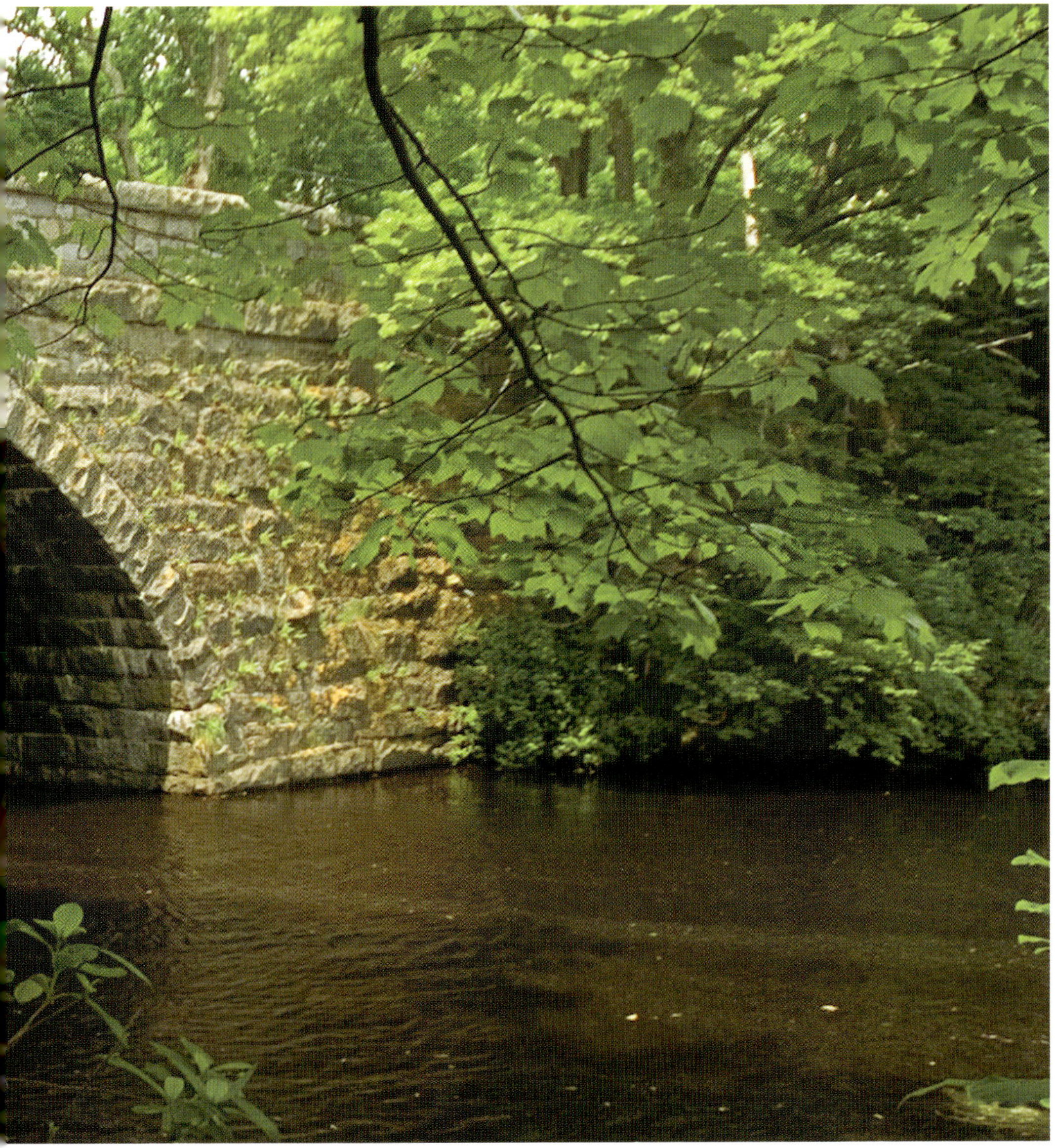

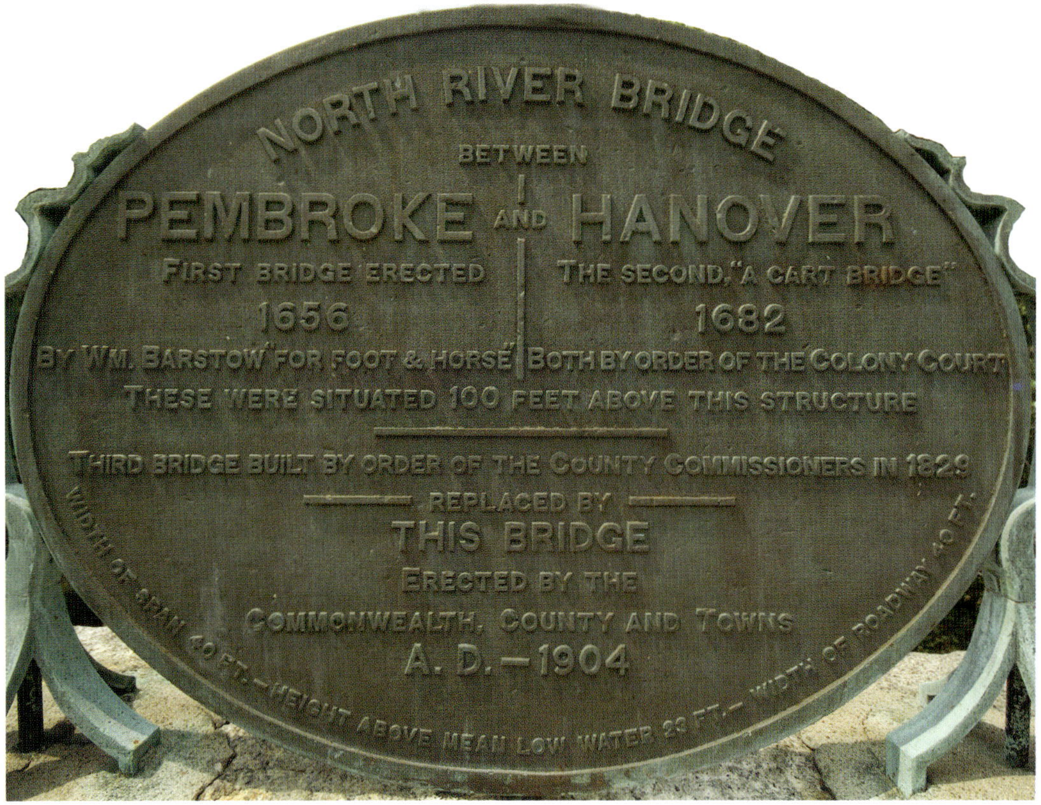
NORTH RIVER BRIDGE
BETWEEN
PEMBROKE AND HANOVER
FIRST BRIDGE ERECTED
1656
BY WM. BARSTOW "FOR FOOT & HORSE"
THE SECOND, "A CART BRIDGE"
1682
BOTH BY ORDER OF THE COLONY COURT
THESE WERE SITUATED 100 FEET ABOVE THIS STRUCTURE
THIRD BRIDGE BUILT BY ORDER OF THE COUNTY COMMISSIONERS IN 1829
REPLACED BY
THIS BRIDGE
ERECTED BY THE
COMMONWEALTH, COUNTY AND TOWNS
A. D. — 1904
WIDTH OF SPAN 40 FT. — HEIGHT ABOVE MEAN LOW WATER 23 FT. — WIDTH OF ROADWAY 40 FT.

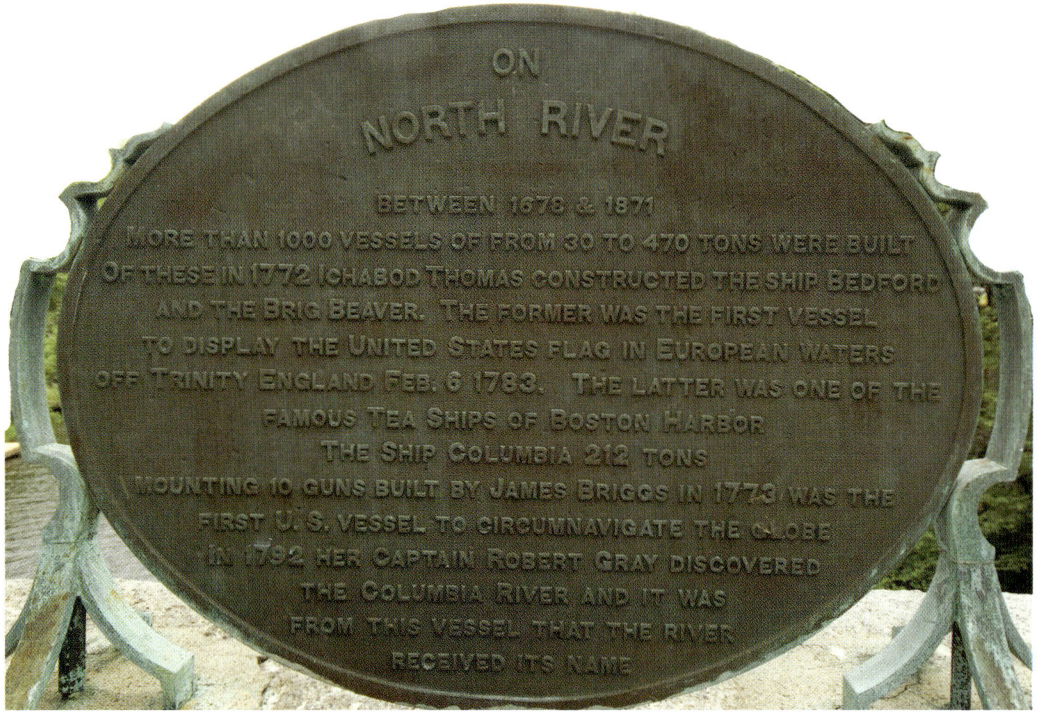
ON
NORTH RIVER
BETWEEN 1678 & 1871
MORE THAN 1000 VESSELS OF FROM 30 TO 470 TONS WERE BUILT
OF THESE IN 1772 ICHABOD THOMAS CONSTRUCTED THE SHIP BEDFORD
AND THE BRIG BEAVER. THE FORMER WAS THE FIRST VESSEL
TO DISPLAY THE UNITED STATES FLAG IN EUROPEAN WATERS
OFF TRINITY ENGLAND FEB. 6 1783. THE LATTER WAS ONE OF THE
FAMOUS TEA SHIPS OF BOSTON HARBOR
THE SHIP COLUMBIA 212 TONS
MOUNTING 10 GUNS BUILT BY JAMES BRIGGS IN 1773 WAS THE
FIRST U. S. VESSEL TO CIRCUMNAVIGATE THE GLOBE
IN 1792 HER CAPTAIN ROBERT GRAY DISCOVERED
THE COLUMBIA RIVER AND IT WAS
FROM THIS VESSEL THAT THE RIVER
RECEIVED ITS NAME

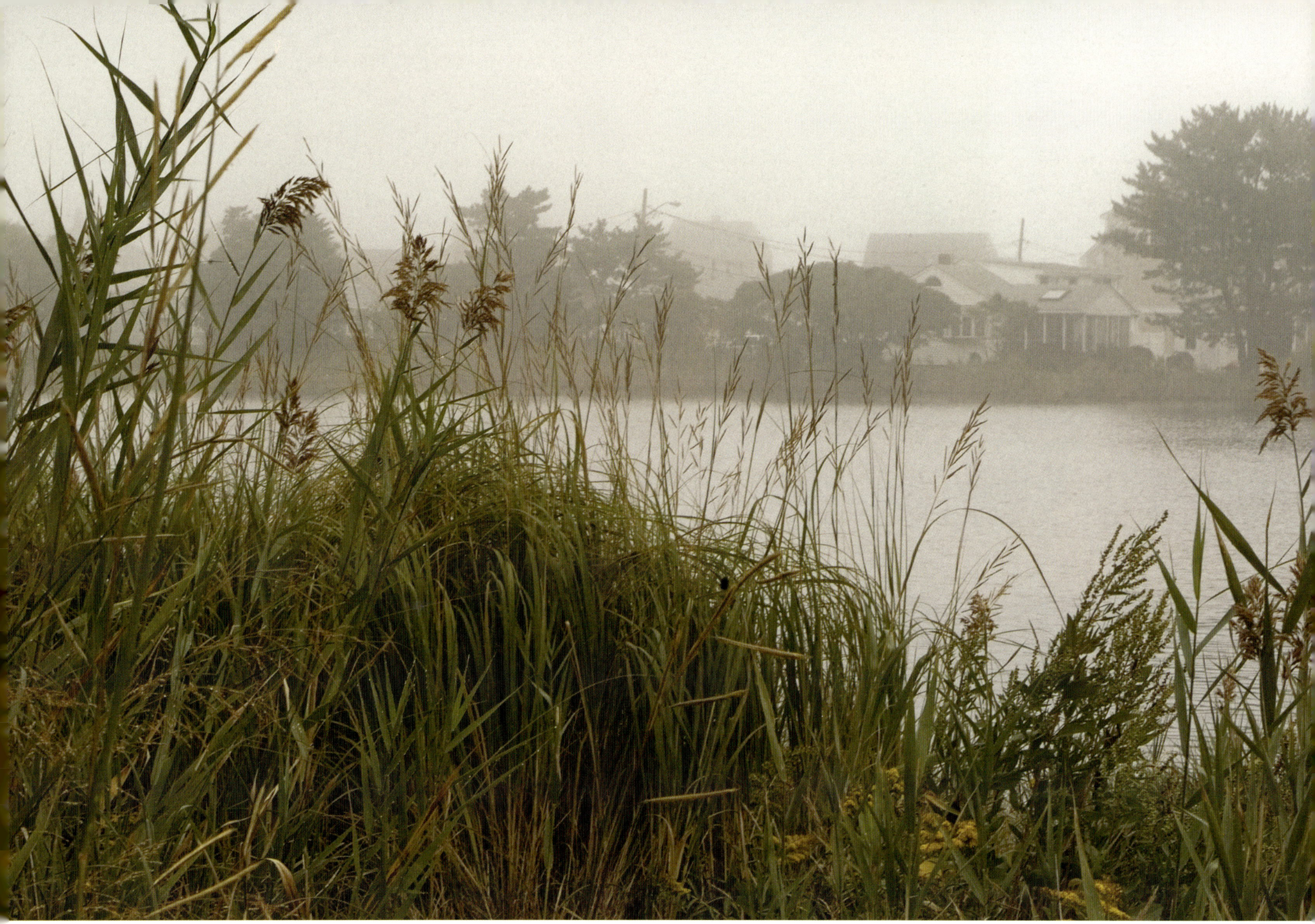

Musquashicut Pond is located just behind North Scituate Beach.

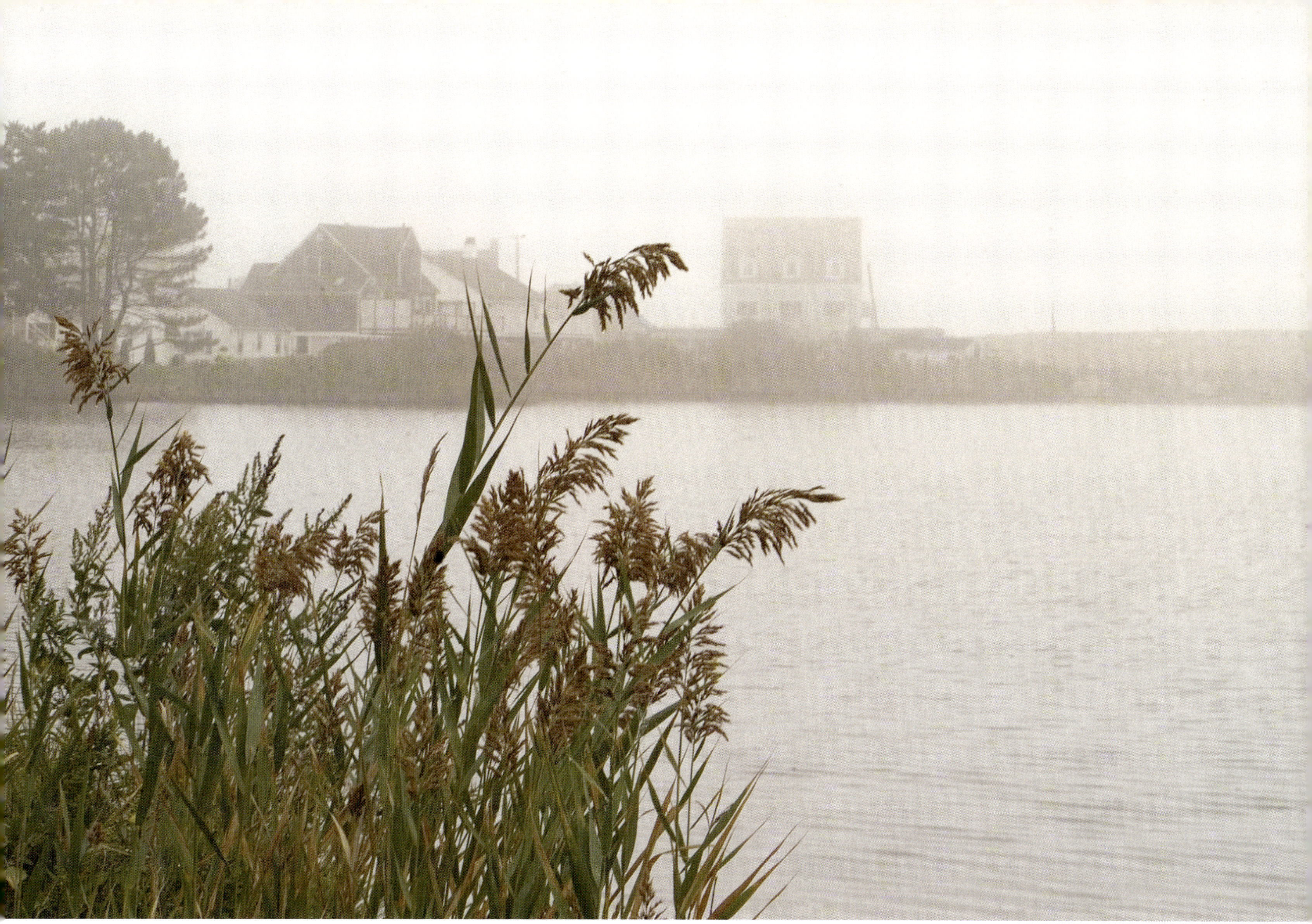

Lawson Park in Scituate is surrounded by colonial homes and features a fountain with three spouting elephants.

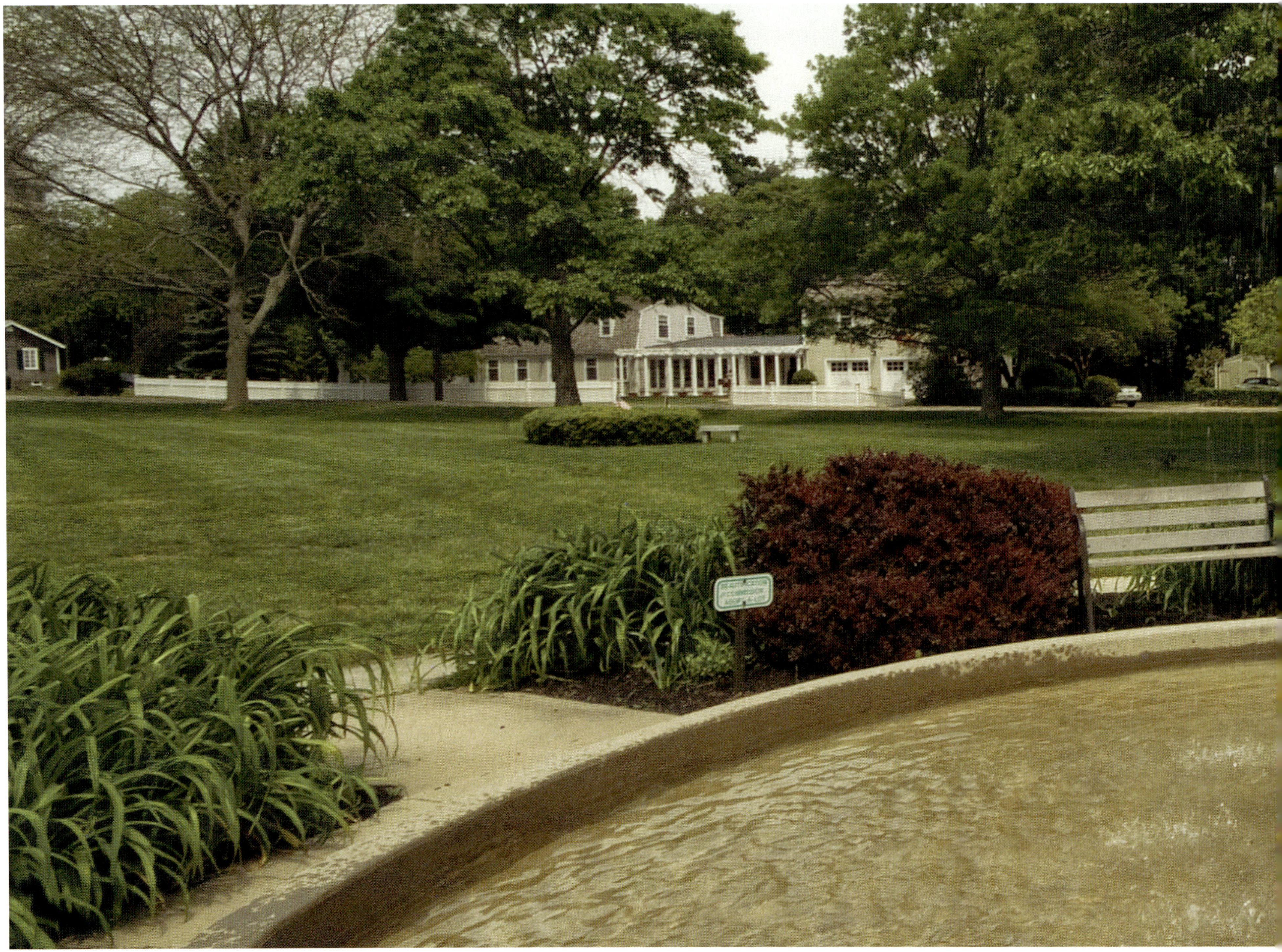

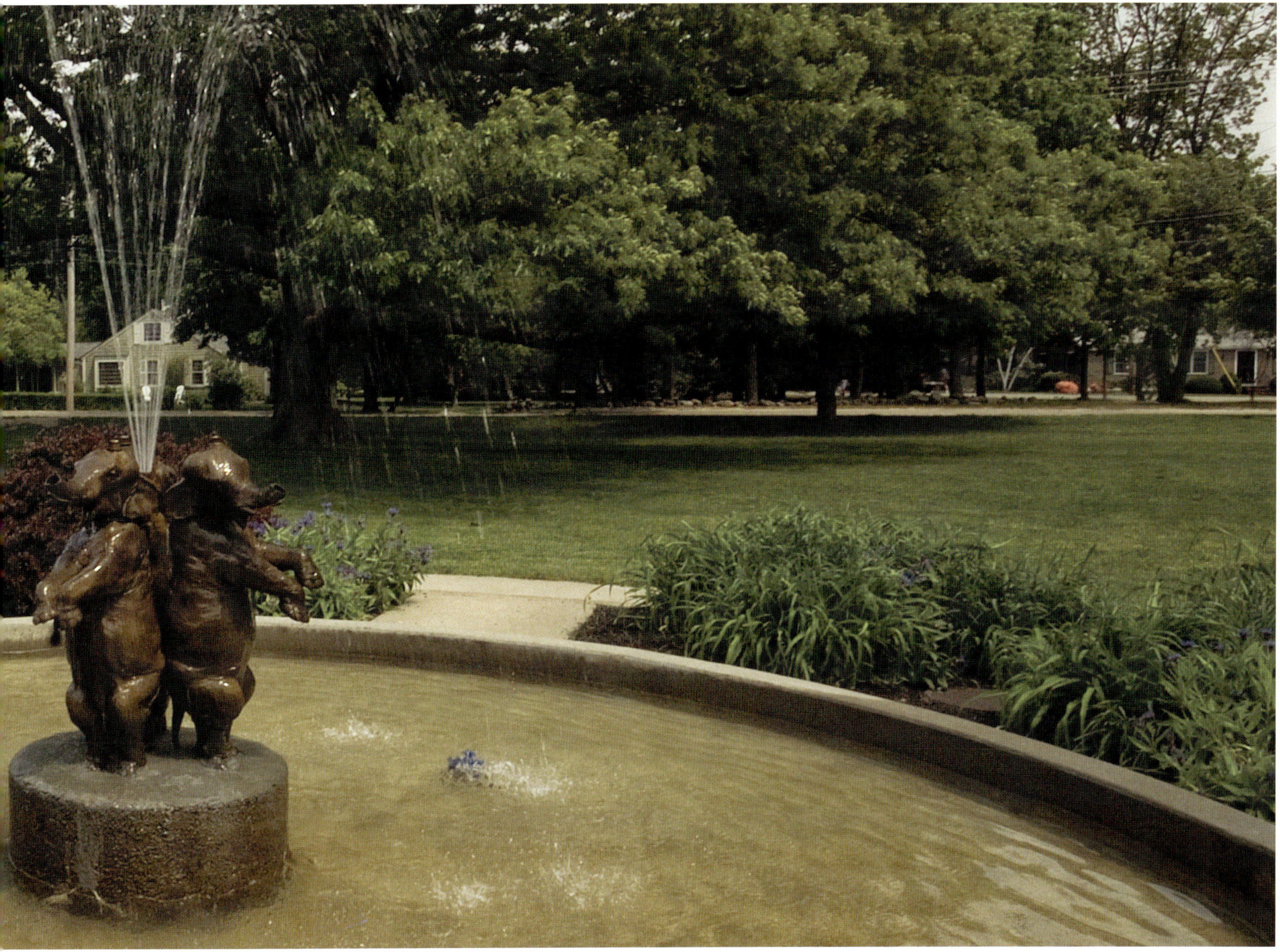

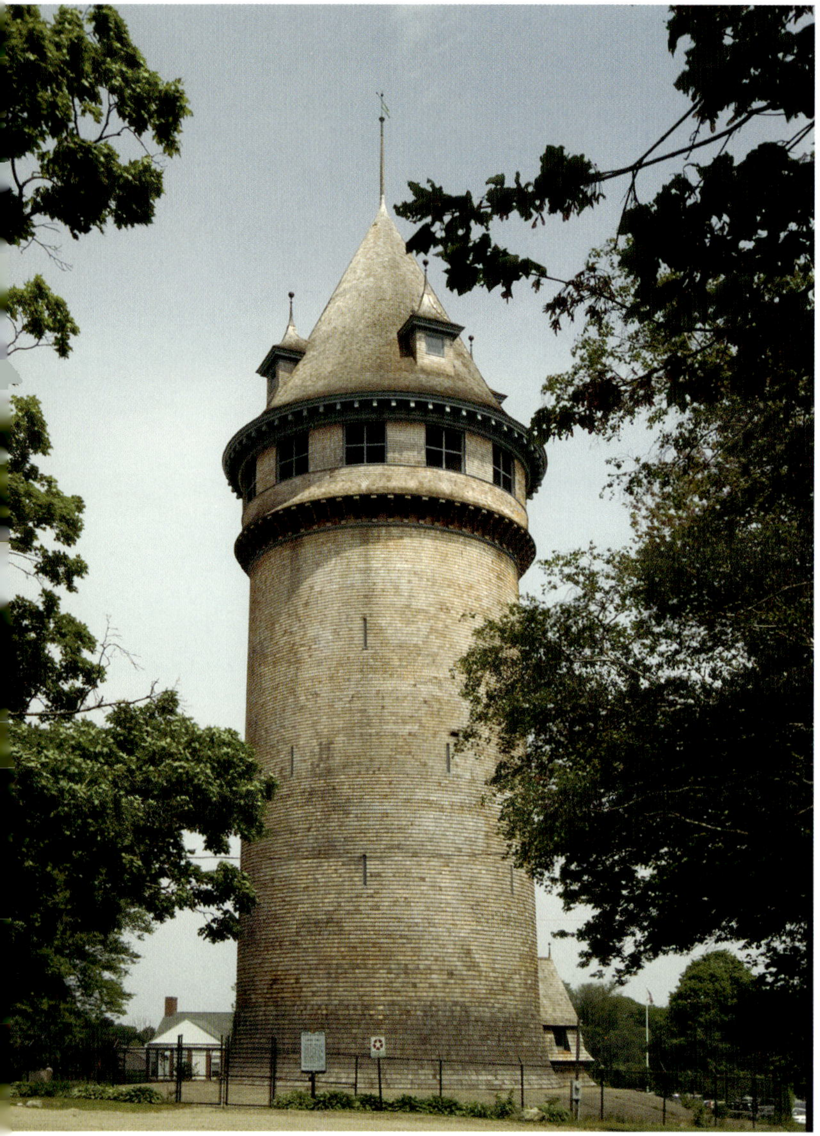

One distinctive landmarks in Scituate is the Lawson Tower.

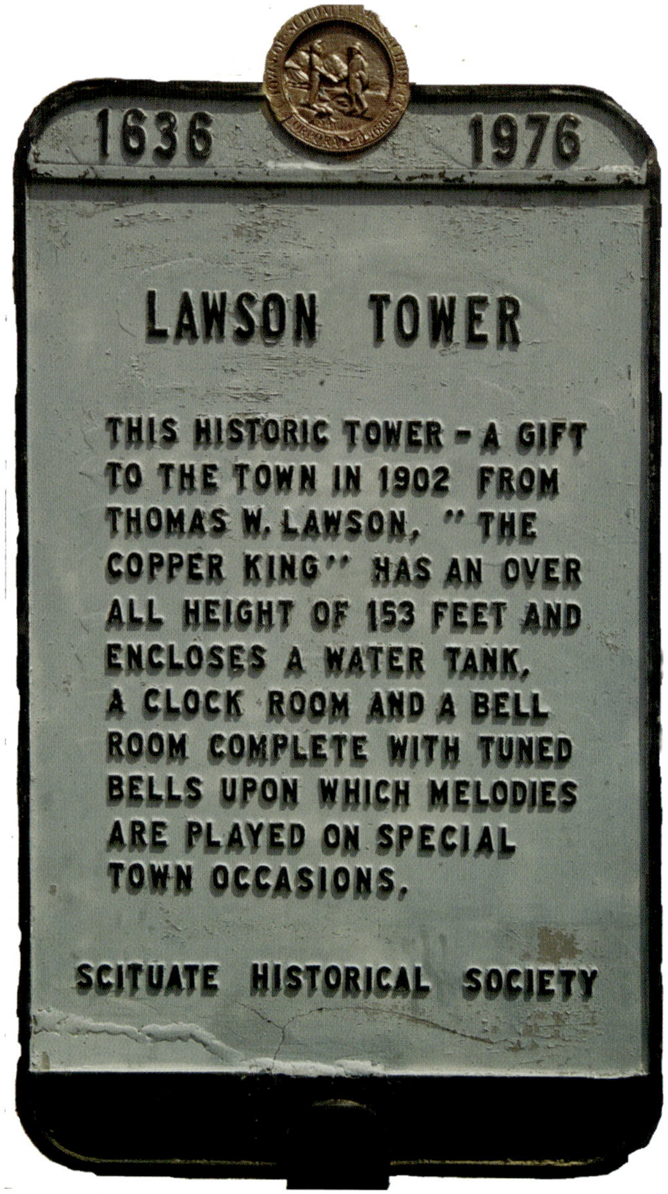

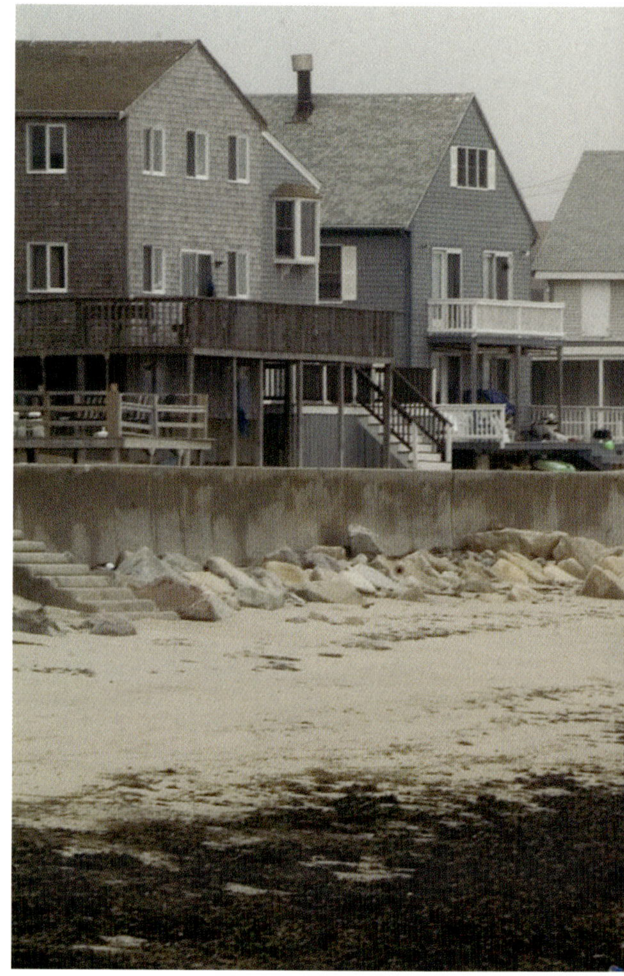

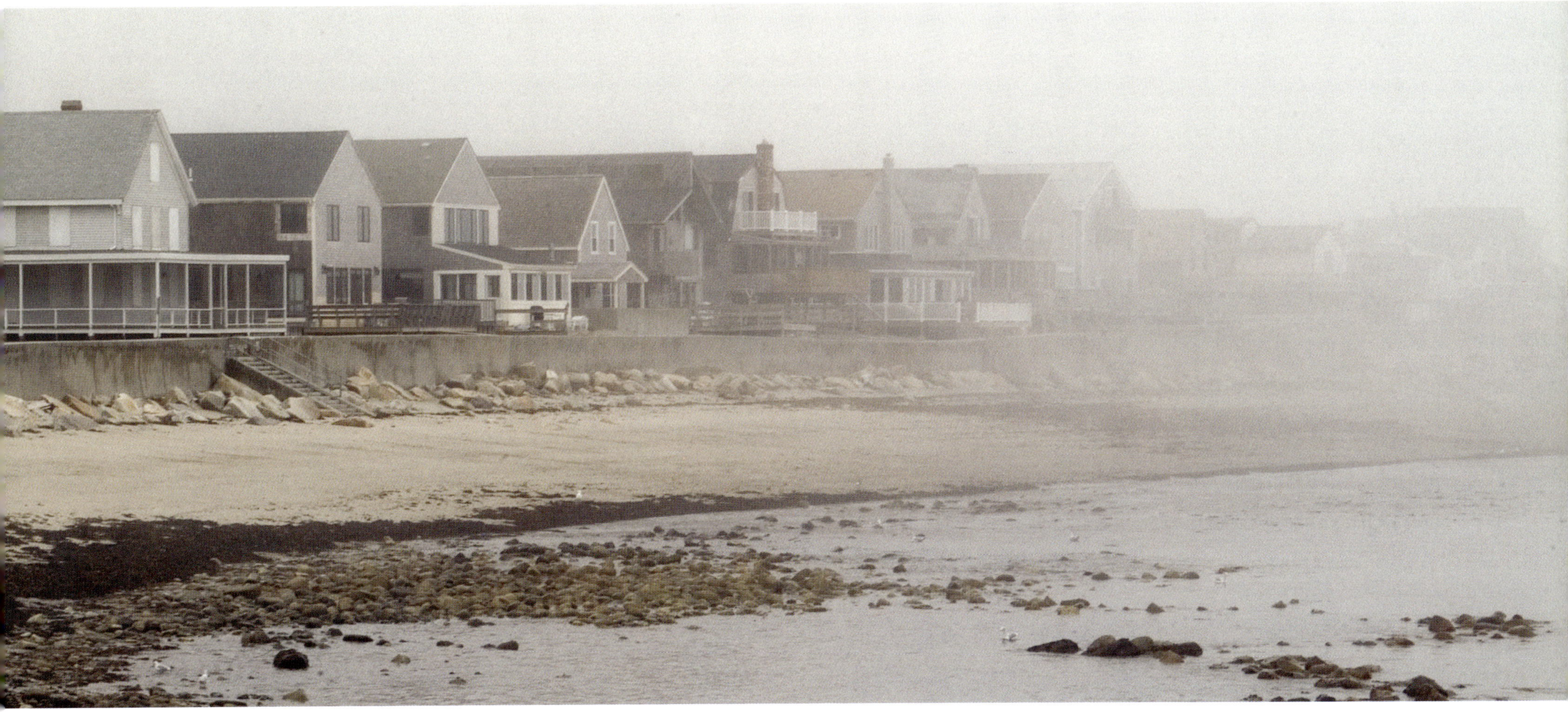

On a foggy morning, houses in the Sand Hills section of Scituate overlook the beach.

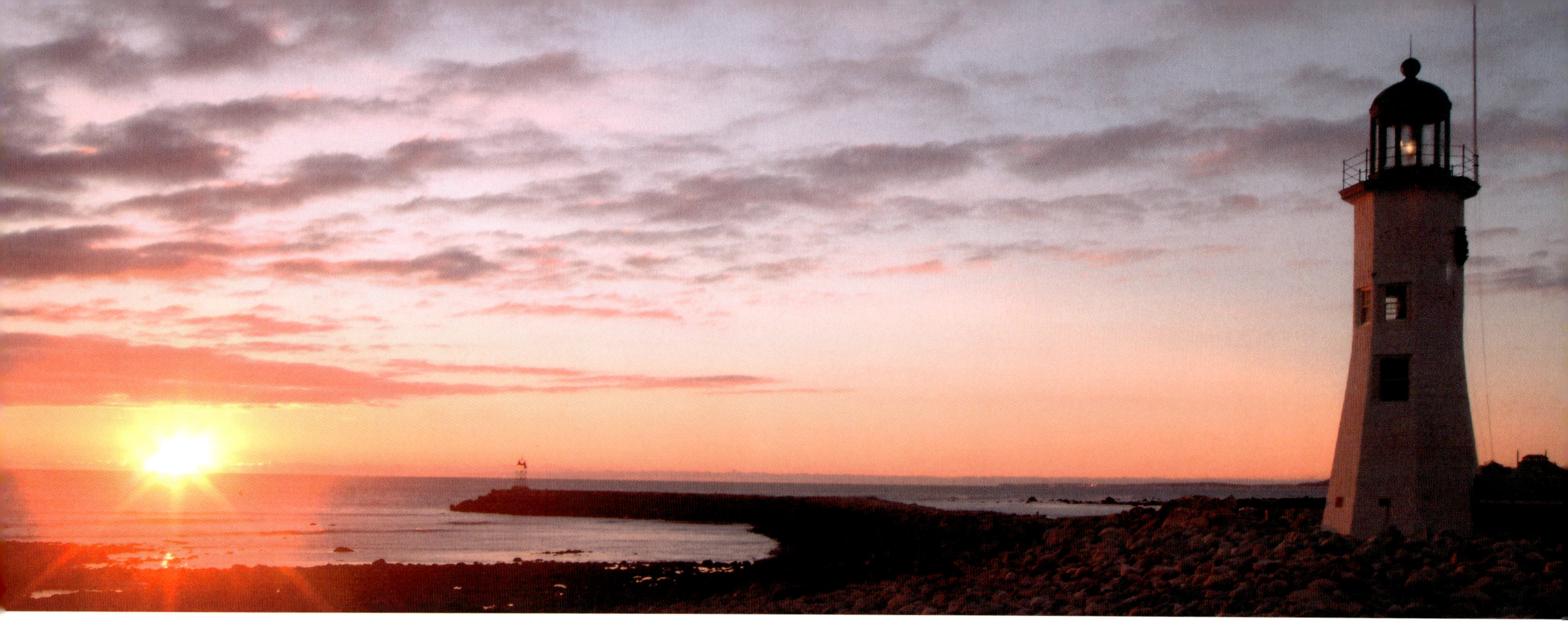

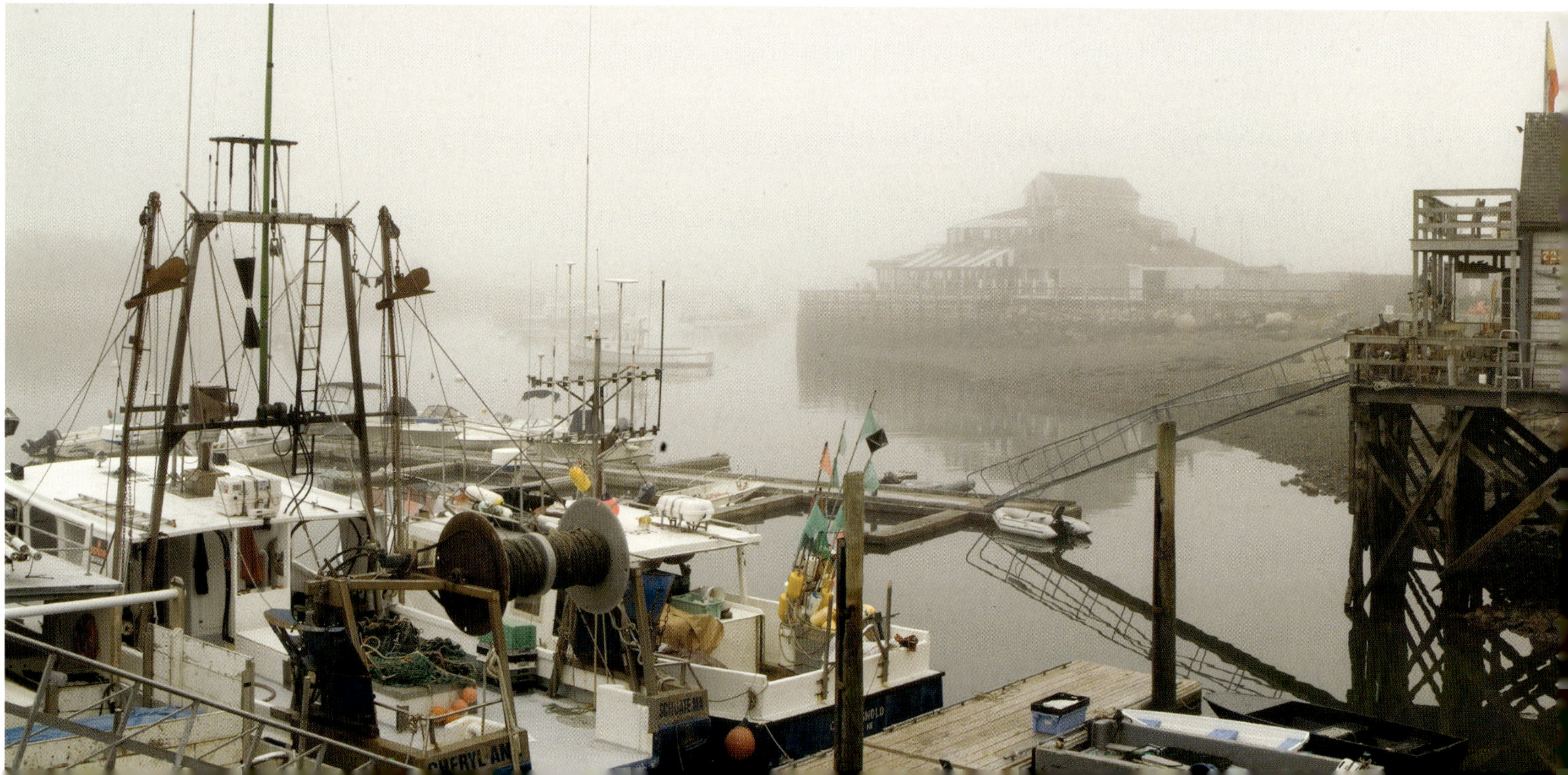
SCITUATE MA

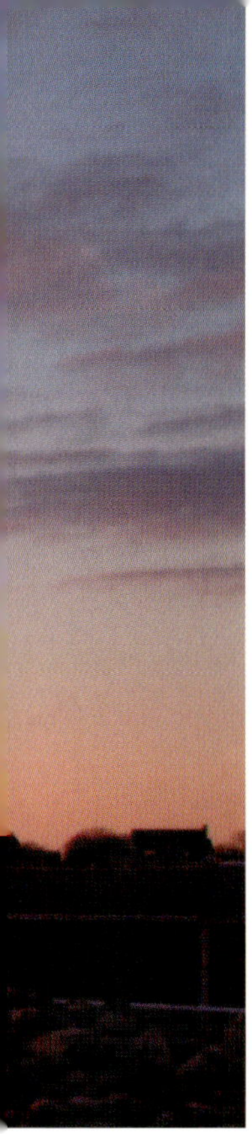

Sunrise at Scituate Lighthouse.

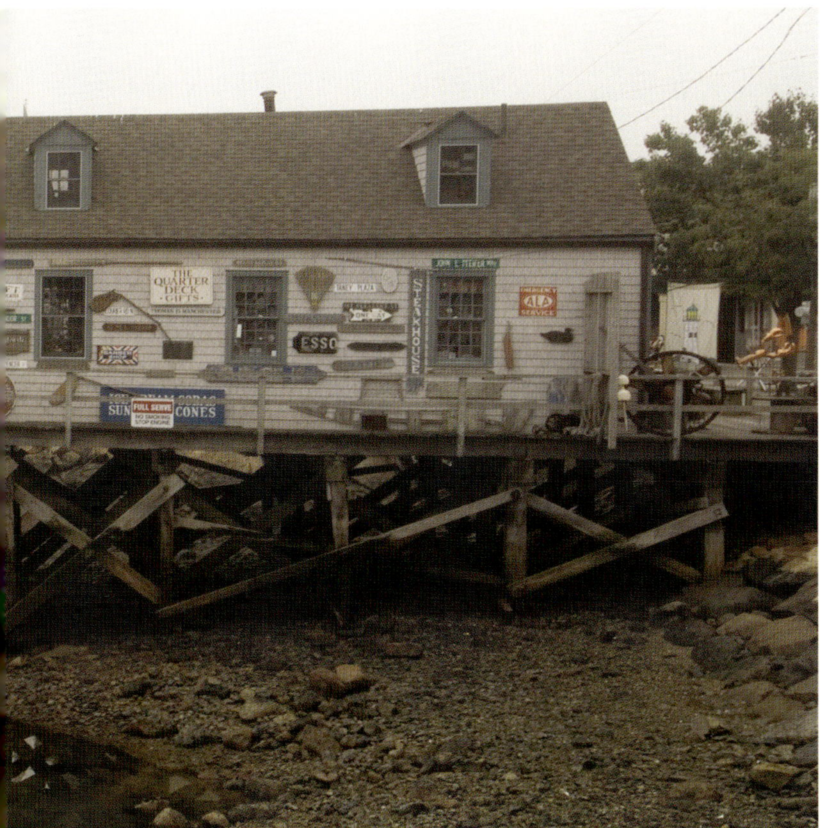

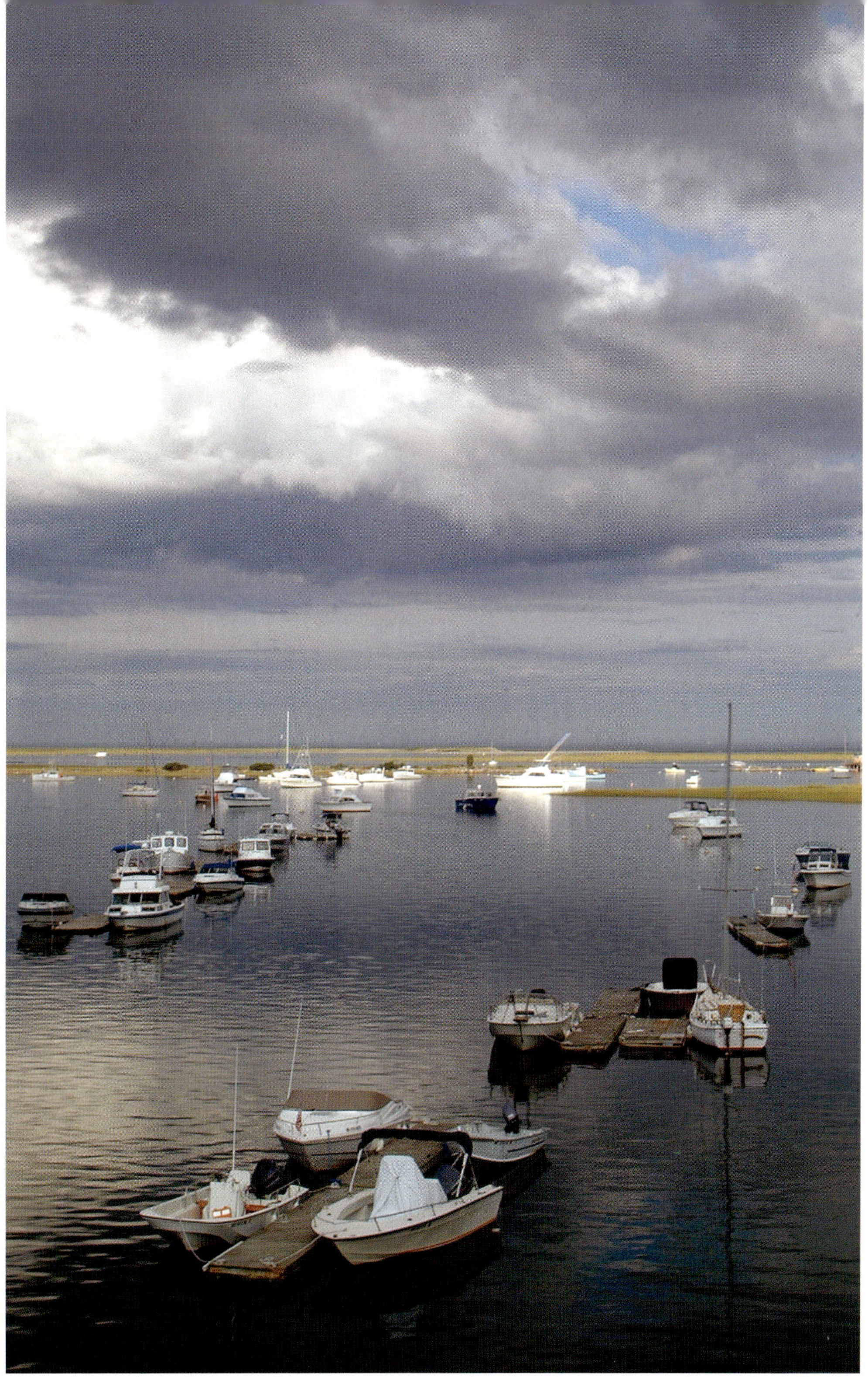

Boats swing at their moorings in Scituate Harbor.

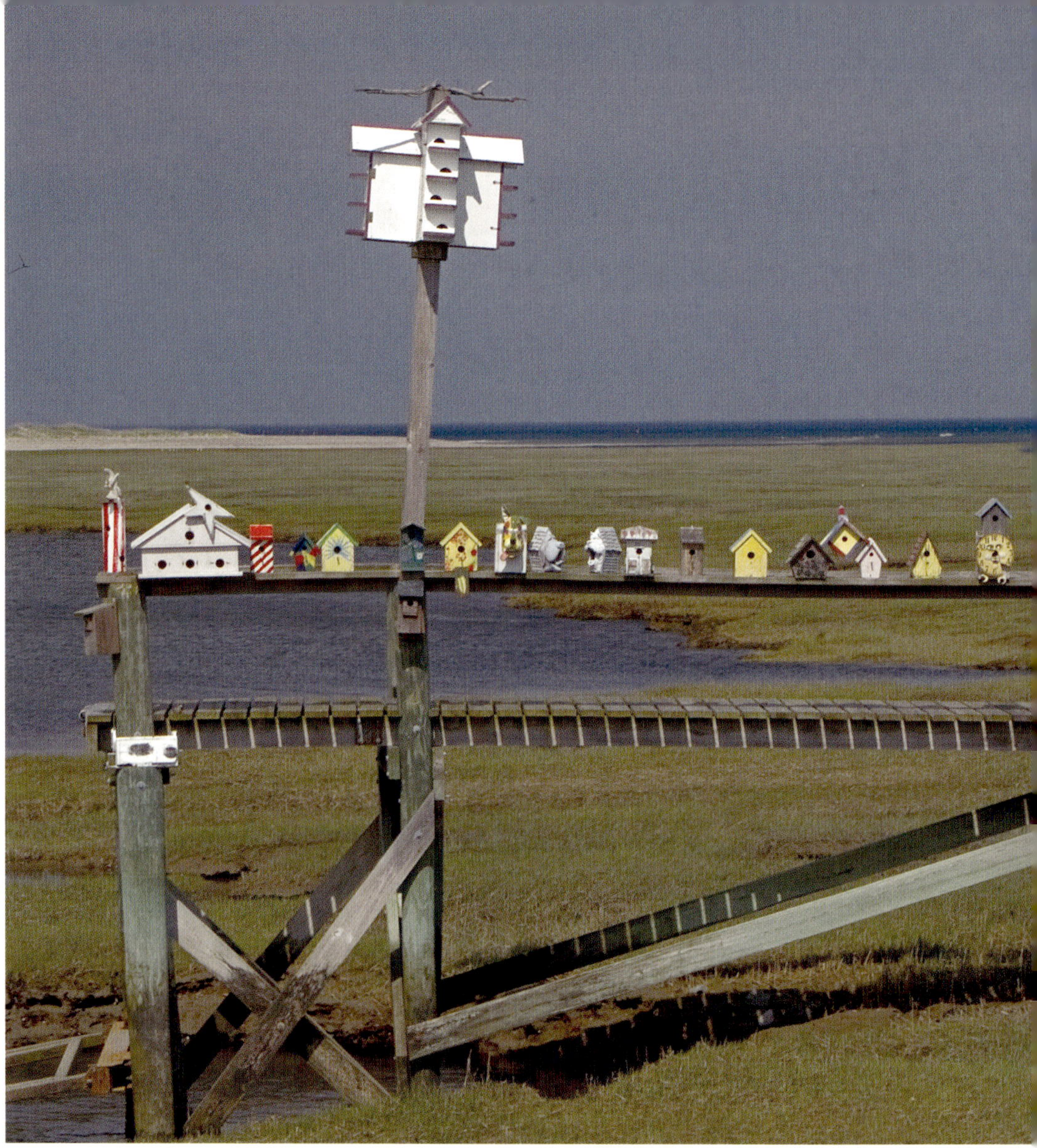

Birdhouses decorate this boardwalk that leads to the North River.

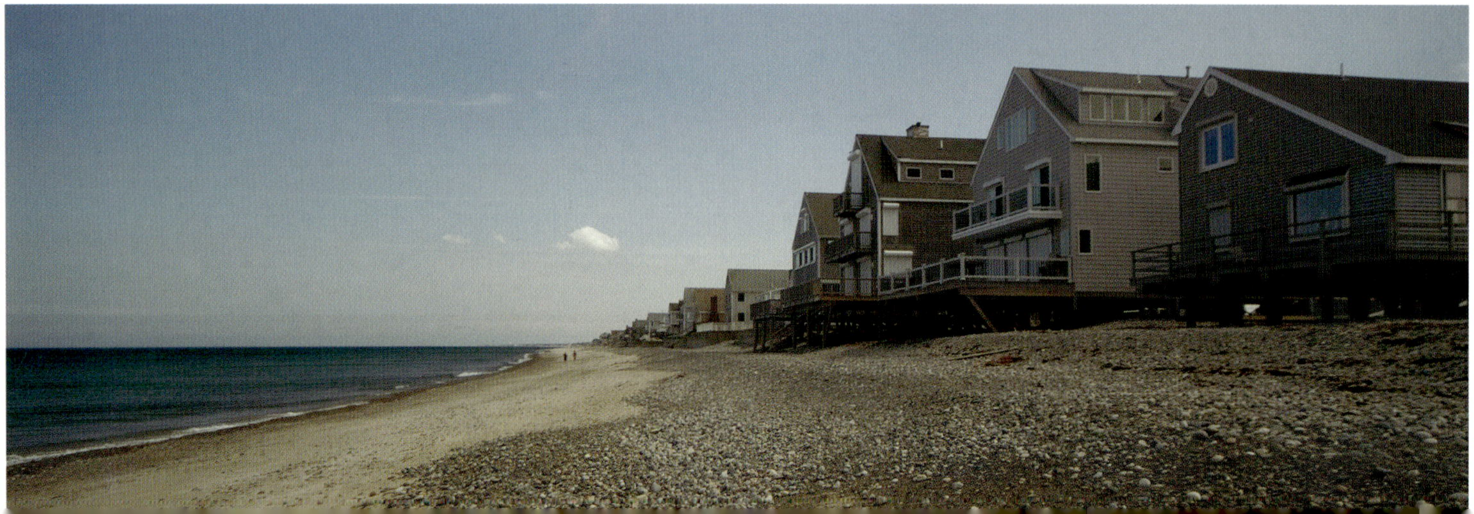

Houses line the beach in Humarock.

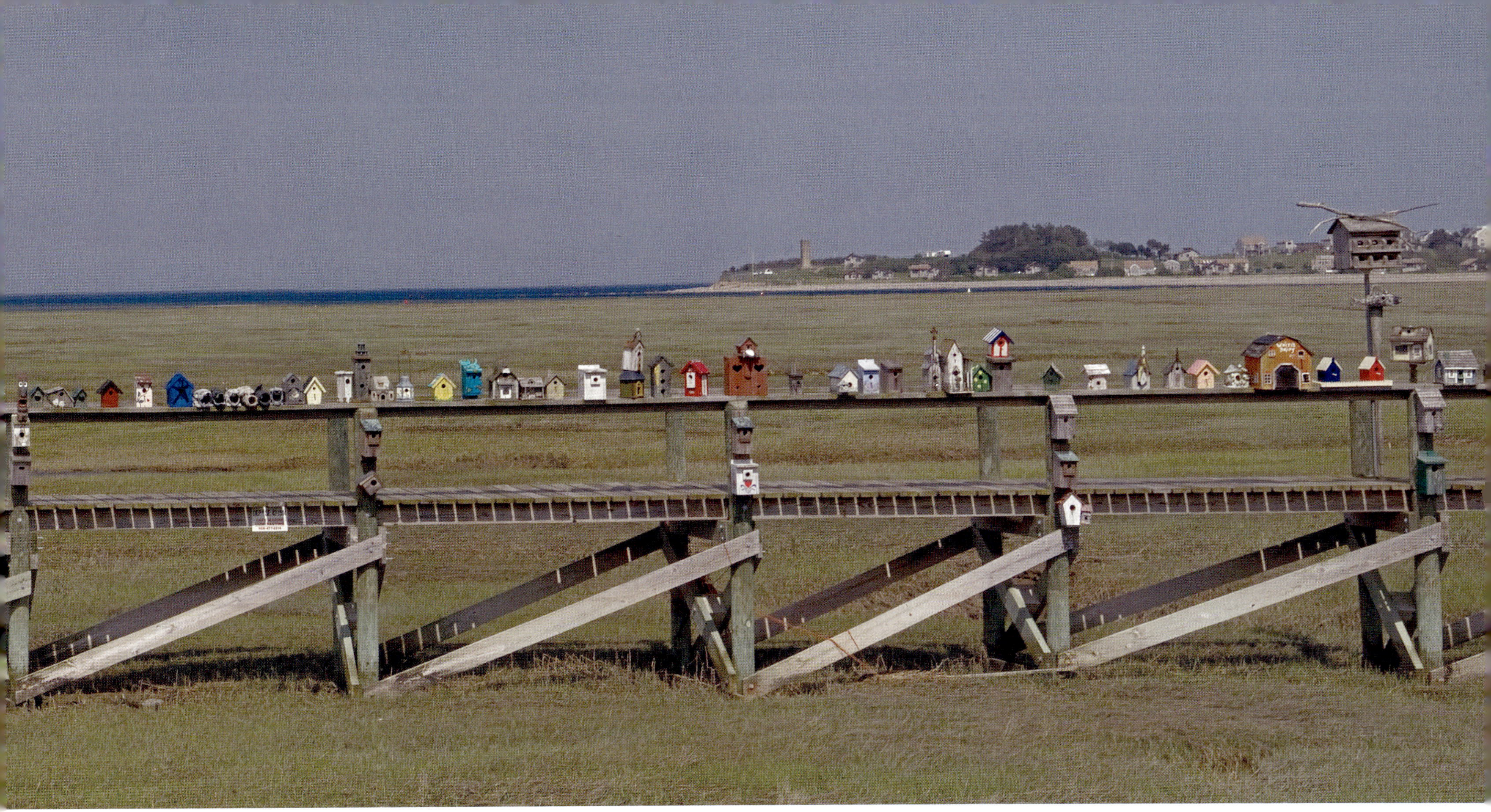

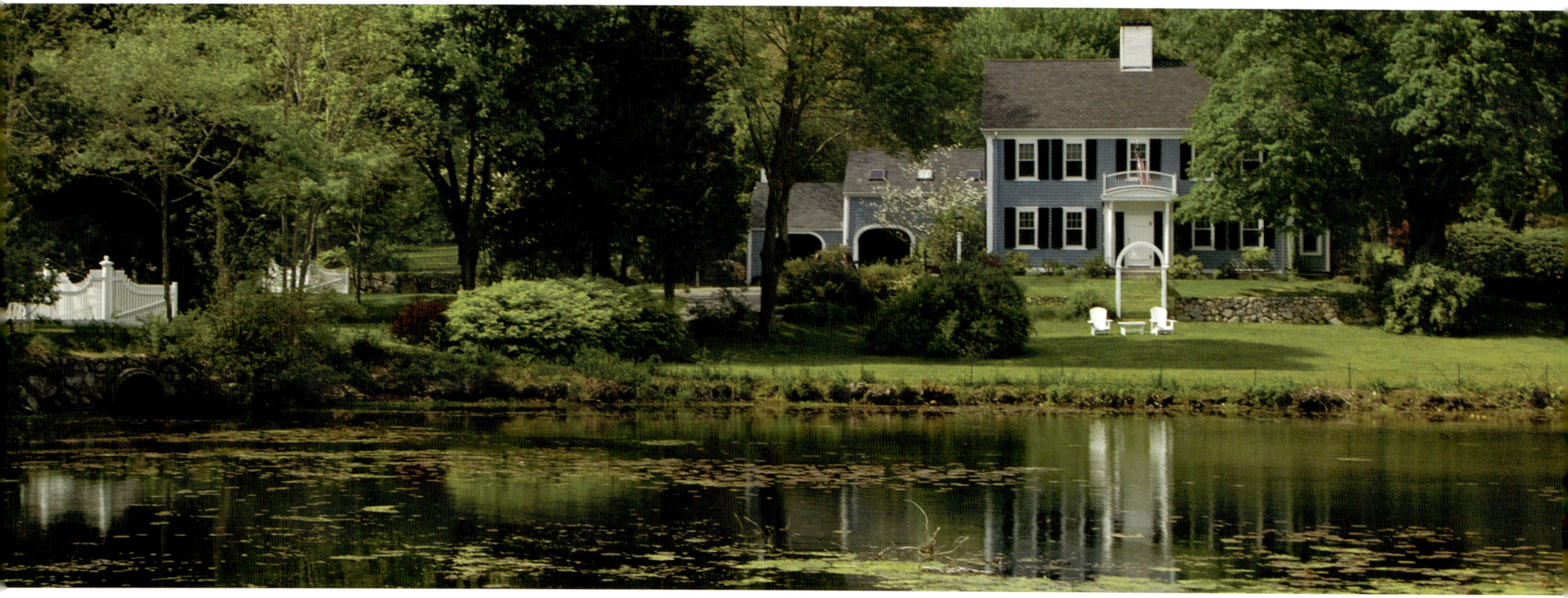

This antique colonial overlooks a pond in Marshfield.

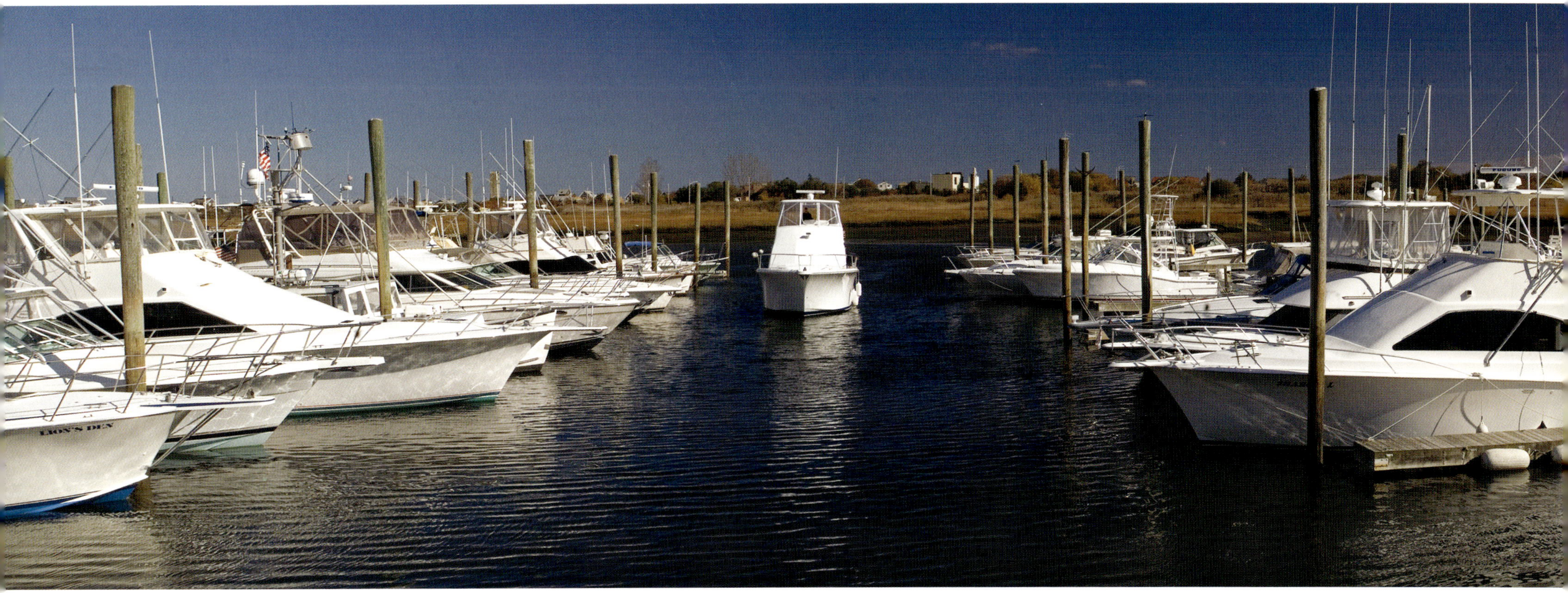

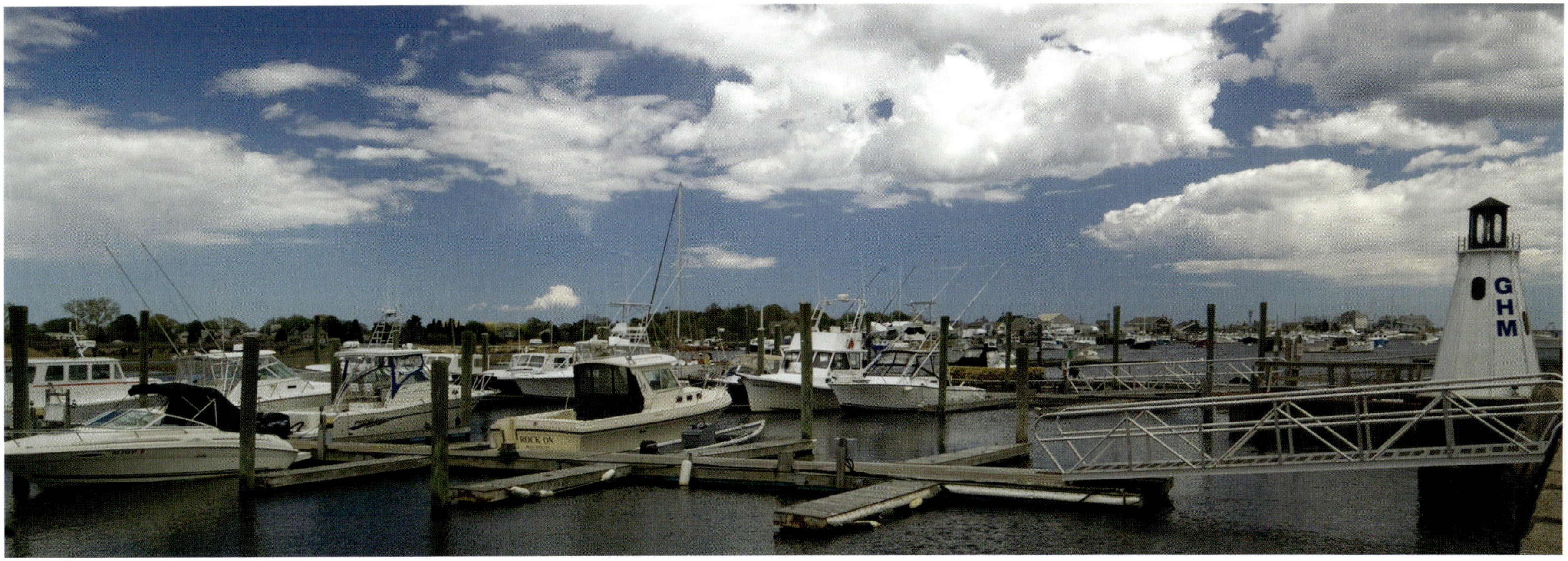

Two views of the boats and slips at the Green Harbor Marina in Marshfield.

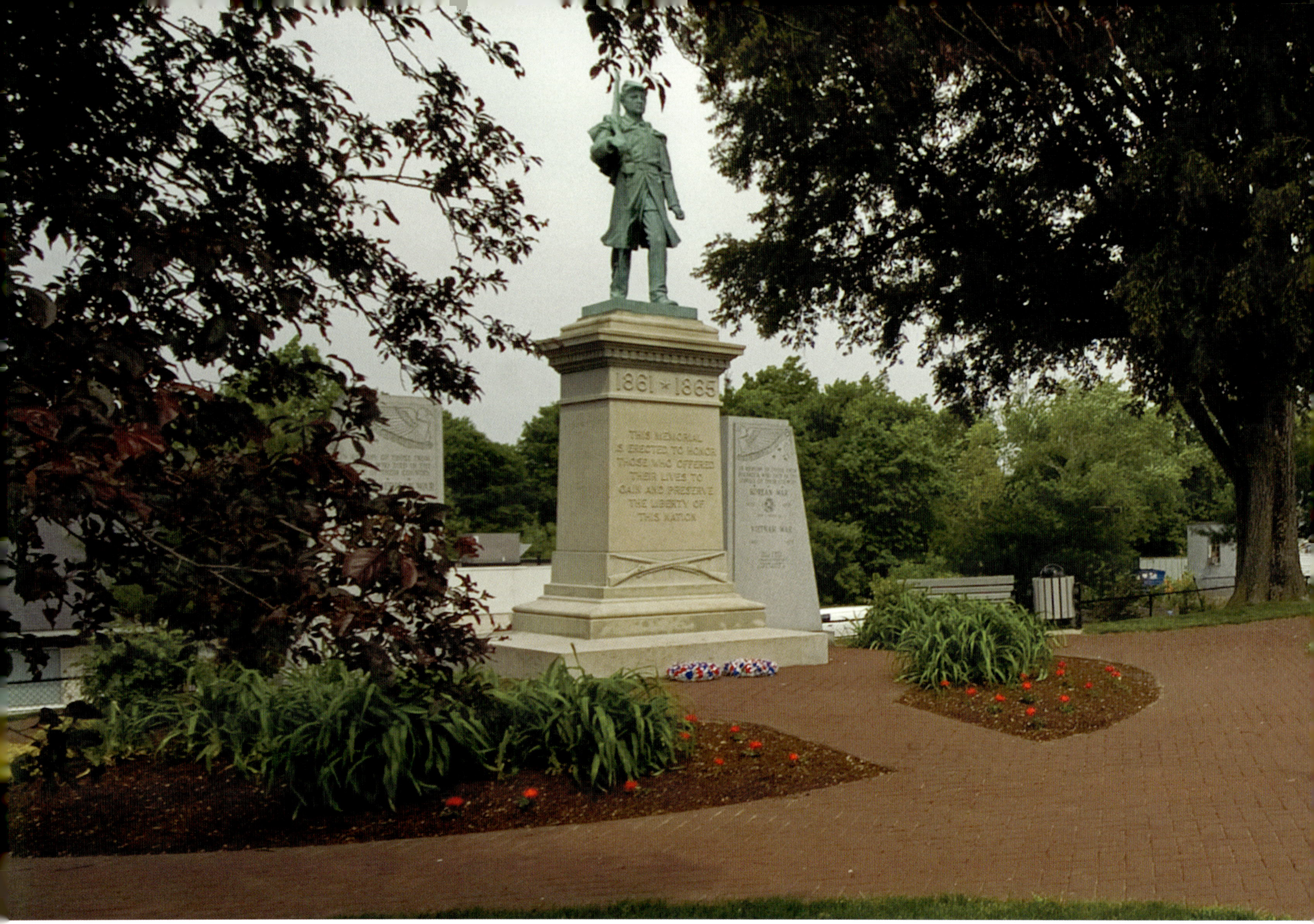

The Town Green in Holbrook has a Civil War Memorial, Town Hall, and a distinctive white church with steeple.

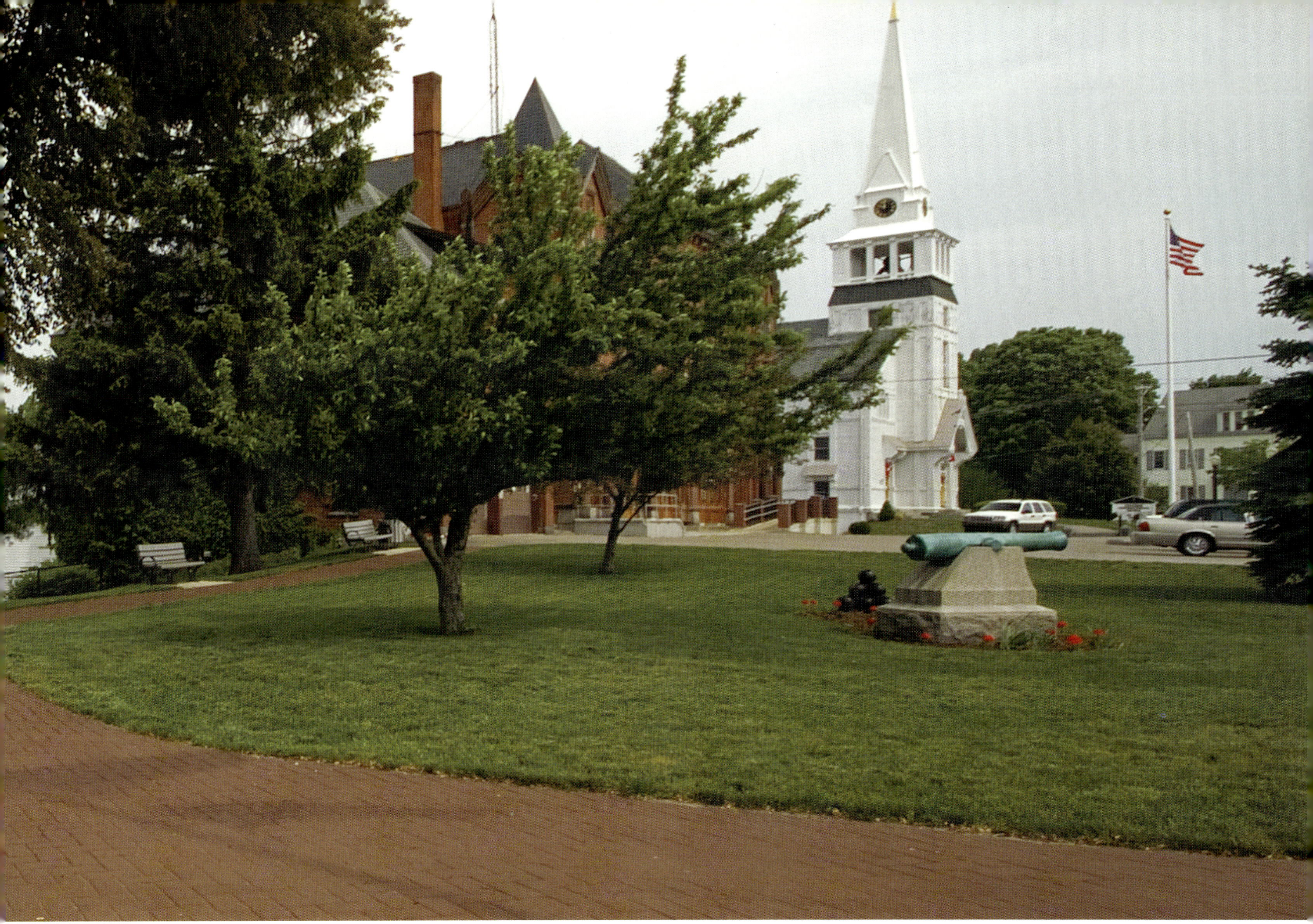

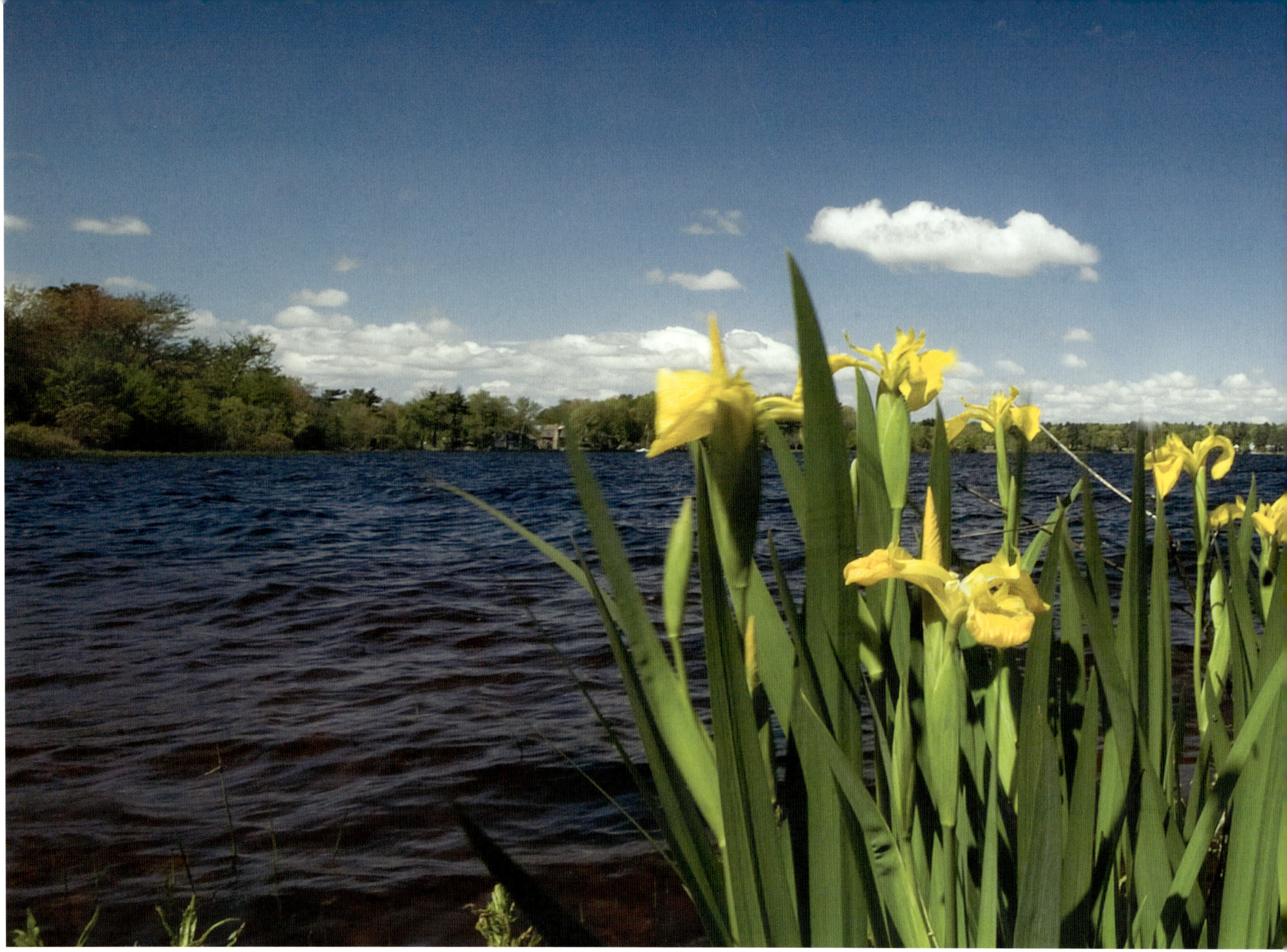

Iris bloom along the shore of Lake Nippennicket in Bridgewater.

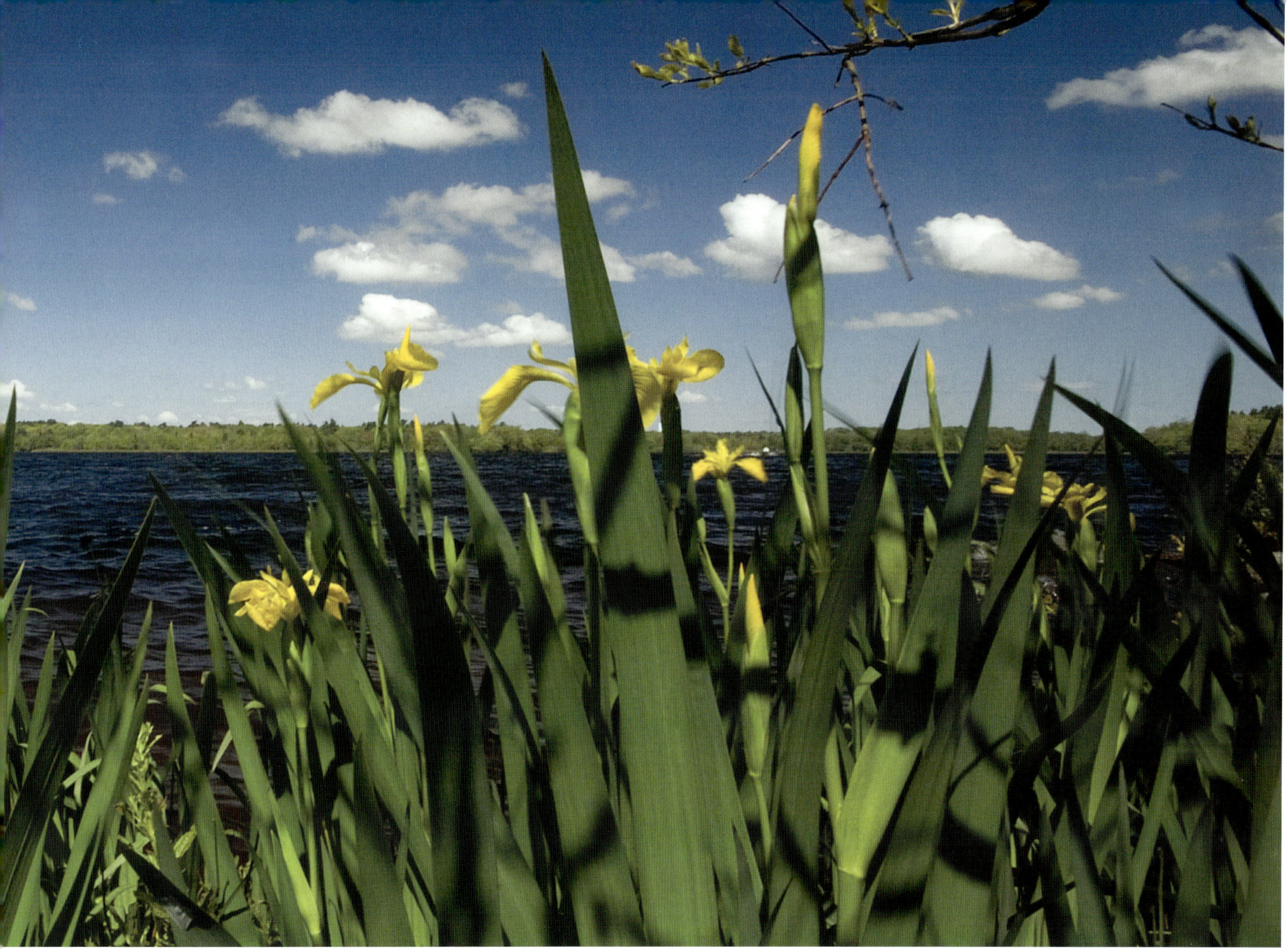

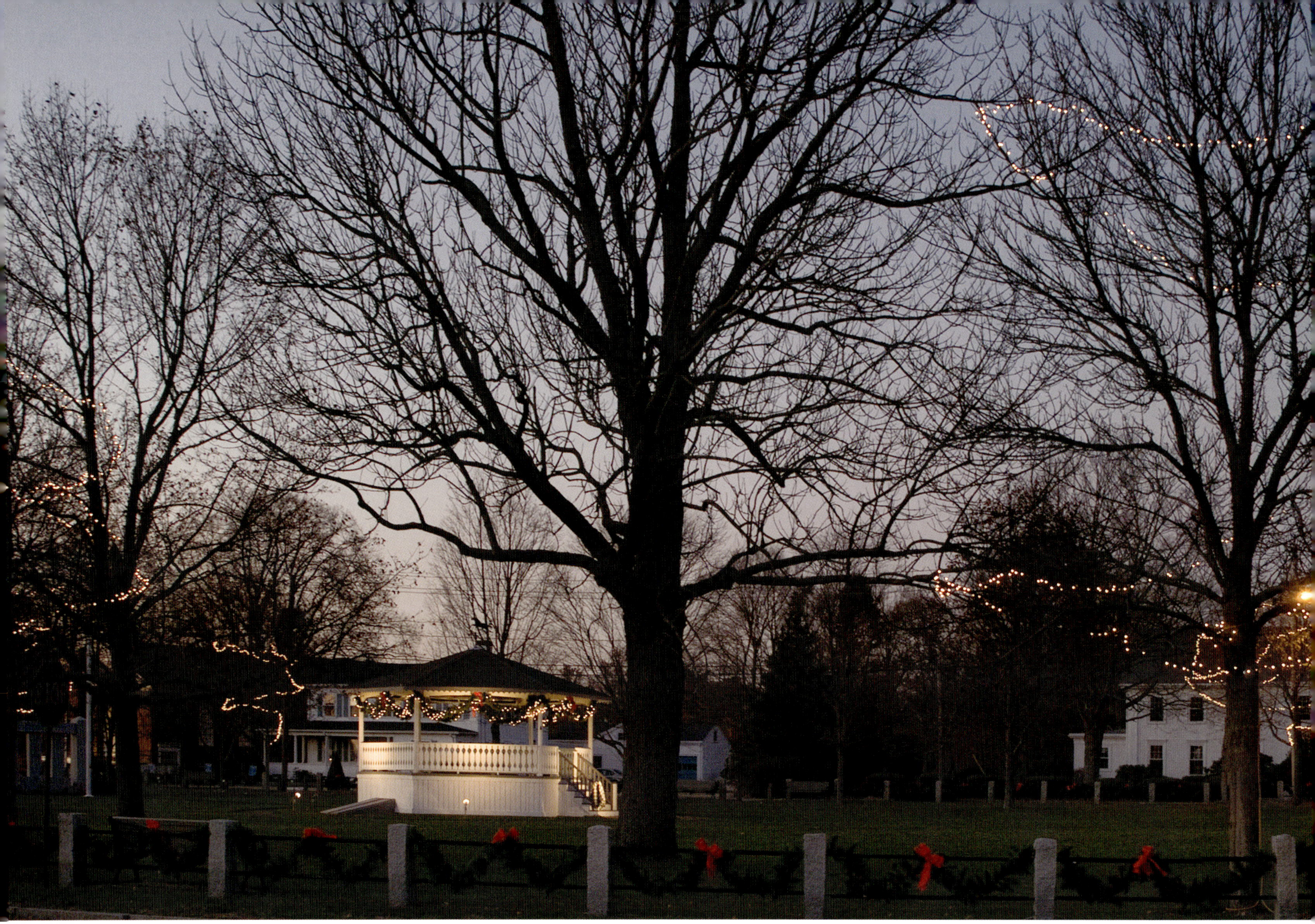

The East Bridgewater town green decorated for the winter holiday season.

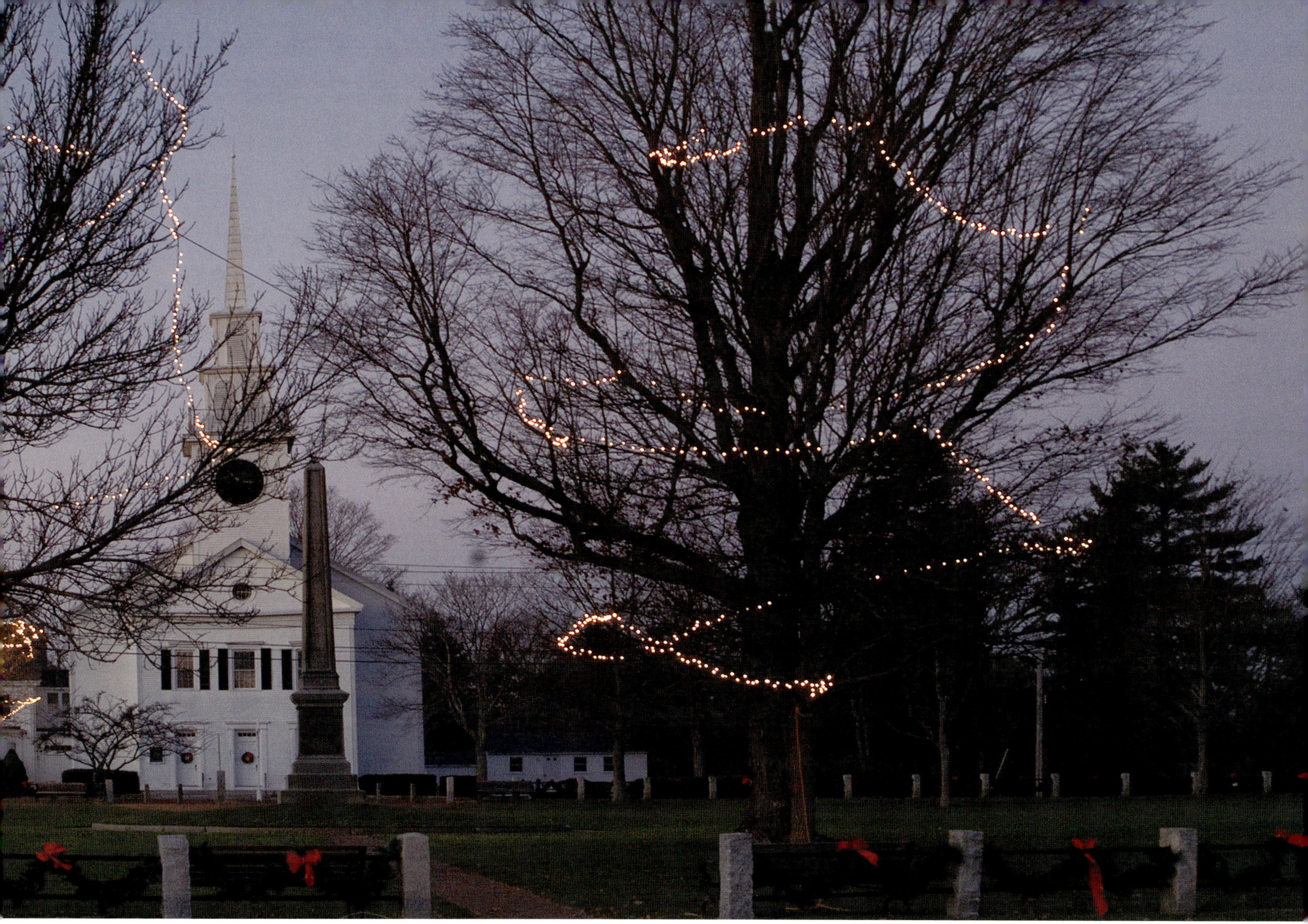

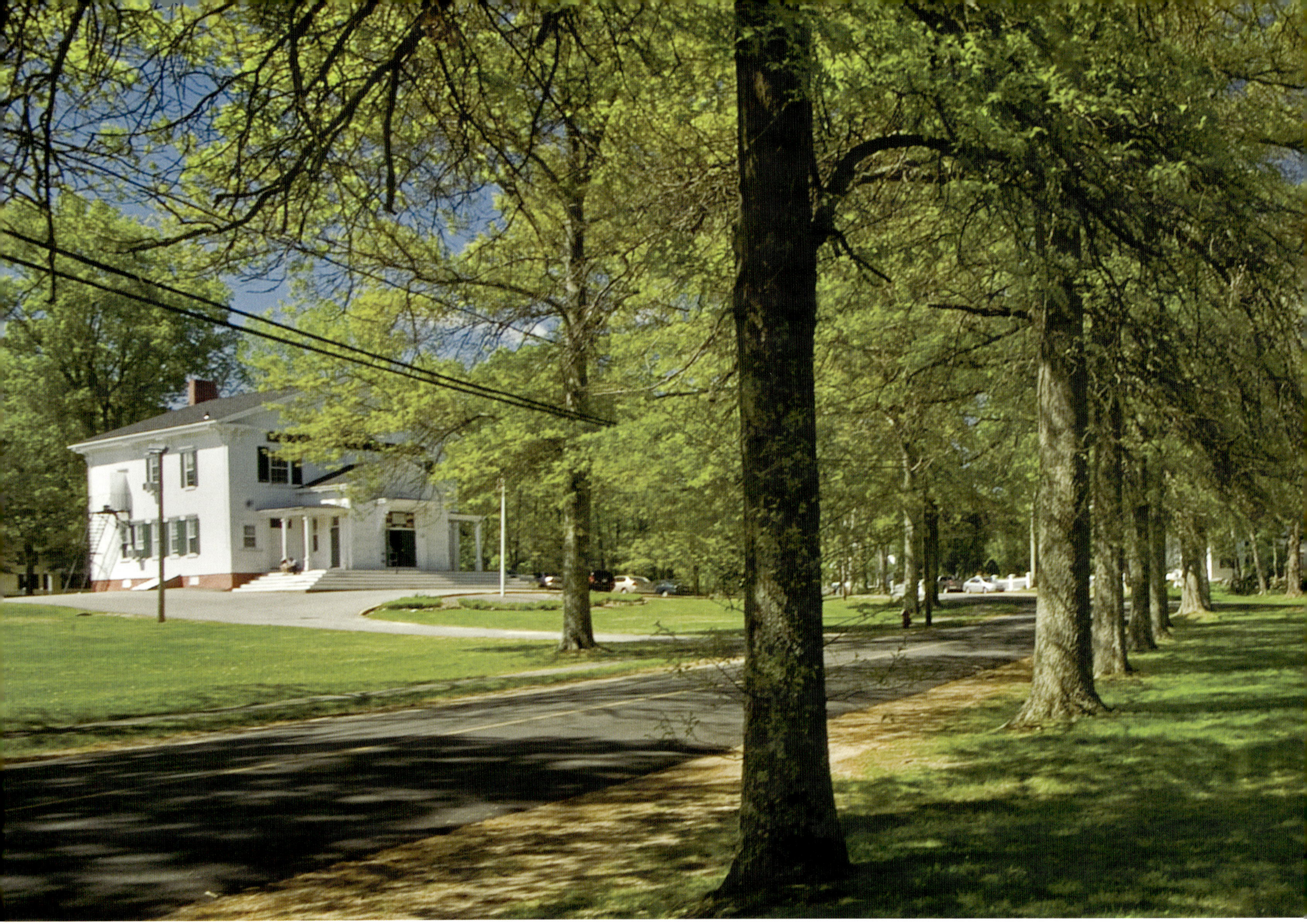

The Titicut Parish Green in North Middleborough.

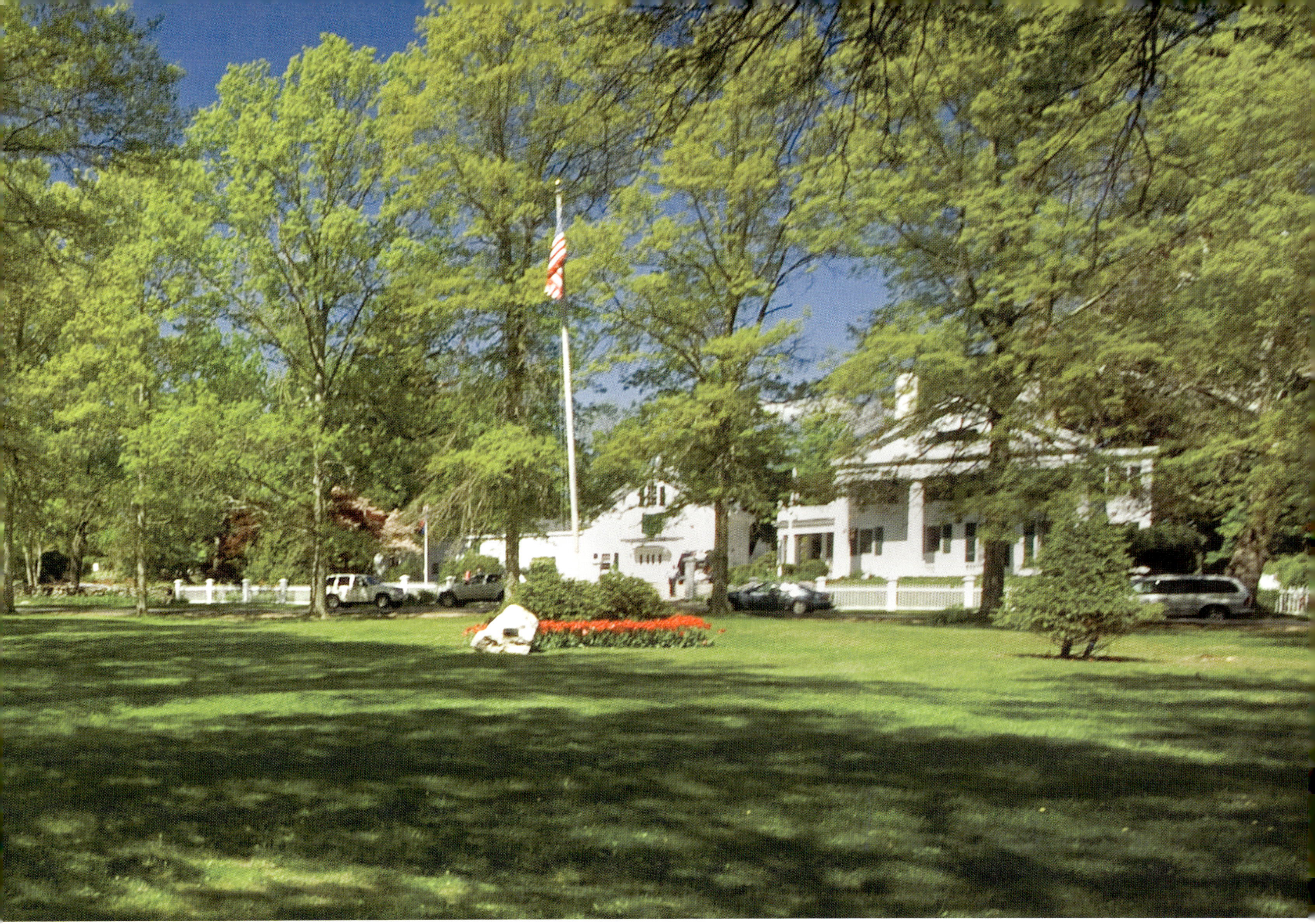

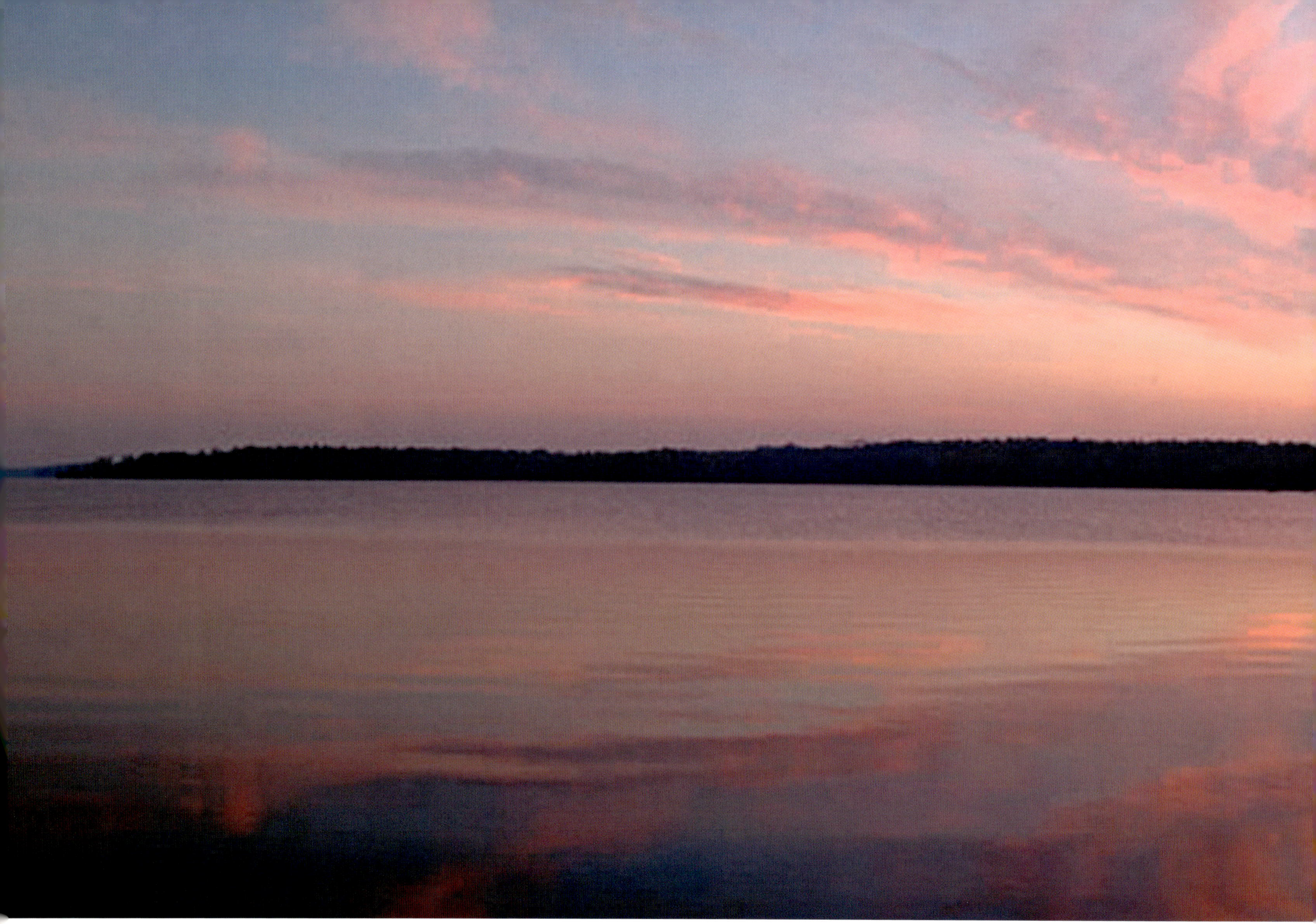

Lakeville has more ponds than any other town in Massachusetts; this is sunrise over Pocksha Pond.

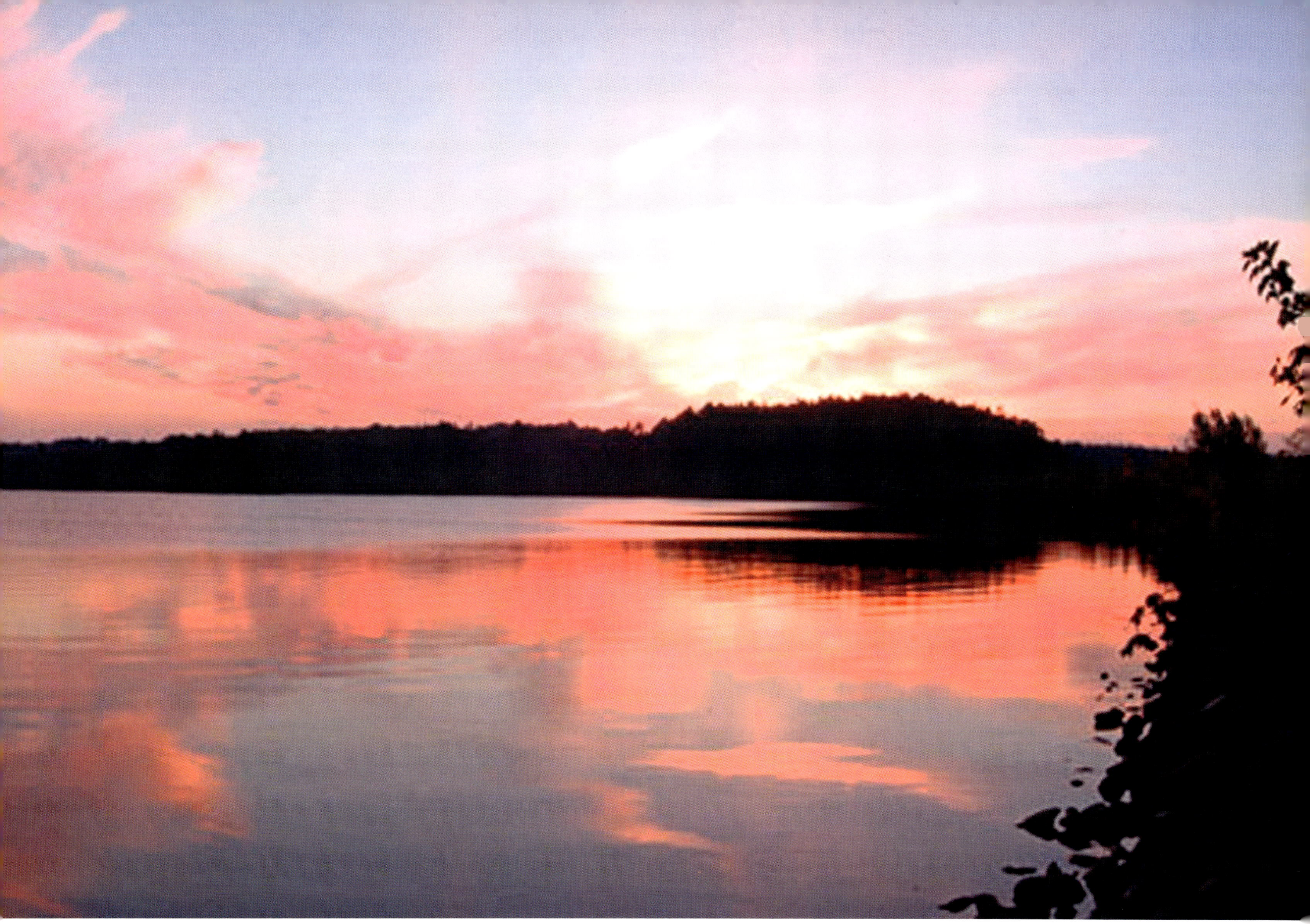

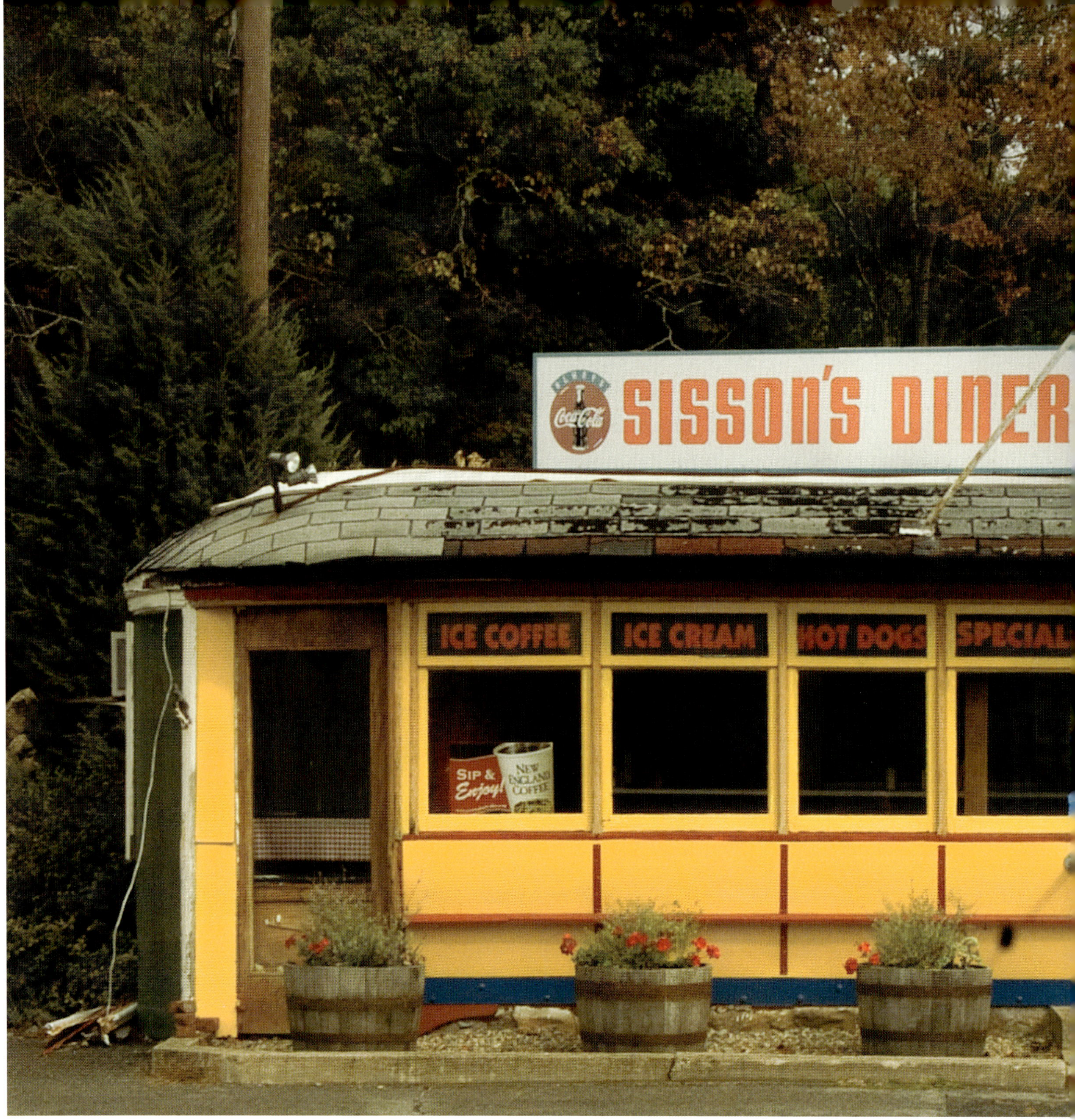

Sisson's Diner is in South Middleborough.

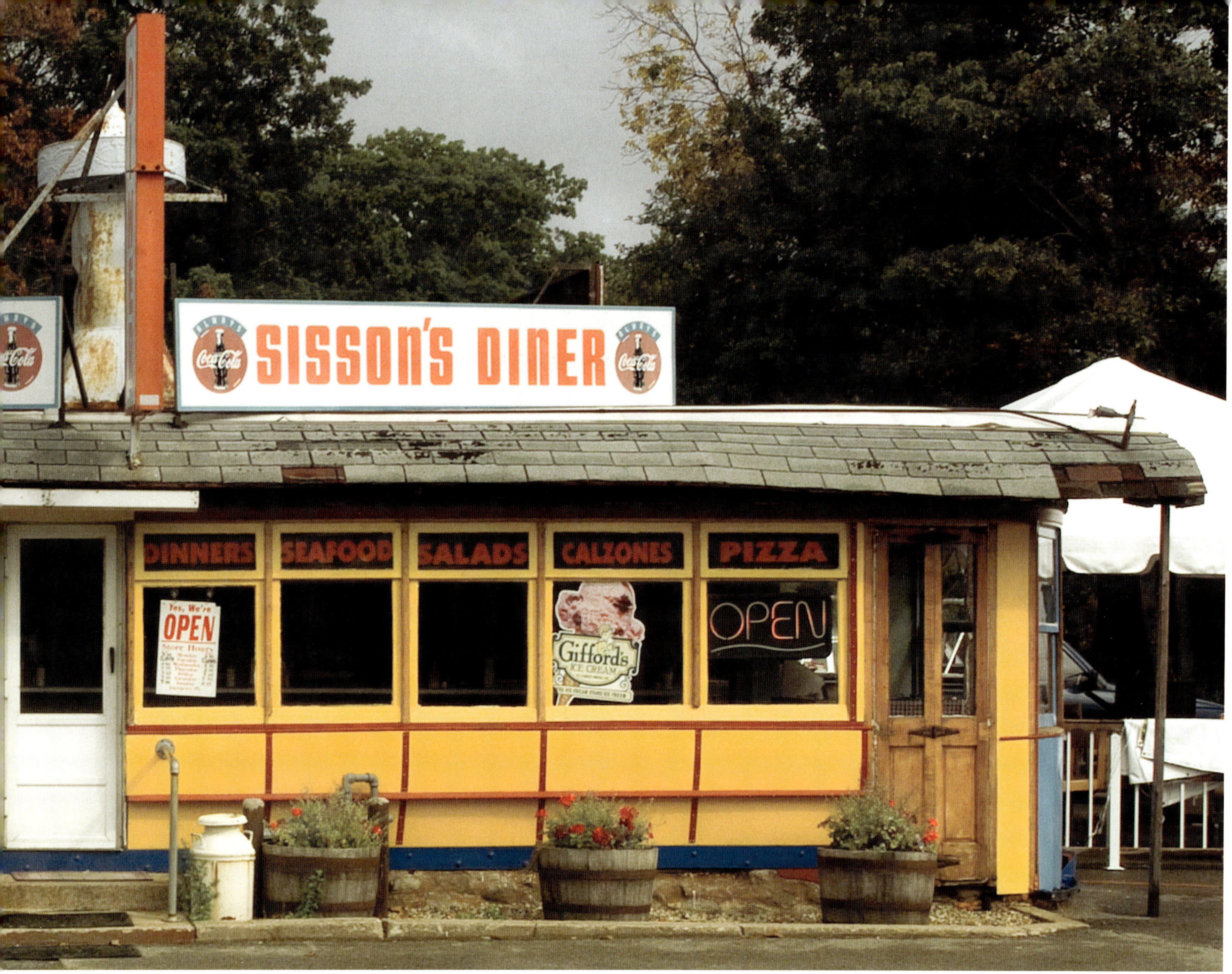
SISSON'S DINER
Coca-Cola
Coca-Cola
Coca-Cola
DINNERS
SEAFOOD
SALADS
CALZONES
PIZZA
Yes, We're
OPEN
Store Hours
Gifford's
ICE CREAM
OPEN

A quiet fall morning on a pond in Lakeville.

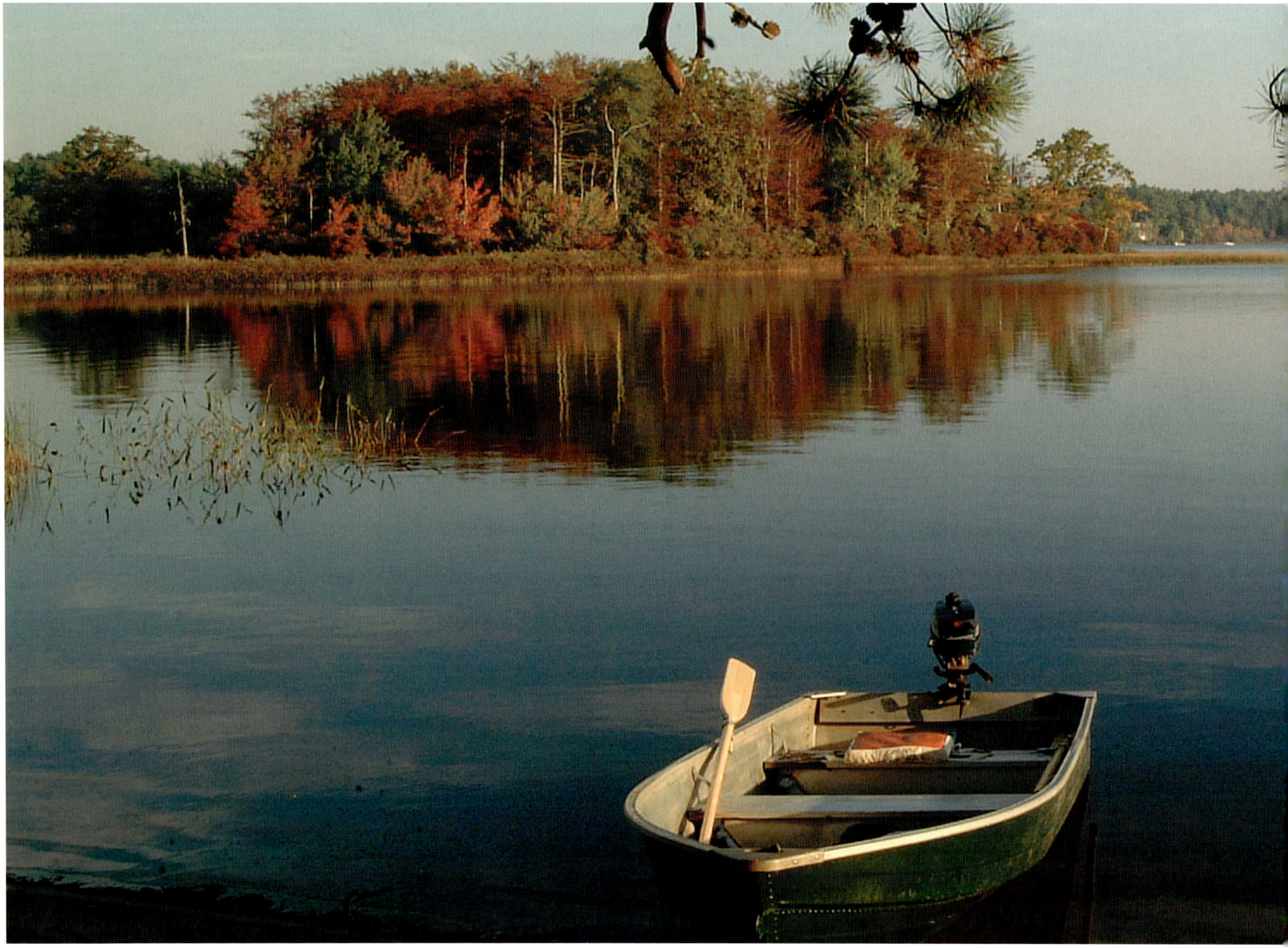

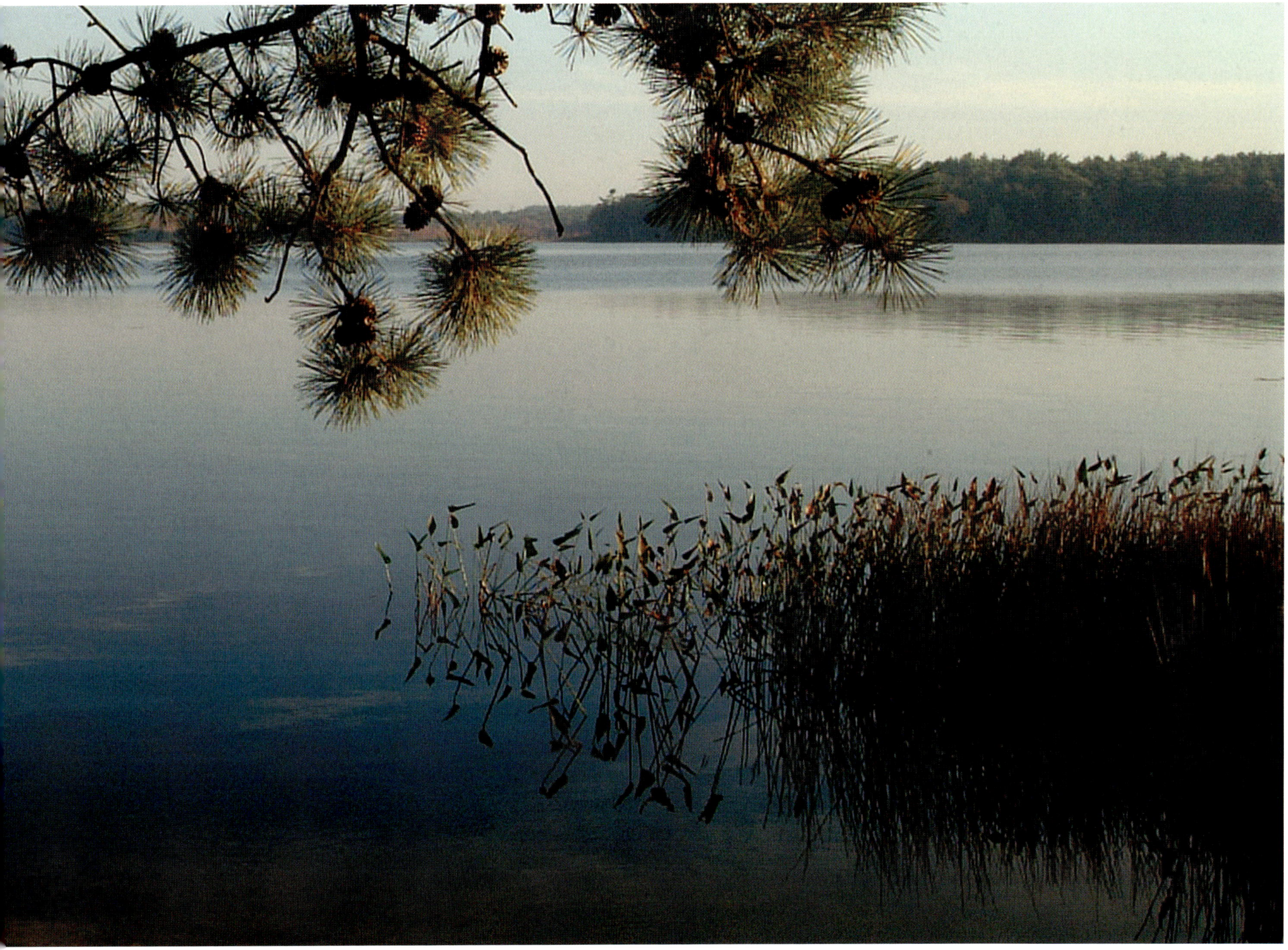

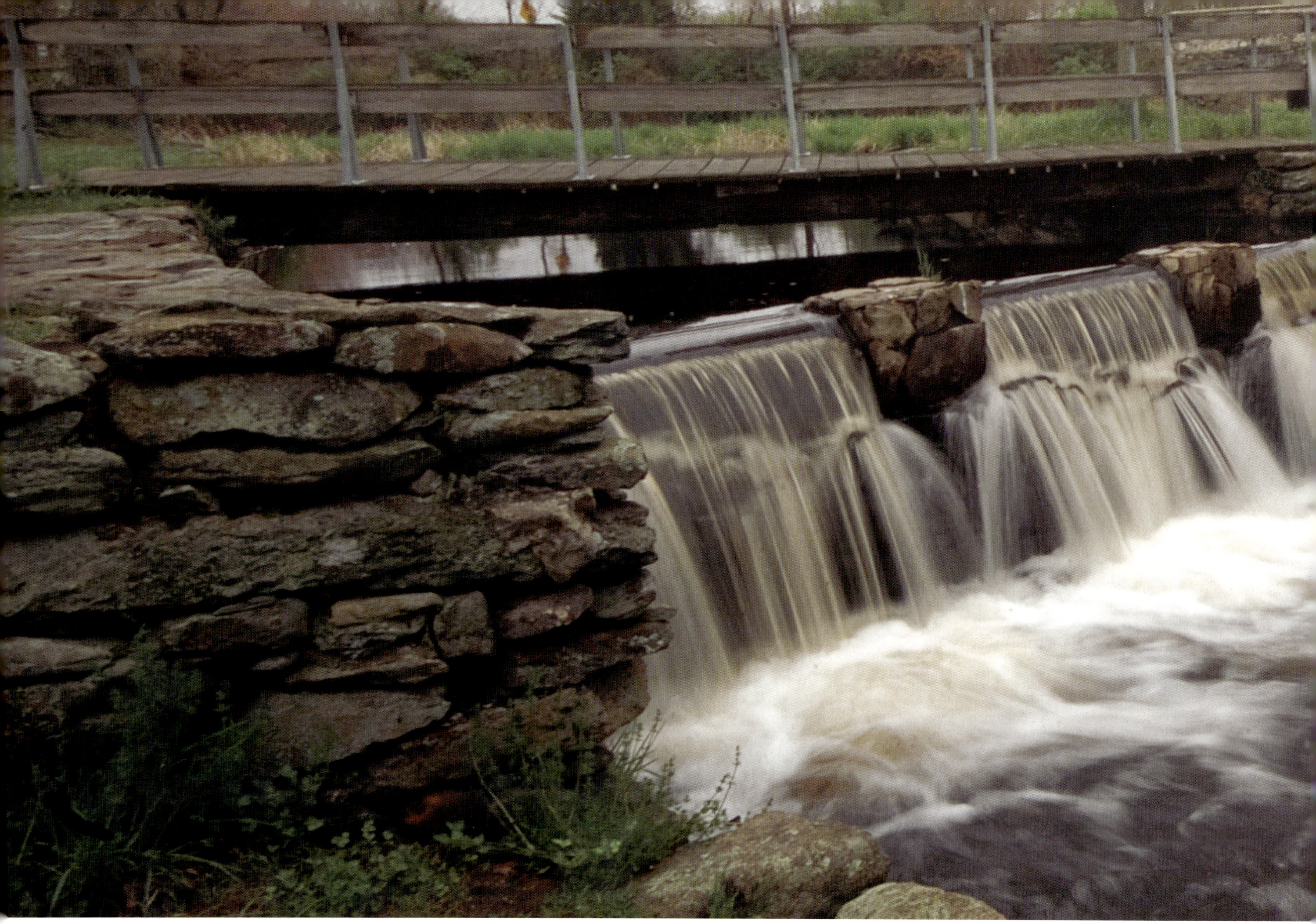

Oliver Mill Park on the Nemasket River in Middleborough, dates from the late 1700's.

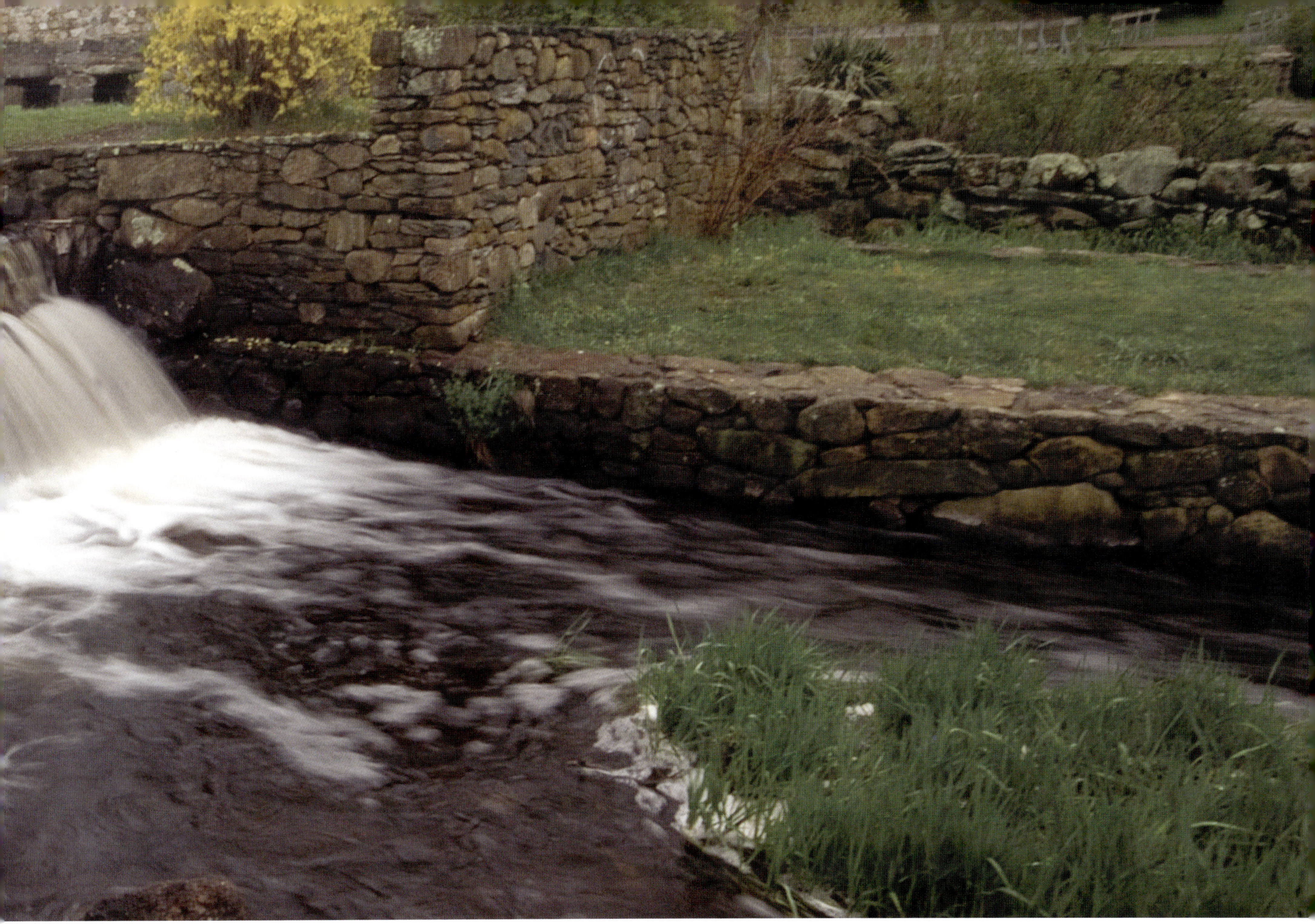

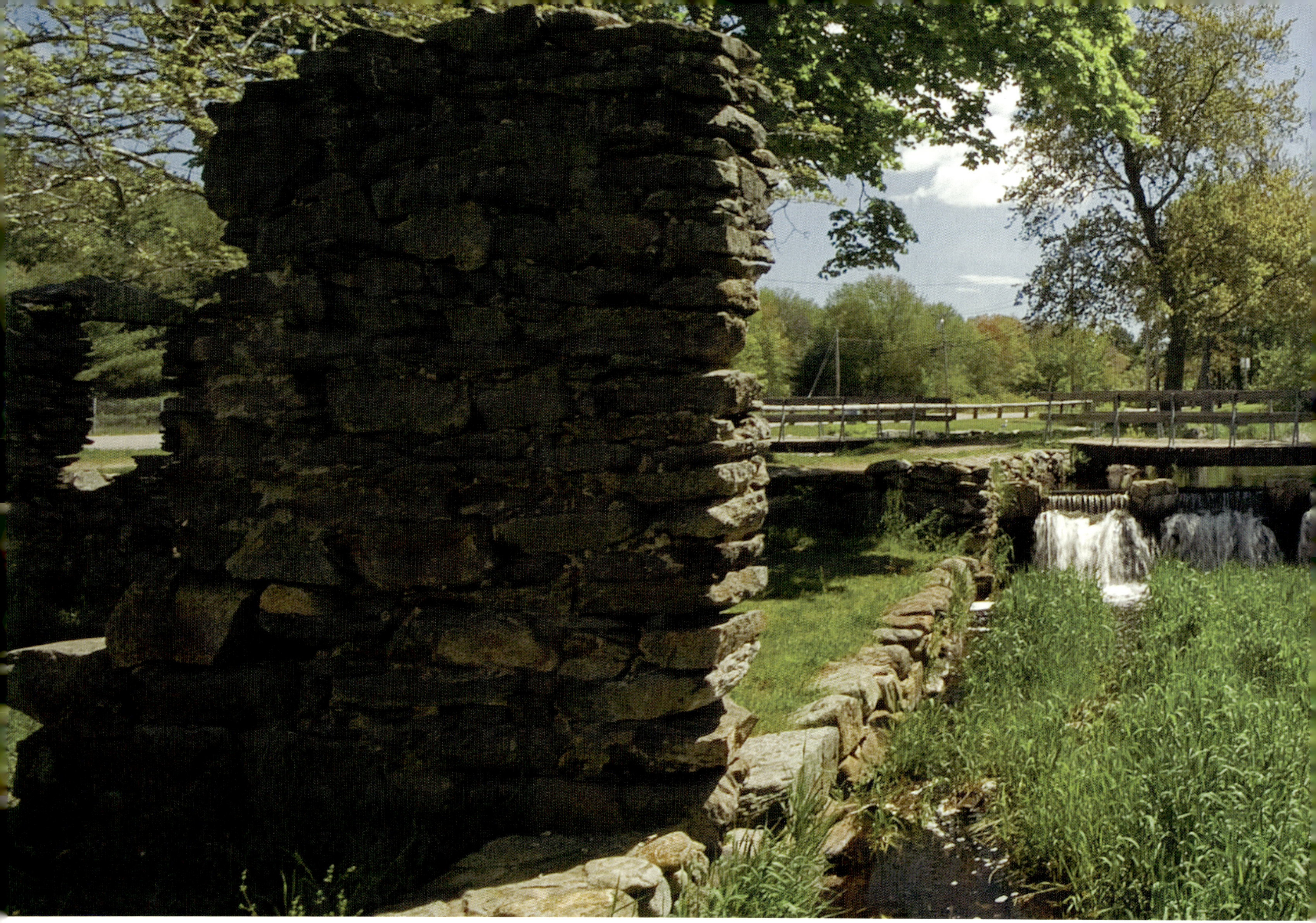

Scenes of the original water channels and walls at Oliver Mill Park.

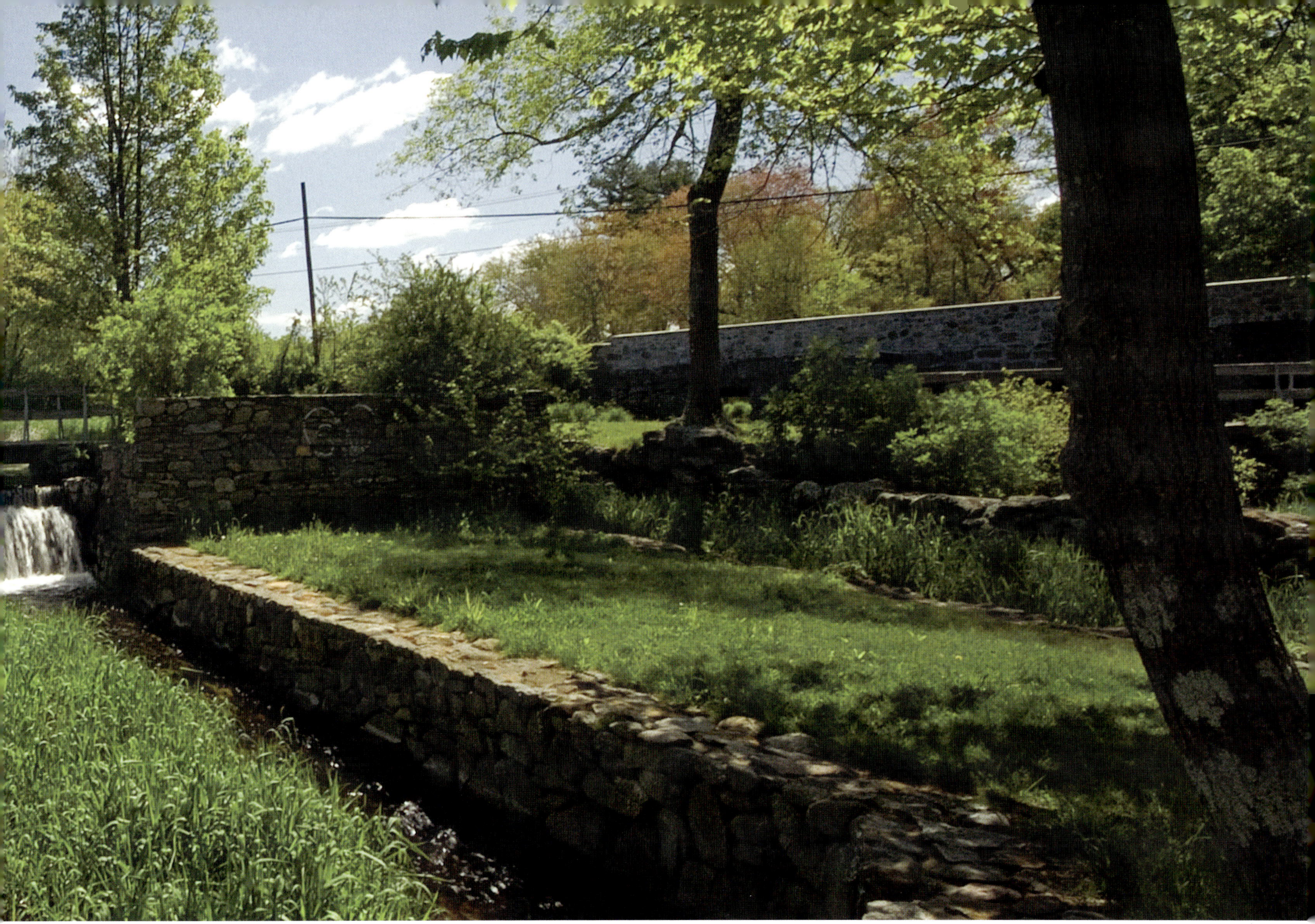

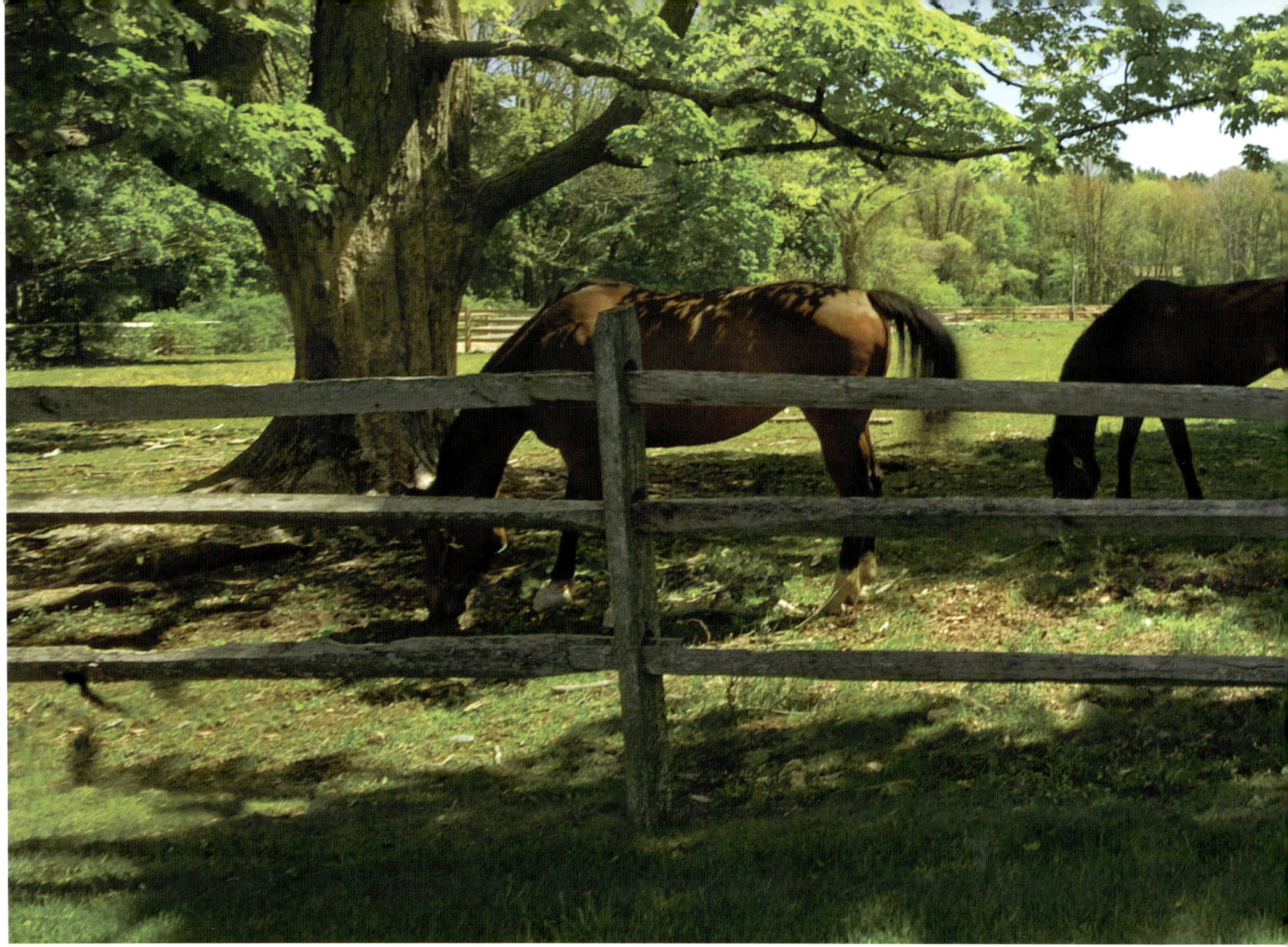

Plympton is a rural community on the South Shore. Here horses graze near the center of town.

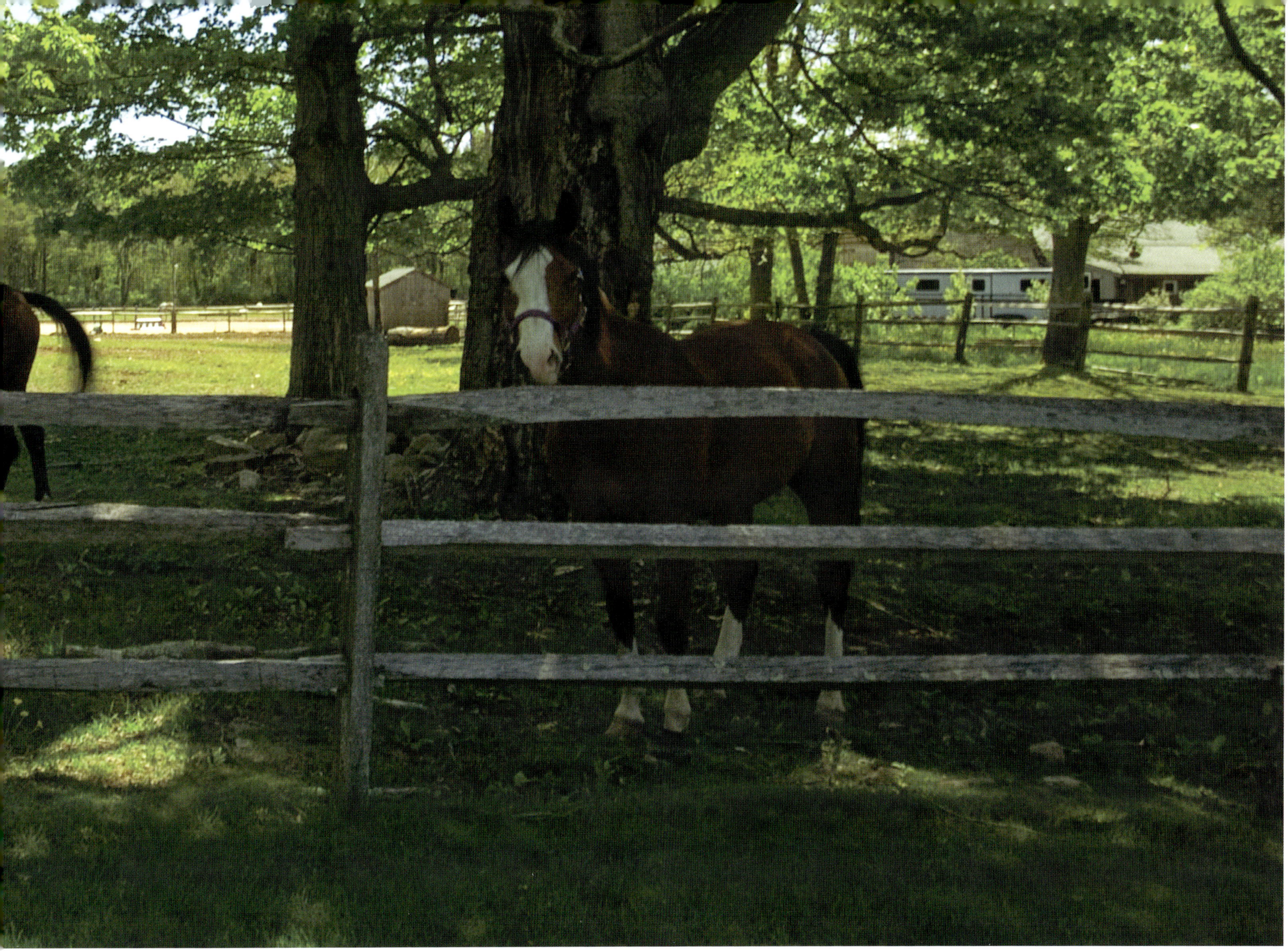

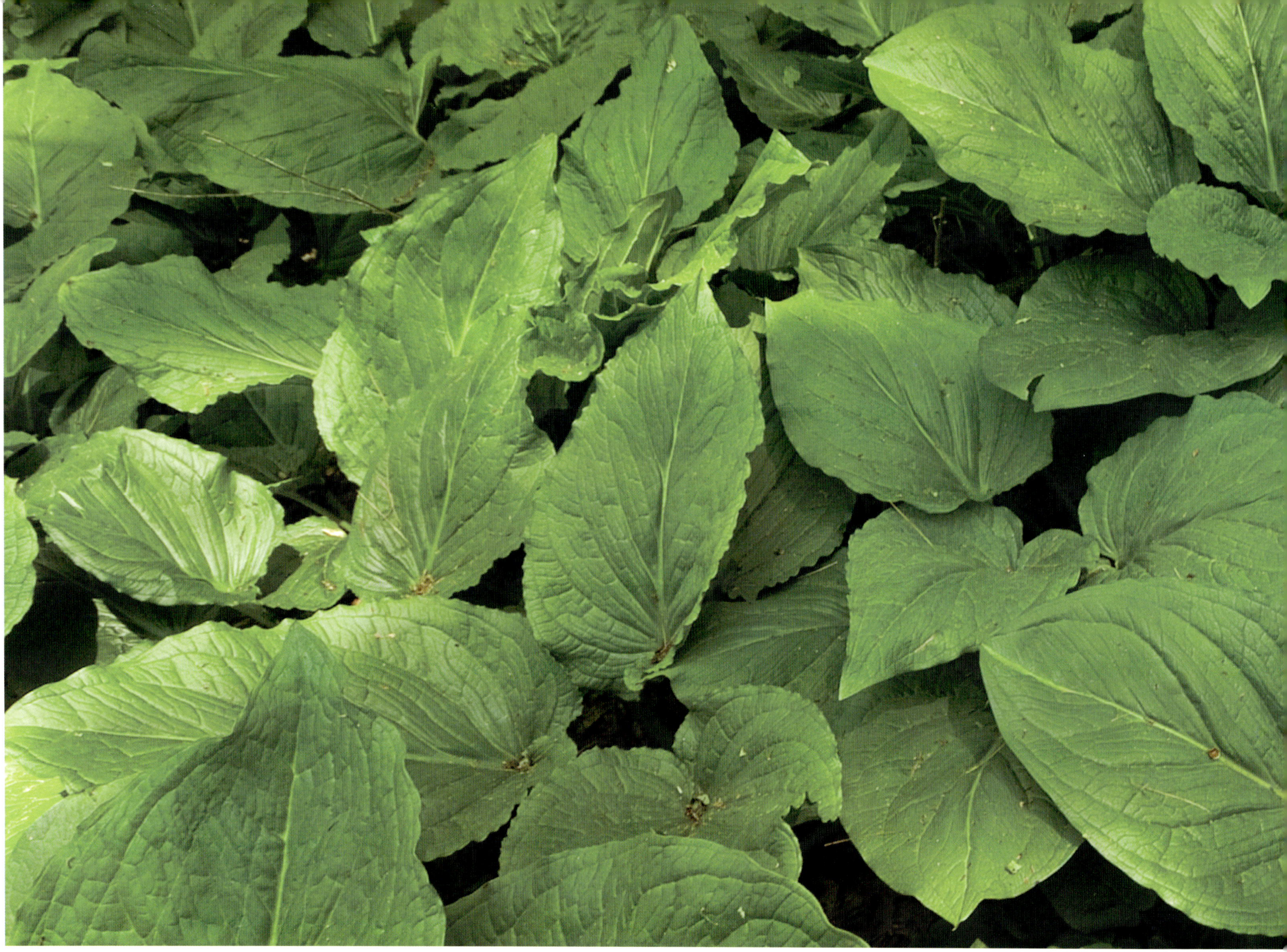

Skunk cabbage forms dense green foliage in the springtime.

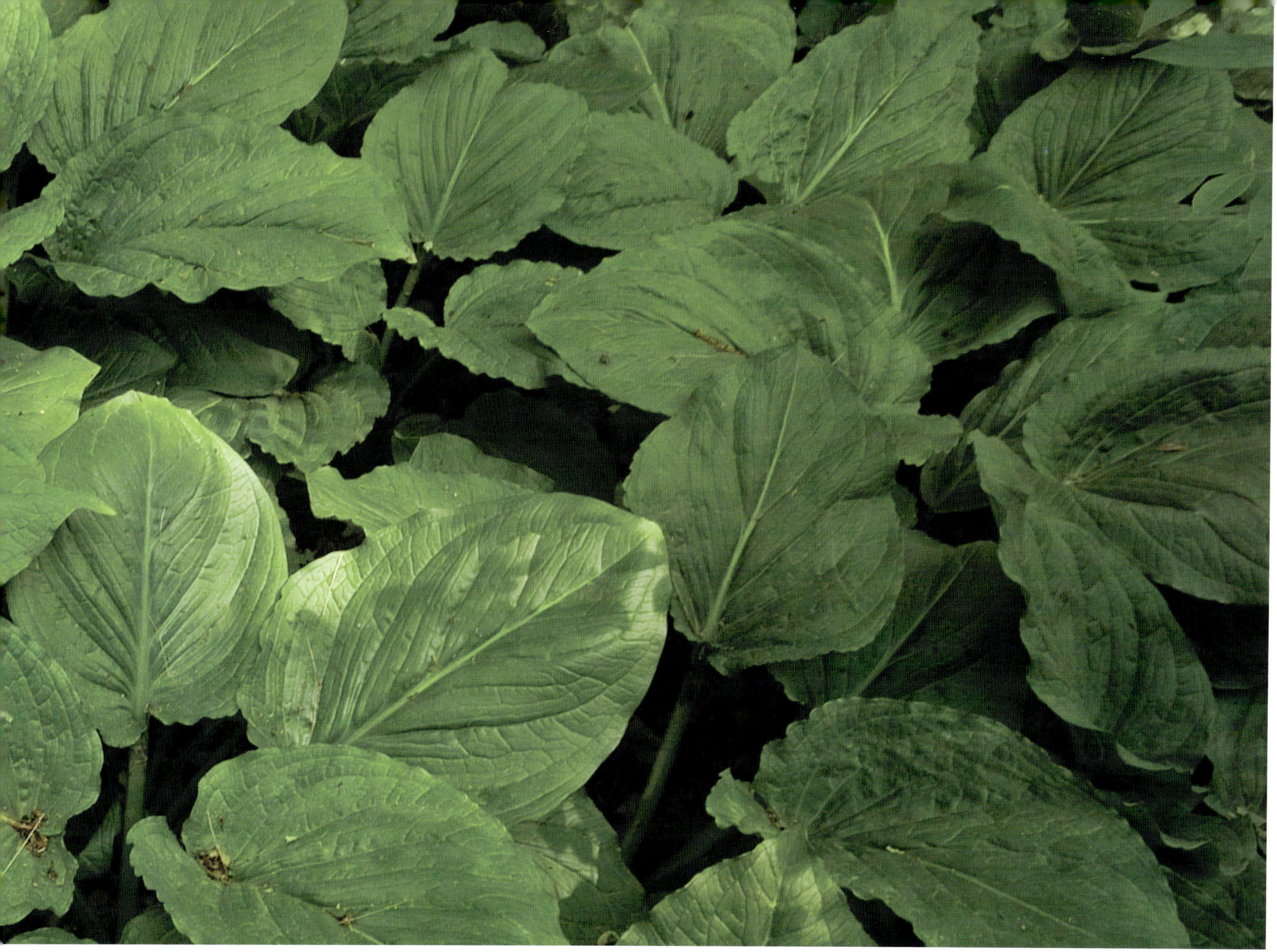

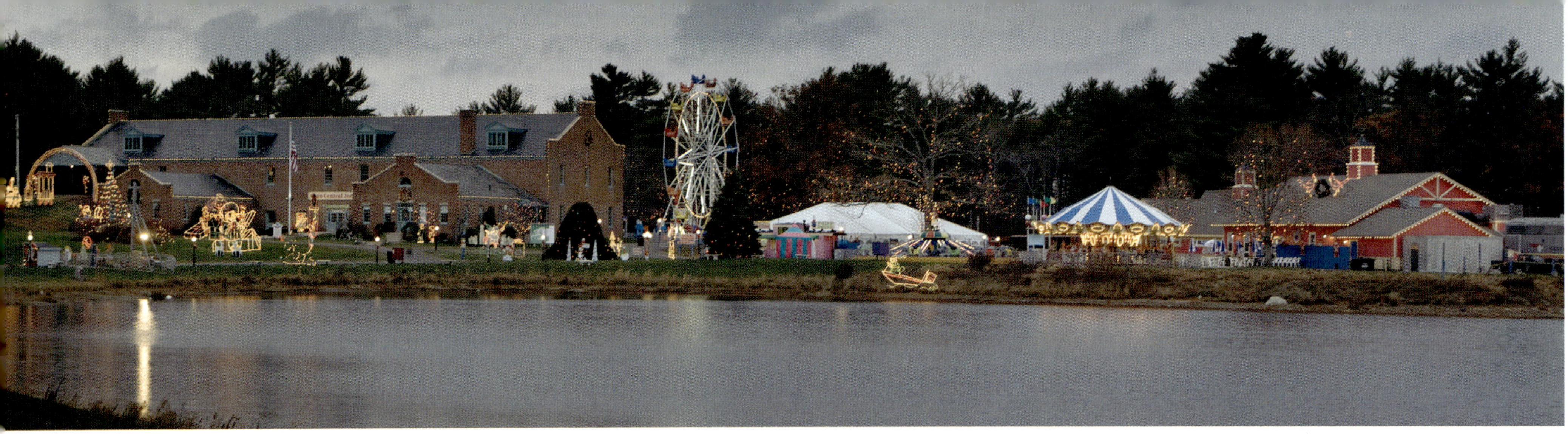

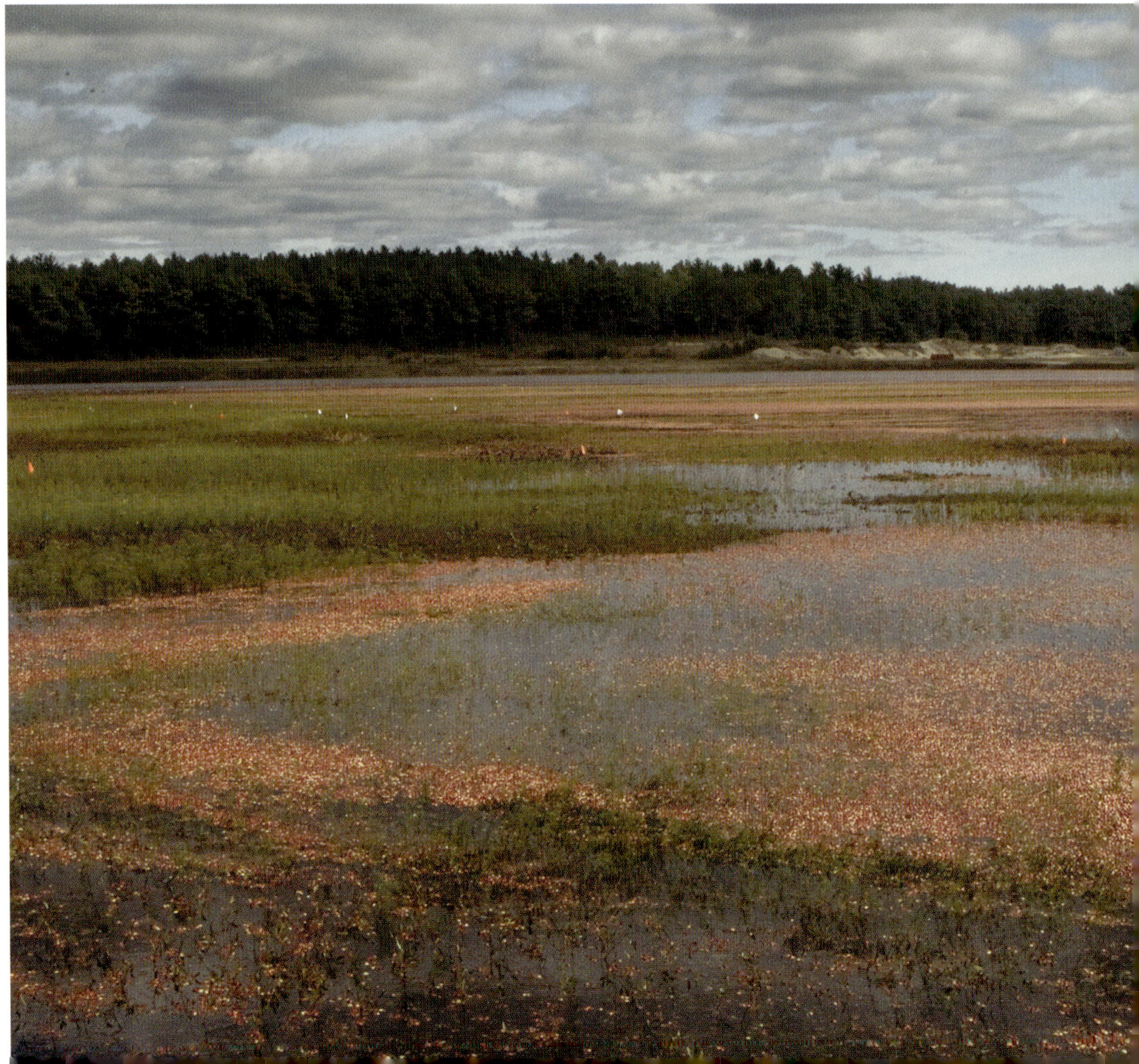

Cranberries floating in a bog waiting to be harvested. Introduced to the Pilgrims by the Native Americans, the round red berries were named by the new inhabitants because the flowers in the springtime resembled the head of a crane found in the Old World.

Opposite:
Edaville Railroad in Carver, decorated for the winter season, offers train rides through the local cranberry bogs.

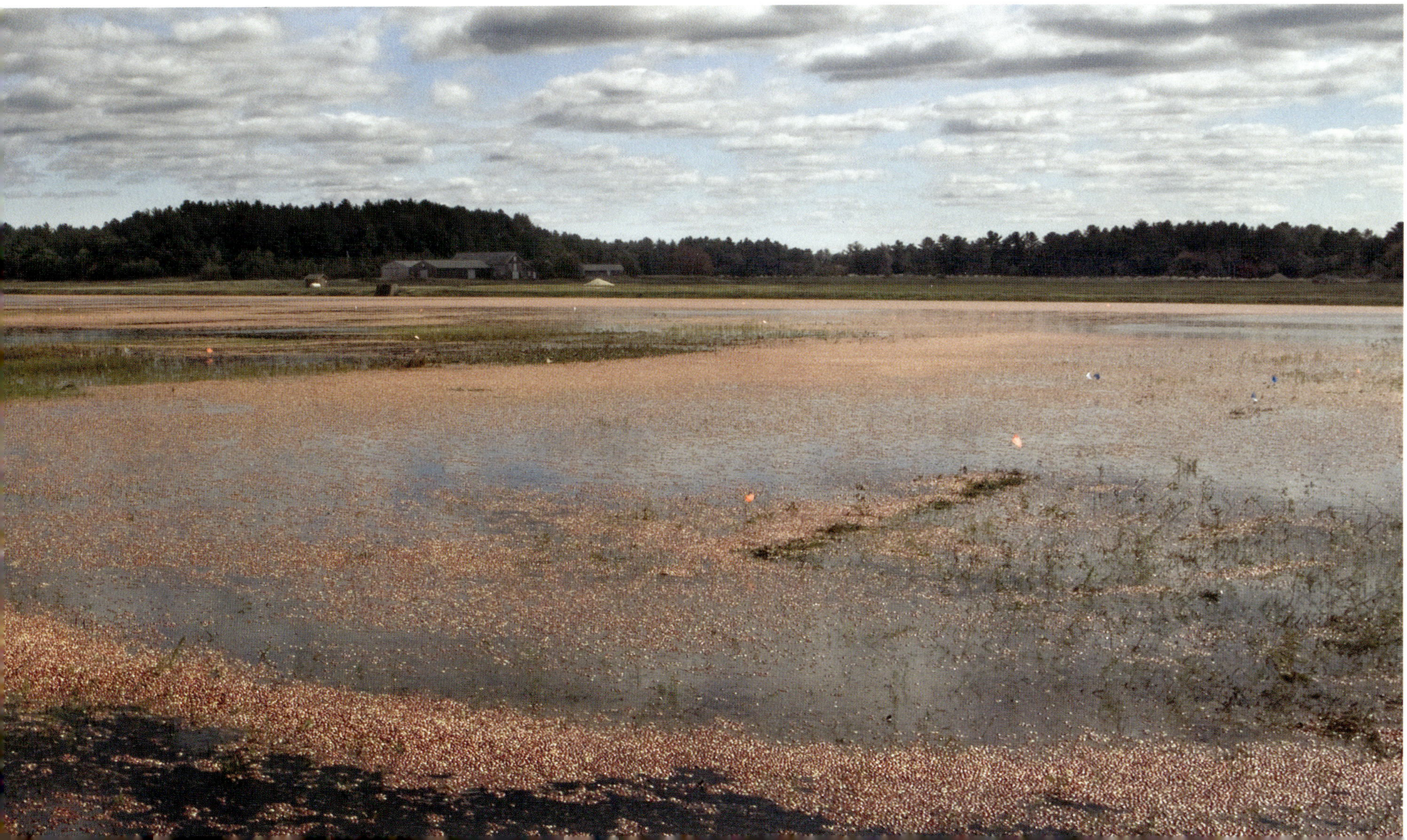

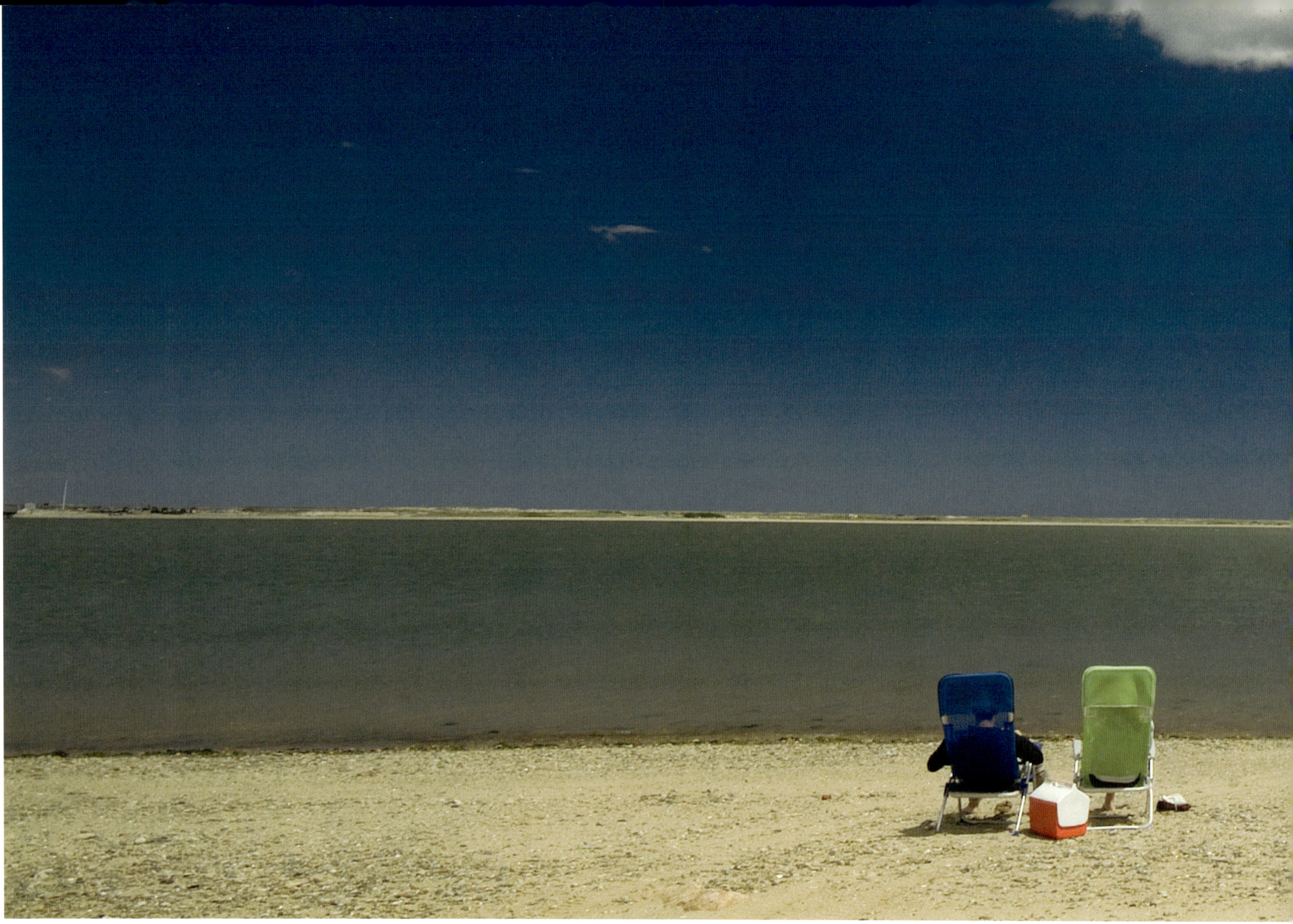

Enjoying the beach at Powder Point in Duxbury.

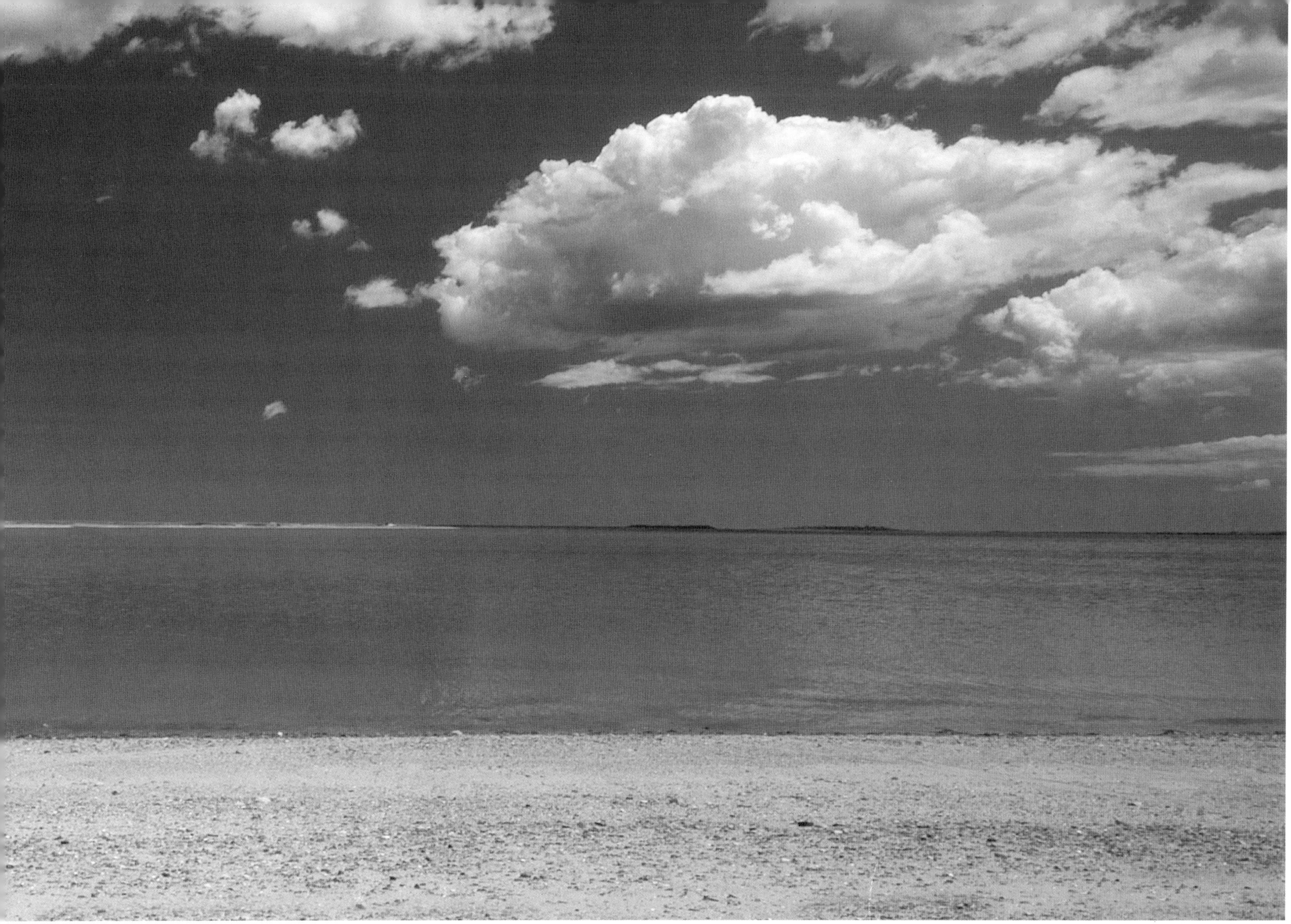

Powder Point Bridge looking towards Duxbury Beach.

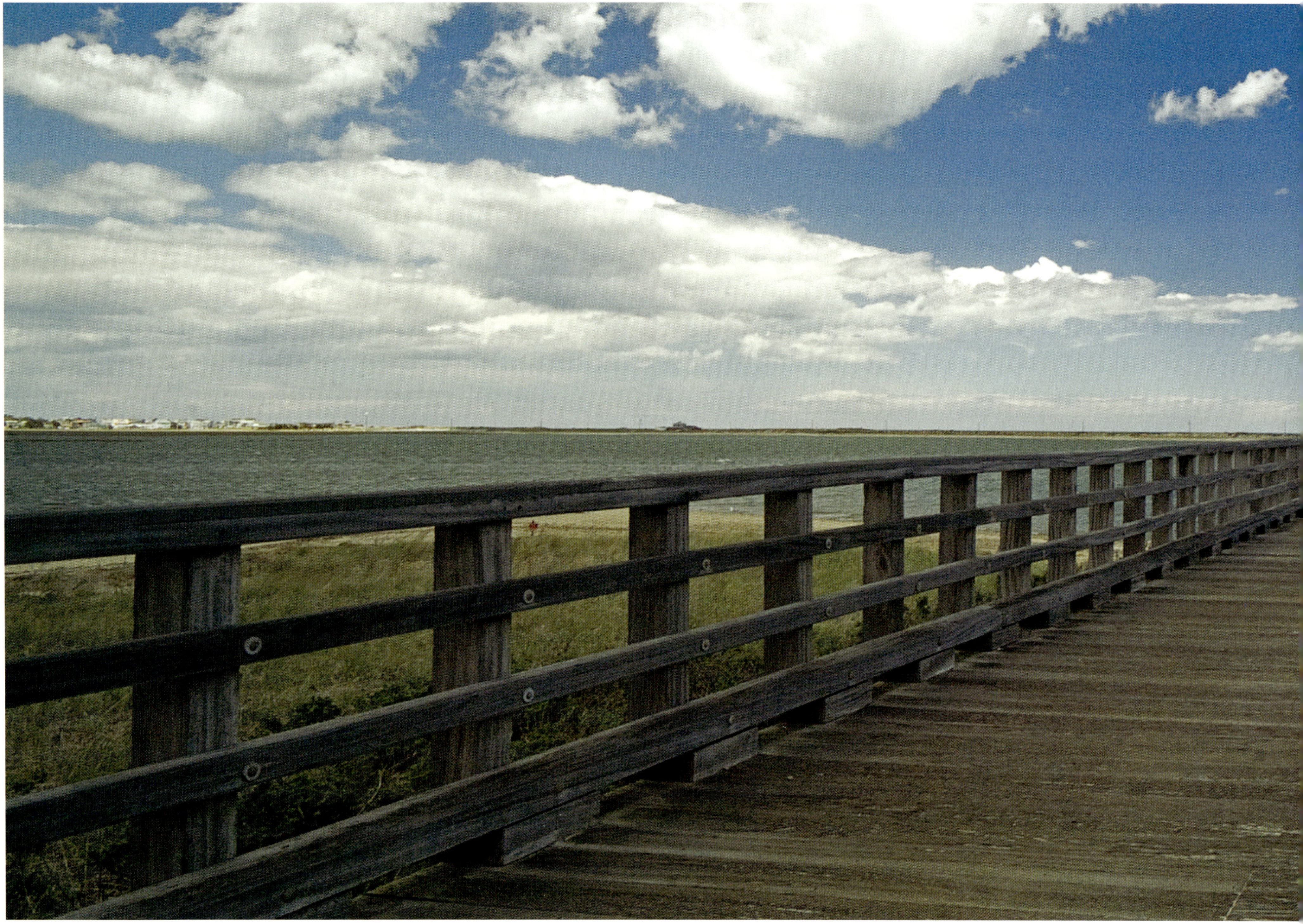

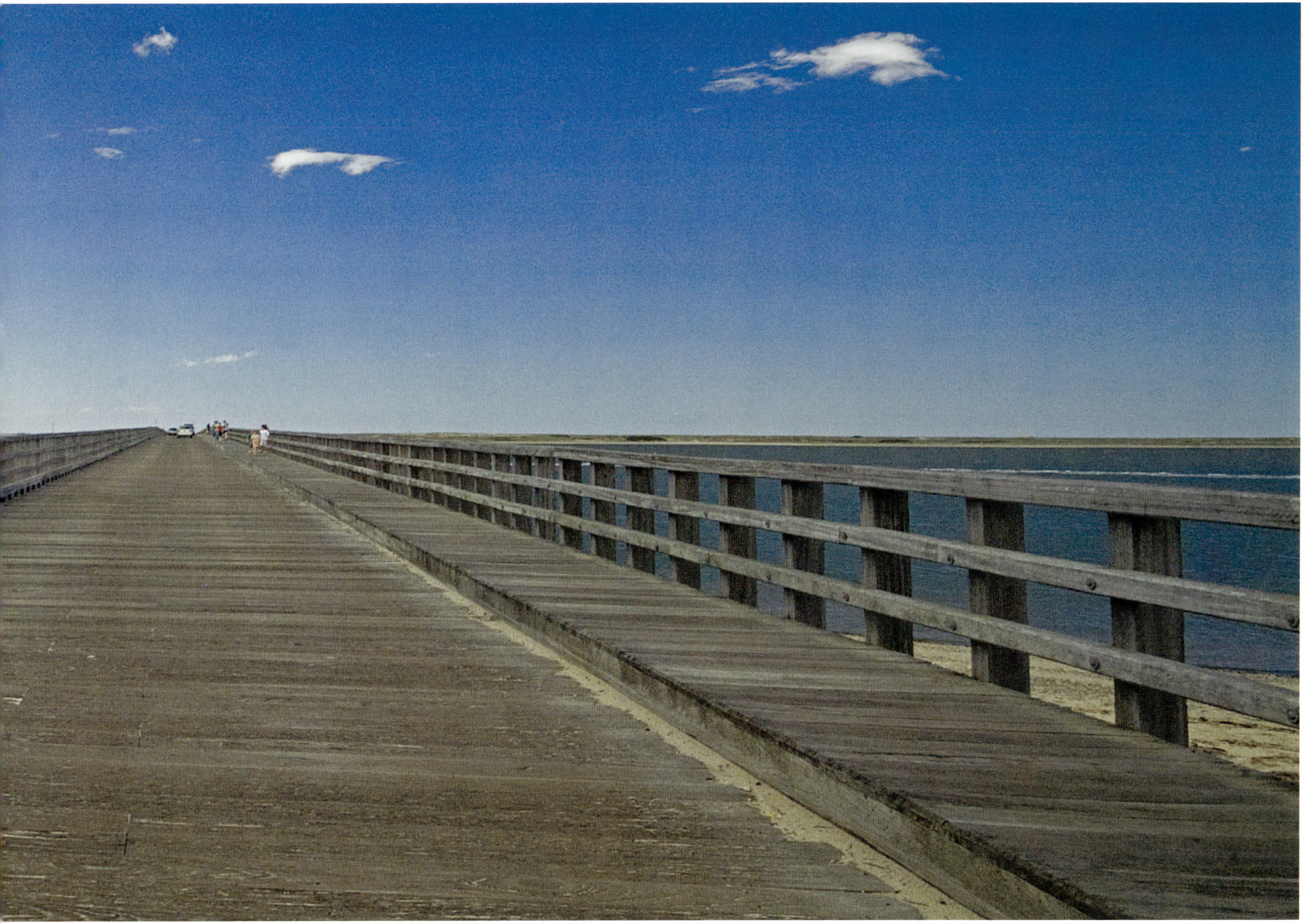

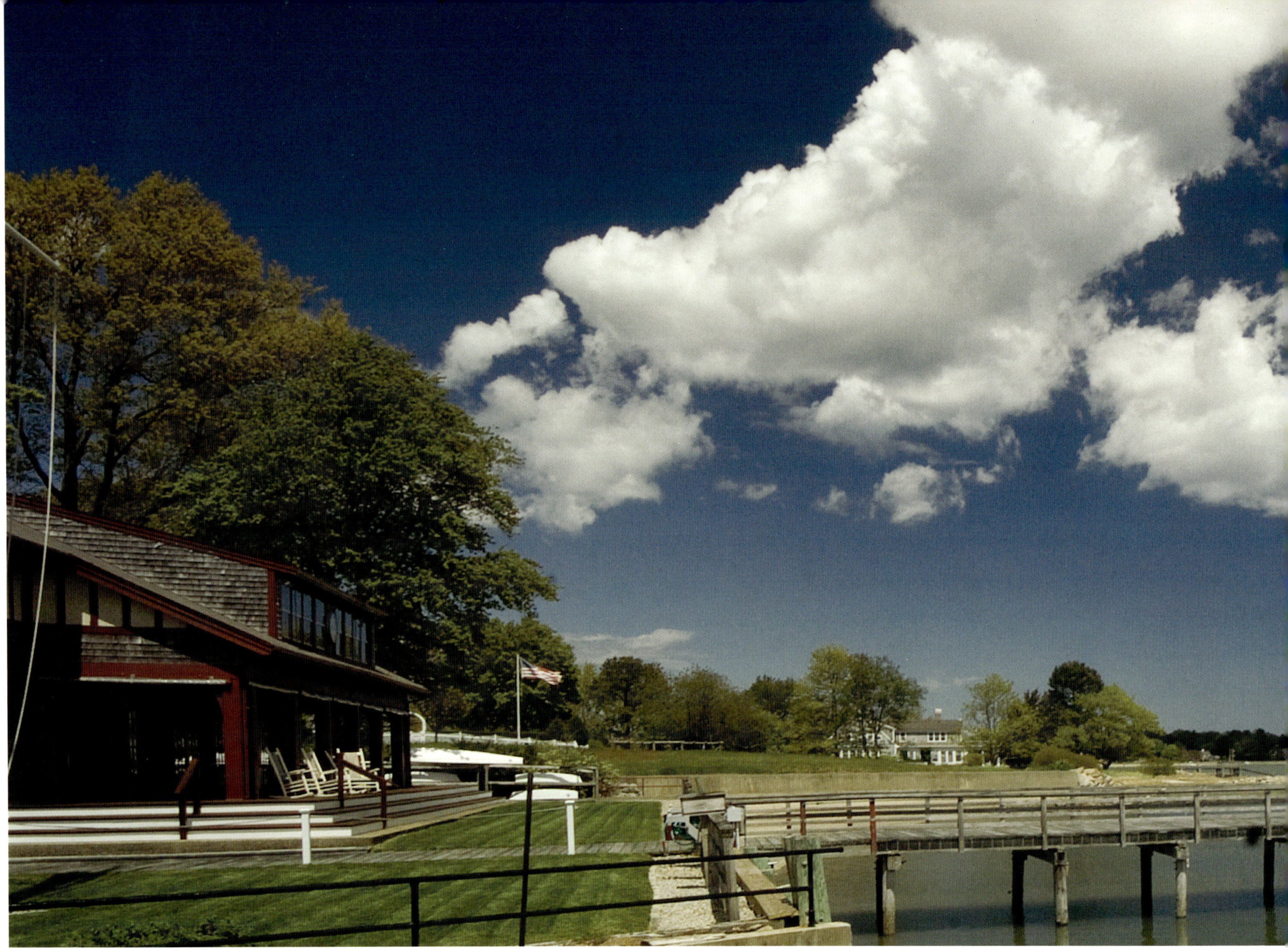

The Duxbury Yacht Club.

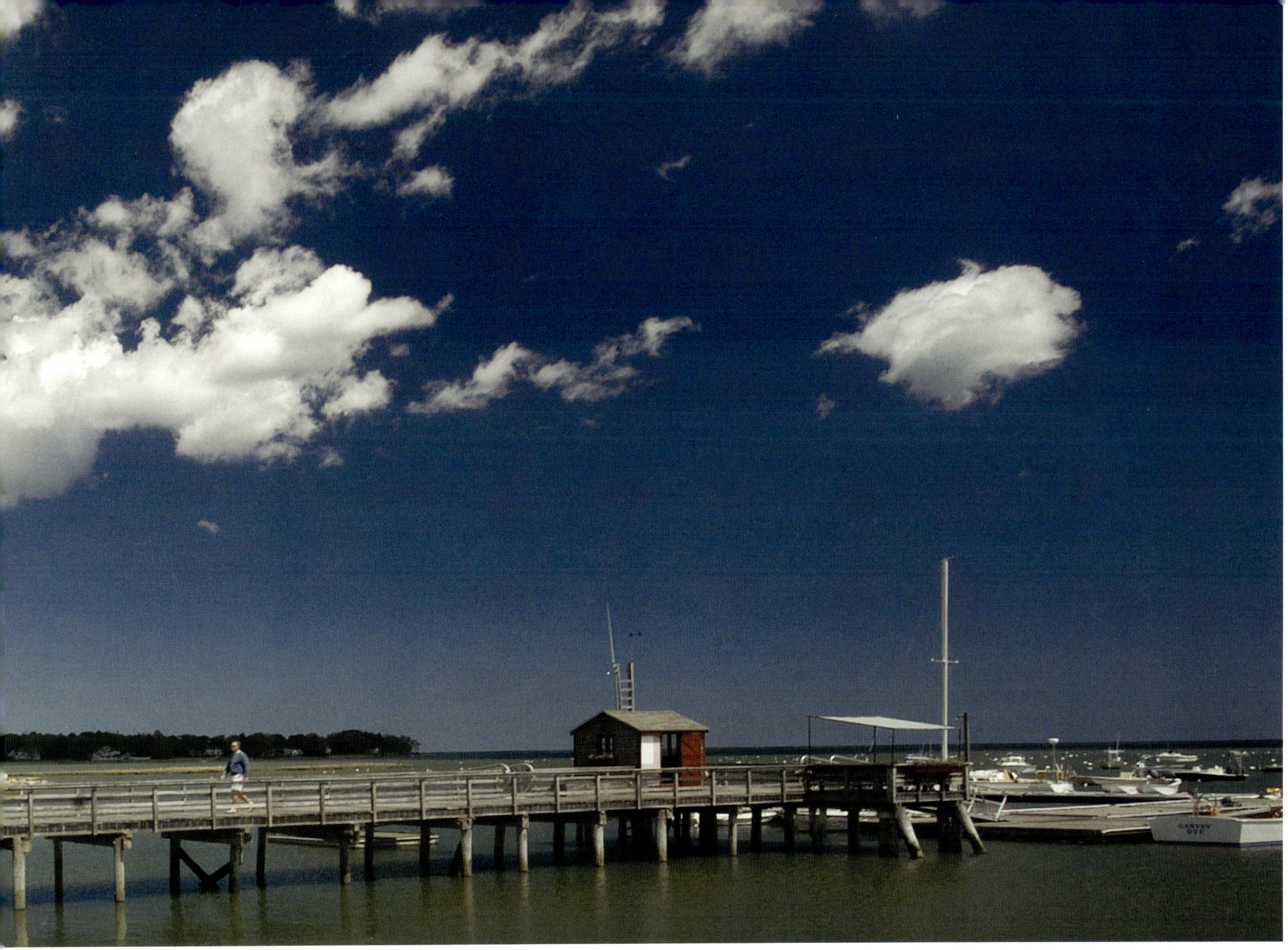

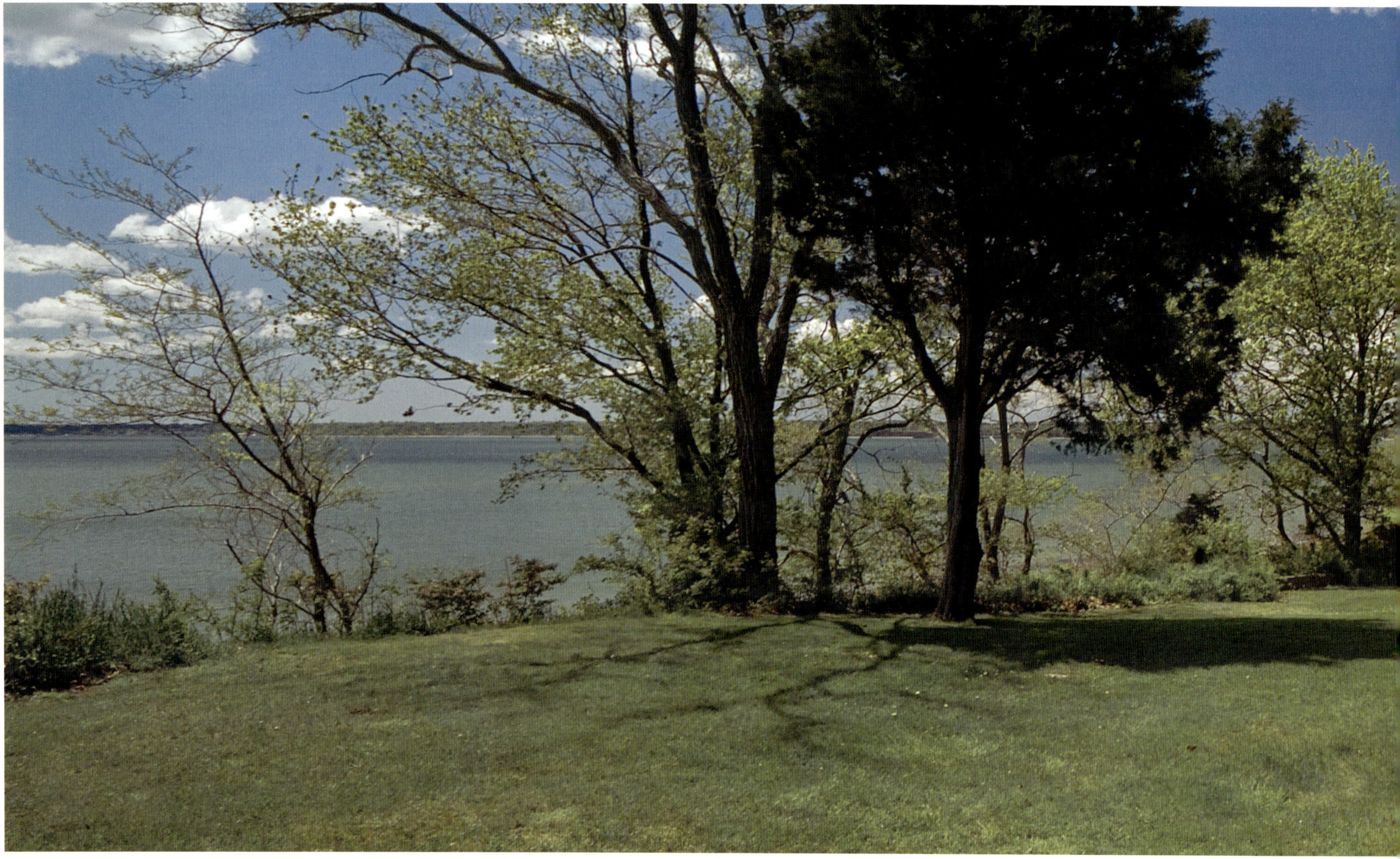

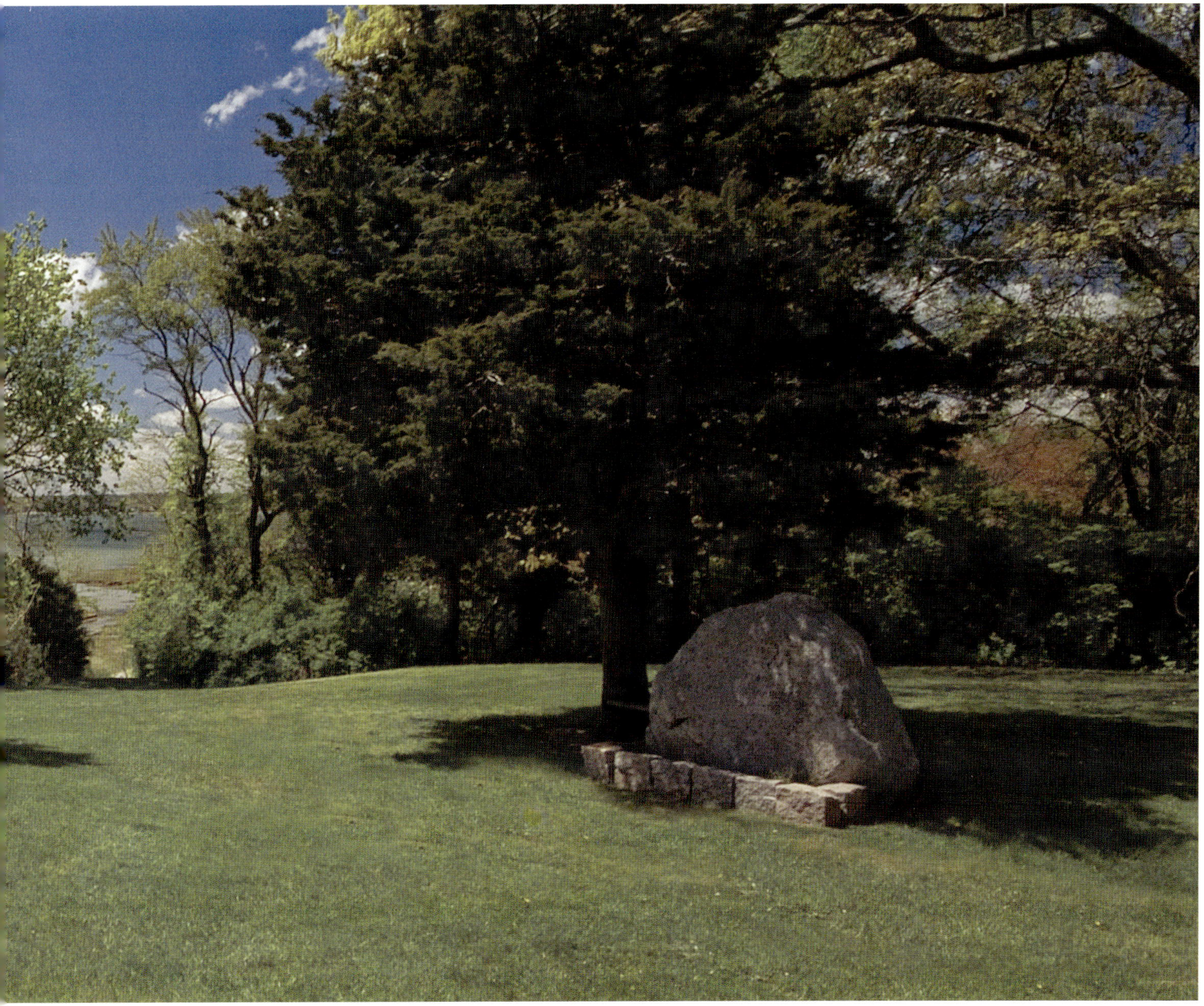

On the Standish Shore section of Duxbury, Myles Standish built his original homestead overlooking Plymouth Bay.

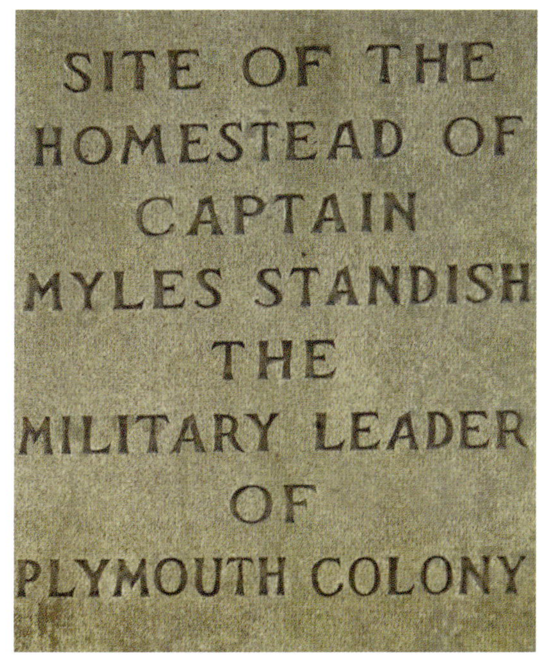

Two children wait for the tide to come in at Shipyard Landing Beach in Duxbury.

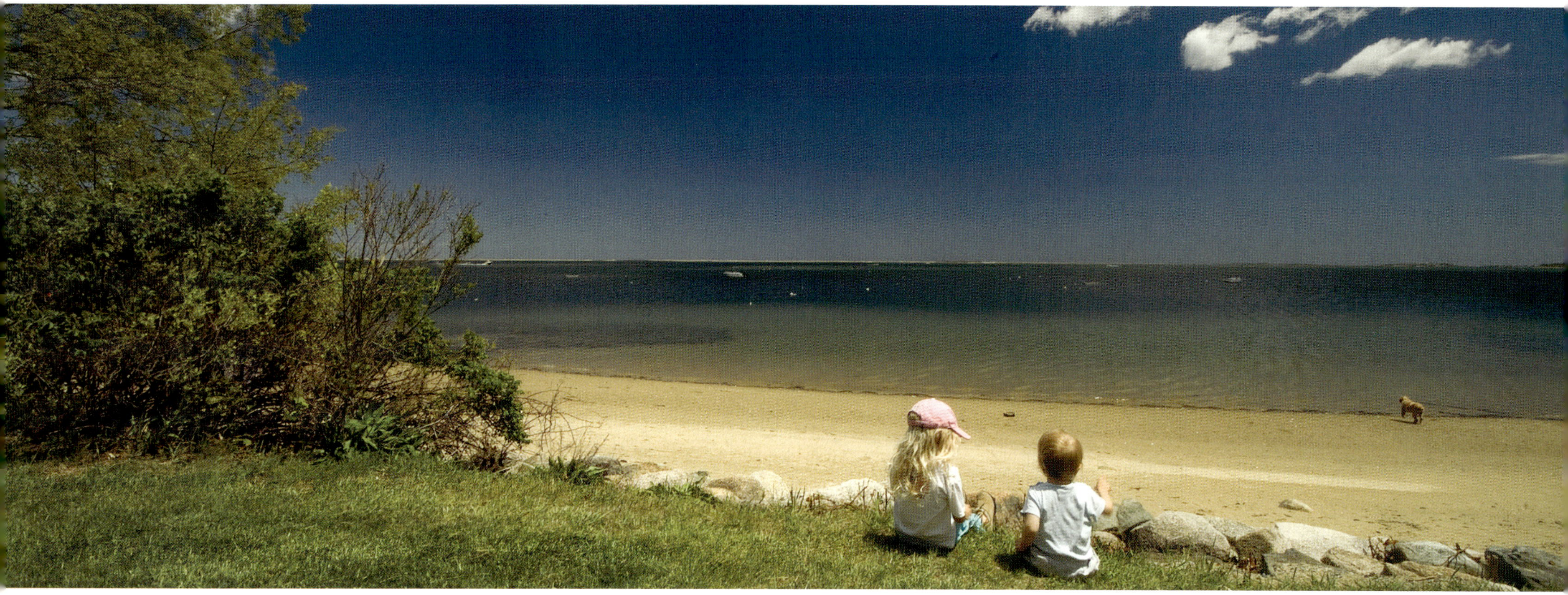

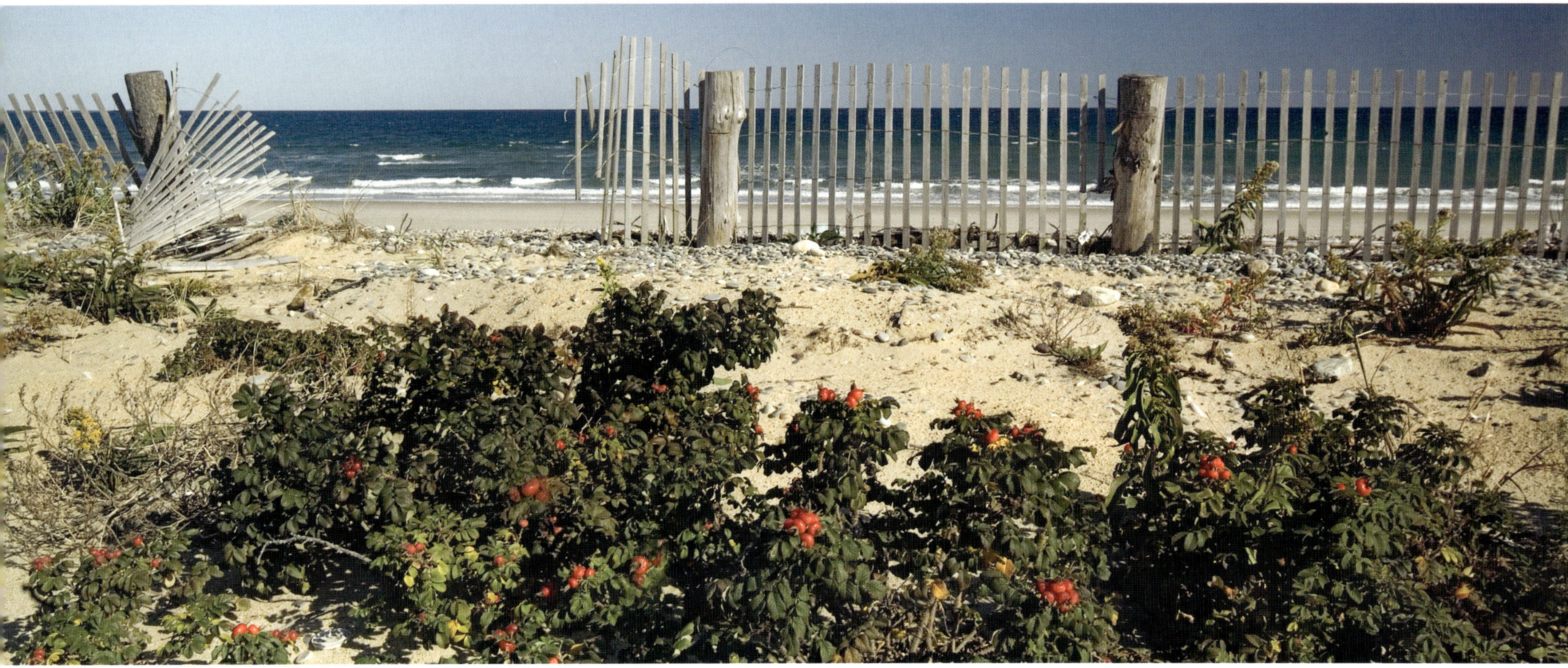

Beach roses with rose hips in the fall, just behind Duxbury Beach.

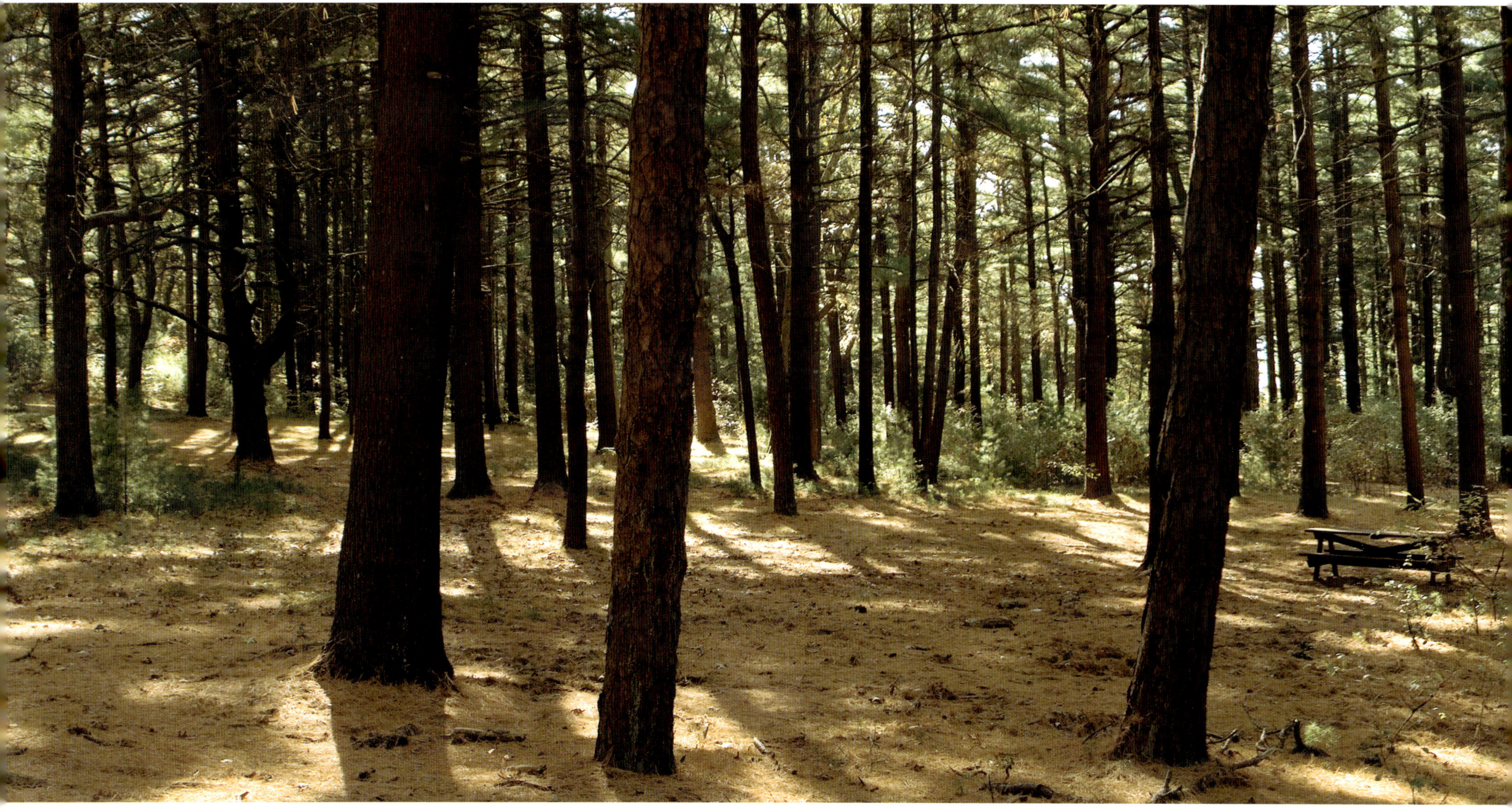

The Myles Standish Monument State Reservation includes a 116 foot tower with panoramic views of the South Shore. A pine forest, with hiking trails, surrounds the tower.

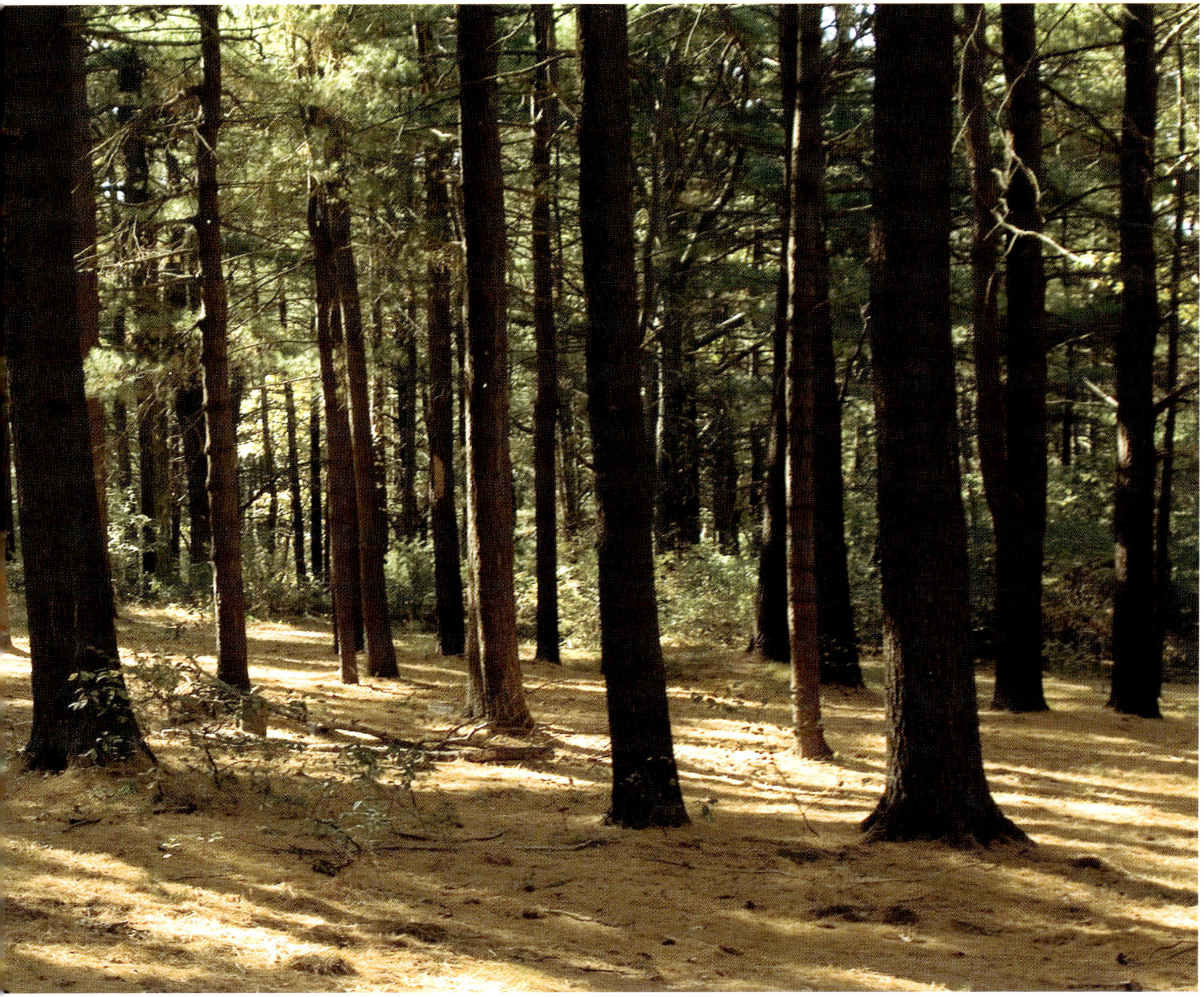

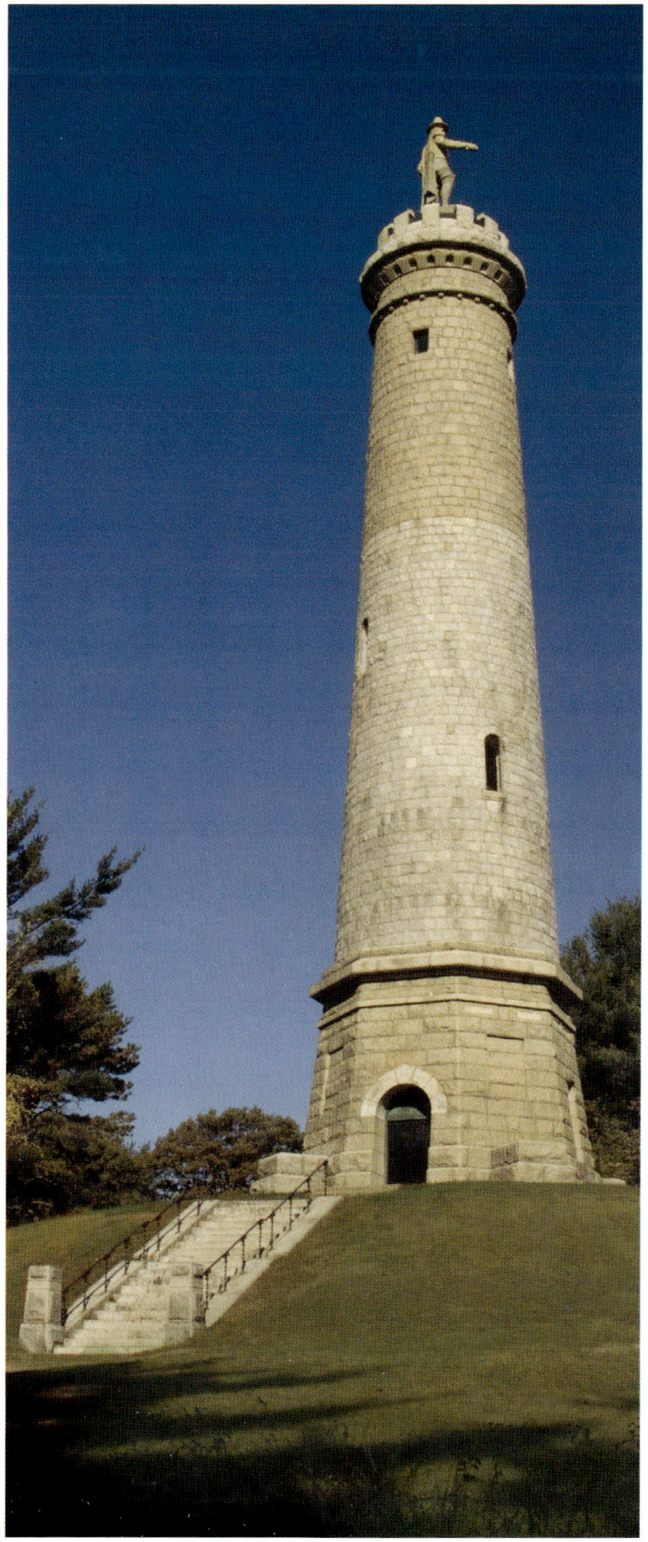

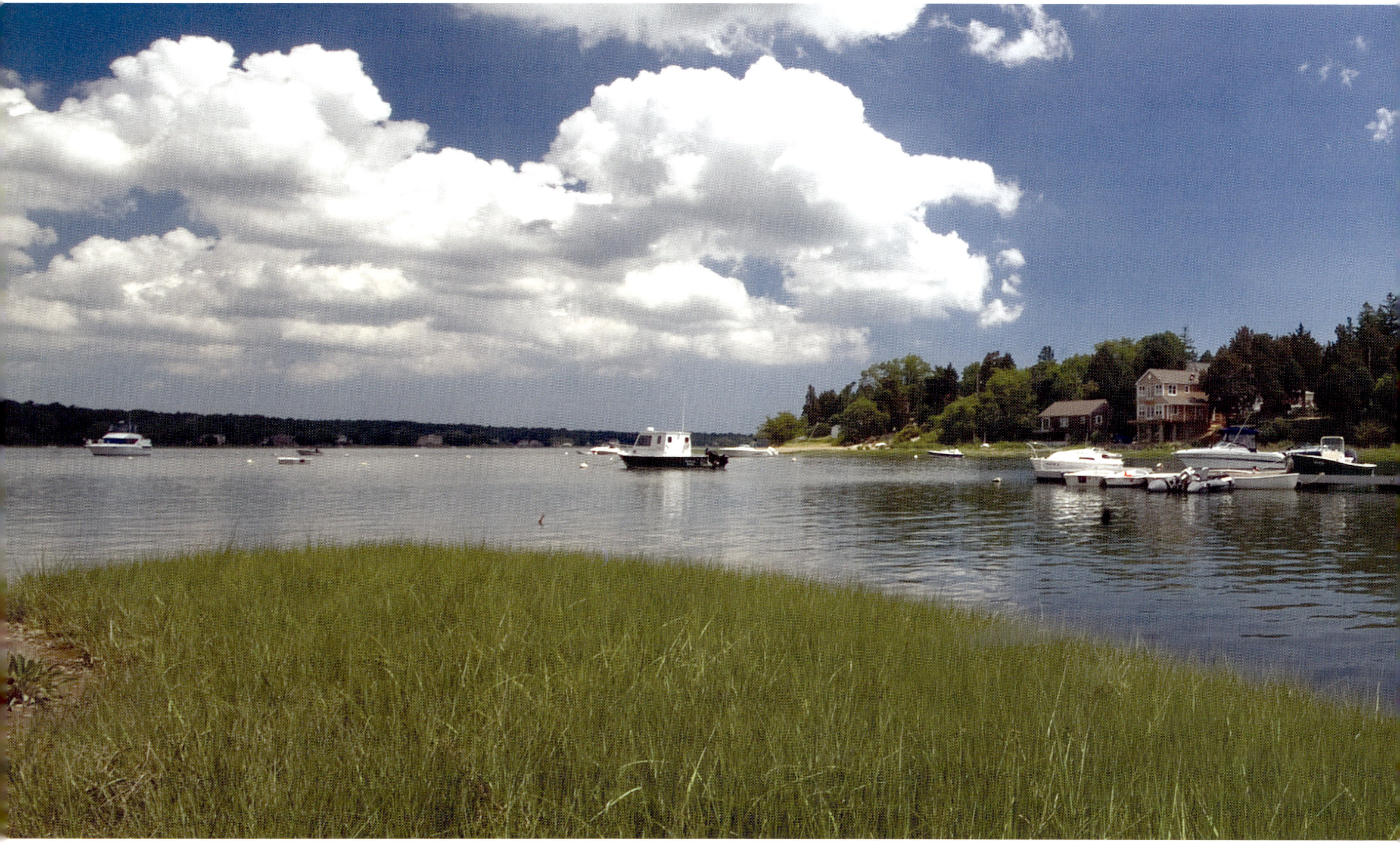

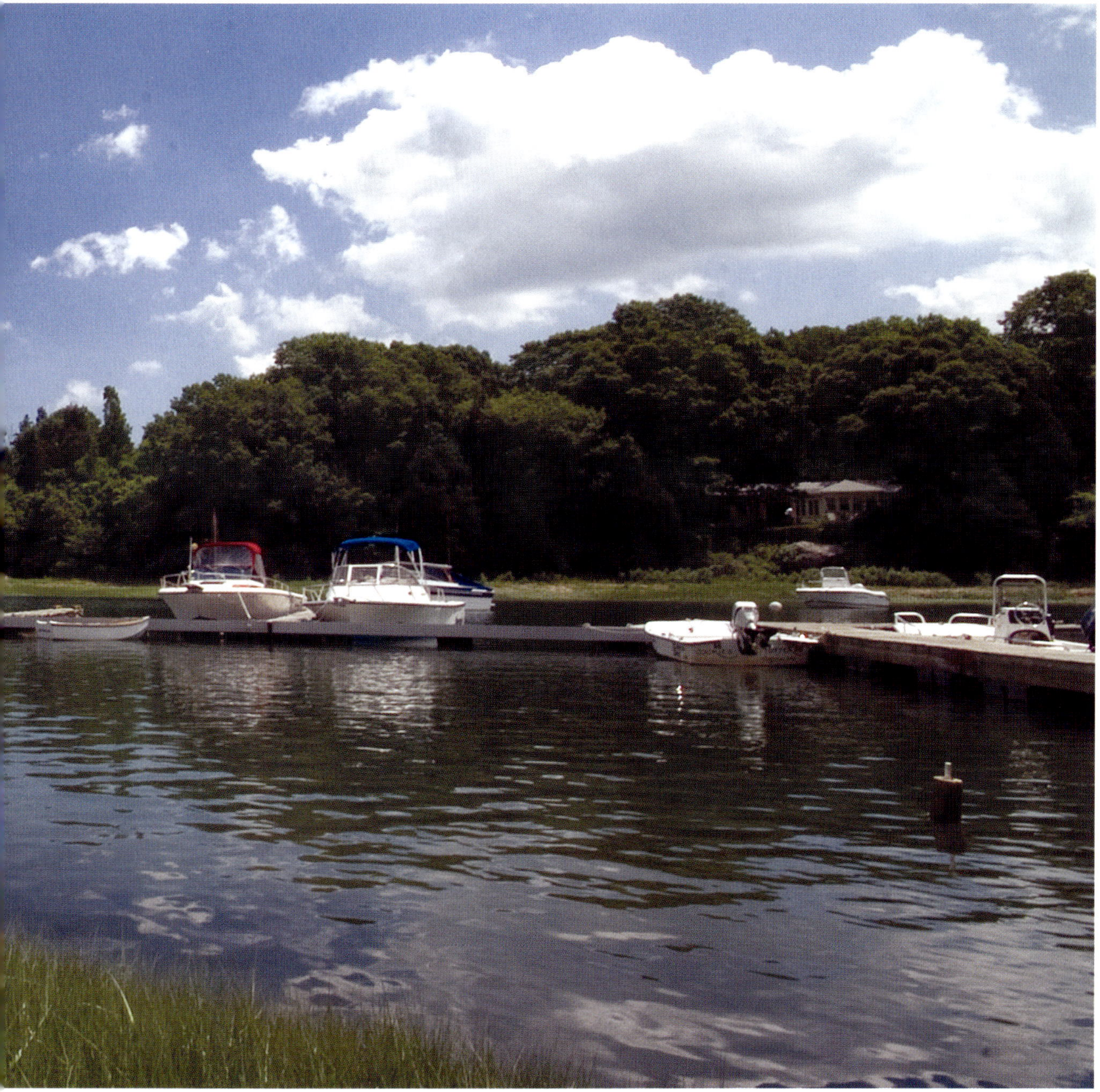

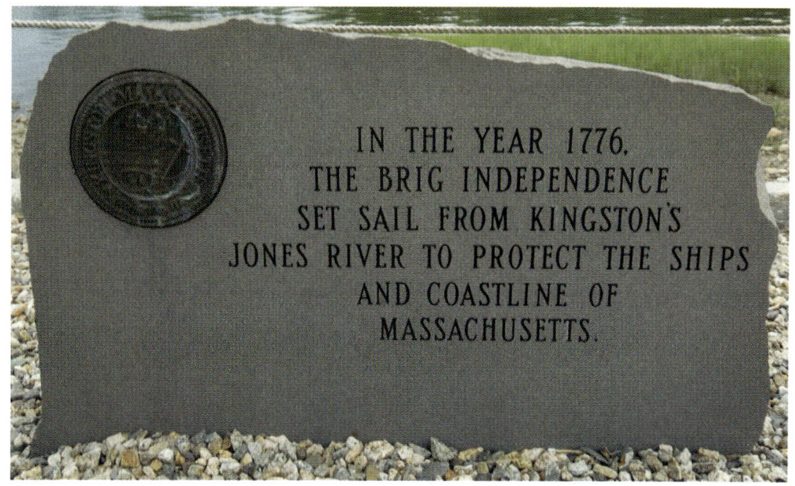

The Jones River, in Kingston, now has mostly recreational craft, and can trace its history back to the Revolutionary War.

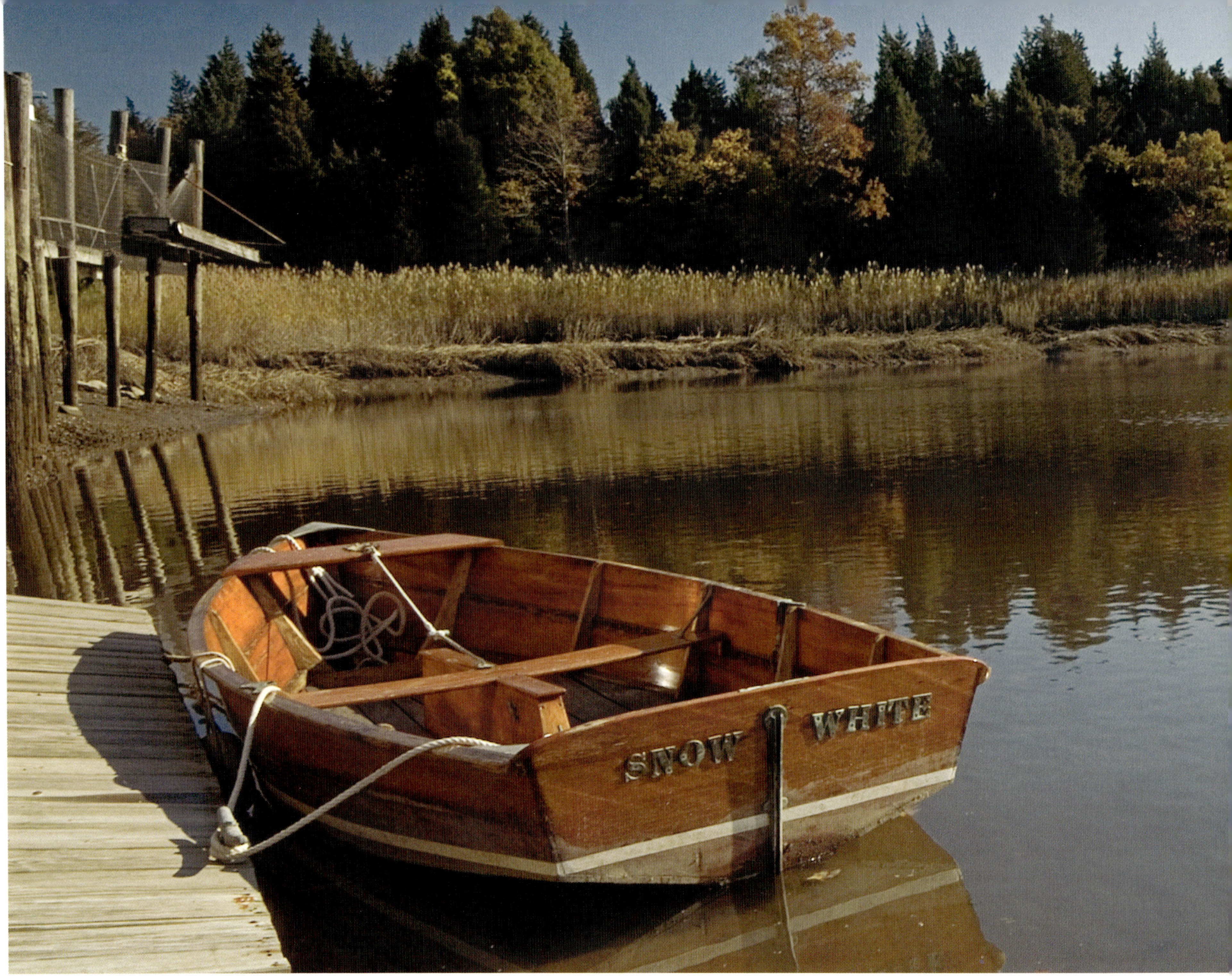

A dinghy sits at a dock on the Jones River.

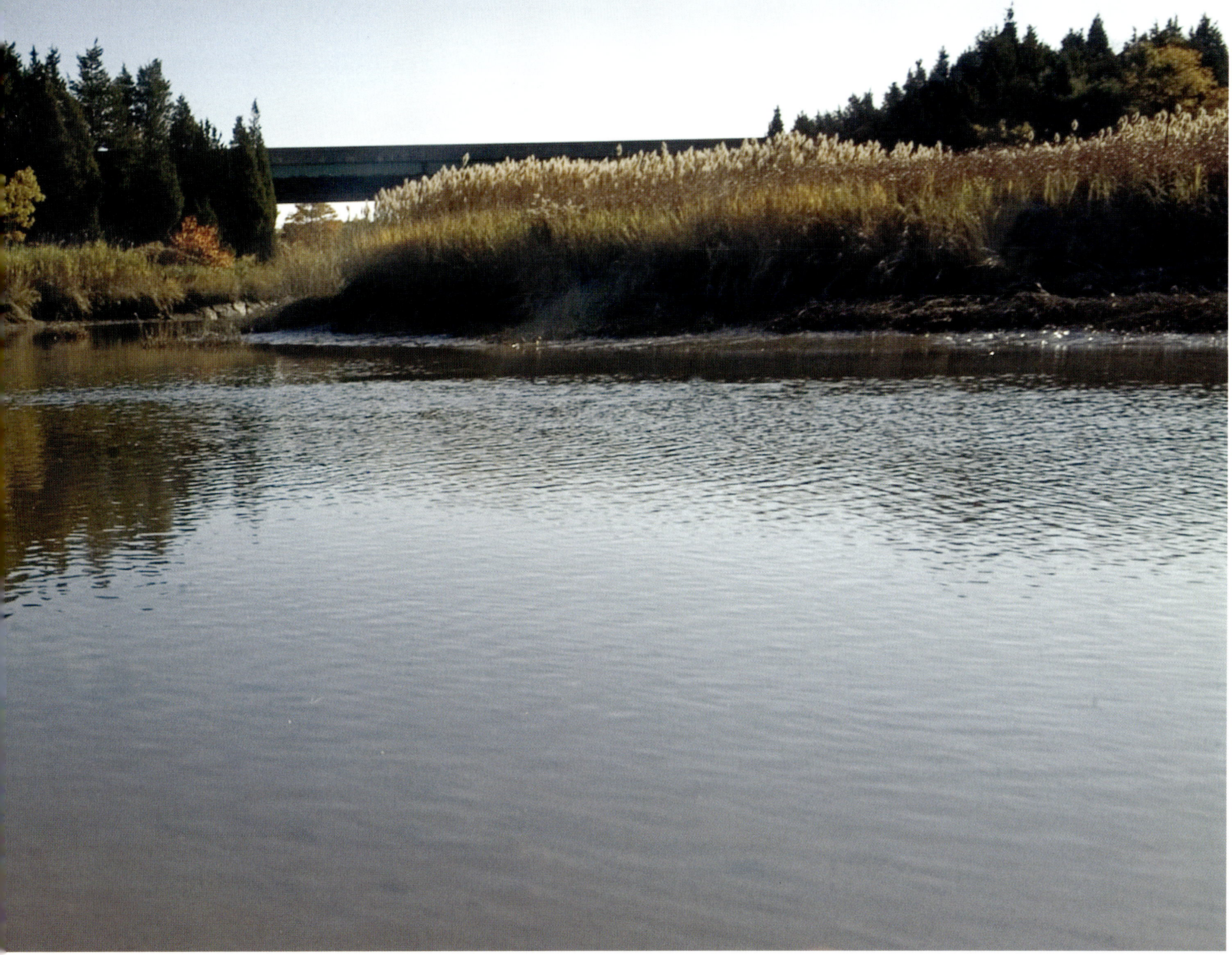

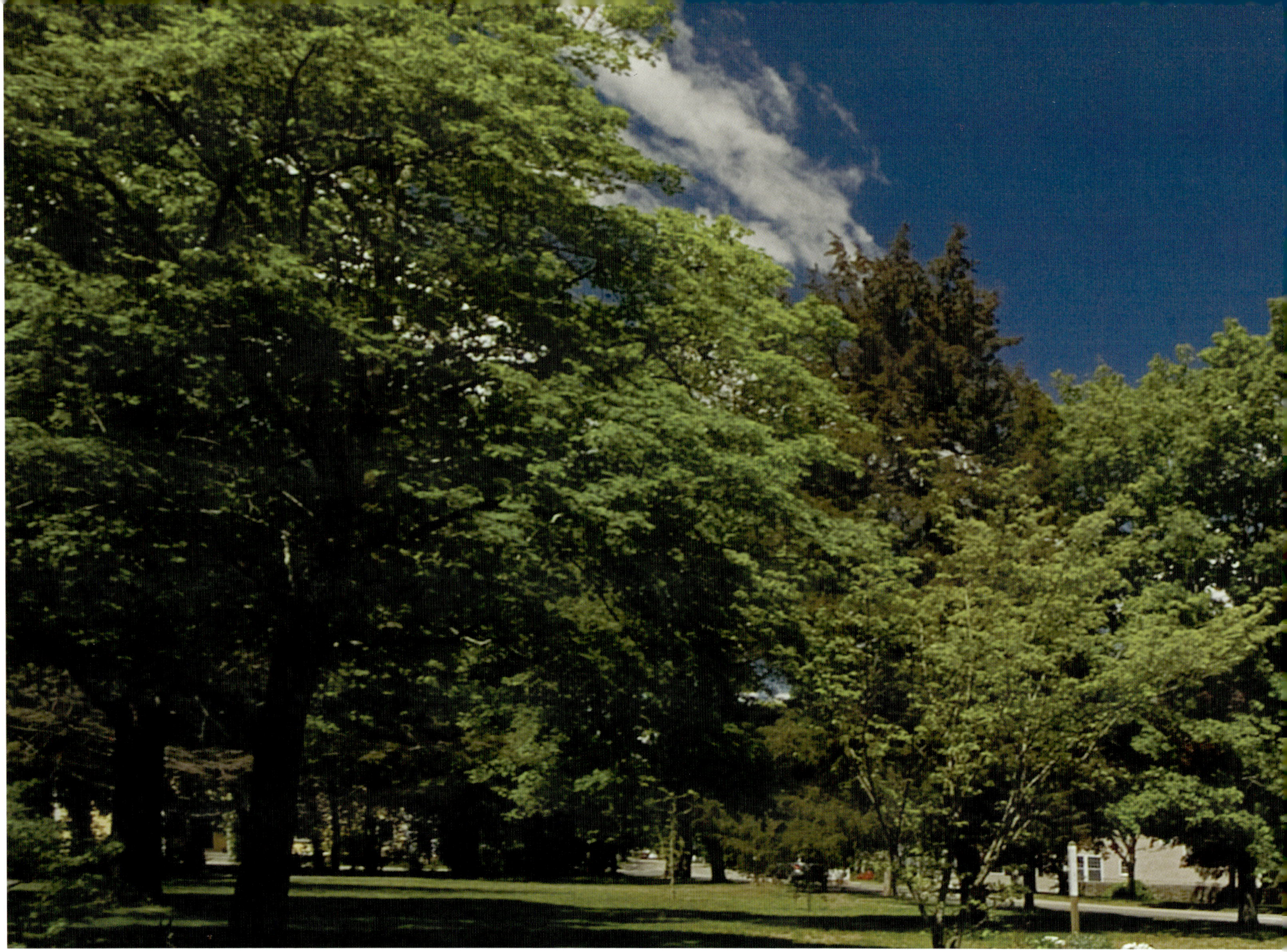

The First Parish Universalist Unitarian Church in Kingston.

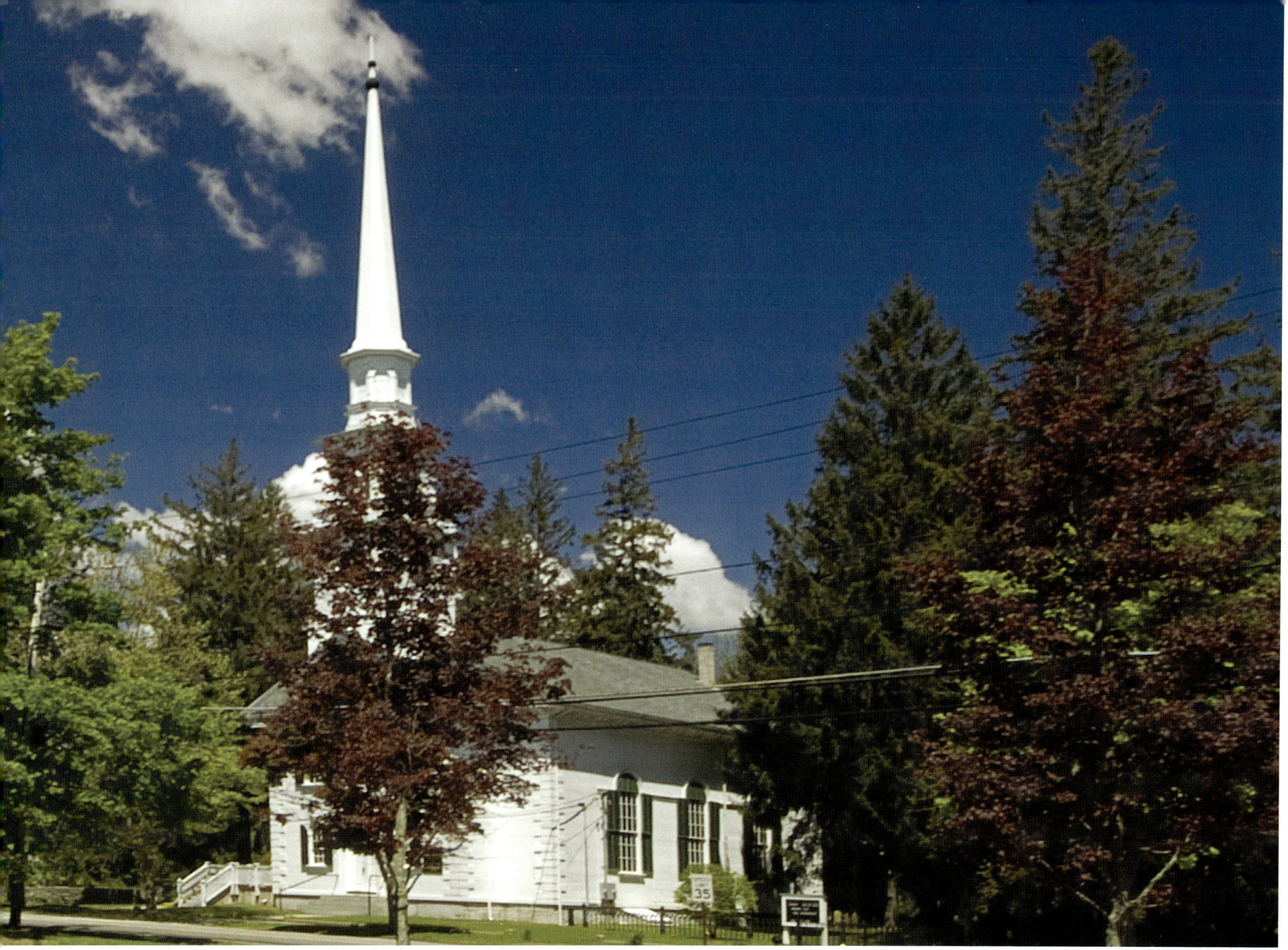
35

Gurnet Light sits on a hill in Plymouth, overlooking Plymouth Bay. The only way to reach the light is to drive south on the 5 mile Duxbury Beach.

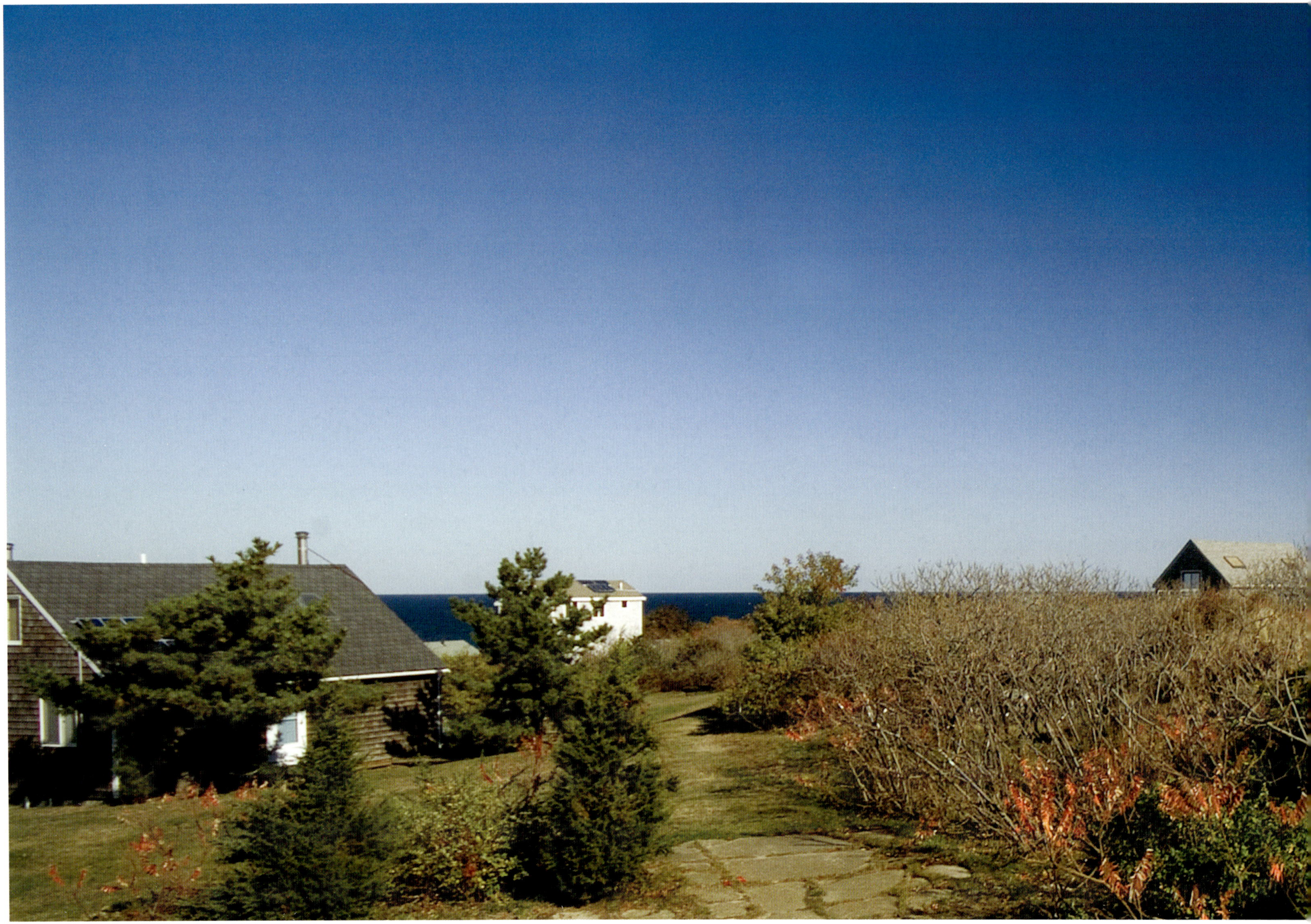

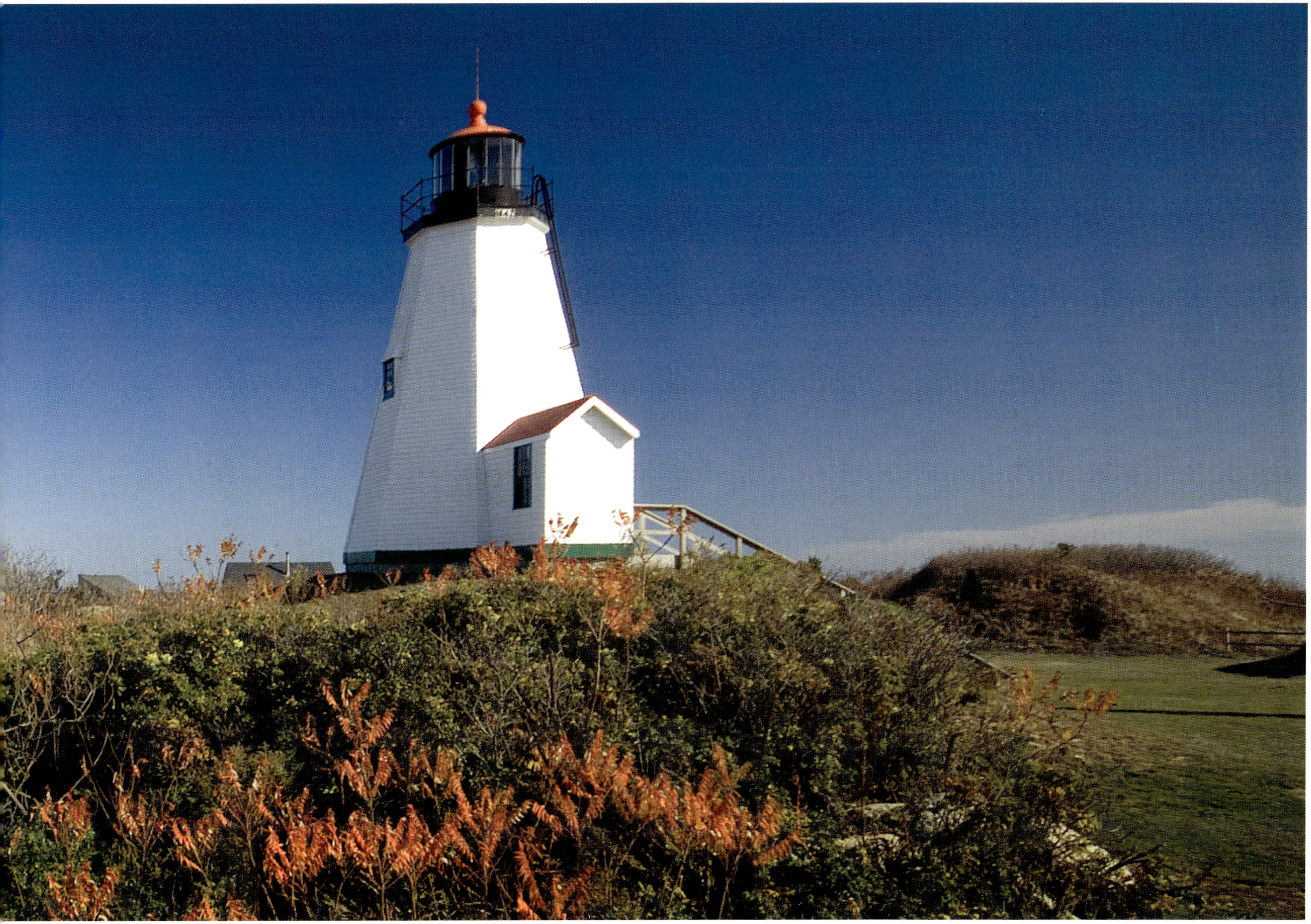

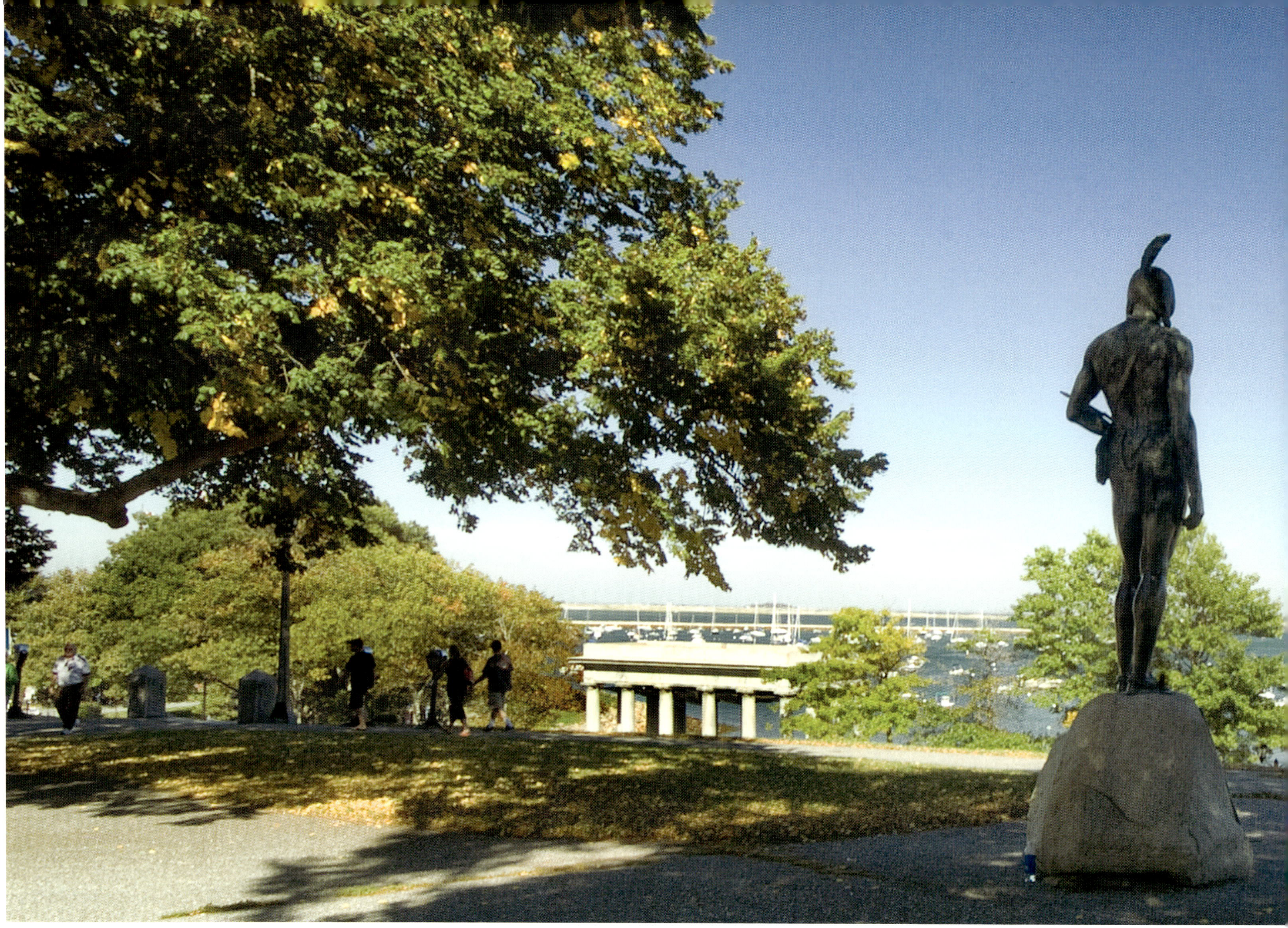

A statue of Massasoit, an Indian chief who lived to be over 80 years old, forged peace between the Wampanoag confederacy and the English colonists, overlooks Plymouth Rock and the harbor beyond. A local community college and a state park are named after him.

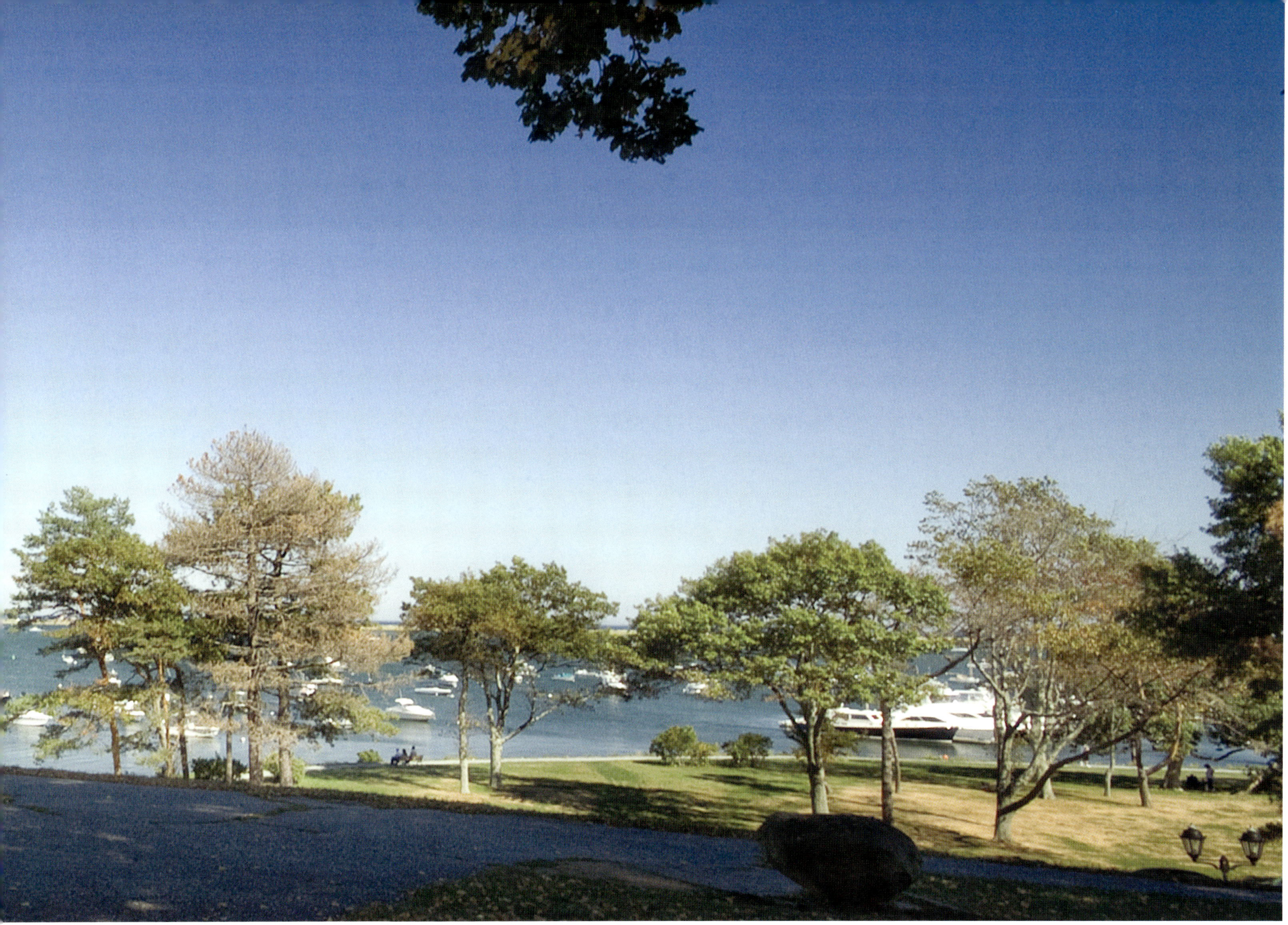

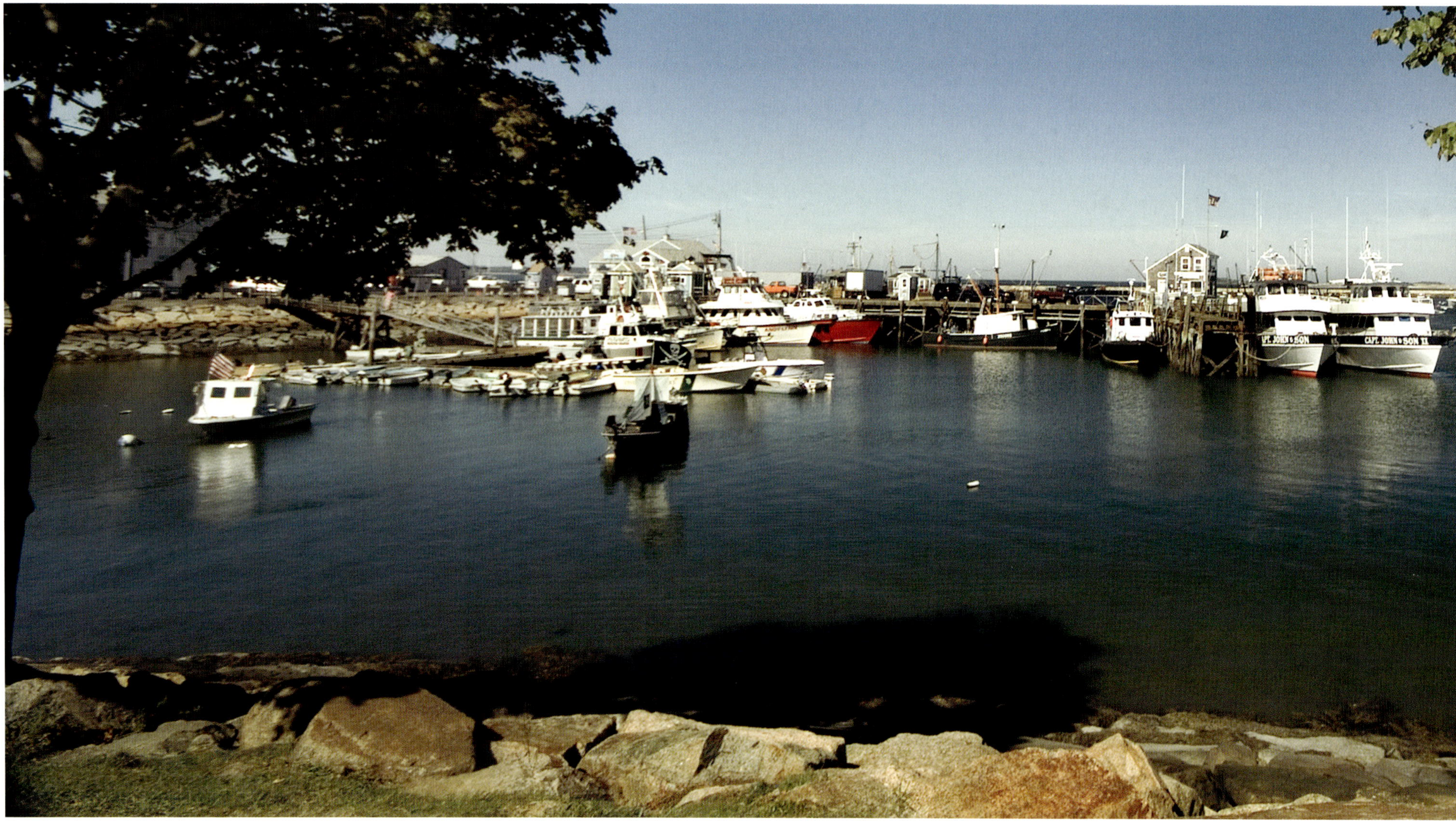

The commercial dock in Plymouth has fishing boats as well as whale watch vessels. Dinghies lined up at the dock, carry boat owners to their moorings.

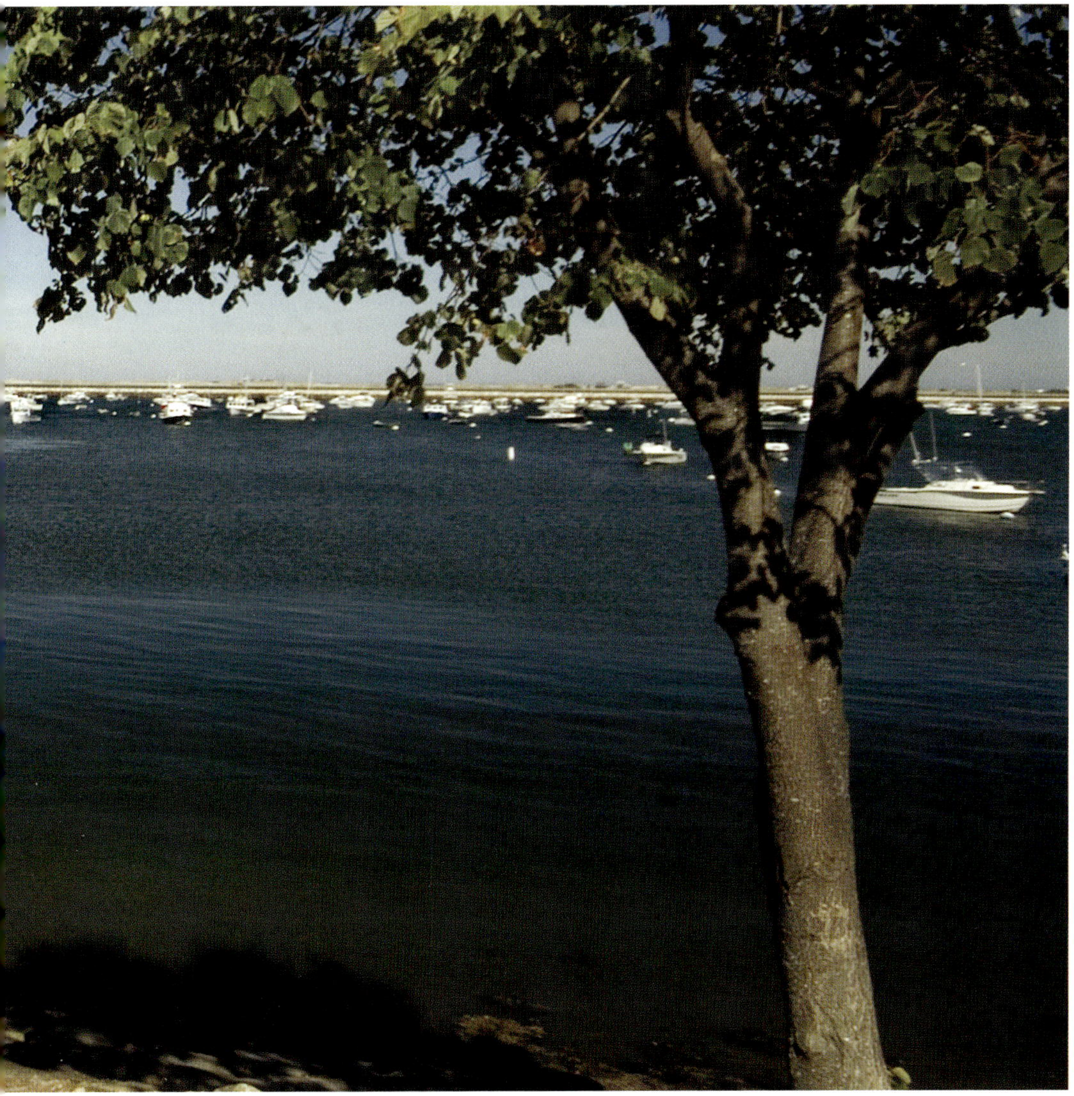

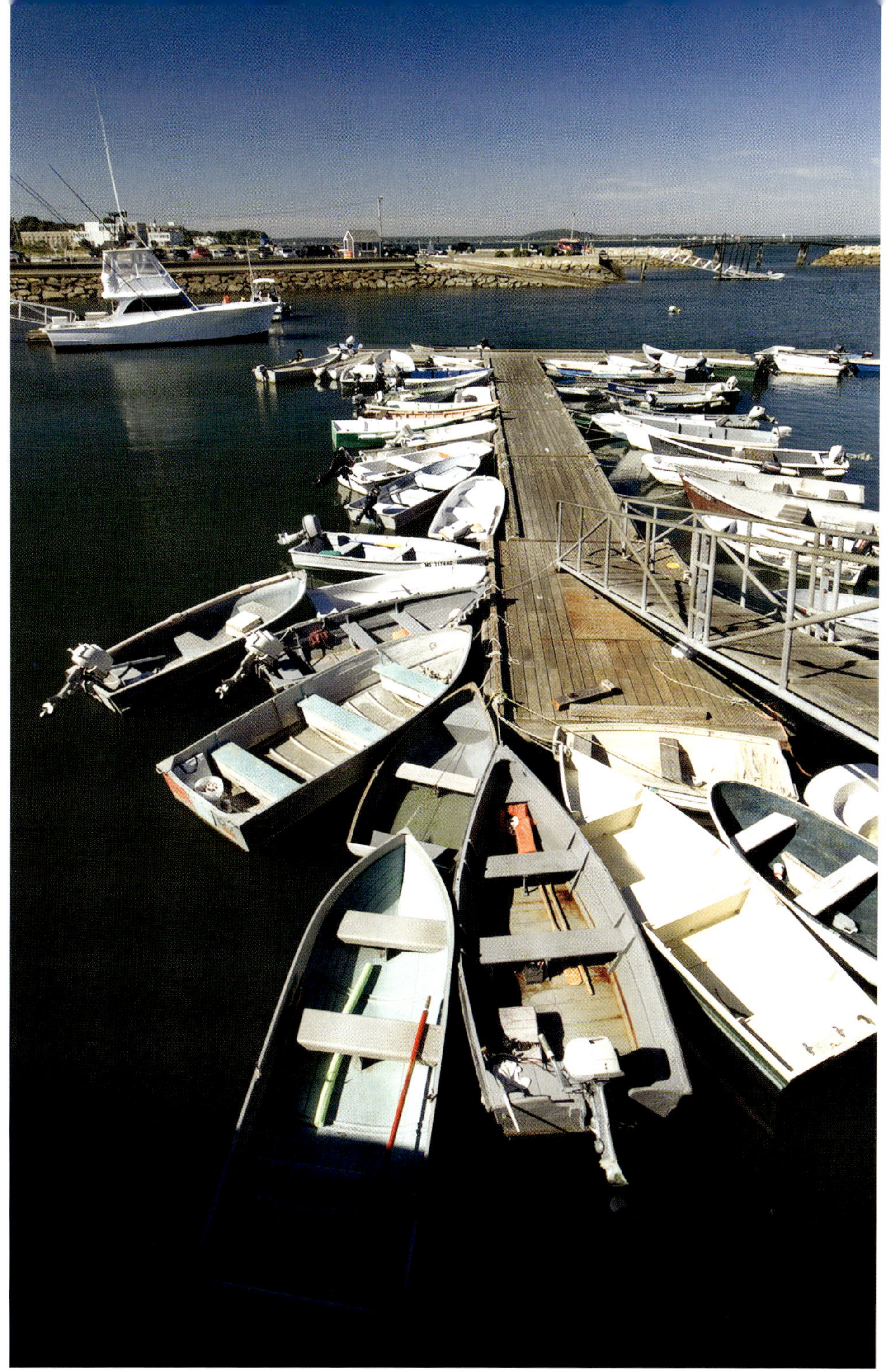

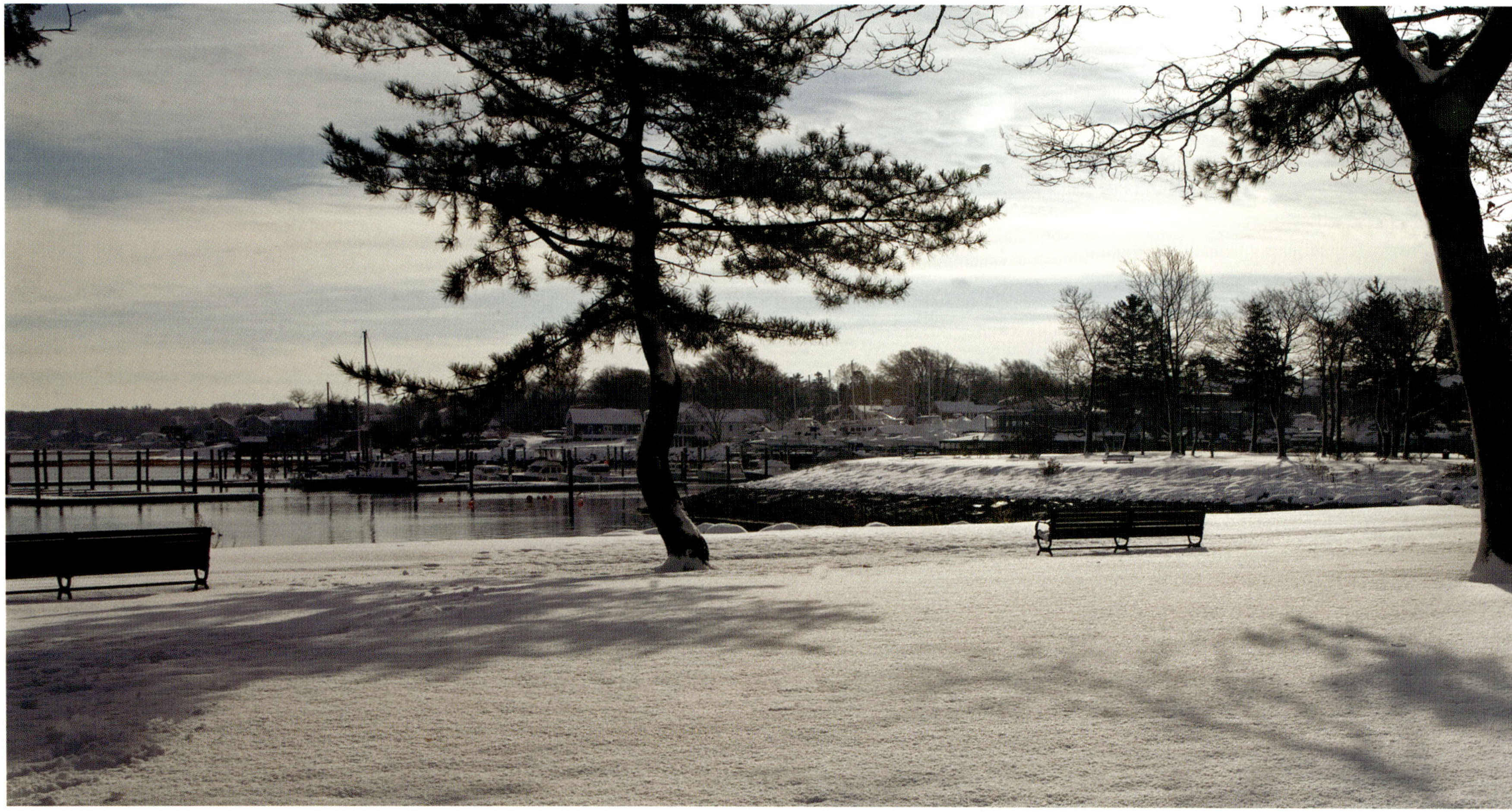

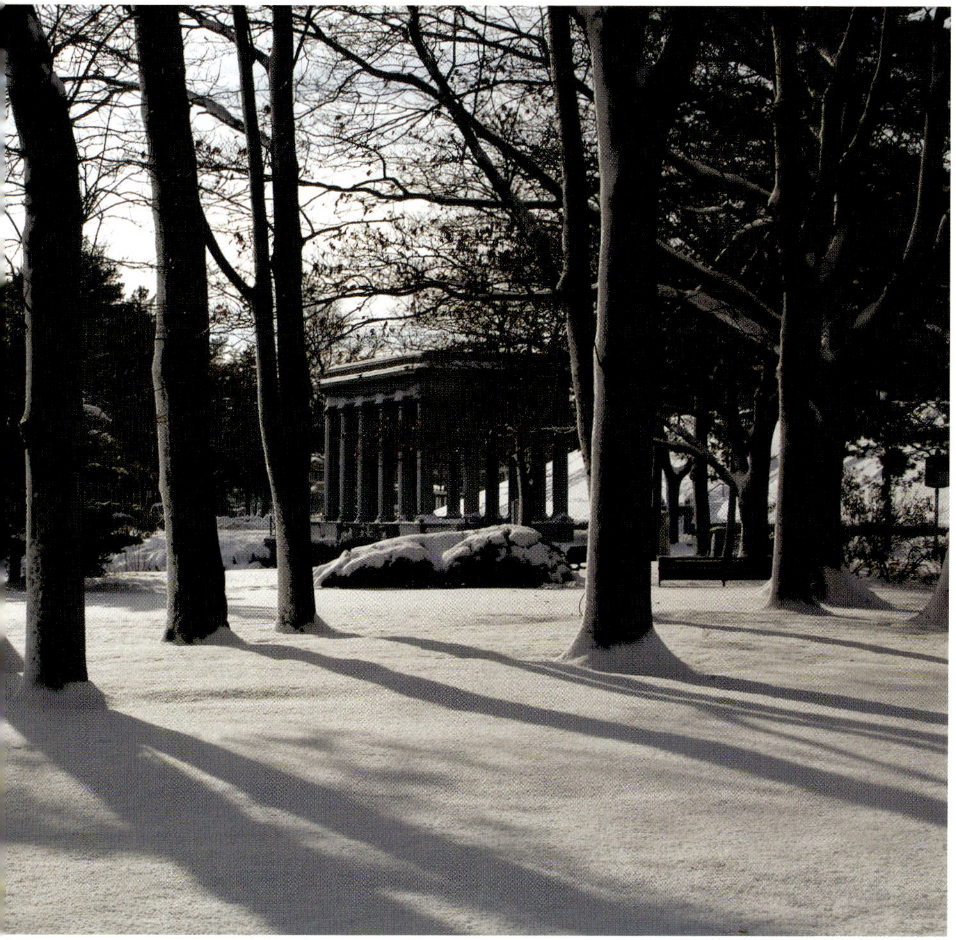

Plymouth Rock is probably one of the most visited sites in town.

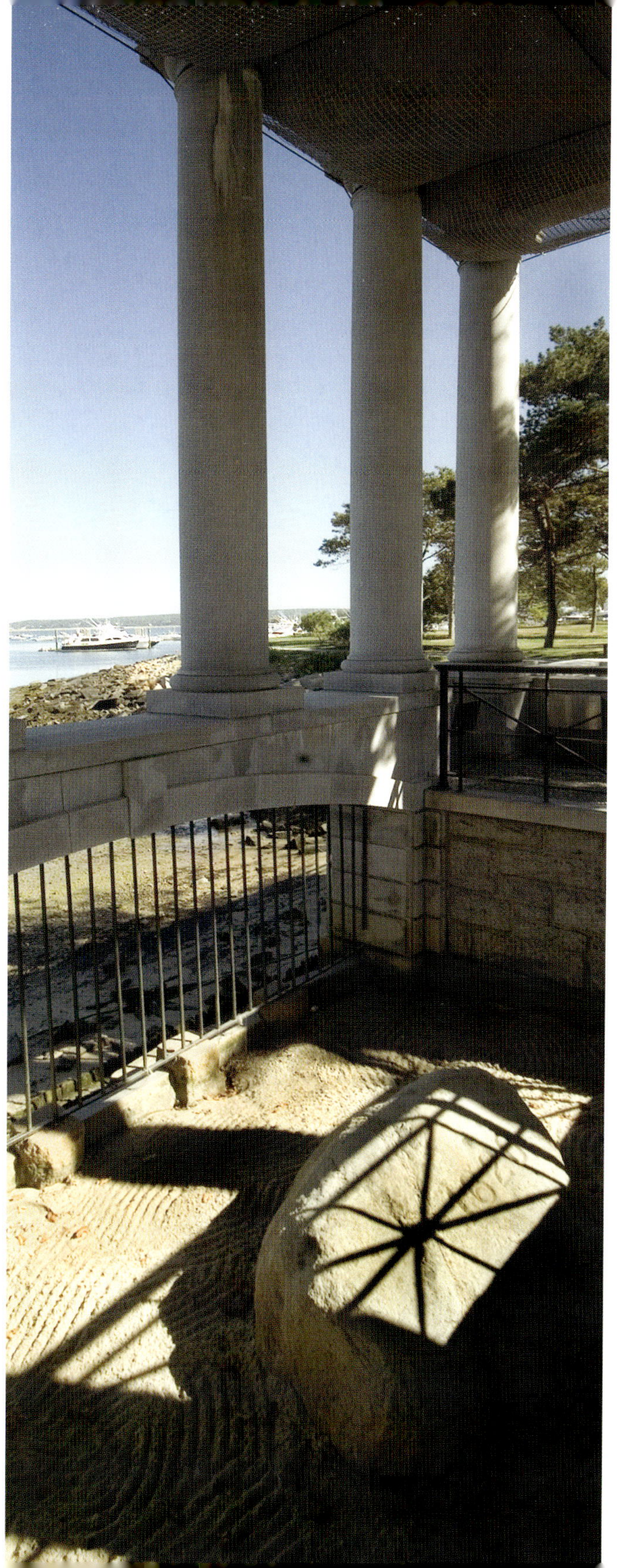

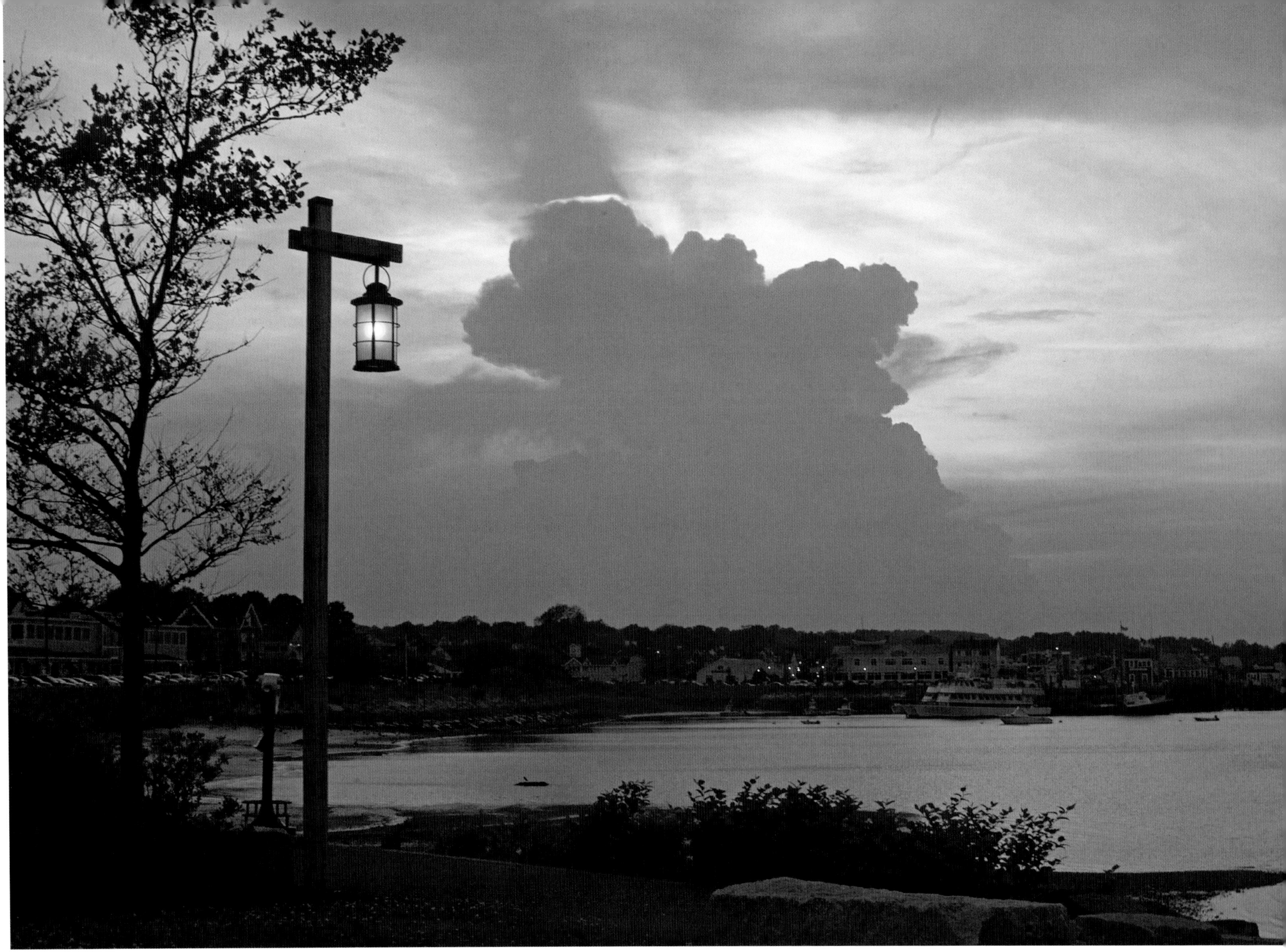

An approaching storm in Plymouth Harbor.

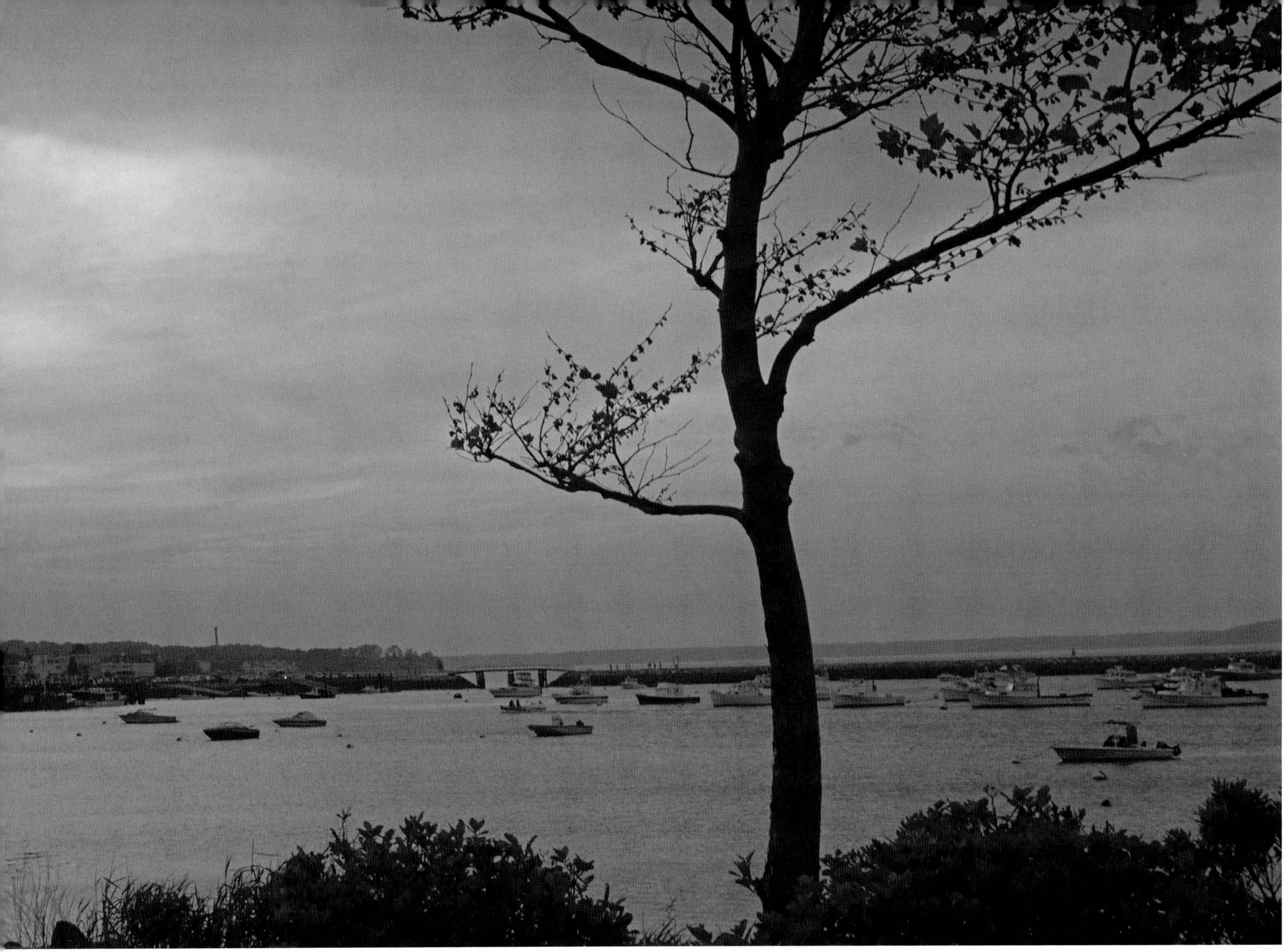

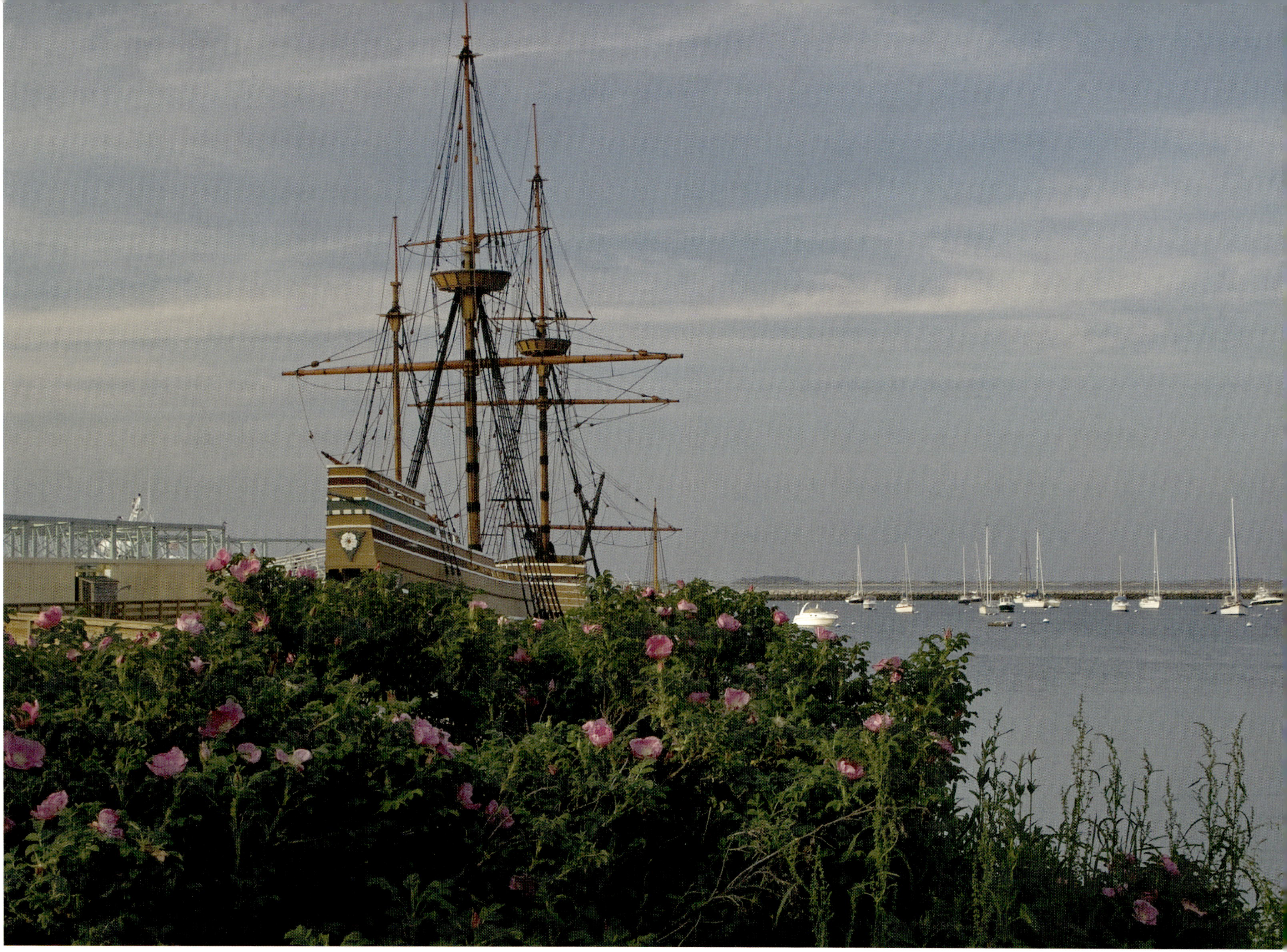

The Mayflower II sits at the dock facing Plymouth Harbor.

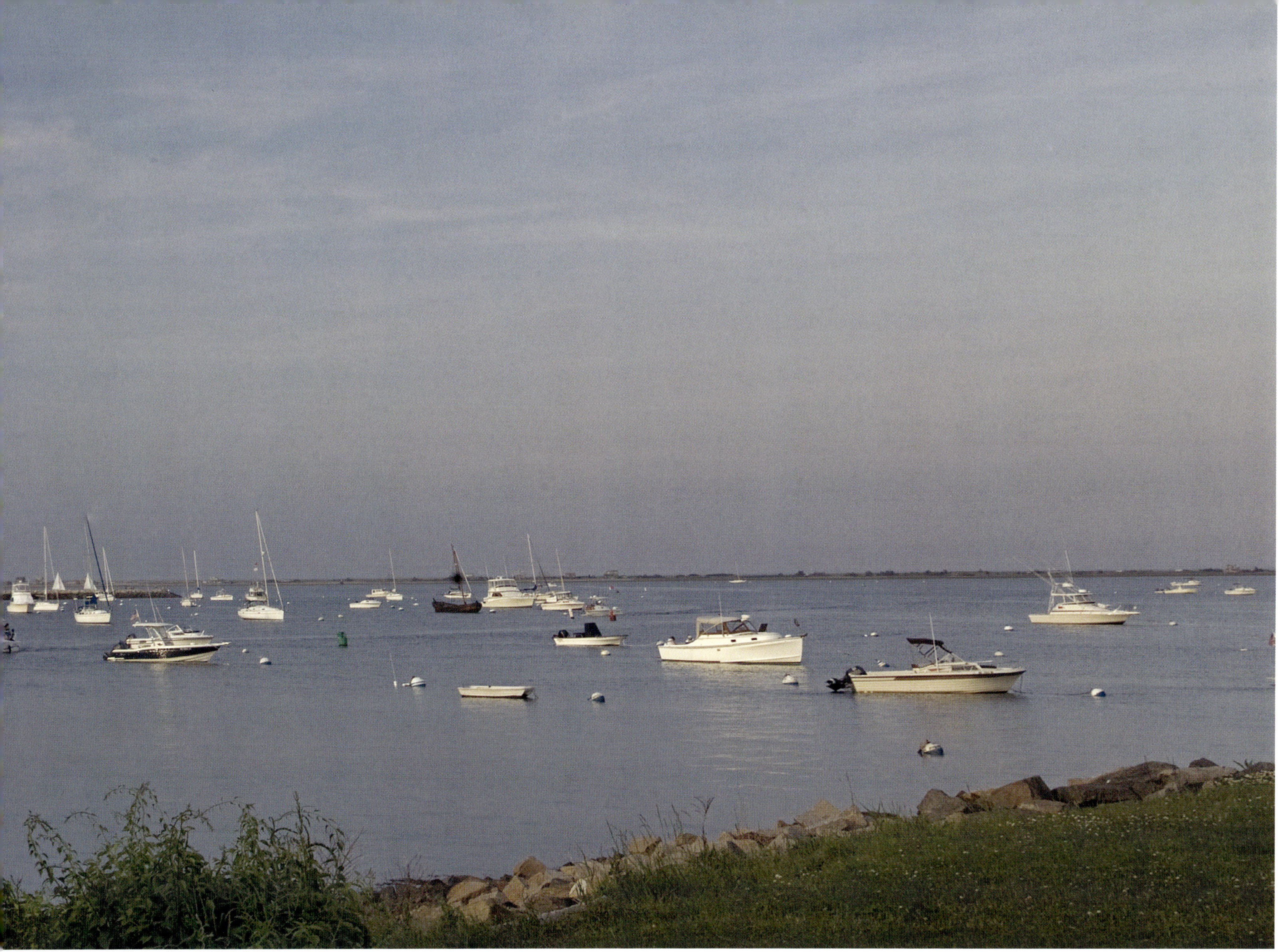

The dock in Plymouth Harbor.

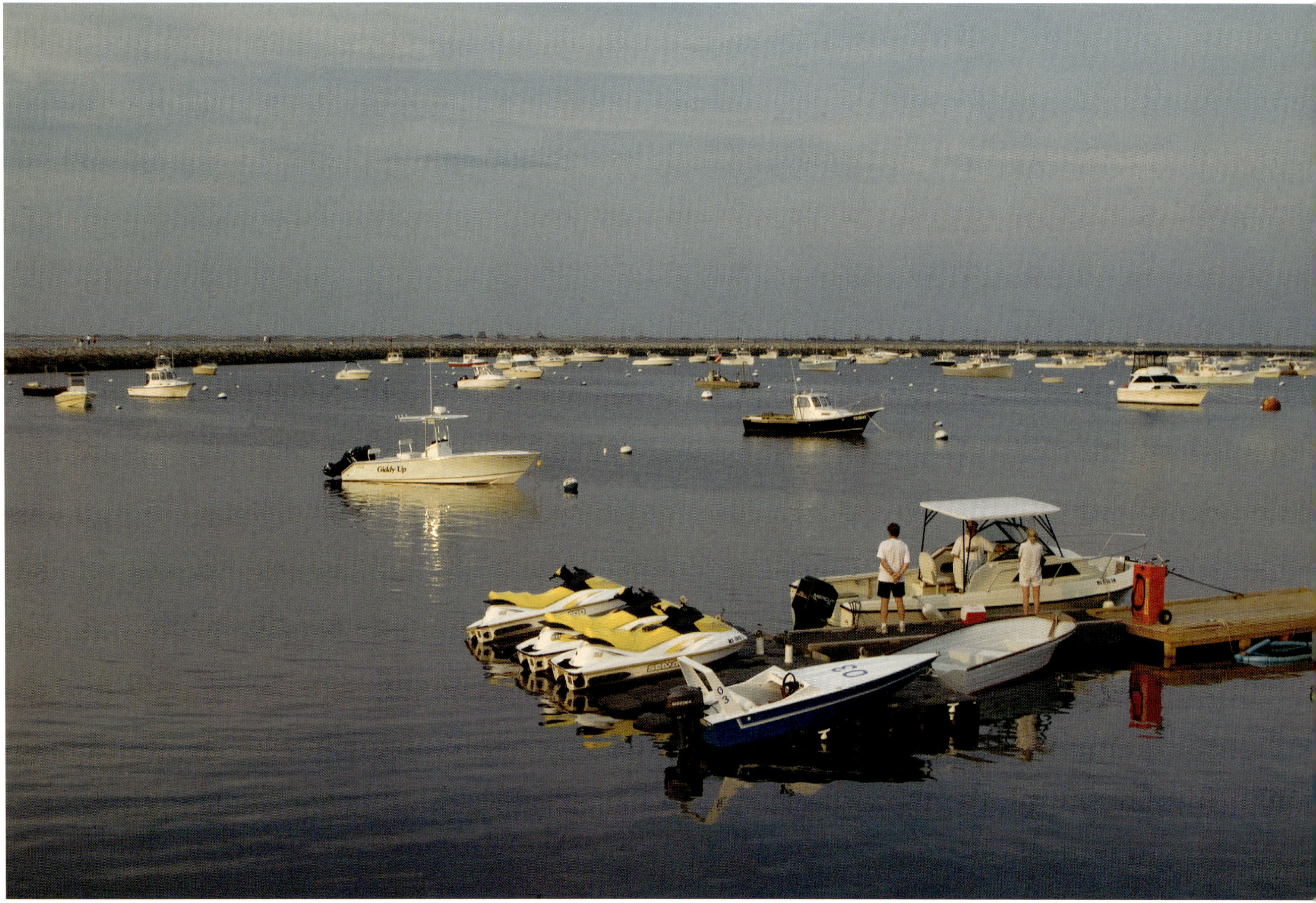

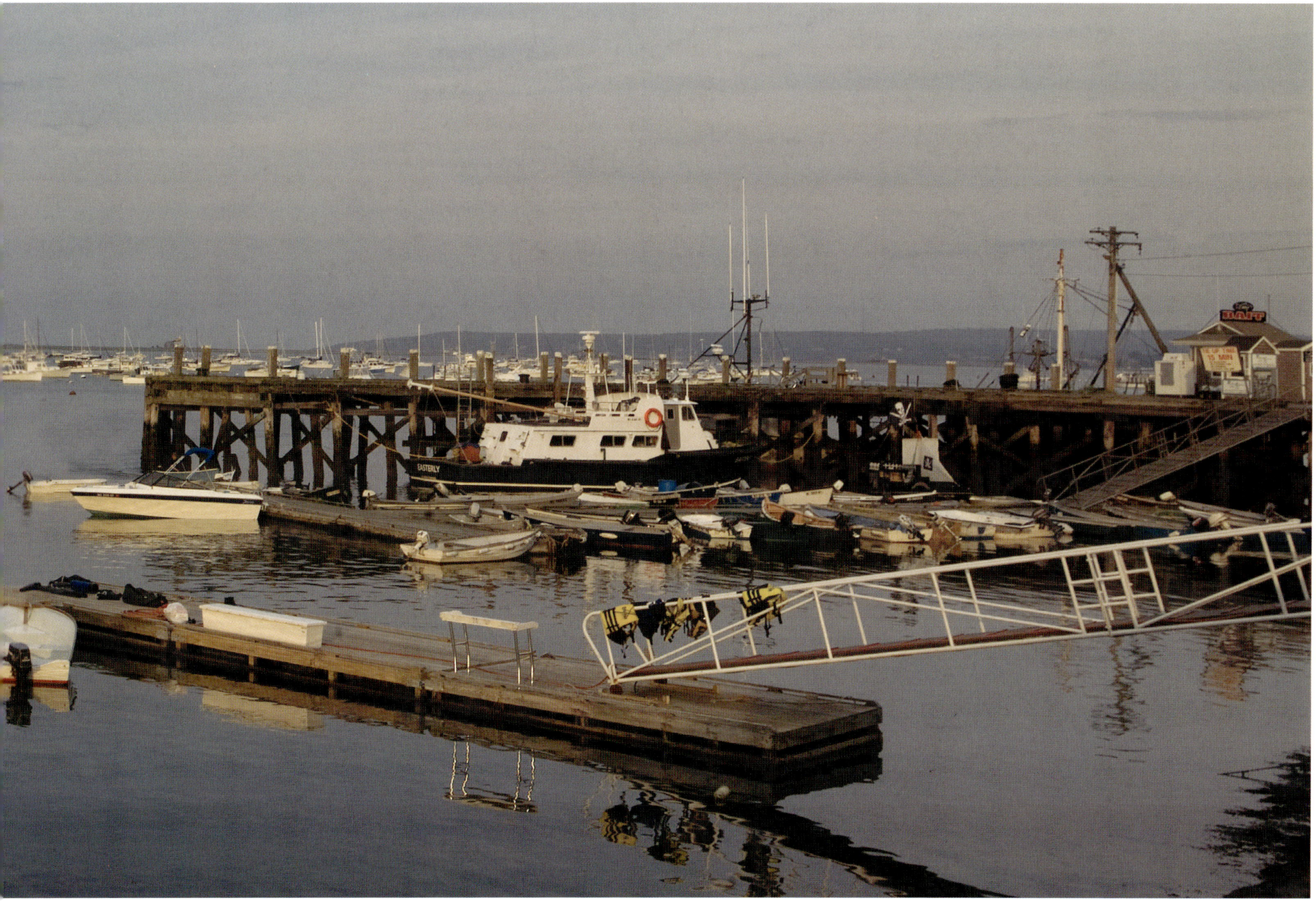
BAIT
EASTERLY

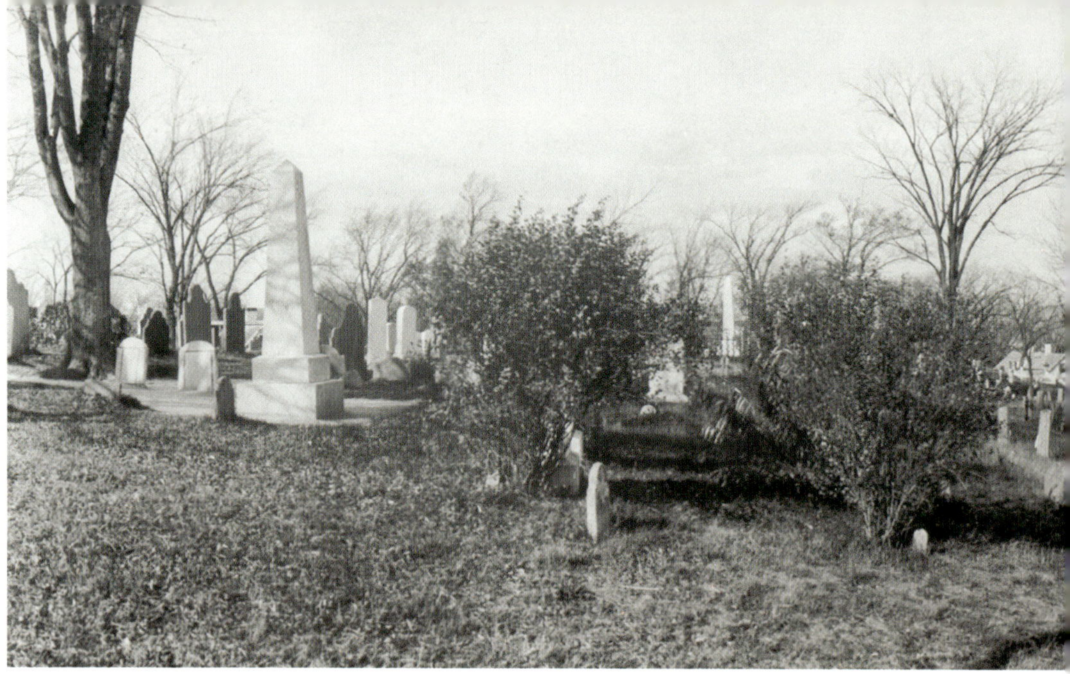

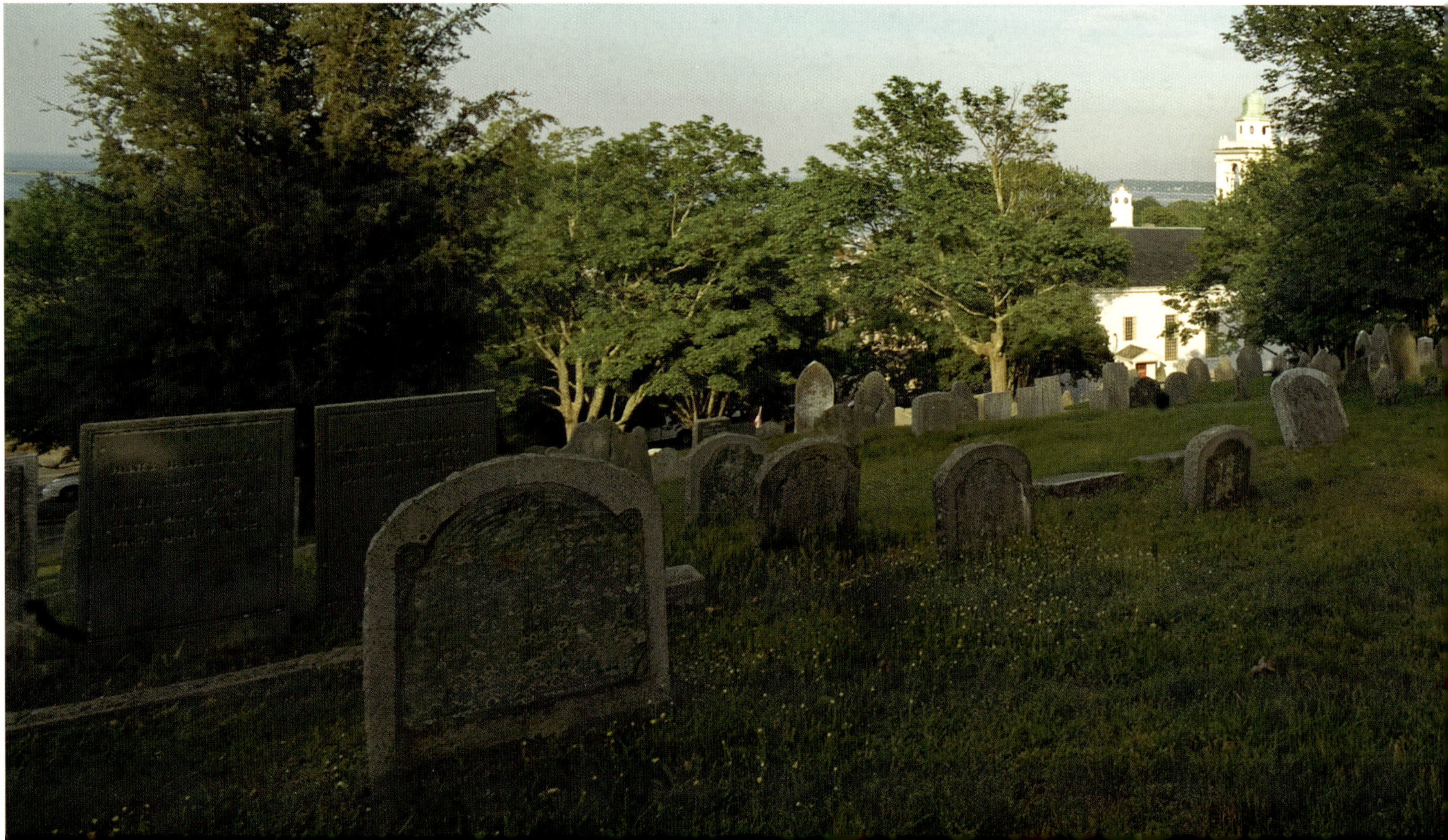

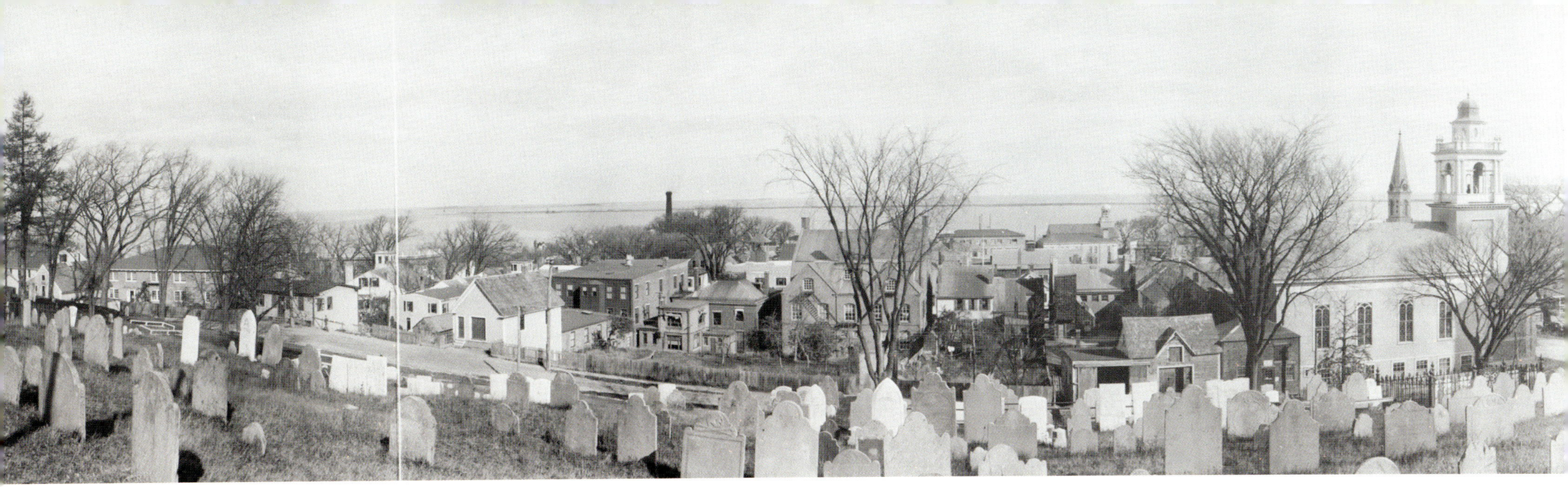

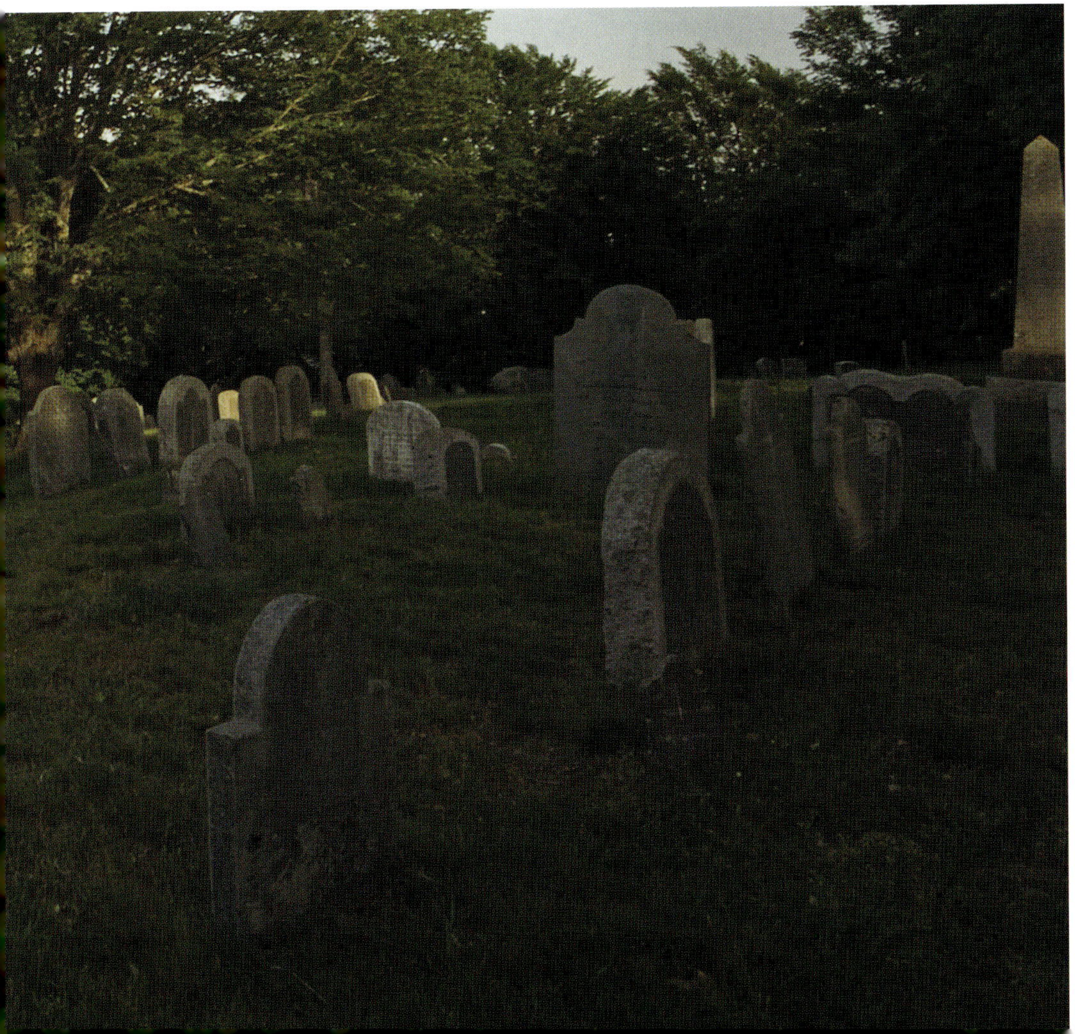

Located on a knoll overlooking the harbor, Burial Hill was first used as a fort and later as a cemetery that includes the graves of many of the original Pilgrims. A panorama of the burial ground nearly 100 years ago was photographed by the Haines Photo Co. of Conneaut, Ohio. A gelatin silver print measured 9" by 34". (Courtesy of Library of Congress)

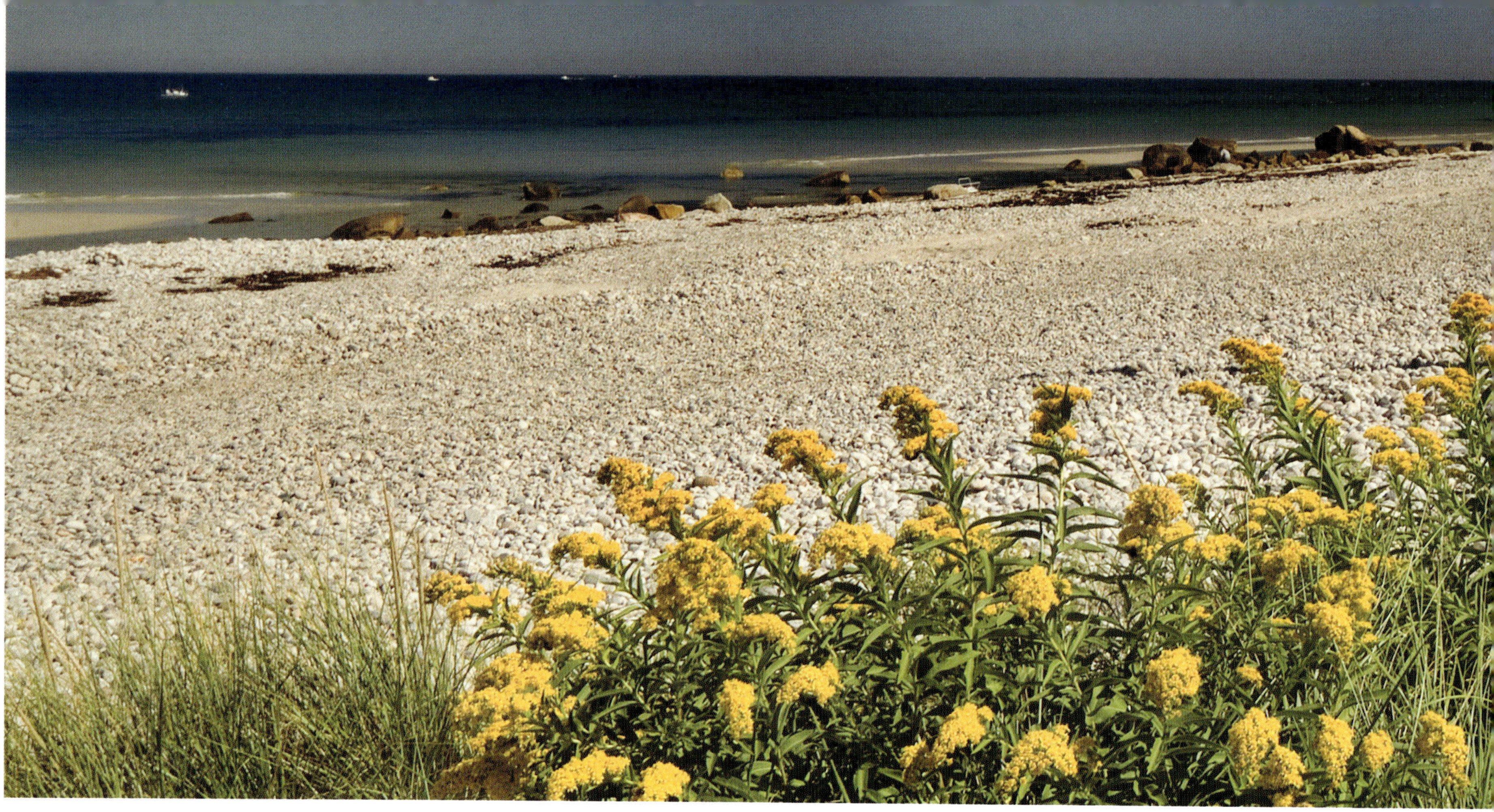

Goldenrod blooms along the shore in the fall in the Manomet area of Plymouth.

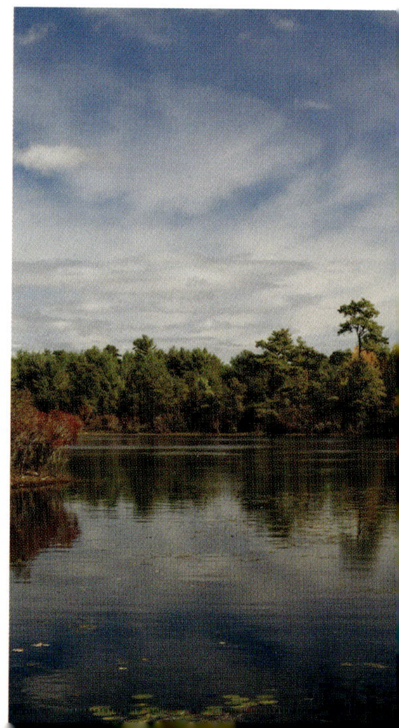

One of the many ponds in the Myles Standish State Forest.

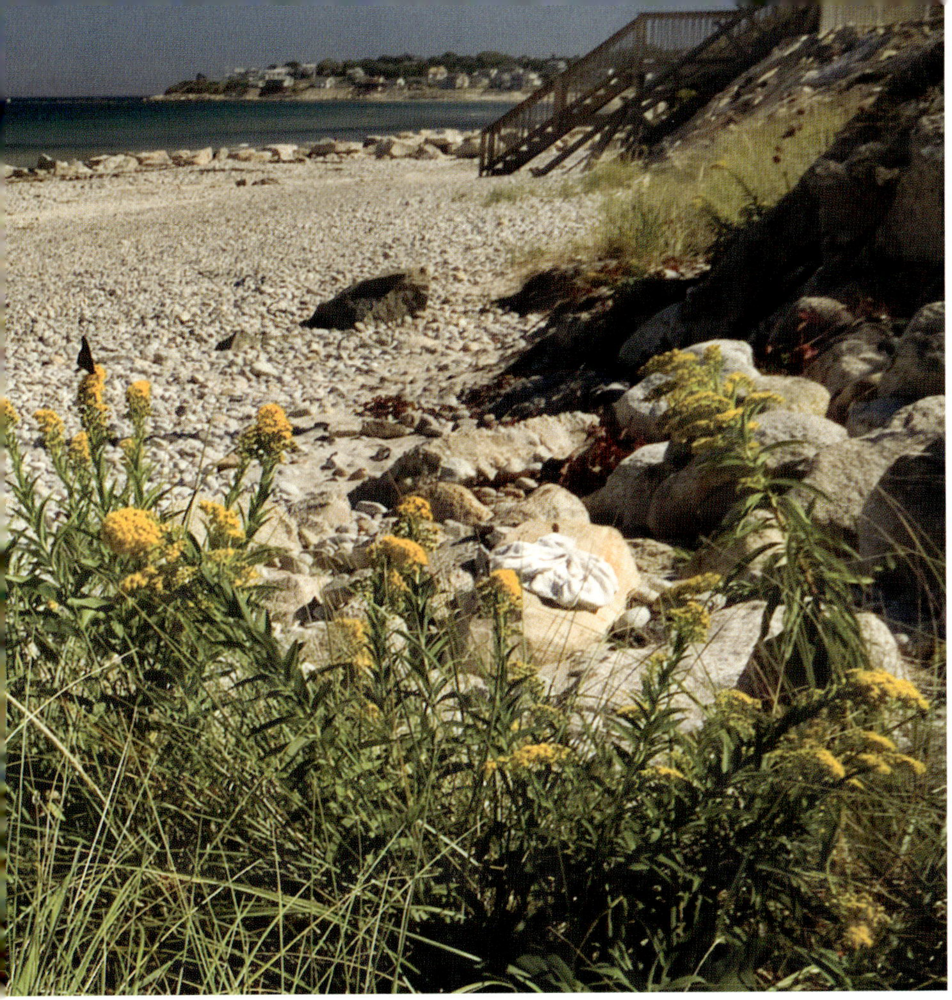

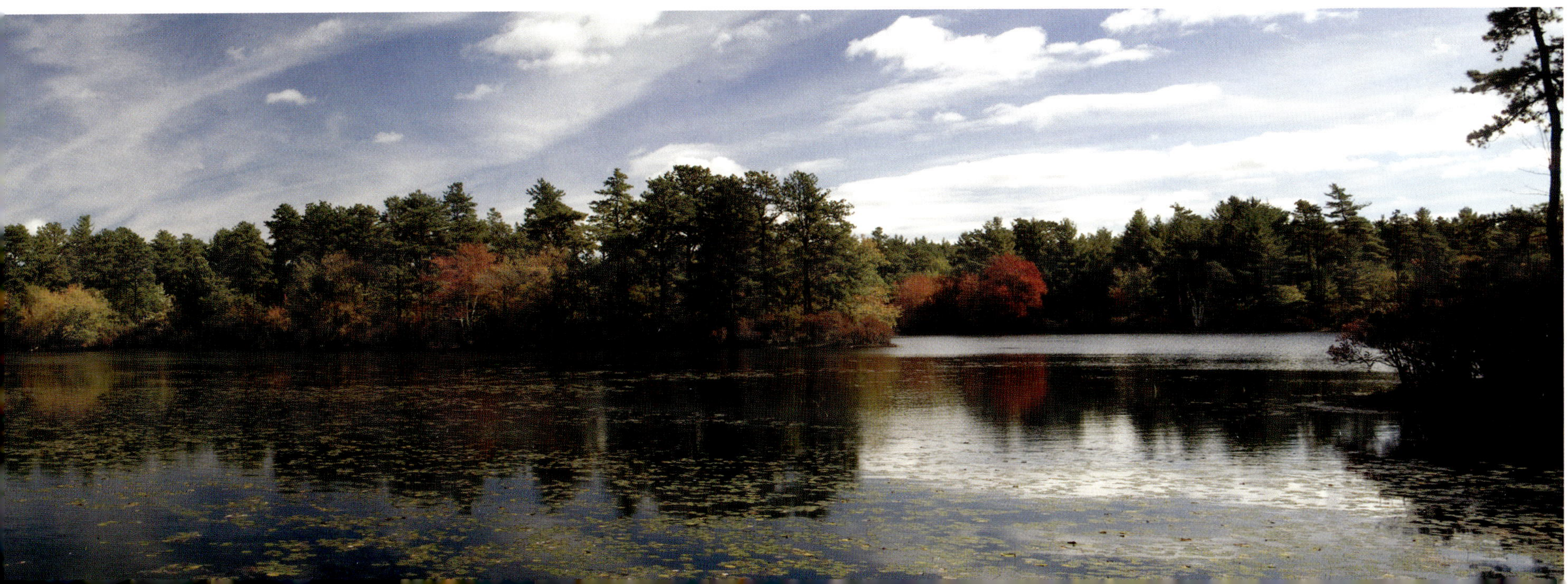

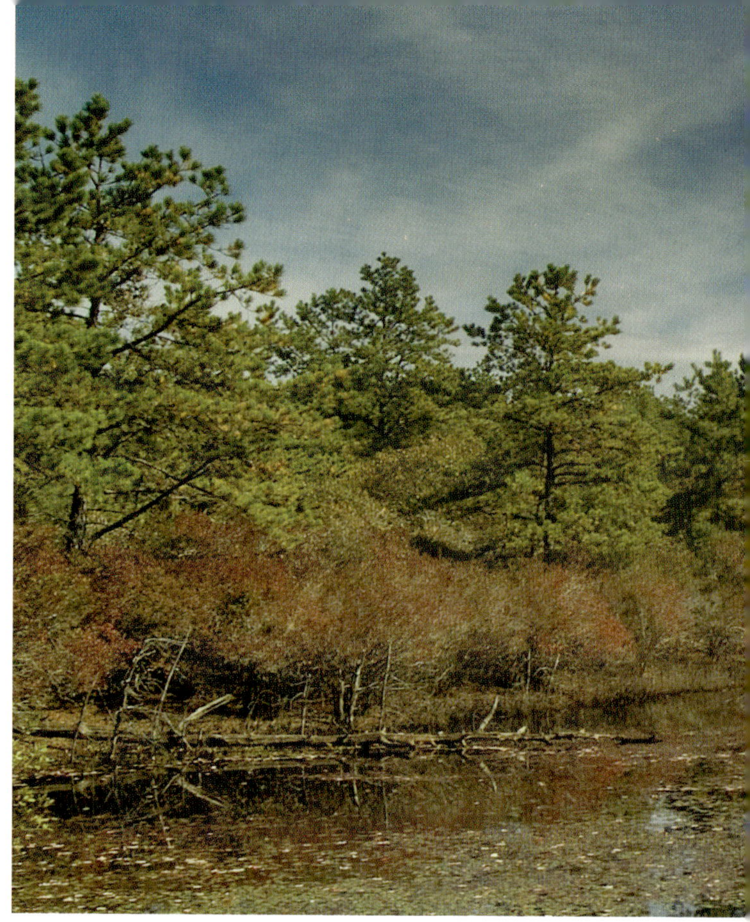

Pitch pine and scrub oak trees within Myles Standish State Forest constitute the largest contiguous forest of this type in the region. With numerous scattered ponds, wide-angle, picturesque vistas abound.

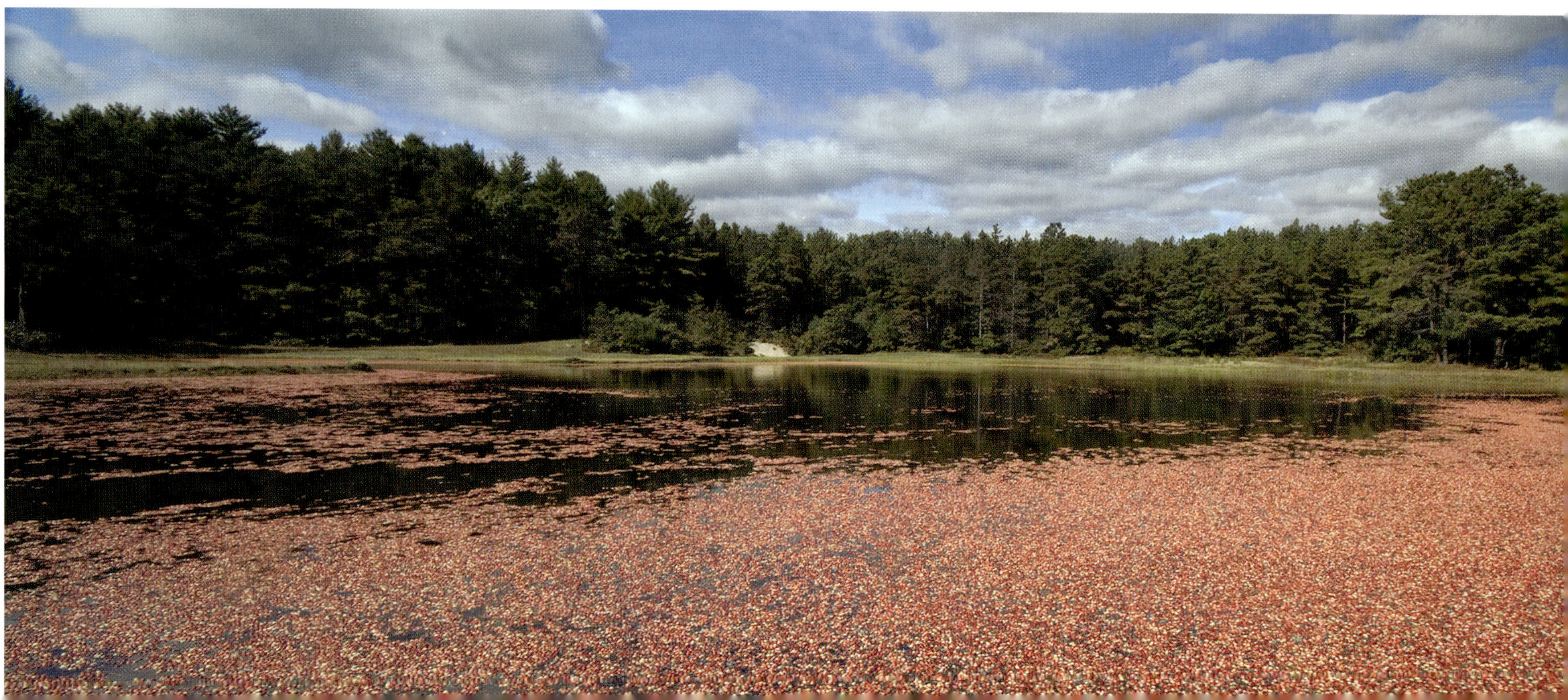

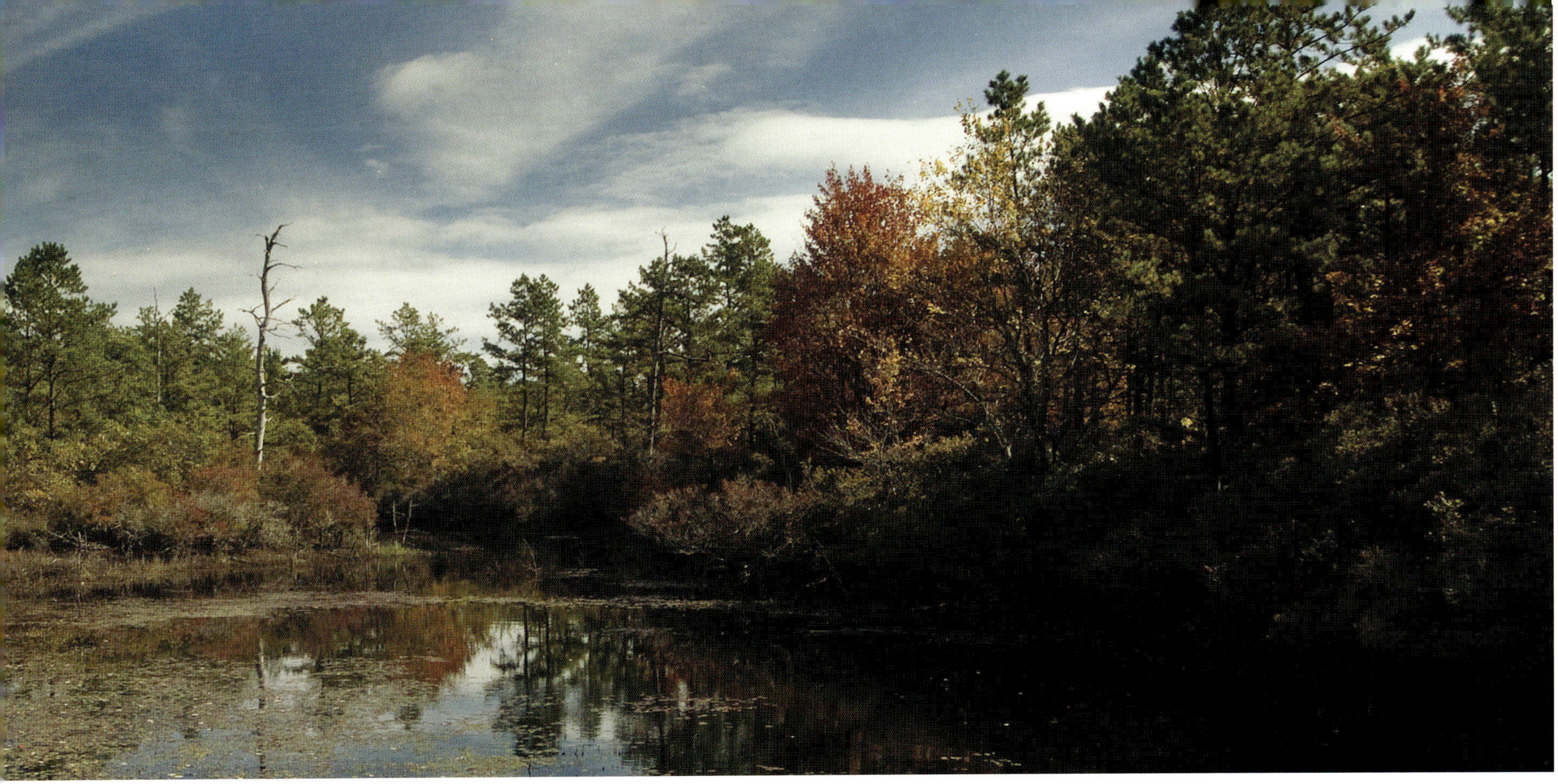

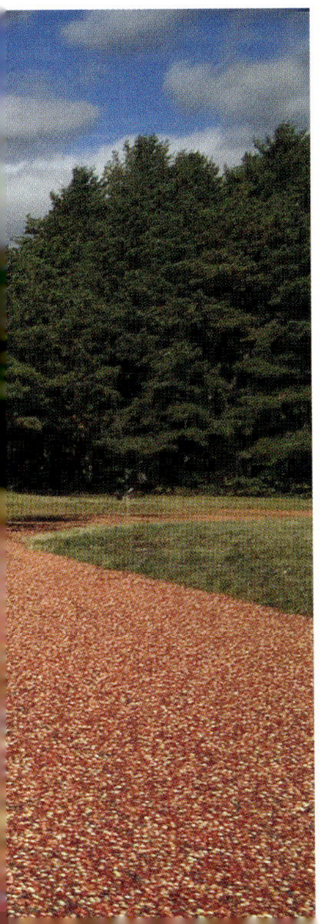

Cranberry bogs are flooded in the early fall to harvest the crop. Canals surround the bogs to provide a water supply.

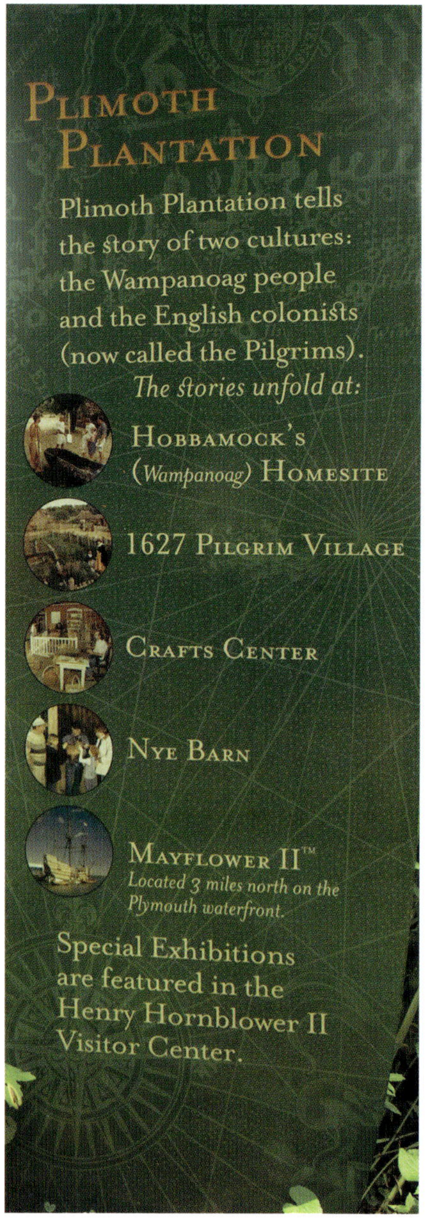

Plimoth Plantation is a bi-cultural museum that takes the visitor back in time to the mid 1620's to the re-creation of a small town built by English colonists in the same locale as the Wampanoag homeland. Self-guided, a tour through both villages will enlighten the guest to activities and give perspective to what life was like nearly 400 years ago. Individuals dressed in period dress enhance the experience and explain viewpoints and histories as it applies to each village. These two views show each village

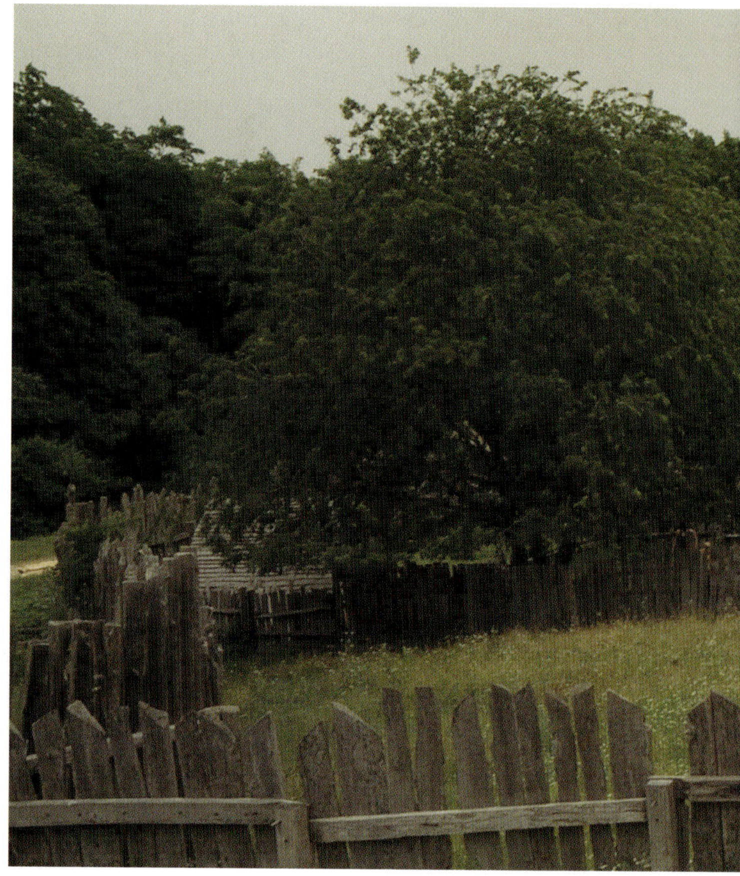

From the fort, this spectacular view shows the street of Plimoth Plantation's 1627 English Village, with Plymouth Bay in the background.

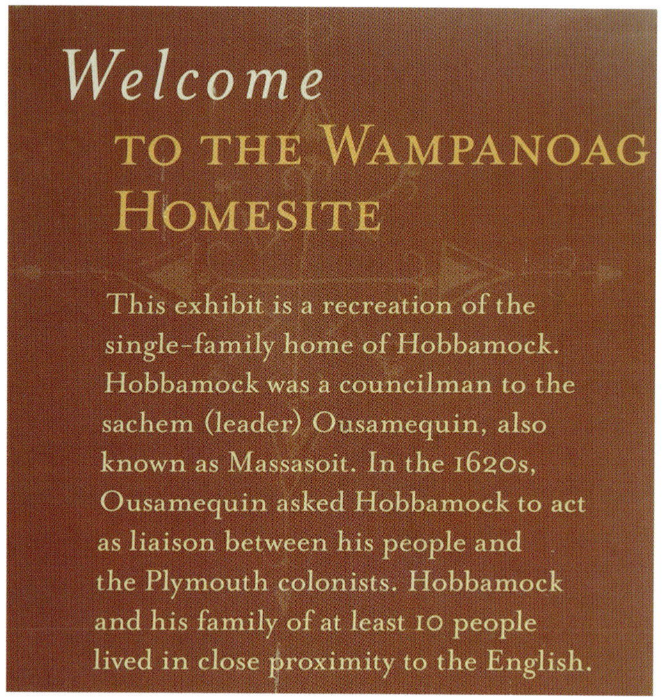

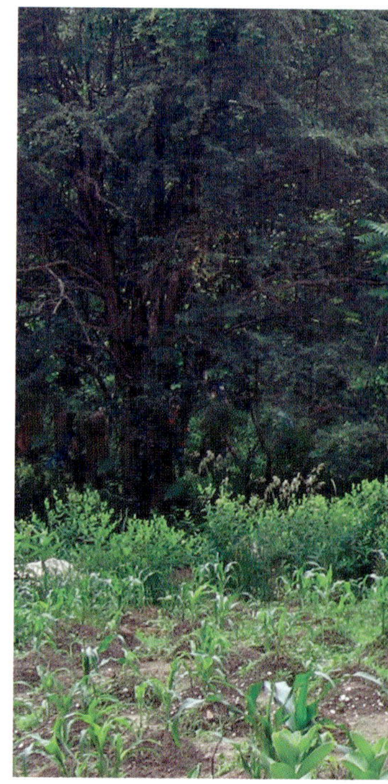

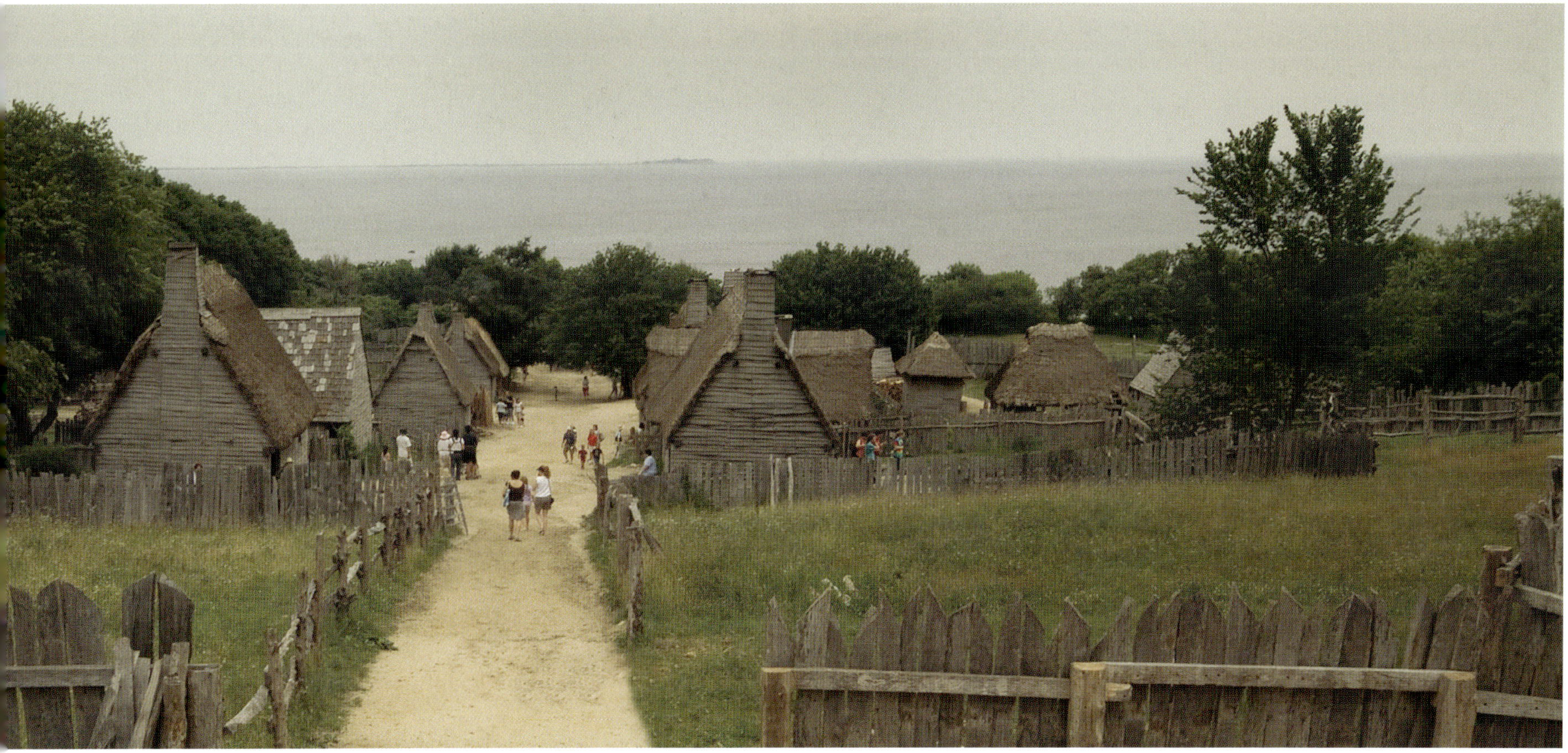

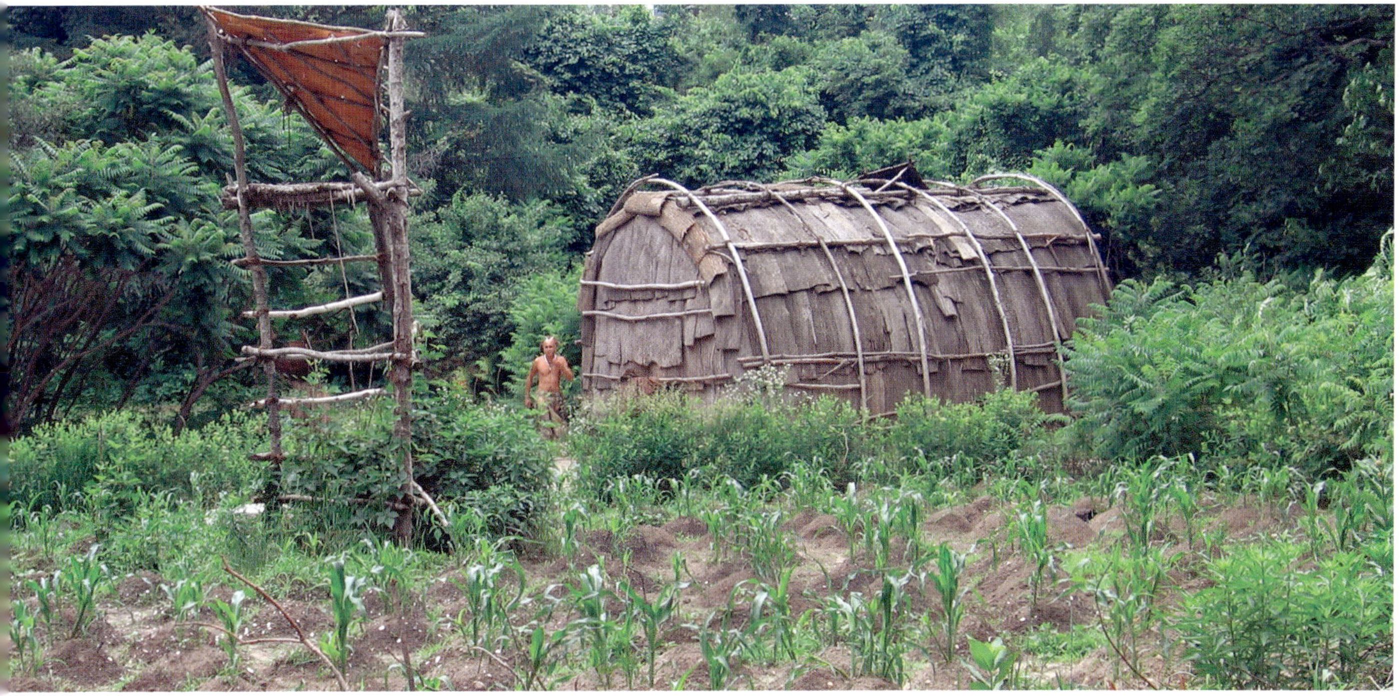

Stepping out of a "nush wetu," the Wampanoag term for a home with three fires, a Wampanoag fisherman overlooks a traditional garden of corn. The tall structure in the middle is called a "corn watch," where children would sit and toss stones to frighten off animals.

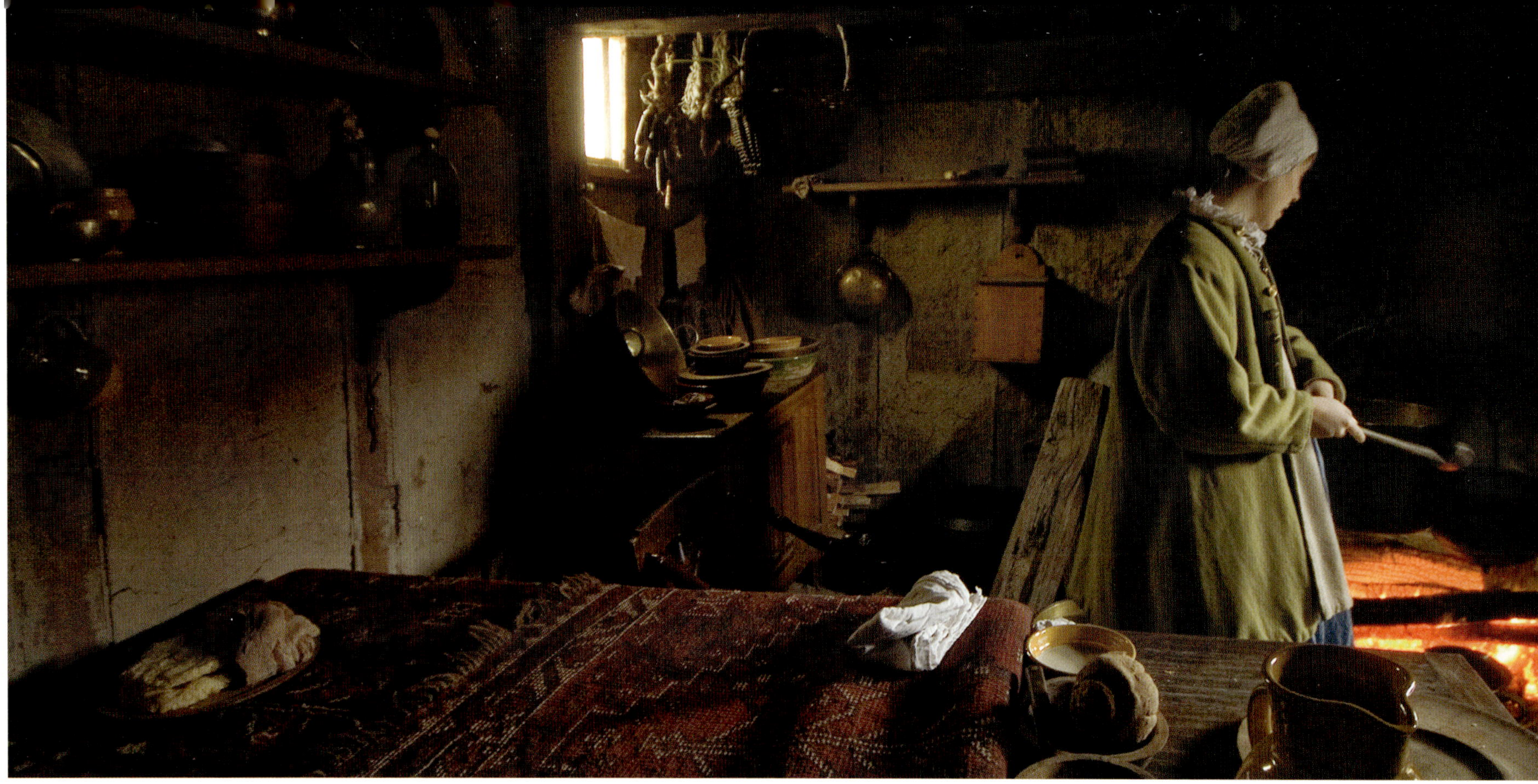

A hearth fire cooks and warms this 17th century English home.

A fire was an important element in each village at Plimoth Plantation.

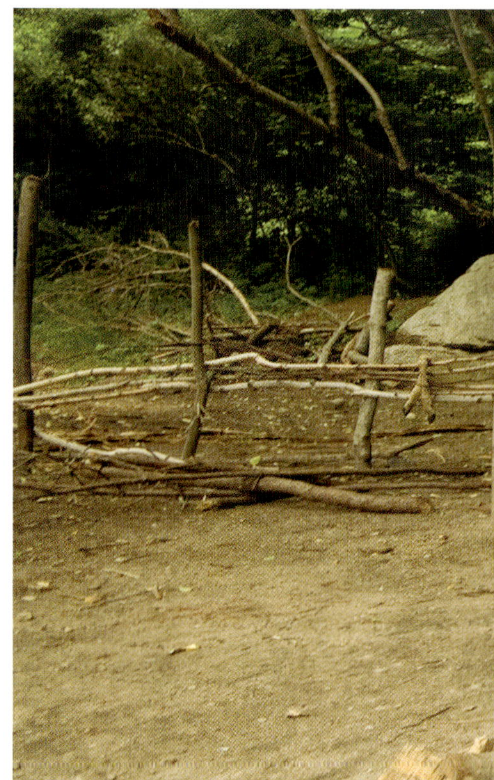

For Wampanoag women, cooking on an open fire, was also a time for socializing.

Gardening was an important activity in each village. It was only through the aid and assistance of the local Wampanoags that the Pilgrims were able to survive in the New World. The food was cooked over open fires.

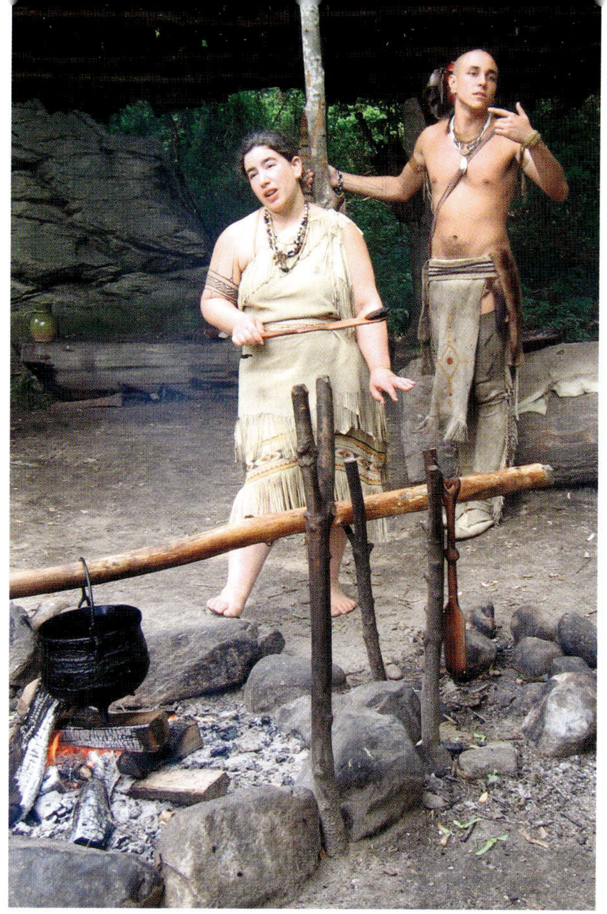

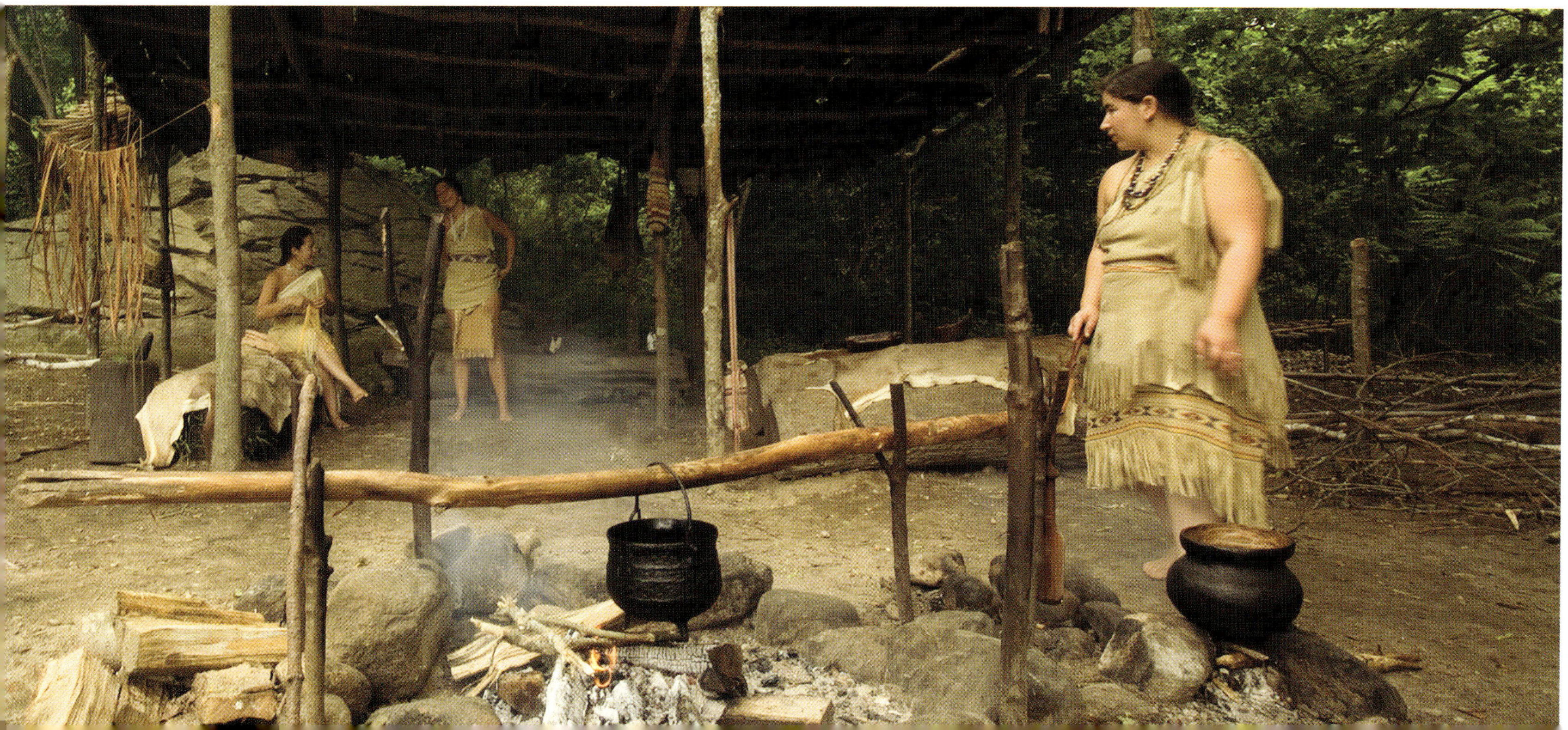

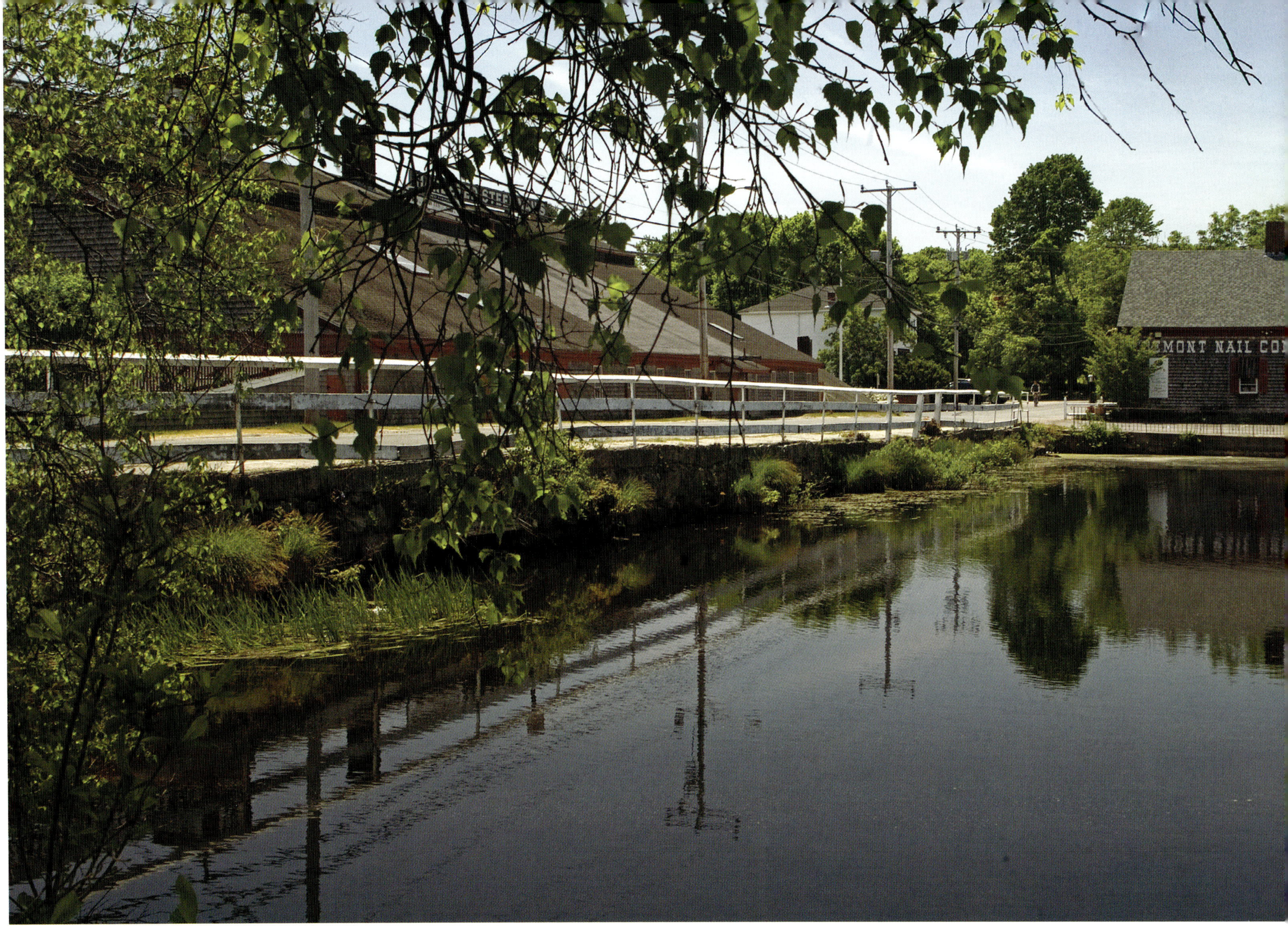

The Tremont Nail Factory in Wareham, was established in 1819, and is one of the earliest continuous manufacturing plants in America. Until the 1920s, power for the plant was provided by the water in the foreground. Even today, the nails produced here are of superior quality and sold worldwide.

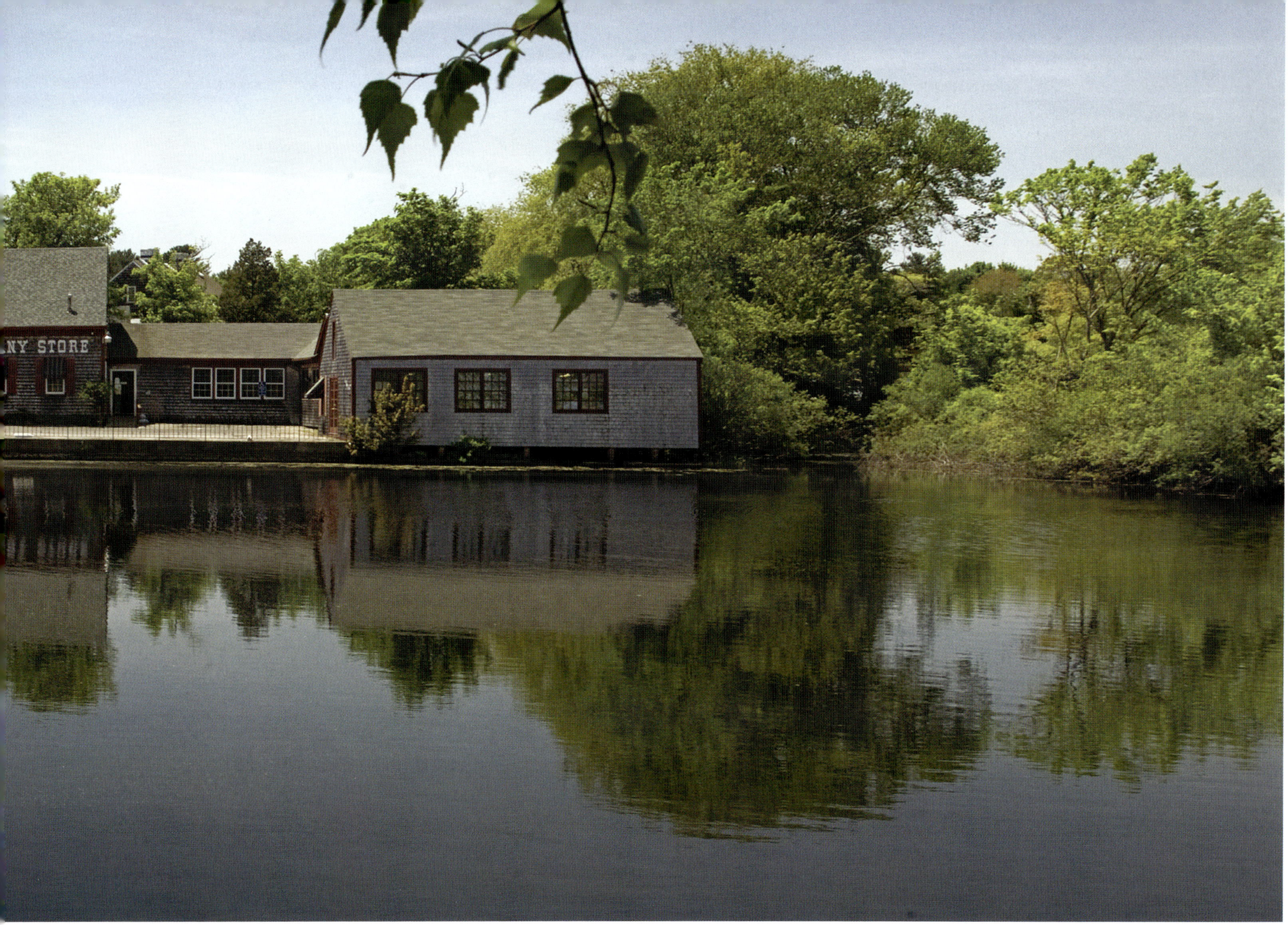
NY STORE

Ellisville Harbor State Park is a shoreline park with a salt marsh, beach front, and a red pine forest. Walking trails, fishing, and picnicking are some of the activities available. Evidence of pre-historic Native Americans shows that more than 2500 years ago, they hunted, fished and made tools in the vicinity.

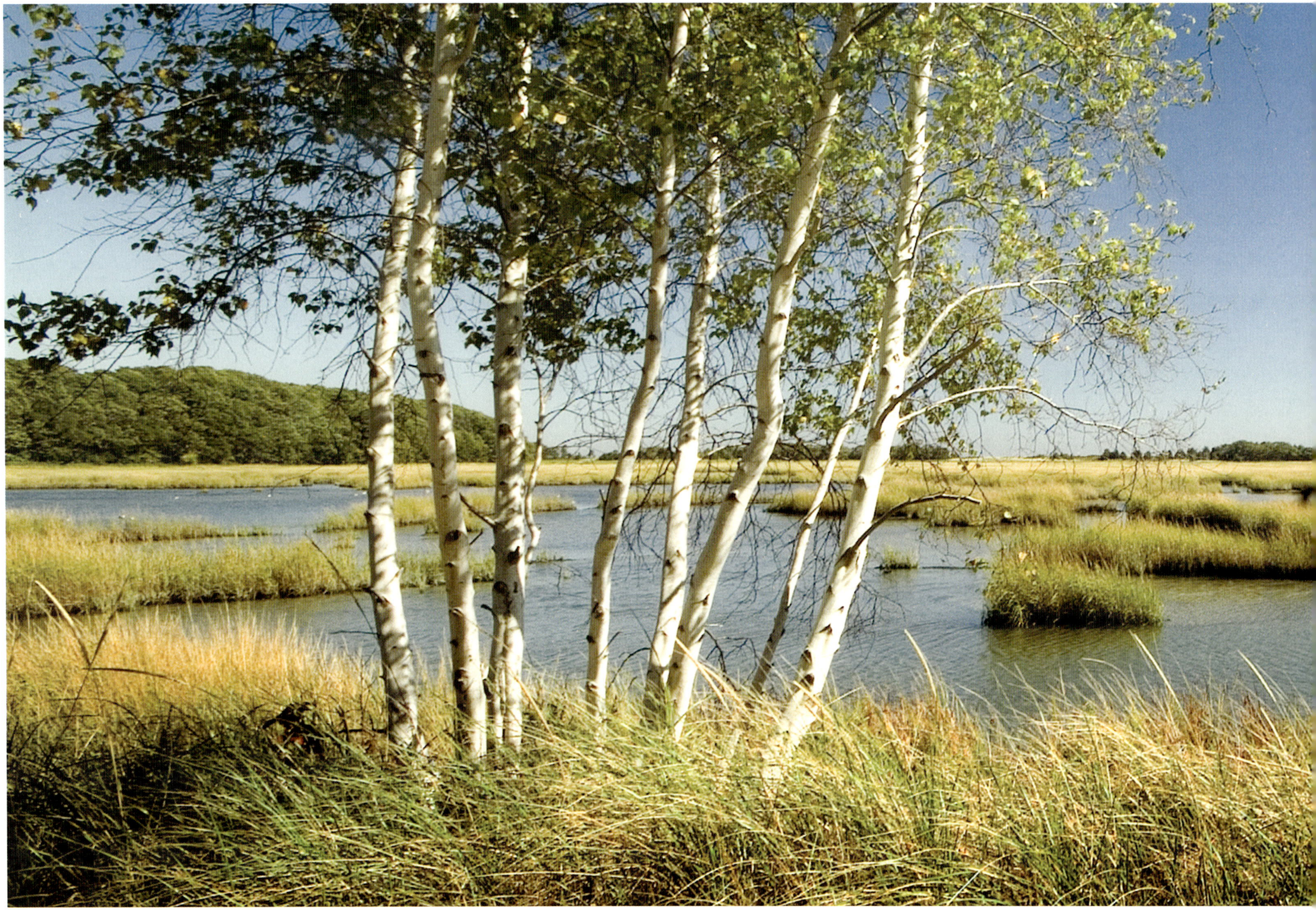

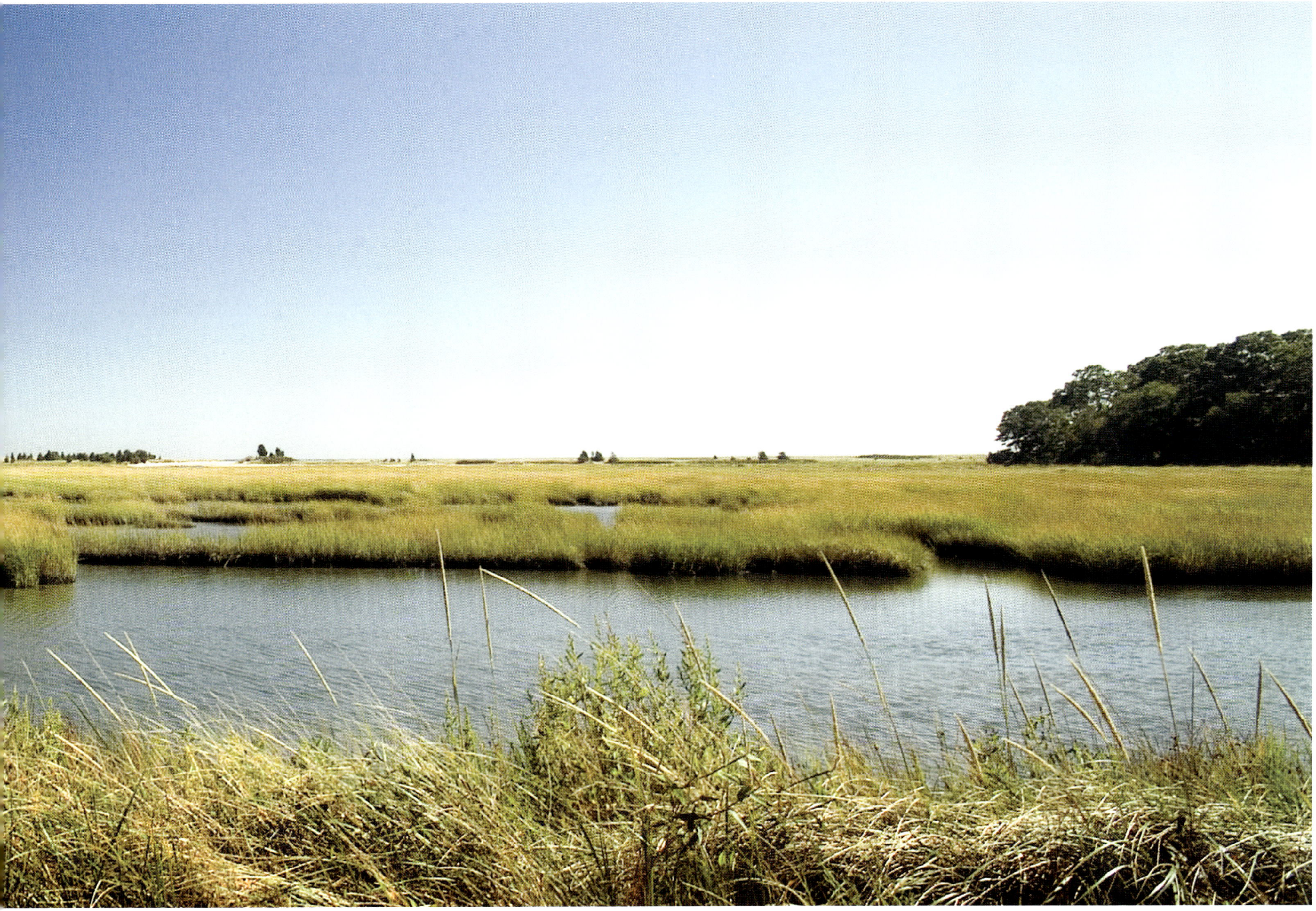

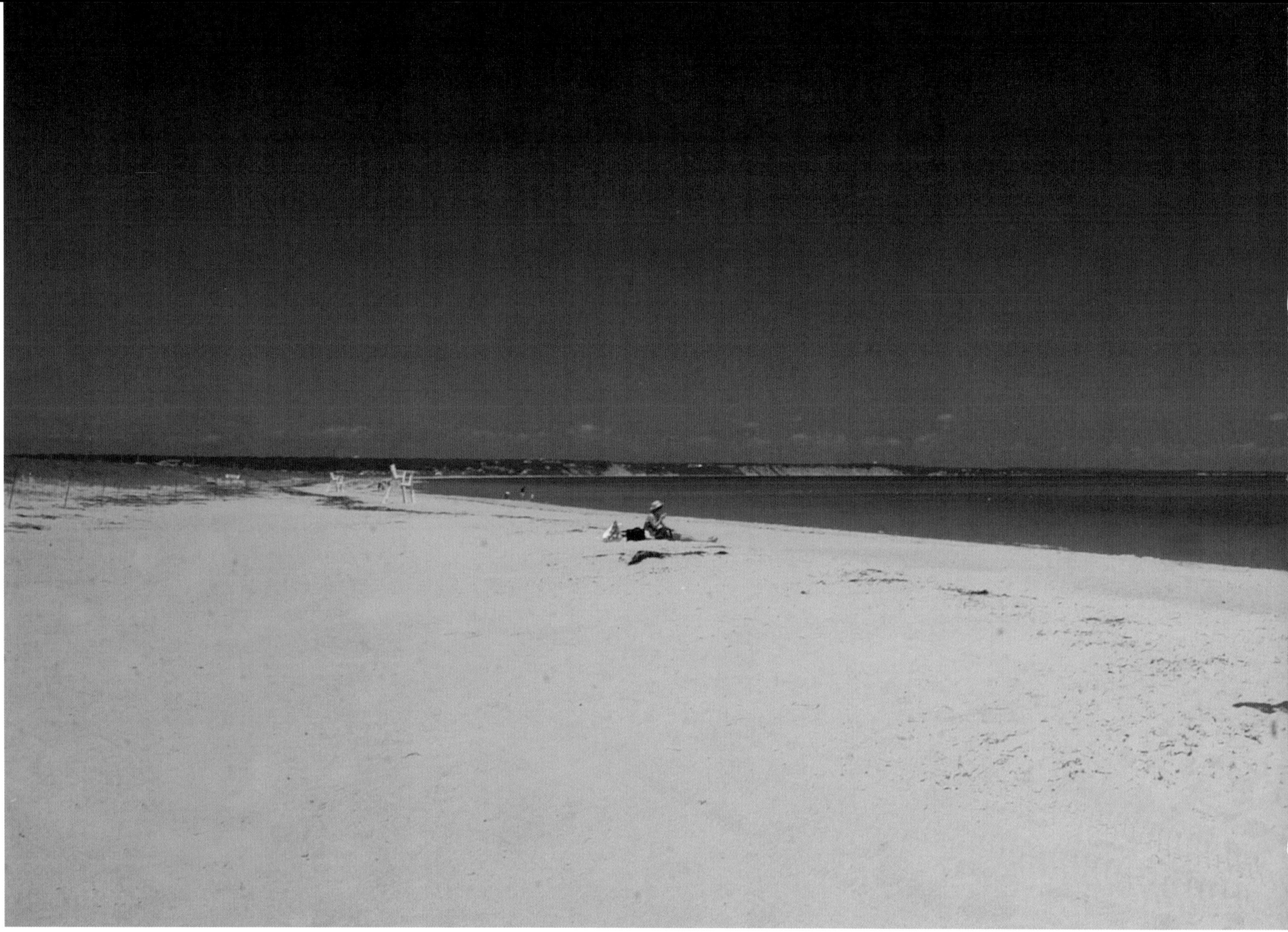

The shore at Scusset Beach State Park, looking north towards Ellisville. This park, on Cape Cod Bay, is located at the east end of the Canal, and in addition to the beach also has a fishing pier, almost 100 campsites, bicycle and walking trails.

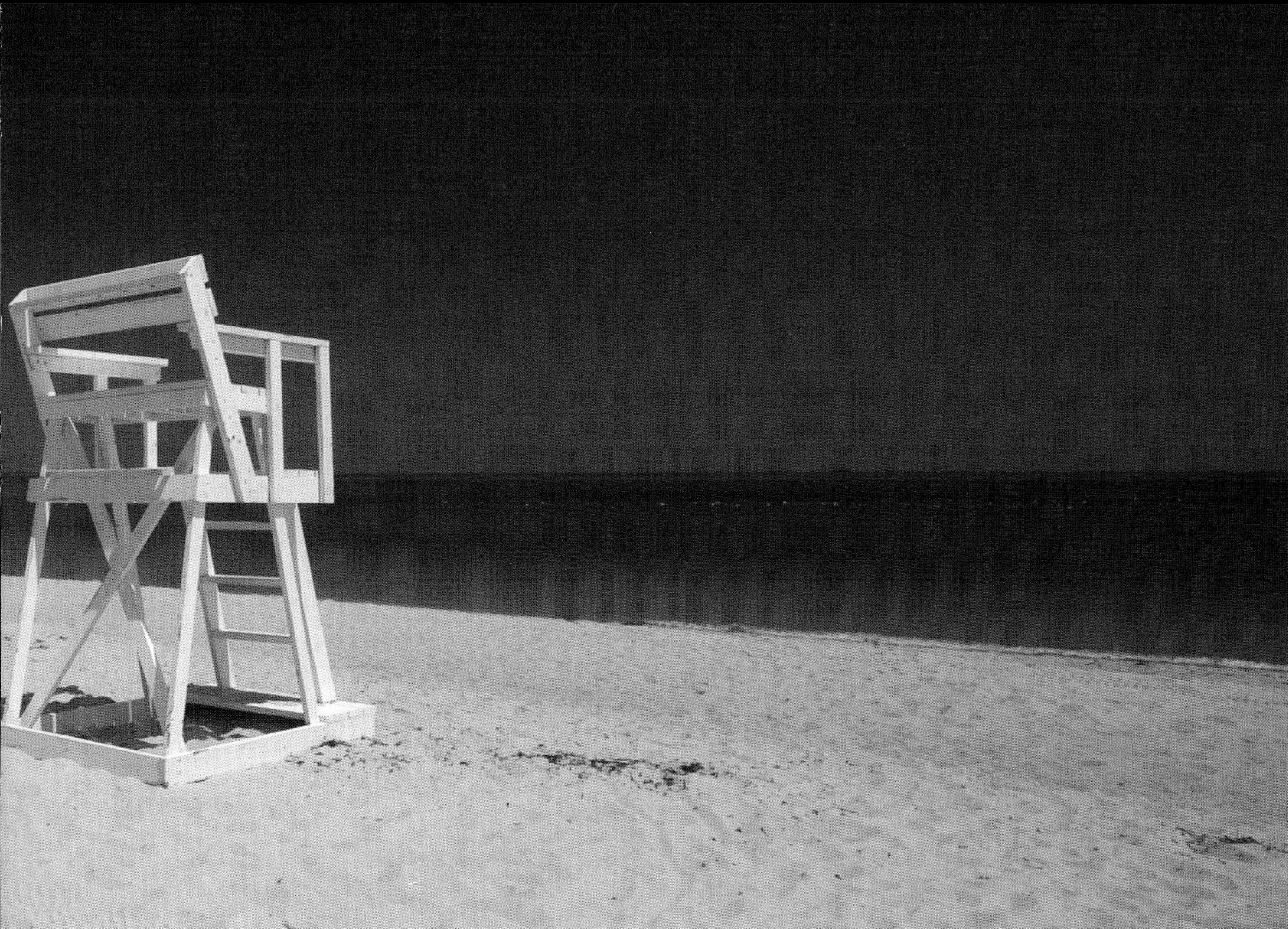

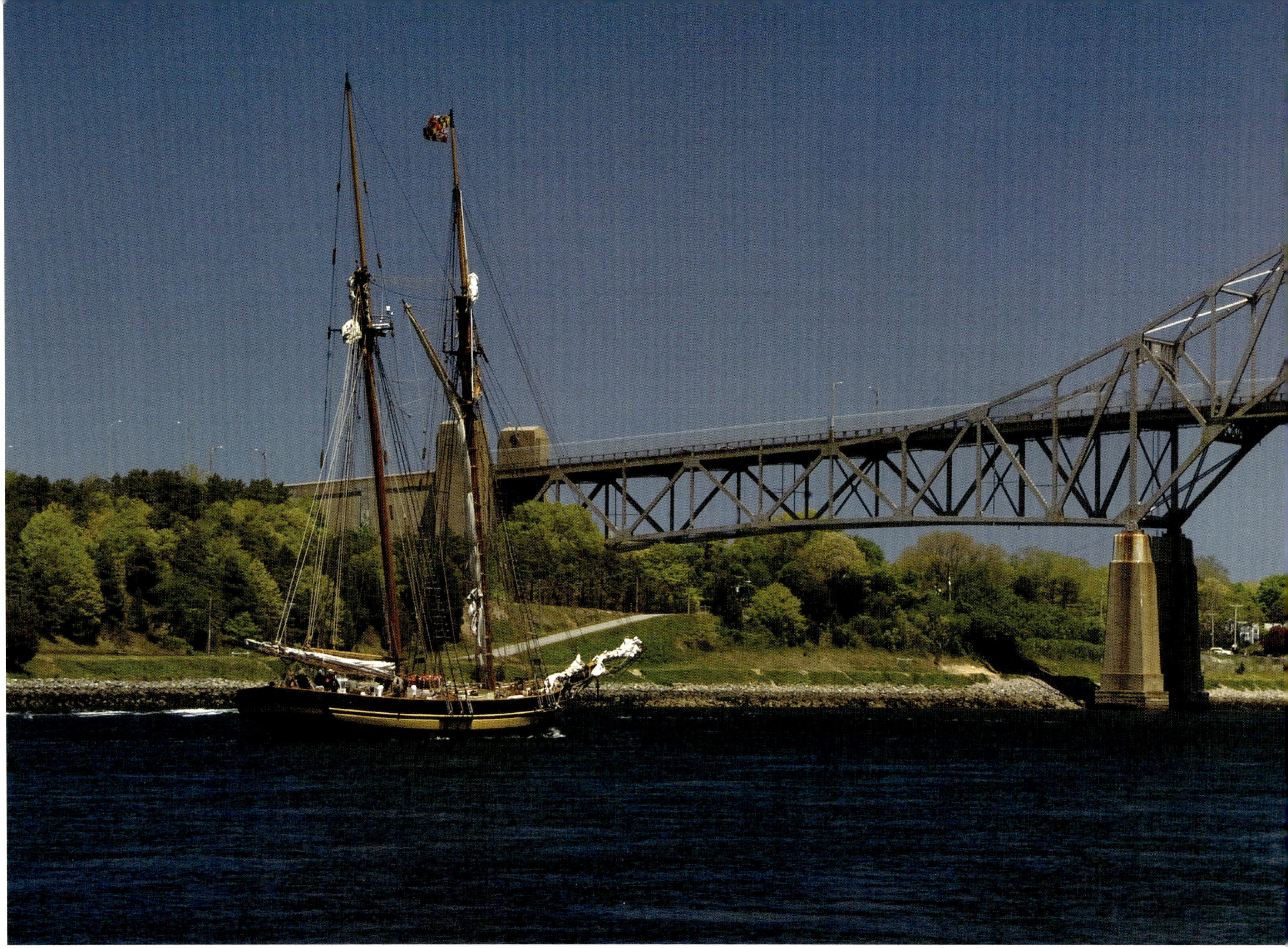

With the Sagamore Bridge in the background and looking north, a sailboat, using power navigates the Cape Cod Canal.

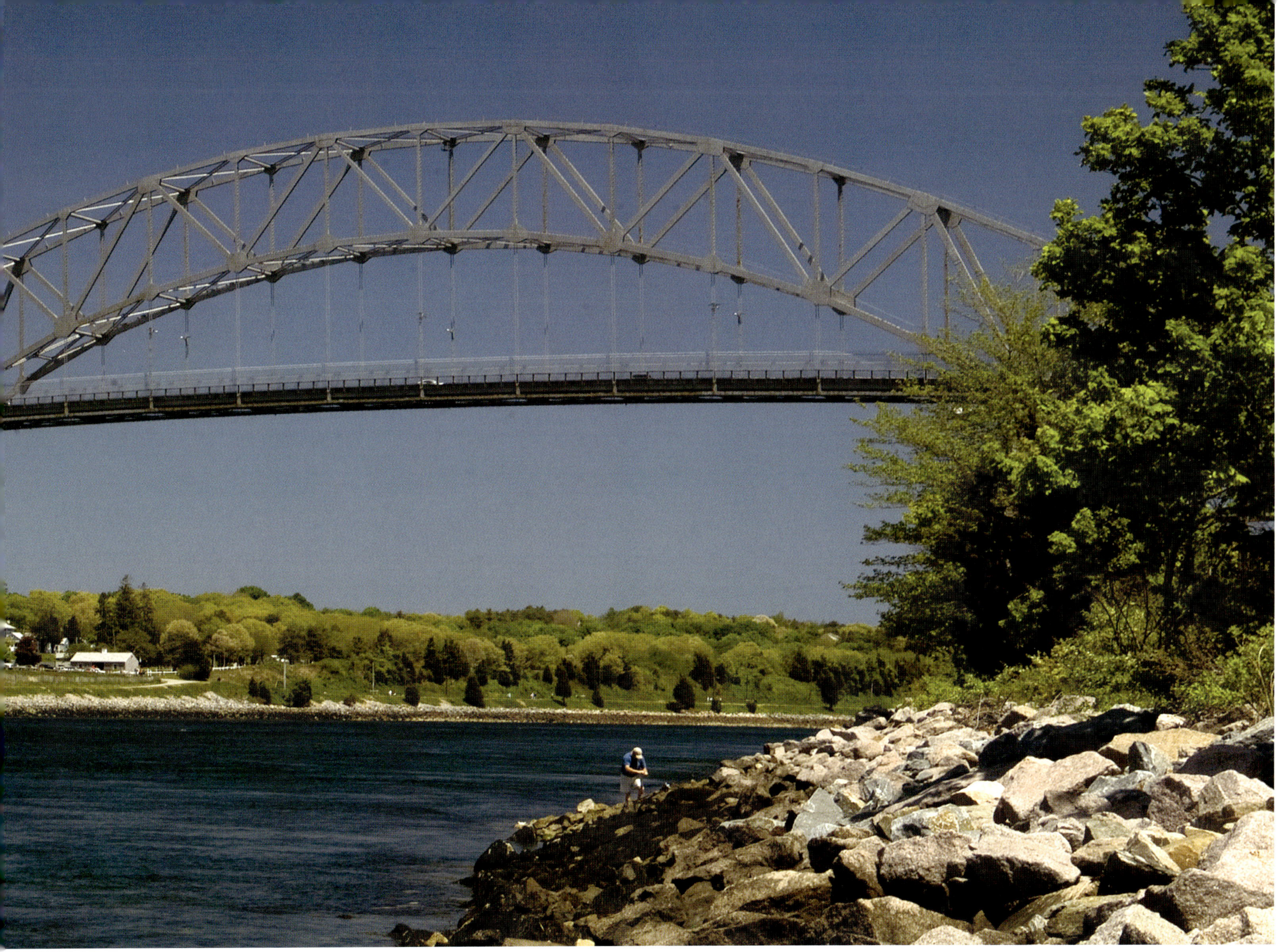

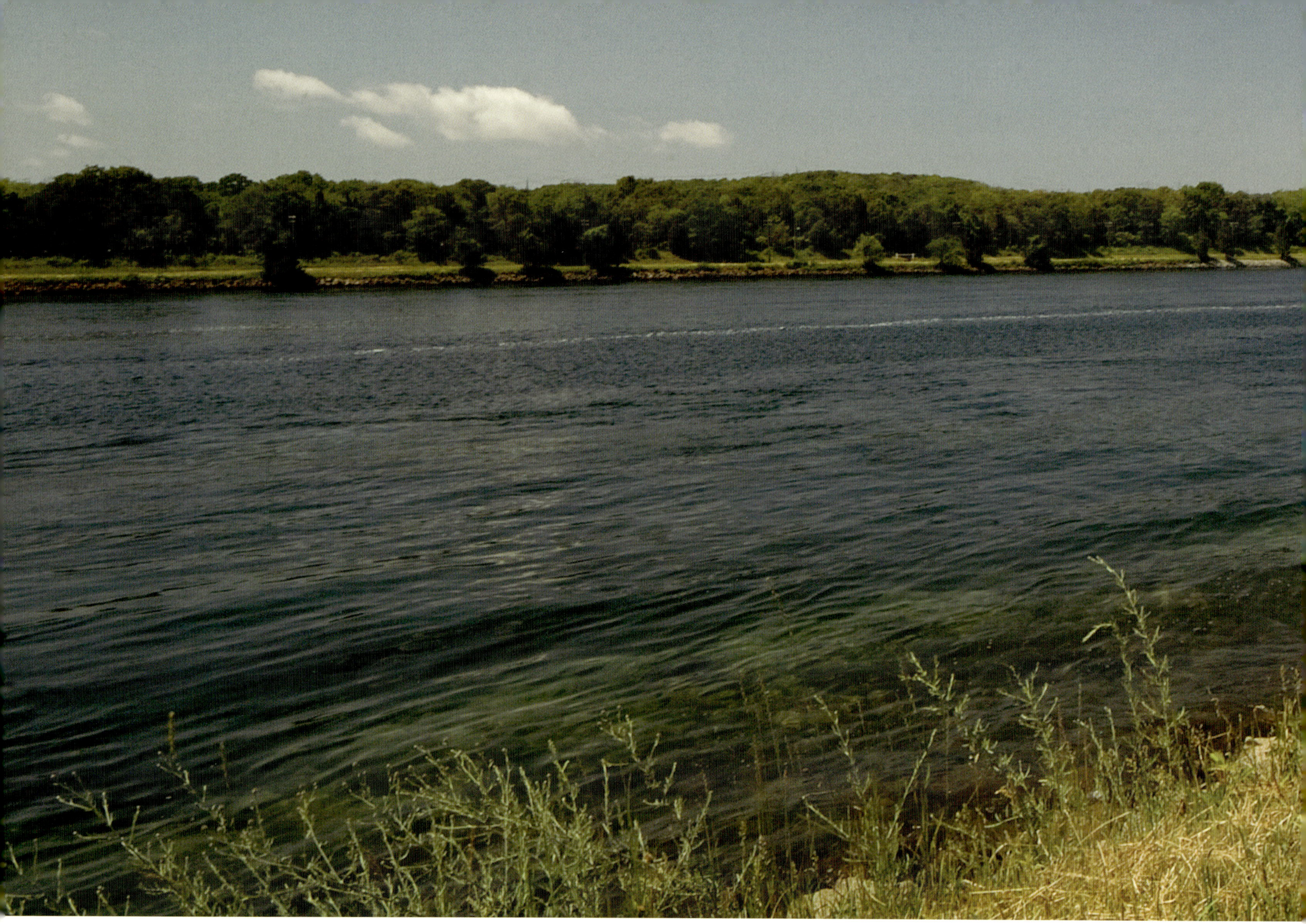

Salty Dog, in the foreground, and Morgan, watch for boats passing through the Canal.

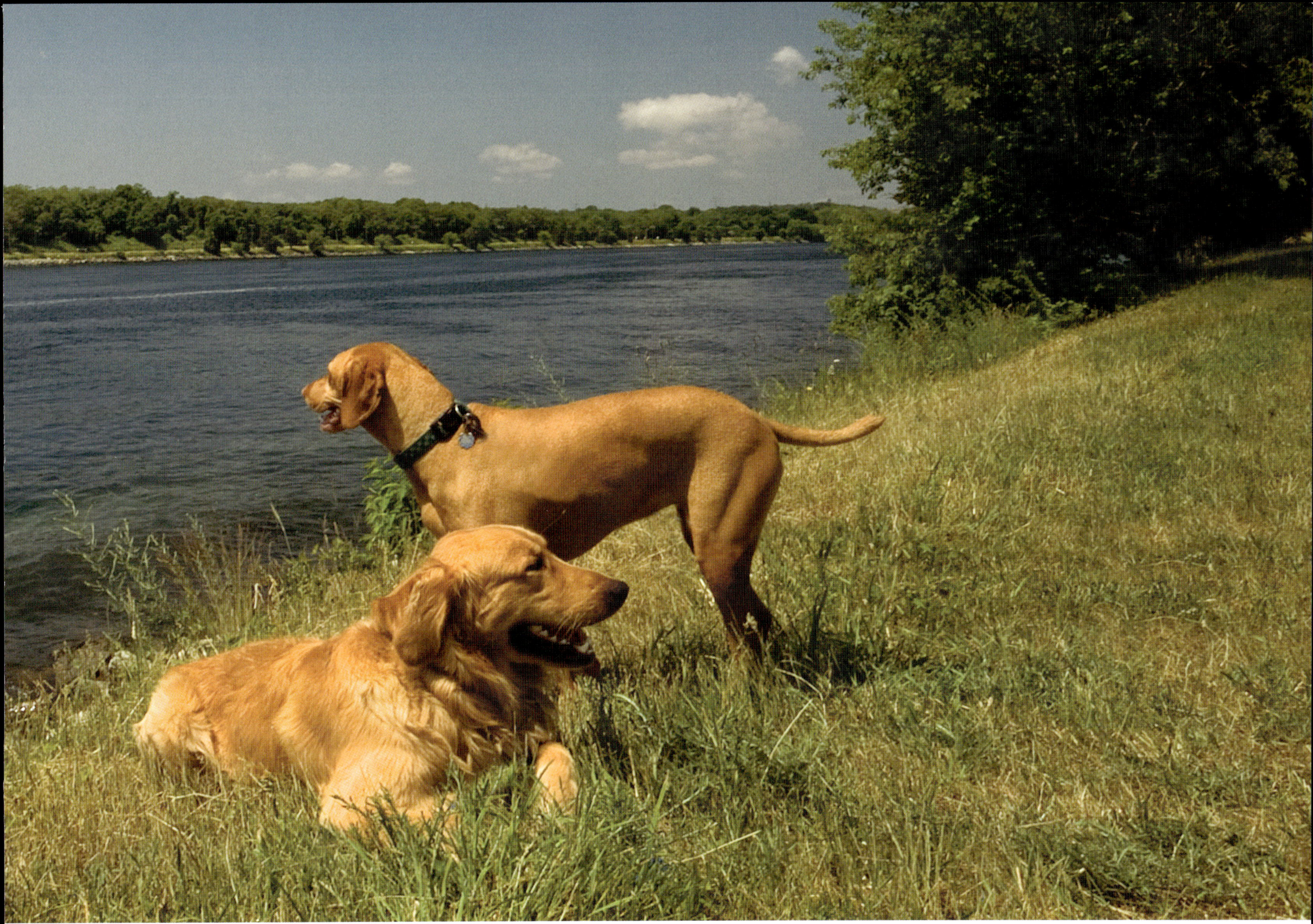

WINTER MEDLEY

Throughout the South Shore, winter brings snow and picturesque scenes.

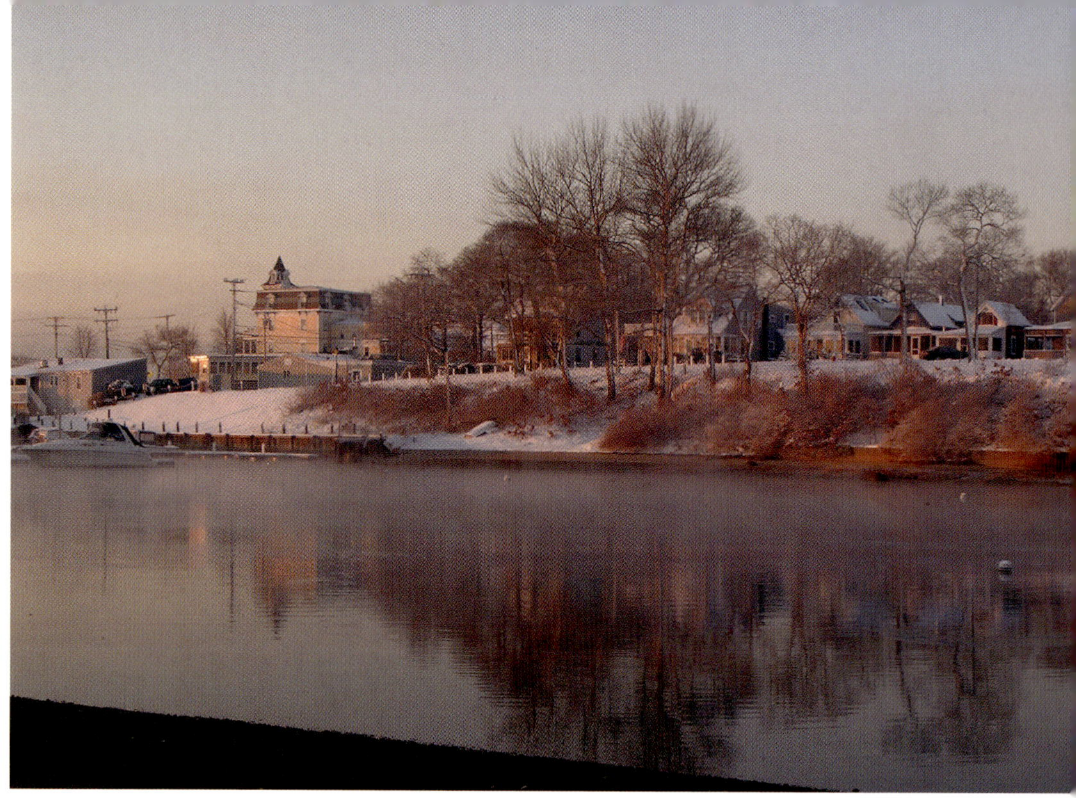

New fallen snow, blankets the ground in Onset.

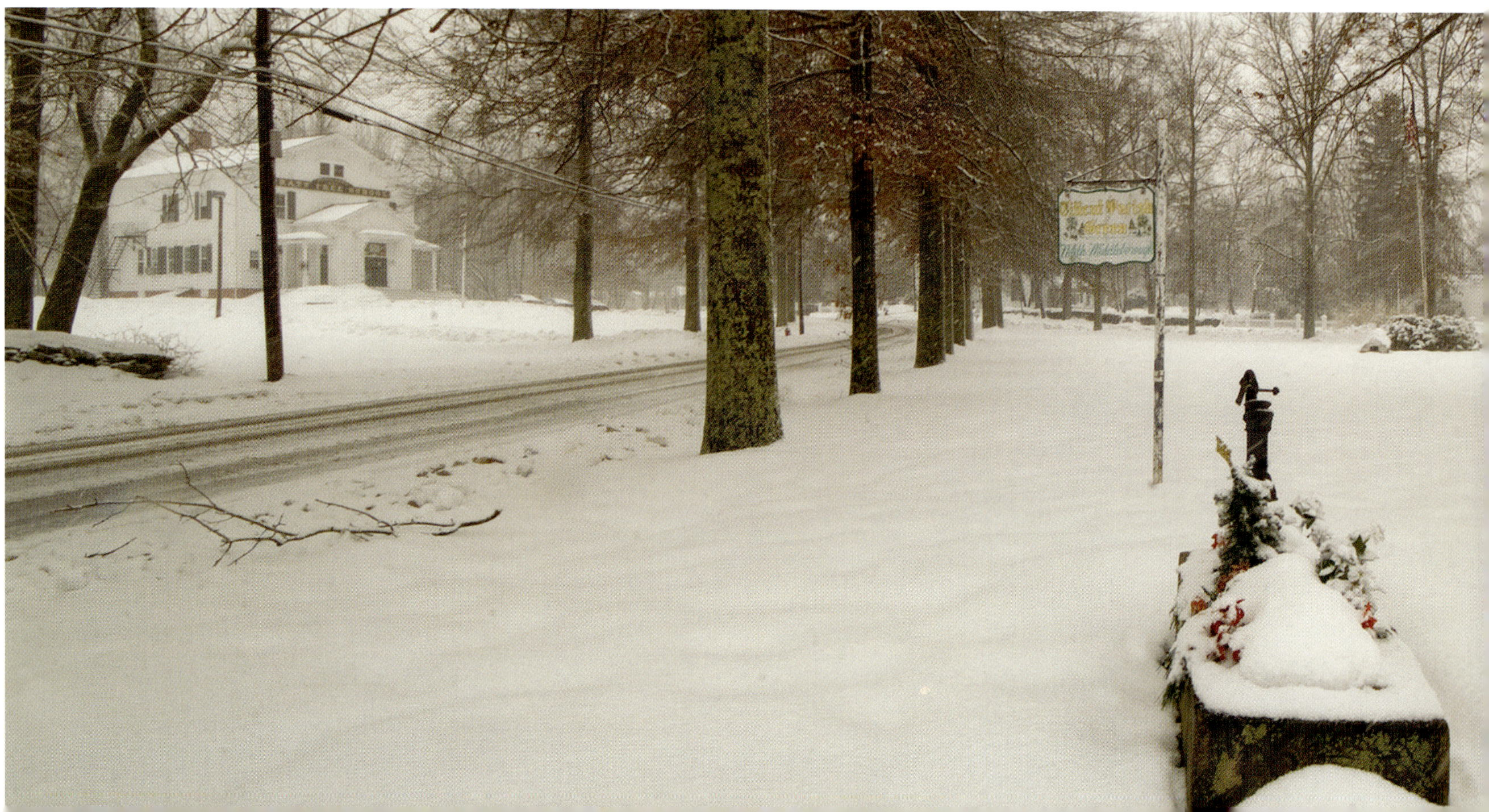

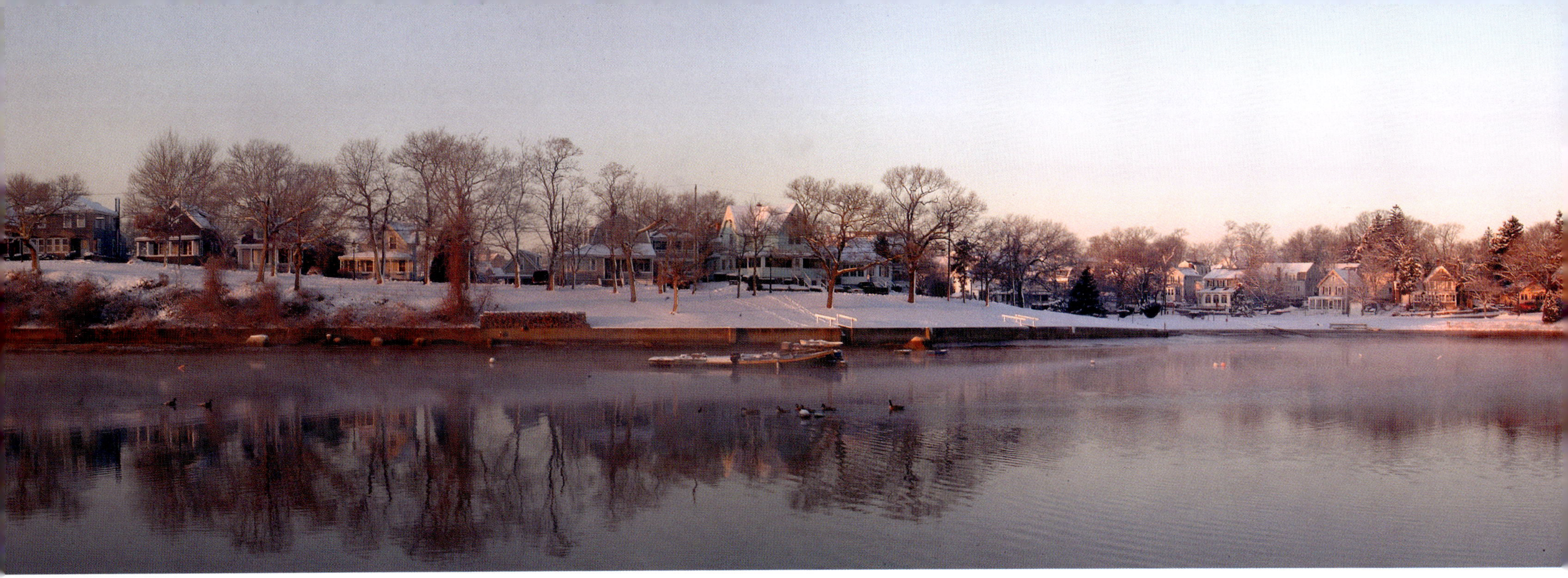

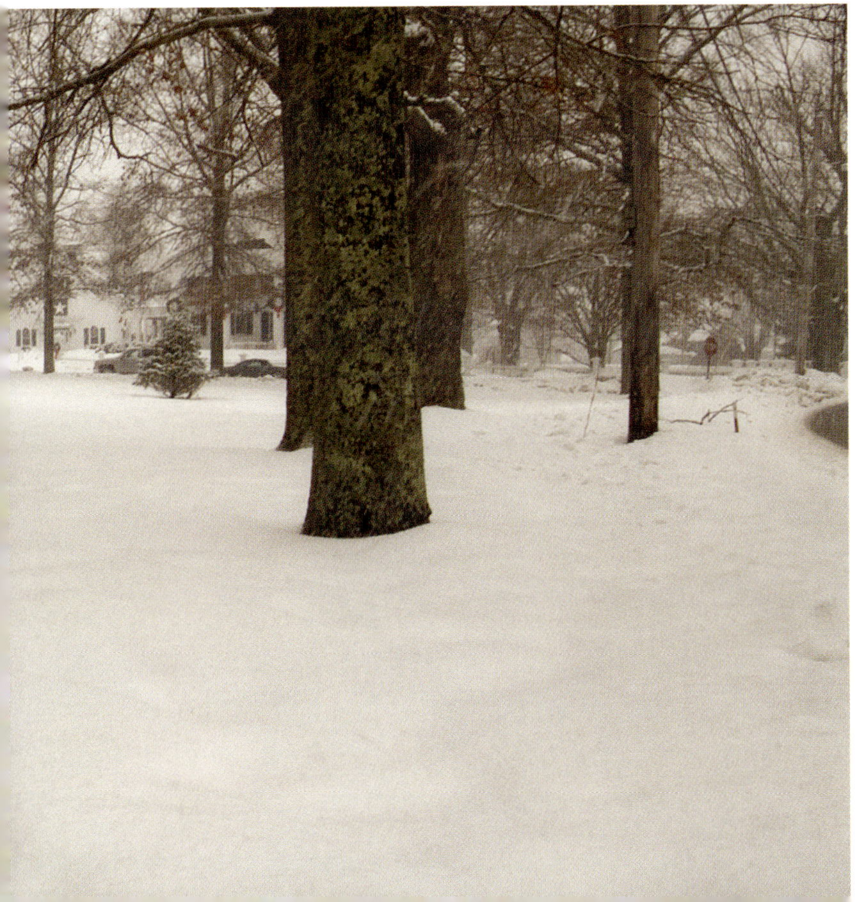

Titicut Parish Green in North Middleborough with the Pratt Free School in the left background.

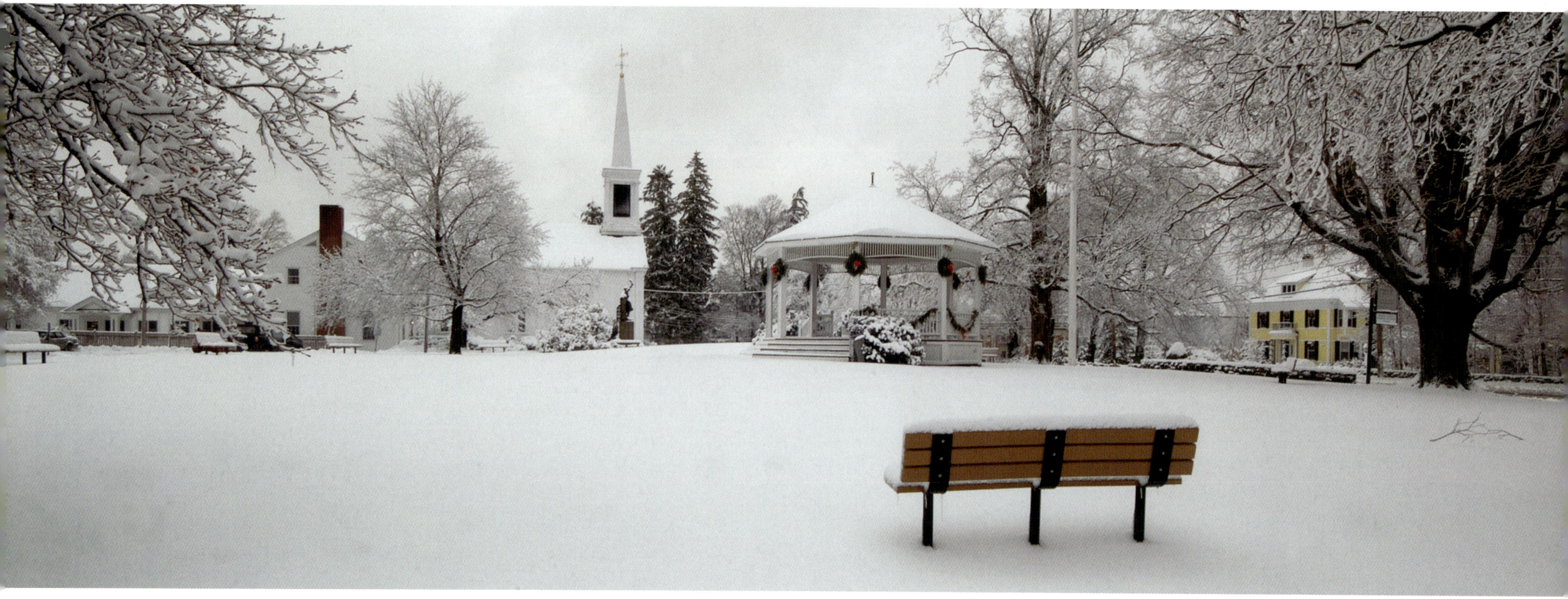

The Milton Town Green, with a classic colonial home across the street.

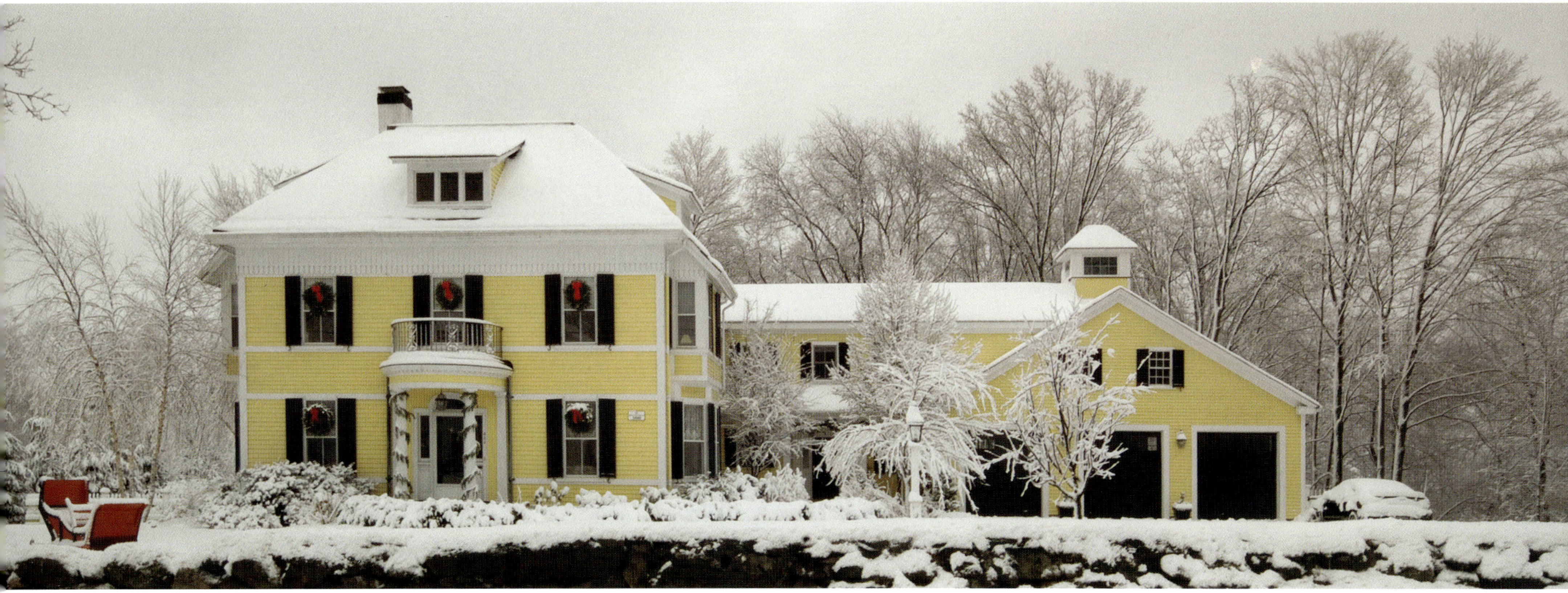

The Scituate Town Green with the Lawson Tower in the background.

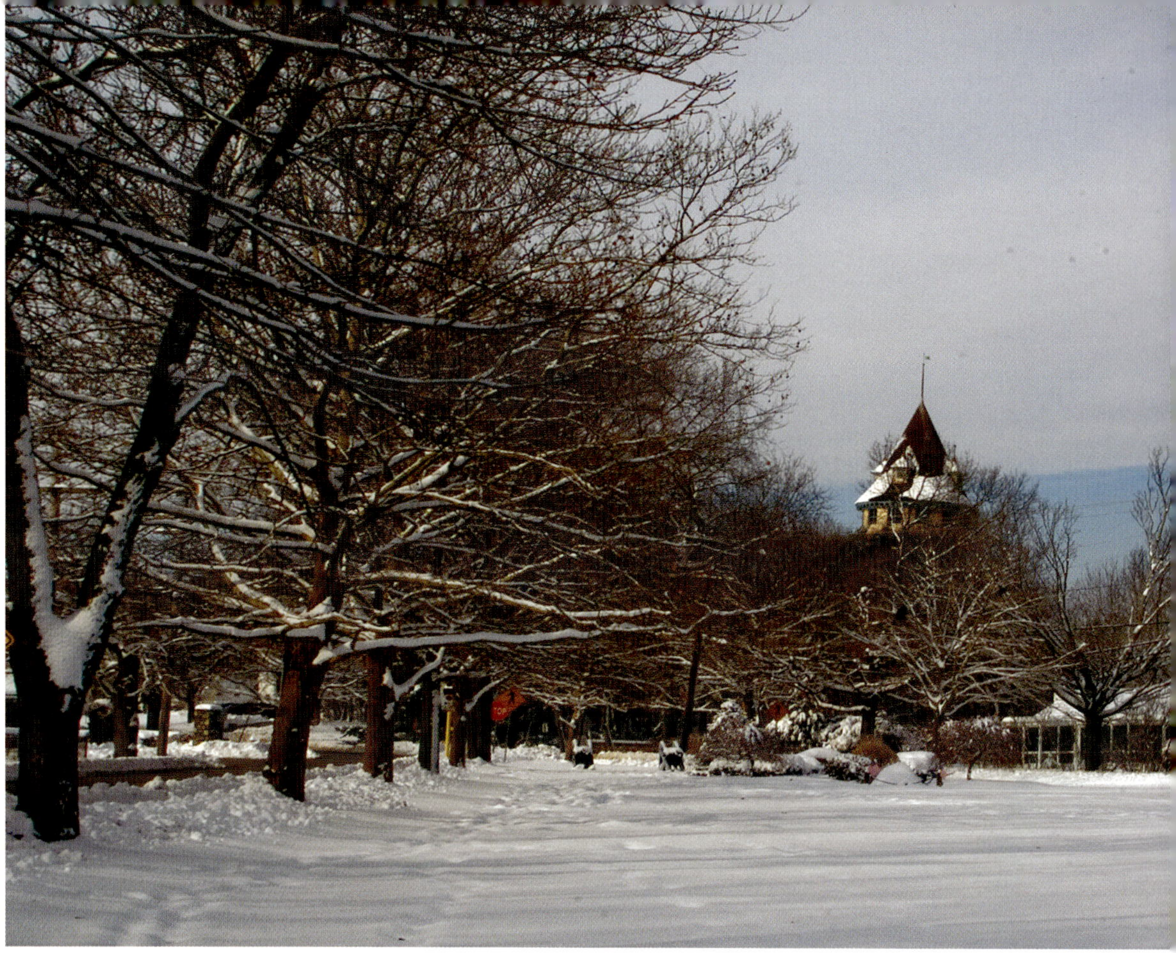

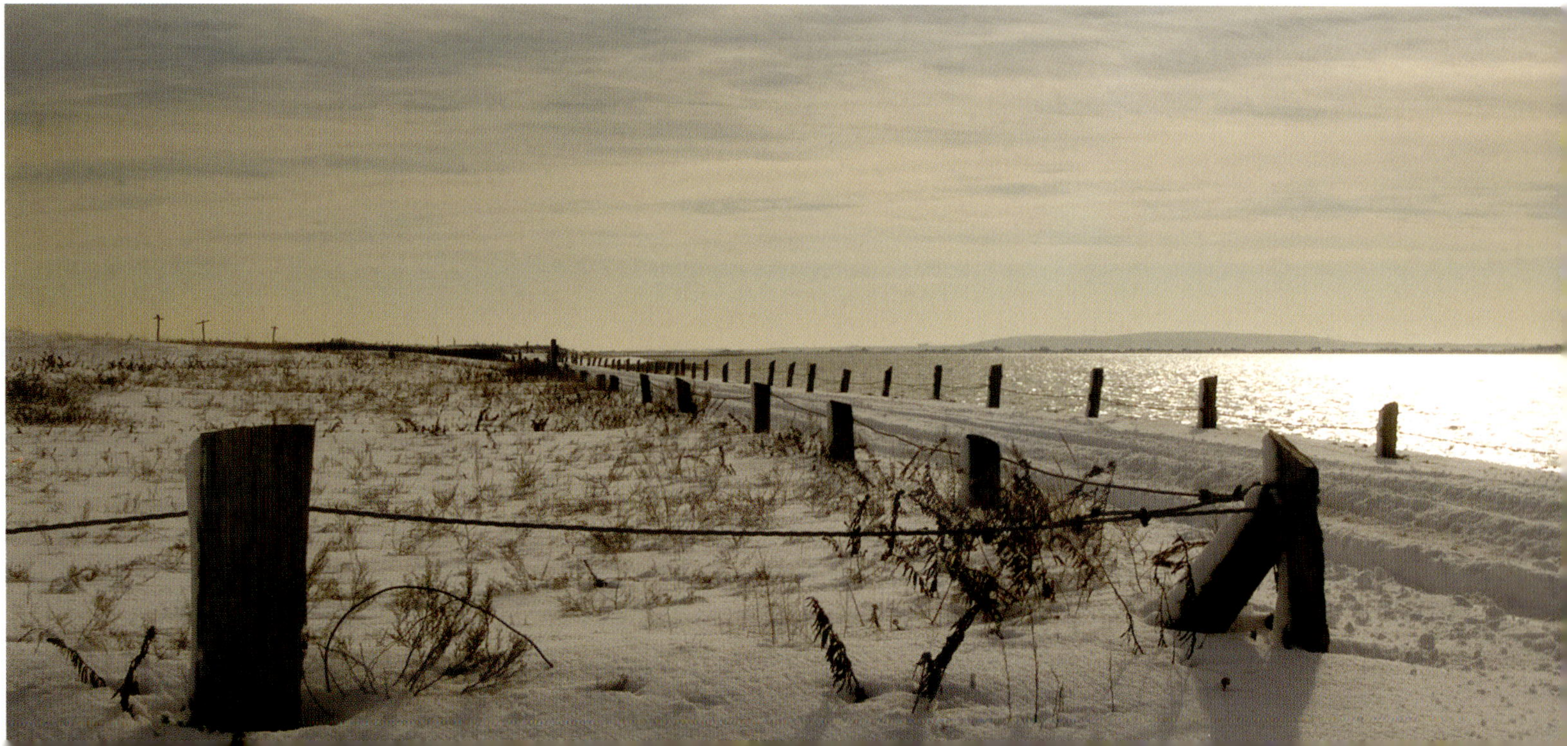

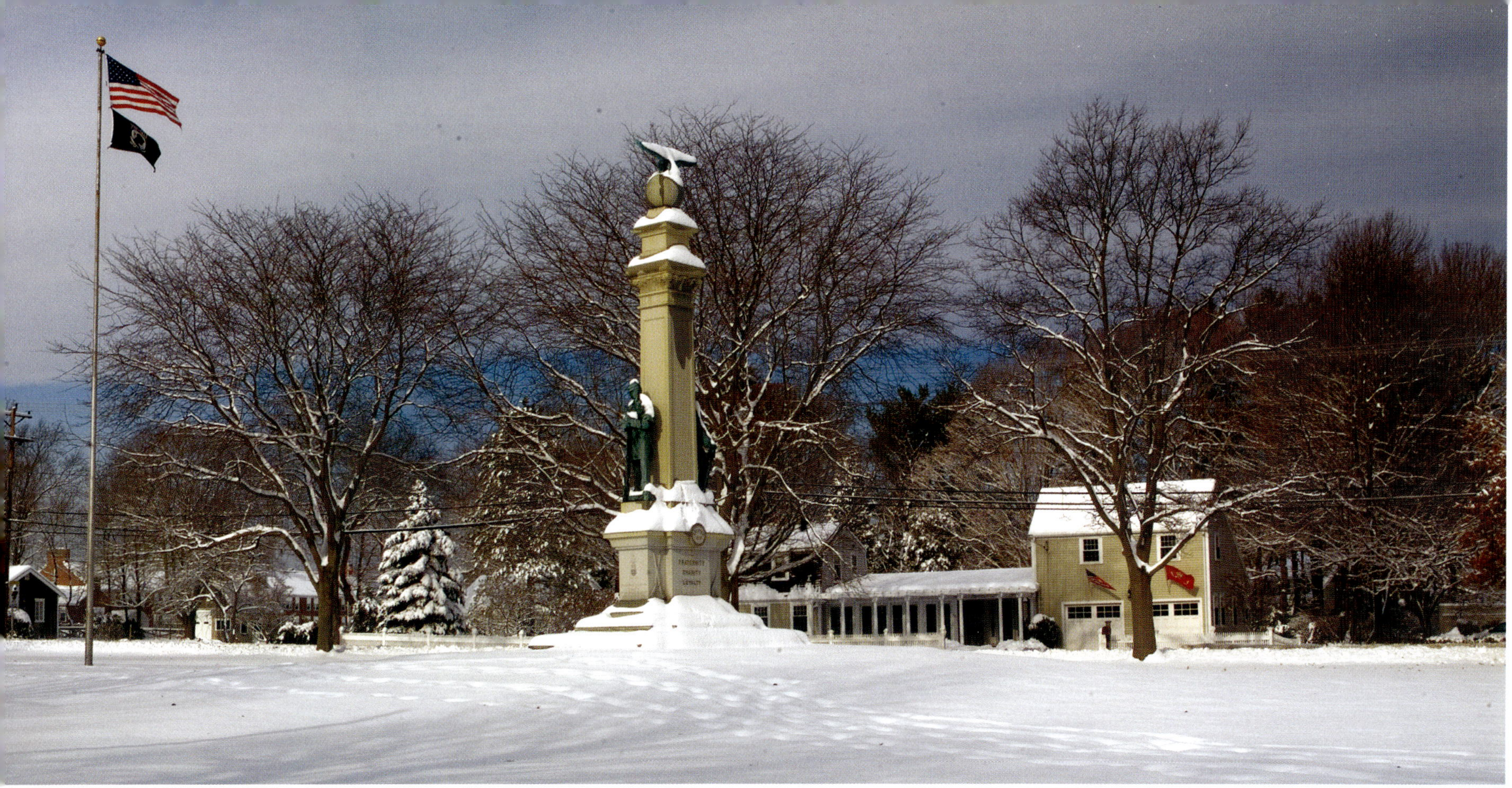

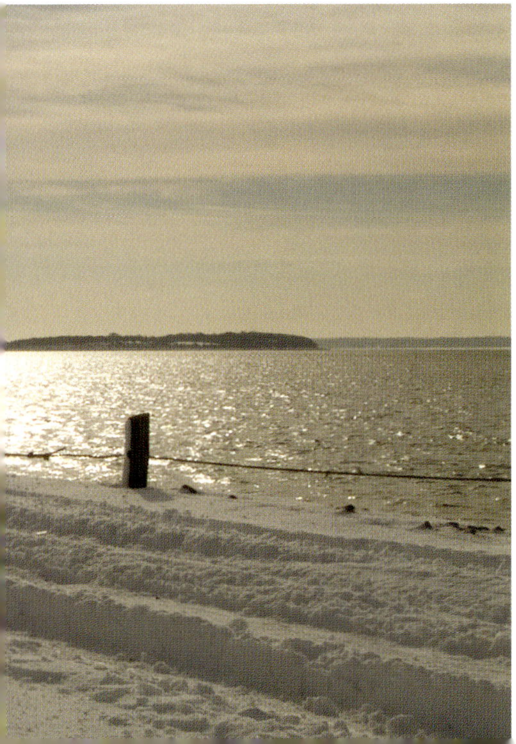

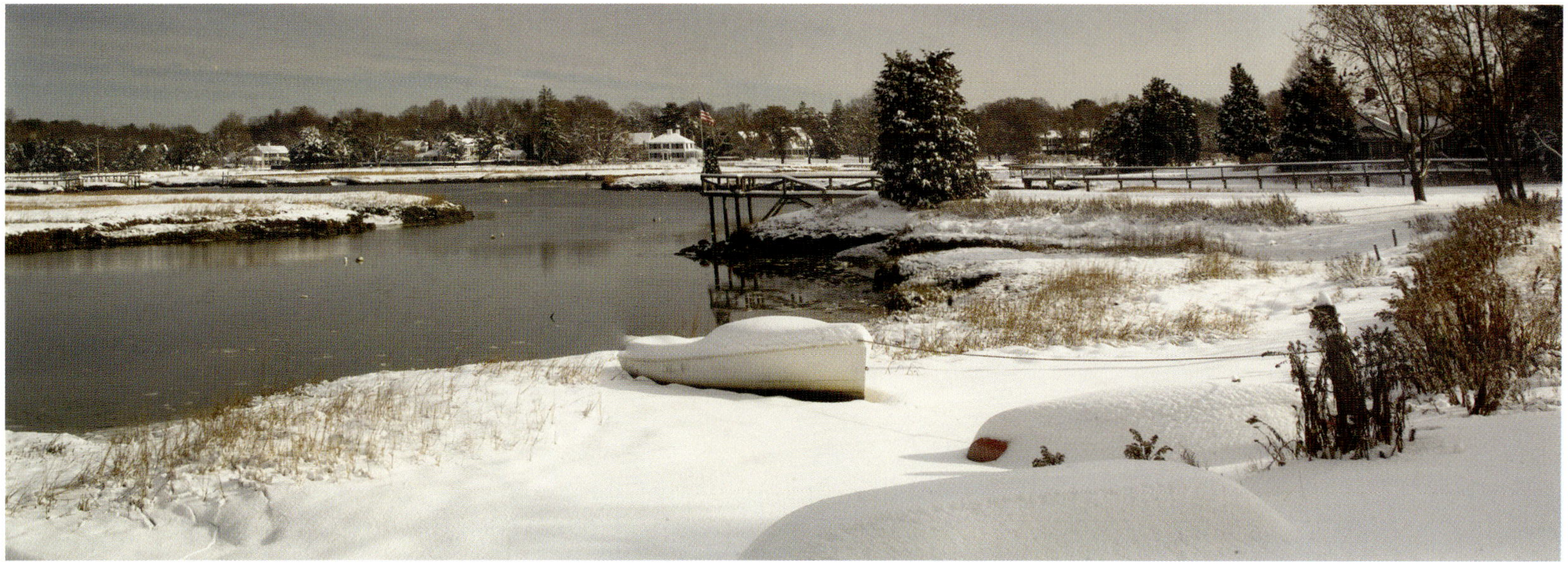

These two scenes of Duxbury show the Gurnet Road on the outer beach, and a snow covered sailboat along the Bluefish River.

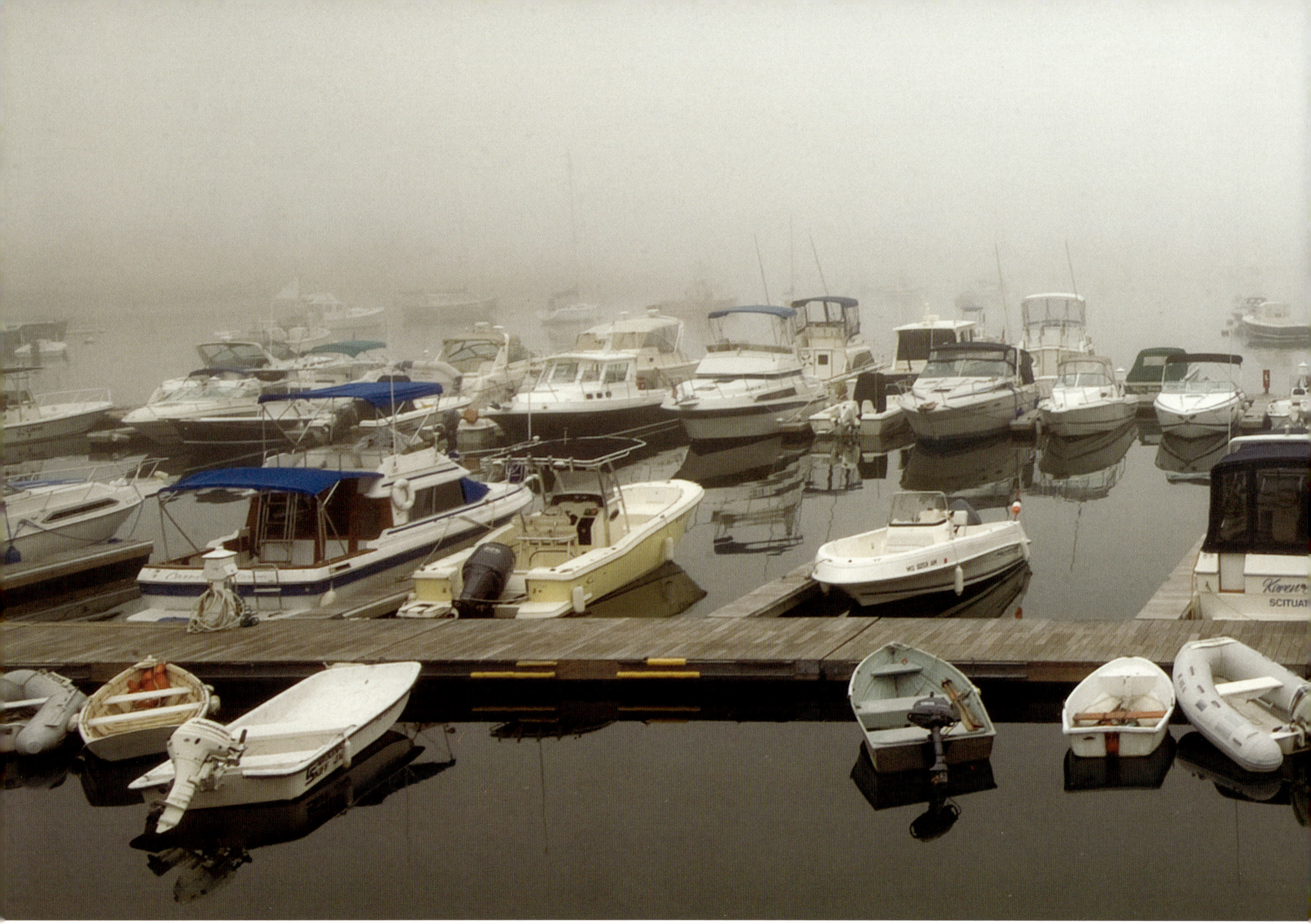

Boats moored in slips in Scituate Harbor.

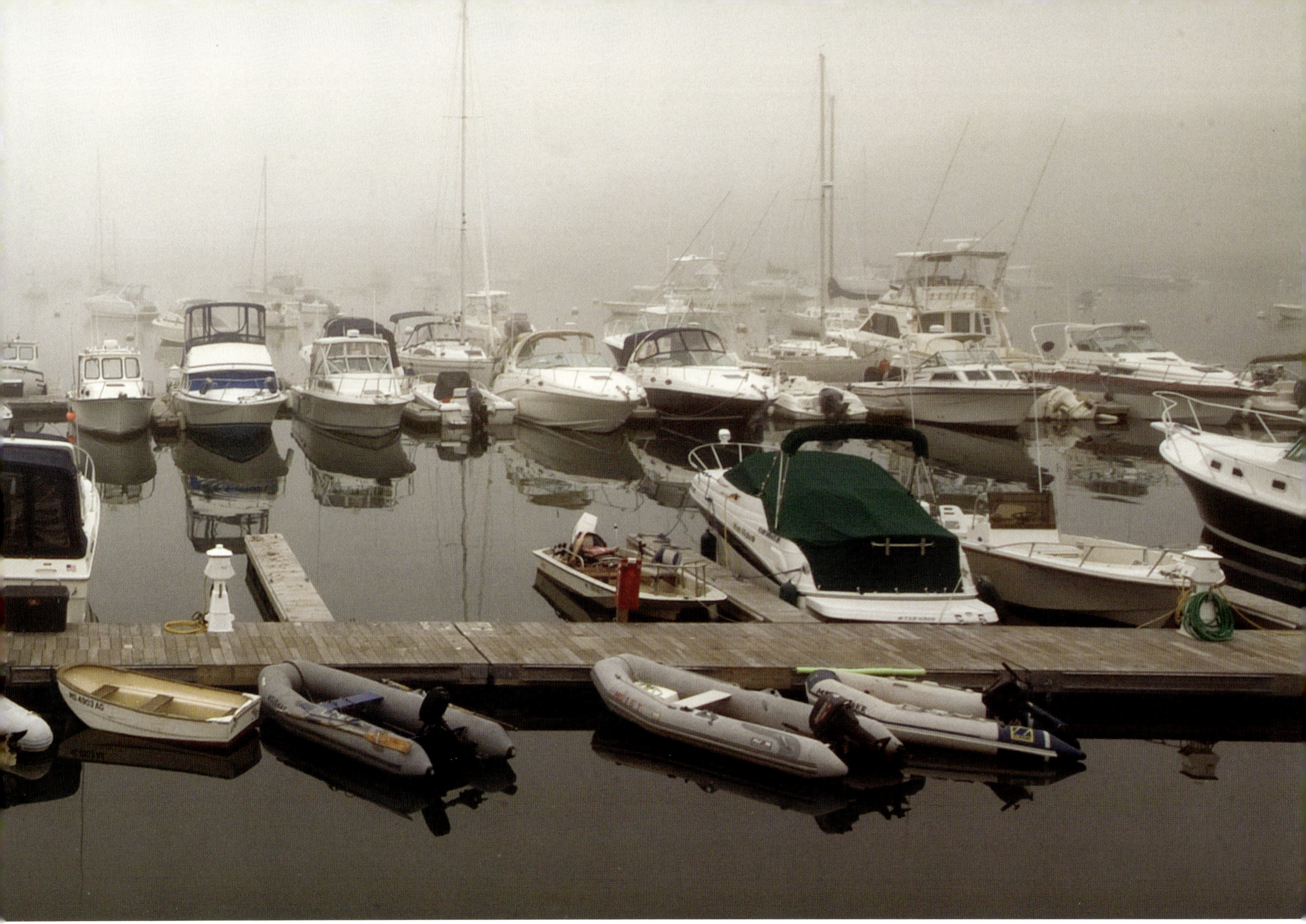

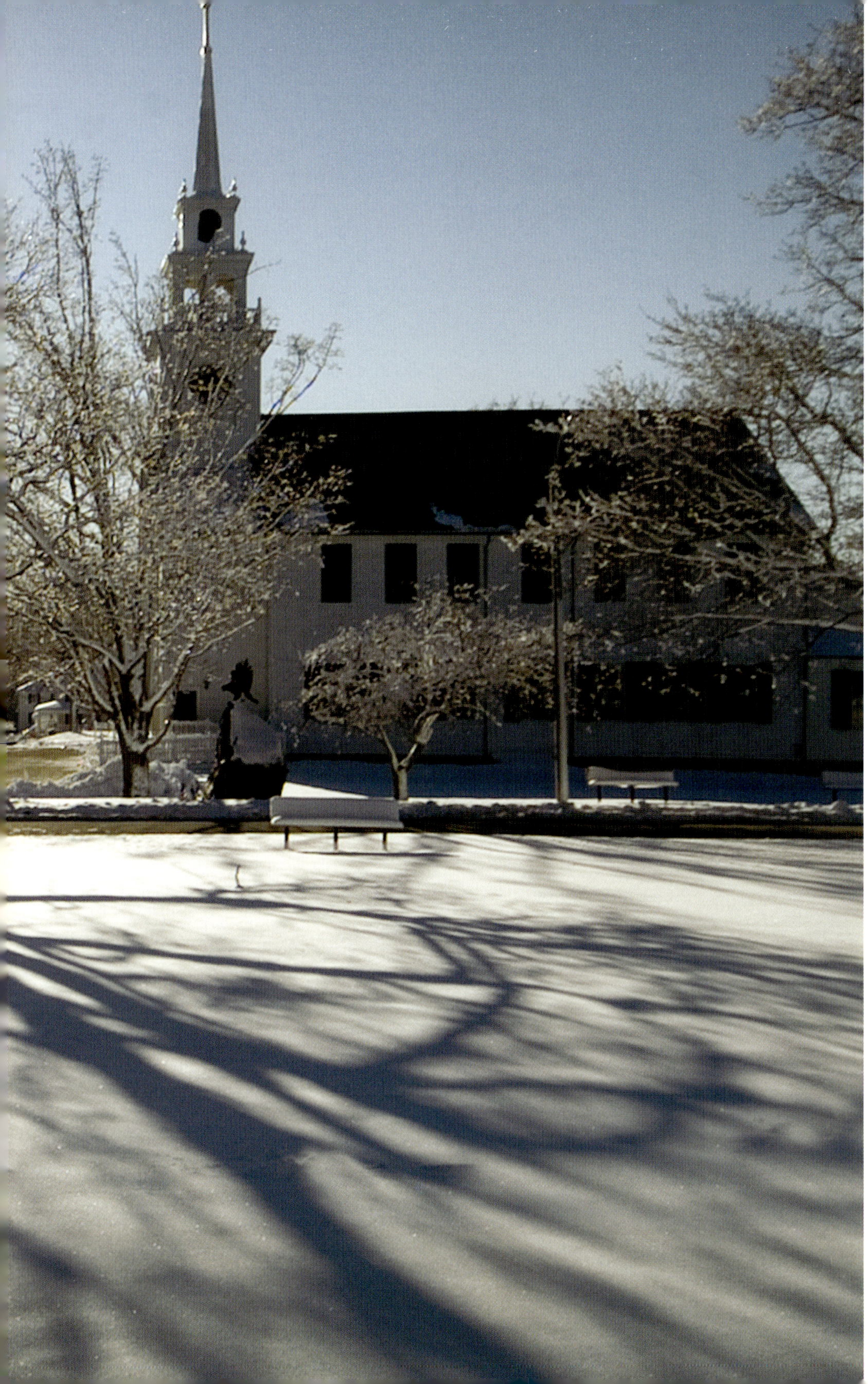

Author's Notes

Any book requires a tremendous amount of work, knowledge, coordination, and the skills of a variety of people involved in the process and that doesn't even include the author/photographer. To have one book published is a success; to be working on the third book in this series is amazing. Well received and highly acclaimed, *Cape Cod Wide* was my first panoramic photography book; it included wide- angled images from Provincetown to the Cape Cod Canal.

The original inspiration for the images in *Cape Cod Wide* was the customers who visited galleries and craft shows and wanted to purchase a wide-angled print of a local vista. Not possible with a typical camera, digital photography opened the door to the process of stitching images together and producing a print that could be up to a 360 degree panorama. Most of the images in these books are about 120 degrees because that is about the field of view for human vision.

Originally designed as a course book to explain the process of producing a panoramic image, *Cape Cod Wide* was editorially conceived rather as a photographic journey across some of the most beautiful and magnificent areas of that bended arm of Massachusetts. There was no intention to cover specific areas of the Cape, but instead to capture scenes that were the most photogenic and memorable. Included at the back of *Cape Cod Wide*, is a tutorial explaining the ins and outs of creating a panoramic image. If anyone is interested in how many of these images are produced or wishes to produce their own panoramas, the explanation can be found in *CCW*.

North Shore Wide followed and included images from Revere Beach northward towards the coast of New Hampshire. An endeavor was made to highlight each community on the North Shore, selecting commonly identifiable scenes, including both landscapes and seascapes. Some scenes were easily recognizable; others were hidden gems found on back roads and less traveled ways. Most of the panoramas are stitched together using dedicated software and photo editing programs. No attempt has been made to significantly alter the scene; what you see in the print is what was there when the image was photographed.

This book is larger and more inclusive than the previous Wide books. The shoreline towns of Plymouth County, including Hingham, Scituate, Duxbury, Kingston, and Plymouth are considered the South Shore, but this book expands beyond those towns to encompass parts of Norfolk County, comprised of Milton, Cohasset, and Quincy. It also includes images of historically famous places and landmarks not normally considered as subjects for panoramic photography. The photographic boundaries of South Shore Wide are defined as south of Boston, west to Route 24 and east of Routes 495 and 25 to the Cape Cod Canal. Each town within that area offers numerous opportunities for panoramic images.

Bibliography

Tree, Christina and Davis, William, *An Explorer's Guide, Massachusetts, The North Shore, South Coast, Central Massachusetts, and The Berkshires.* The Countryman Press, Woodstock, Vermont. 2000.

The WPA Guide to Massachusetts, *The Federal Writers' Project Guide to 1930's Massachusetts,* Pantheon Books, New York, 1937.

Rogers, Barbara Radcliffe and Stillman Rogers, *Insiders' Guide, Off the Beaten Path*, Globe Pequot Press, Guilford, Connecticut, 2007.

Also, the brochures, pamphlets and guides found at the visitor's centers throughout the South Shore that have proved invaluable.

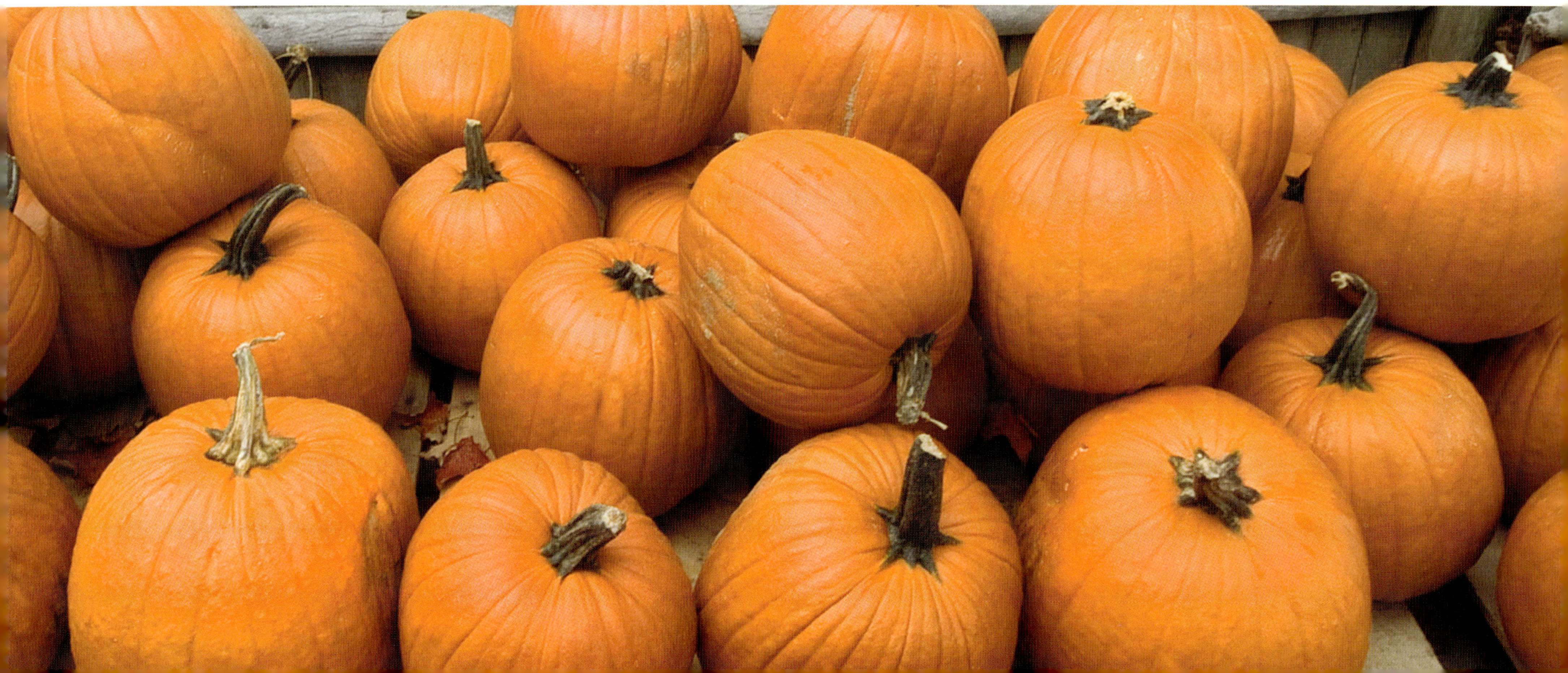

Index

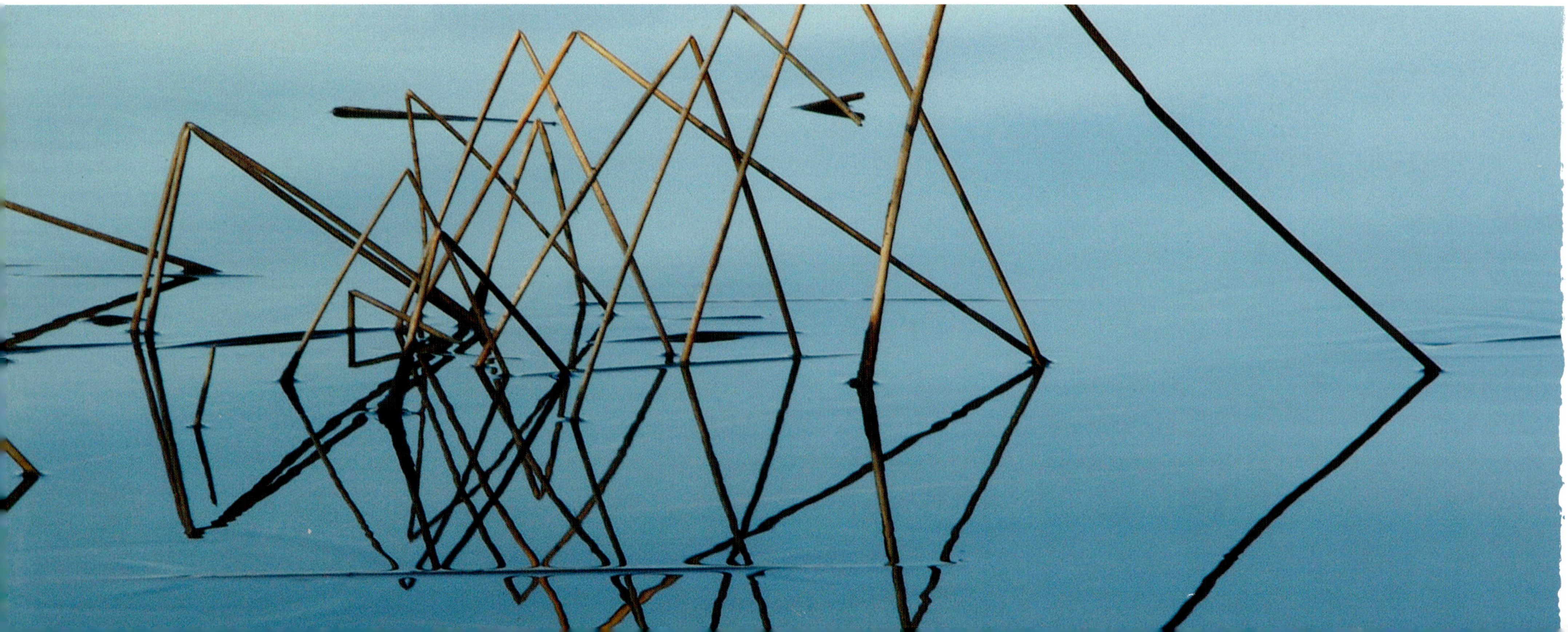

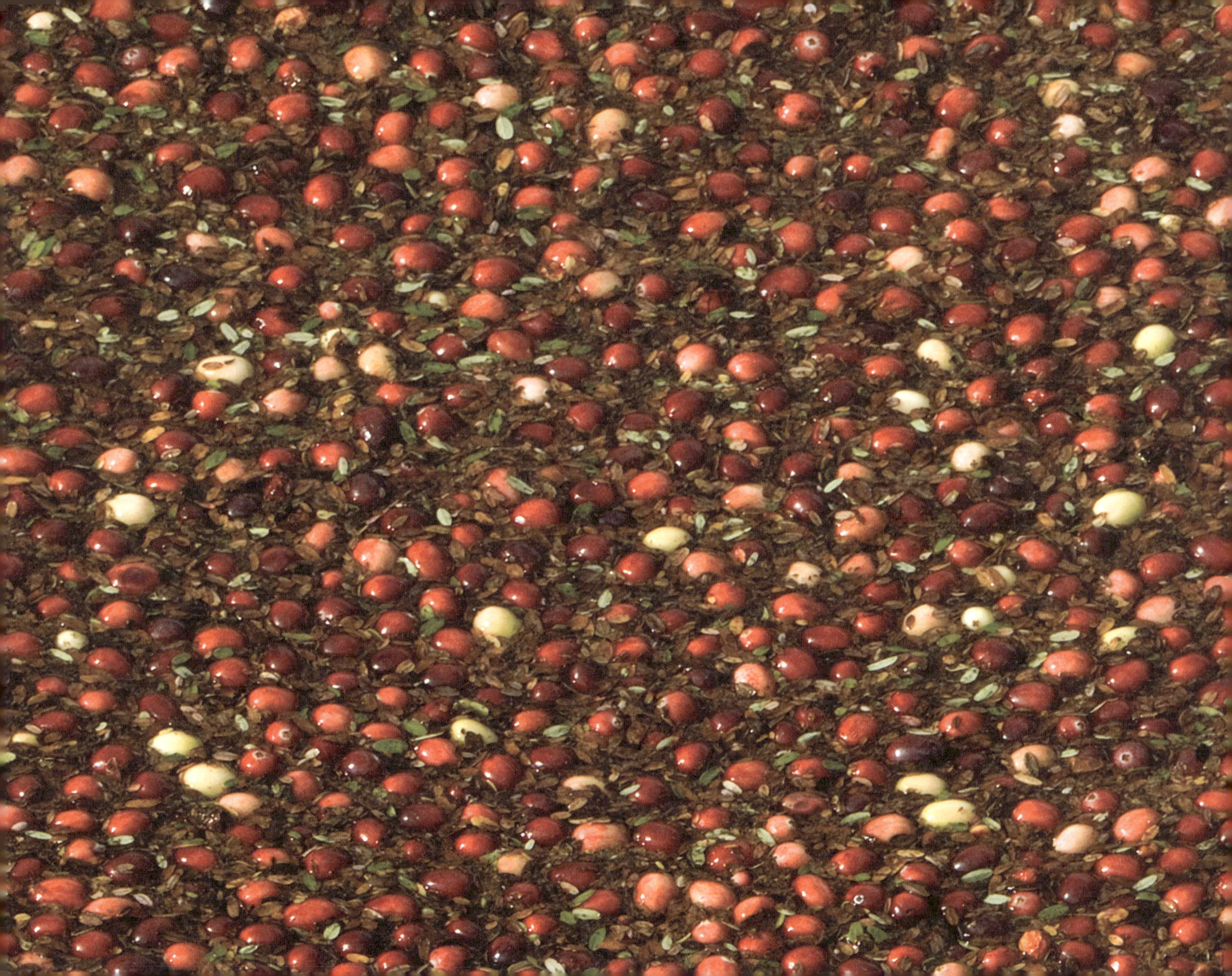